# In Pursuit of Psychic C

The members of the Betty Joseph workshop have provided major contributions to psychoanalytic thinking since the meeting's inception in 1962. This book is a celebration of Betty Joseph's work, and the work of a group of analysts who have joined her to discuss obstacles to psychic change in psychoanalytic treatment.

A prestigious line up of contributors presents clinical material for discussion on a range of topics including:

- Supporting psychic change: Betty Joseph
- Complacency in analysis and everyday life
- Containment, enactment and communication

The history of psychoanalysis is one of an ongoing struggle to reach a new understanding of the human psyche and develop more effective methods of treatment. *In Pursuit of Psychic Change* reflects this tradition – discussions of each contribution by other members of the group provide an in-depth exploration of the merits and limitations of a developing analytic technique, in the hope of achieving true psychic change.

All psychoanalysts will benefit from the insights provided into the original and stimulating work of the members of the Betty Joseph workshop.

**Edith Hargreaves** is a training analyst of the British Psychoanalytic Society.

**Arturo Varchevker** is a Psychoanalyst and a member of the British Psychoanalytical Society.

THE NEW LIBRARY OF PSYCHOANALYSIS



The New Library of Psychoanalysis was launched in 1987 in association with the Institute of Psychoanalysis, London. It took over from the International Psychoanalytical Library, which published many of the early translations of the works of Freud and the writings of most of the leading British and Continental psychoanalysts.

The purpose of the New Library of Psychoanalysis is to facilitate a greater and more widespread appreciation of psychoanalysis and to provide a forum for increasing mutual understanding between psychoanalysts and those working in other disciplines such as history, film studies, literature, medicine, philosophy and the social sciences. It aims to represent different trends both in British psychoanalysis and in psychoanalysis generally. The New Library of Psychoanalysis is well placed to make available to the English speaking world psychoanalytic writings from other European countries and to increase the interchange of ideas between British and American psychoanalysts.

The Institute, together with the British Psychoanalytical Society, runs a low-fee psychoanalytic clinic, organises lectures and scientific events concerned with psychoanalysis and publishes The *International Journal of Psychoanalysis*. It also runs the only UK training course in psychoanalysis which leads to membership of the International Psychoanalytical Association – the body which preserves internationally agreed standards of training, of professional entry, and of professional ethics and practice of psychoanalysis as initiated and developed by Sigmund Freud. Distinguished members of the Institute have included Michael Balint, Wilfred Bion, Ronald Fairbairn, Anna Freud, Ernest Jones, Melanie Klein, John Rickman and Donald Winnicott.

Previous General Editors include David Tuckett, Elizabeth Bott Spillius and Susan Budd. Previous Associate Editors and Members of the Advisory Board include Christopher Bollas, Ronald Britton, Donald Campbell, Stephen Grosz, John Keene, Eglé Laufer, Juliet Mitchell, Michael Parsons, Rosine Jozef Perelberg and David Taylor.

This book was commissioned under the general editorship of Susan Budd. The current general editor of the New Library of Pyschoanalysis is Dana Birksted-Breen.

## ALSO IN THIS SERIES

*Impasse and Interpretation* Herbert Rosenfeld
*Psychoanalysis and Discourse* Patrick Mahony
*The Suppressed Madness of Sane Men* Marion Milner
*The Riddle of Freud* Estelle Roith
*Thinking, Feeling, and Being* Ignacio Matte-Blanco
*The Theatre of the Dream* Salomon Resnik
*Melanie Klein Today: Volume 1, Mainly Theory* Edited by Elizabeth Bott Spillius
*Melanie Klein Today: Volume 2, Mainly Practice* Edited by Elizabeth Bott Spillius
*Psychic Equilibrium and Psychic Change: Selected Papers of Betty Joseph* Edited by Michael Feldman and Elizabeth Bott Spillius
*About Children and Children-No-Longer: Collected Papers 1942–80* Paula Heimann. Edited by Margret Tonnesmann
*The Freud–Klein Controversies 1941–45* Edited by Pearl King and Riccardo Steiner
*Dream, Phantasy and Art* Hanna Segal
*Psychic Experience and Problems of Technique* Harold Stewart
*Clinical Lectures on Klein and Bion* Edited by Robin Anderson
*From Fetus to Child* Alessandra Piontelli
*A Psychoanalytic Theory of Infantile Experience: Conceptual and Clinical Reflections* E. Gaddini. Edited by Adam Limentani
*The Dream Discourse Today* Edited and introduced by Sara Flanders
*The Gender Conundrum: Contemporary Psychoanalytic Perspectives on Feminitity and Masculinity* Edited and introduced by Dana Breen
*Psychic Retreats* John Steiner
*The Taming of Solitude: Separation Anxiety in Psychoanalysis* Jean-Michel Quinodoz
*Unconscious Logic: An Introduction to Matte-Blanco's Bi-logic and its Uses* Eric Rayner
*Understanding Mental Objects* Meir Perlow
*Life, Sex and Death: Selected Writings of William Gillespie* Edited and introduced by Michael Sinason
*What Do Psychoanalysts Want? The Problem of Aims in Psychoanalytic Therapy* Joseph Sandler and Anna Ursula Dreher
*Michael Balint: Object Relations, Pure and Applied* Harold Stewart
*Hope: A Shield in the Economy of Borderline States* Anna Potamianou
*Psychoanalysis, Literature & War: Papers 1972–1995* Hanna Segal
*Emotional Vertigo: Between Anxiety and Pleasure* Danielle Quinodoz
*Early Freud and Late Freud* Ilse Grubrich-Simitis
*A History of Child Psychoanalysis* Claudine and Pierre Geissmann
*Belief and Imagination: Explorations in Psychoanalysis* Ronald Britton
*A Mind of One's Own: A Kleinian View of Self and Object* Robert A. Caper

*Psychoanalytic Understanding of Violence and Suicide* Edited by Rosine Jozef Perelberg

*On Bearing Unbearable States of Mind* Ruth Riesenberg-Malcolm

*Psychoanalysis on the Move: The Work of Joseph Sandler* Edited by Peter Fonagy, Arnold M. Cooper and Robert S. Wallerstein

*The Dead Mother: The Work of André Green* Edited by Gregorio Kohon

*The Fabric of Affect in the Psychoanalytic Discourse* André Green

*The Bi-Personal Field: Experiences of Child Analysis* Antonino Ferro

*The Dove that Returns, the Dove that Vanishes: Paradox and Creativity in Psychoanalysis* Michael Parsons

*Ordinary People, Extra-ordinary Protections: A Post Kleinian Approach to the Treatment of Primitive Mental States* Judith Mitrani

*The Violence of Interpretation: From Pictogram to Statement* Piera Aulagnier. Translated by Alan Sheridan.

*The Importance of Fathers: A Psychoanalytic Re-Evaluation* Judith Trowell and Alicia Etchegoyen

*Dreams that Turn Over a Page: Paradoxical Dreams in Psychoanalysis* Jean-Michel Quinodoz

*The Couch and the Silver Screen: Psychoanalytic Reflections on European Cinema* Edited and introduced by Andrea Sabbadini

*In Pursuit of Psychic Change: The Betty Joseph Workshop* Edited by Edith Hargreaves and Arturo Varchevker

THE NEW LIBRARY OF PSYCHOANALYSIS

General Editor: Dana Birksted-Breen

# In Pursuit of Psychic Change

## The Betty Joseph Workshop

Edited by Edith Hargreaves and Arturo Varchevker

HOVE AND NEW YORK

First published 2004
by Brunner-Routledge
27 Church Road, Hove, East Sussex BN3 2FA

Simultaneously published in the USA and Canada
by Brunner-Routledge
29 West 35th Street, New York NY 10001

Reprinted 2004

*Brunner-Routledge is an imprint of the Taylor & Francis Group*



Typeset in Bembo
by Keystroke, Jacaranda Lodge, Wolverhampton
Printed and bound in Great Britain
by TJ International Ltd, Padstow, Cornwall
Paperback cover design by Sandra Heath



This publication has been produced with paper manufactured to strict environmental standards and with pulp derived from sustainable forests.

*British Library Cataloguing in Publication Data*
A catalogue record for this book is available from the British Library

*Library of Congress Cataloging in Publication Data*
In pursuit of psychic change: the Betty Joseph workshop/[edited by]
Edith Hargreaves and Arturo Varchevker.—1st ed.
p. cm. — (The new library of psychoanalysis)
Includes bibliographical references and index.
ISBN 1–58391–822–1 (hardback) — ISBN 1–58391–823–X (pbk.)
1. Psychoanalysis.
[DNLM: 1. Psychoanalytic Theory. 2. Psychoanalytic Therapy. WM460 P986
2004] I. Hargreaves, Edith. II. Varchevker, Arturo. III. Joseph, Betty. IV. Series:
New library of psychoanalysis (Unnumbered)
RC504.I495 2004
616.89'17—dc22

2003015797

ISBN 1–58391–822–1 (hbk)
ISBN 1–58391–823–X (pbk)

# CONTENTS

# CONTRIBUTORS

**Robin Anderson** is a consultant psychiatrist, formerly chairman of the Adolescent Department, Tavistock Clinic, London. He is a training analyst in child and adult analysis of the British Psychoanalytical Society. His publications include the editing of *Clinical Lectures on Klein and Bion*, and *Facing it Out* with Anna Dartington.

**Irma Brenman Pick** is a training analyst and child analyst of the British Psychoanalytical Society, past president of the British Society, and author of several papers, particularly 'Working through in the counter transference'.

**Ronald Britton** is well known internationally as a psychoanalytic writer and teacher; his writings include *The Oedipus Complex Today*, *Belief and Imagination* and *Sex, Death and the Super-ego*. He is president of the British Psychoanalytical Society and vice-president of the International Psychoanalytical Association, a member of the Melanie Klein Trust and a participant in Betty Joseph's postgraduate workshop since 1980.

**Patricia Daniel** practises psychoanalysis in London and is a training analyst and supervisor of the British Psychoanalytical Society.

**Michael Feldman** is a training analyst of the British Psychoanalytical Society. He was previously also a consultant in the Psychotherapy Unit of the Maudsley Hospital for many years. He is actively involved in teaching and supervising psychoanalytic work in Britain and abroad. His main interests are in relation to psychoanalytic technique, particularly the implications our understanding of the nature of psychic change have for the way we work.

**Gigliola Fornari Spoto** is a training analyst and supervisor of the British Psychoanalytical Society with a full-time psychoanalytic practice. She teaches and supervises extensively in England and internationally.

**Edith Hargreaves** is a training analyst of the British Psychoanalytical Society with a particular interest in teaching psychoanalytic ideas and supervising clinical work. She has been actively involved for many years in the training organisations of the Institute of Psychoanalysis and other psychoanalytic-psychotherapy organisations and is committed to the strengthening of psychoanalysis outside London, and the application of psychoanalytic ideas in the NHS.

**Athol Hughes** is an adult, child and adolescent psychoanalyst of the British Psychoanalytical Society. She has supervised and taught child and adolescent psychotherapy in England and abroad. She edited and introduced the collected papers of Joan Riviere and is currently on the Editorial Board of *Psychoanalysis and History*.

**Betty Joseph** is a training analyst of the British Psychoanalytical Society supervising both child and adult cases. She has travelled extensively in Europe, North and South America, India, Israel and elsewhere, lecturing, participating in conferences and doing clinical seminars and supervisions. In 1995 she was awarded a Mary Sigourney Award for outstanding contributions to psychoanalysis. In 1989 a collection of her papers was published by Routledge edited by Elizabeth Bott Spillius and Michael Feldman, entitled *Psychic Equilibrium and Psychic Change*. Her main interest in psychoanalysis has always been primarily in the clinical and technical aspects.

**Richard Lucas** OBE is consultant psychiatrist at St Ann's Hospital, London and a member of the British Psychoanalytical Society. He is chair of the general psychiatry section of the Association for Psychoanalytic Psychotherapy in the NHS. His particular interest is in the application of analytic concepts within general psychiatry. He has written papers on the analytic contribution in puerperal psychosis, cyclical psychoses, risk assessment and schizophrenia.

**Edna O'Shaughnessy** first encountered Betty Joseph as a supervisor for her latency training case. She is a child and adult training analyst of the British Psychoanalytical Society and supervisor in the Child and Family Department of the Tavistock Clinic. Formerly she was also lecturer in the Department of Child Development, Institute of Education, London. She has published a number of theoretical and technical psychoanalytic papers.

**Martha Papadakis** is a training analyst of the British Psychoanalytical Society, in full-time private practice, active in administration and teaching at the Institute of Psychoanalysis and other organisations, with a special interest in dreams.

**Priscilla Roth** is a training and supervising analyst of the British Psychoanalytical Society. She is a graduate in psychology of the University of California at Berkeley and did research into mental illness in California and Massachusetts before training as a child and adolescent psychotherapist at the

Tavistock Institute, London, and then as a psychoanalyst at the British Institute of Psychoanalysis. She teaches at the Institute of Psychoanalysis, the Tavistock Clinic, the University of London Psychoanalytic Theory course, and abroad.

**Ignes Sodré** is a training and supervising analyst of the British Psychoanalytical Society. She has done extensive teaching in Britain and abroad, and has published papers on clinical psychoanalysis and on literature and a book with Dame Antonia Byatt, *Imagining Characters*.

**John Steiner** is a training analyst of the British Psychoanalytical Society. He was formerly a consultant psychiatrist at the Maudsley Hospital and then until his retirement from the NHS in 1996 he worked as a consultant psychotherapist at the Tavistock Clinic. He is the author of *Psychic Retreats* and has written a variety of papers on psychoanalysis. He now works in private practice as a psychoanalyst in London.

**David Taylor** is a training analyst of the British Psychoanalytical Society in part-time analytic practice. He also works for the Tavistock and Portman NHS Trust, currently as medical director, and is also the clinical lead of a large-scale trial of psychoanalytic psychotherapy in the treatment of refractory depression. His publications include *Talking Cure*, which he edited to accompany a BBC TV series about the Tavistock, along with papers on Bion, psychotic parts of the personality, and the nature of psychic conflict. He supervises and teaches in Heidelberg as well as more occasionally in other German centres.

**Jane Temperley** has a BA in modern history from St Anne's College Oxford, studied social work at Bristol University and obtained a master's degree in social work from the University of Connecticut. She worked as a psychiatric social worker at St Mary's Hospital Paddington and then at the Tavistock Clinic where she became principal social worker in the Adult Department. She qualified as a psychoanalyst in 1975, is a member of the British Psychoanalytical Society and teaches at the Institute of Psychoanalysis and for a number of psychotherapy trainings.

**Arturo Varchevker** MD. Social Psychol. Psychoanalyst. He is a member of the British Psychoanalytical Society. He is in private practice and he also works in the NHS. He is actively involved in teaching and supervises in England and abroad.

# PREFACE

Since 1962 Betty Joseph has been chairing a workshop which we as editors believe has constituted an important contribution to psychoanalytic thinking. This book is a celebration of Betty Joseph's work, and the work of a group of analysts who have joined her to think about particular kinds of difficulties encountered in the analytic situation, and to discuss technical issues.

Obstacles to treatment have always constituted the basis for important developments in psychoanalytic theory and technique. In her writing, Joseph has explored some of these obstacles, and has developed a technique which emphasises awareness of what Melanie Klein called the 'total transference situation'. This includes not only verbal communication, but also the subtle non-verbal atmospheres and pressures that lead analyst and patient to enact aspects of the internal world of the patient.

The workshop has become a kind of psychoanalytic laboratory in which the members present detailed clinical material of such puzzling situations, which are discussed sometimes over many years. This enables members to become familiar with each other's particular ways of working, making possible an in-depth exploration of the merits and limitations of a developing analytic technique, in the hope of achieving true psychic change.

All the contributions in this volume come from members, past and present, of the workshop. All have been influenced by Betty Joseph's ideas, but, as will become immediately apparent, there are no Betty Joseph clones! Each contributor has his or her own style, theoretical emphasis and approach to analytic technique, influenced by his or her own personality, by past and present mentors, and by each other.

We hope that the chapters in the book, and a selection of discussions of papers by past and present members of the workshop which we have included, will convey the particular tradition which has evolved within the workshop: a tradition of constant attention to the 'total transference situation' as revealed in the subtle awareness of enactment that has become the hallmark of the technique that Betty Joseph has developed.

Edith Hargreaves and
Arturo Varchevker

# ACKNOWLEDGEMENTS

We would like to thank Betty Joseph and all the members of the workshop for their continuous support during the long gestation of this book.

We are indebted to Elizabeth Bott Spillius, Susan Budd and Dana Birksted-Breen for their helpful advice and encouragement with the editorial work. David Bell generously gave of his time and experience, reading and commenting on parts of the manuscript.

We want to thank Routledge, London for permission to use Ronald Britton's 'Complacency in analysis and everyday life' from Britton's (1998) *Belief and Imagination: Explorations in Psychoanalysis*, London: Routledge, and to quote from Betty Joseph's (1989) *Psychic Equilibrium and Psychic Change: Selected Papers of Betty Joseph*, M. Feldman and E. Bott Spillius (eds), London: Routledge.

We thank the *International Journal of Psychoanalysis* for permission to use John Steiner's (2000) 'Containment, enactment and communication', 81(2): 245–255, and Priscilla Roth's (2001) 'Mapping the landscape: levels of transference interpretation', 82(3): 533–543.

# INTRODUCTION

*Edith Hargreaves and Arturo Varchevker*

The development of psychoanalytic technique, from its beginnings in hypnosis to the present day, has been a history of the struggle to overcome obstacles to the understanding of the human psyche and its disorders, and to develop an effective therapy which would lead to 'cure'. At every step, alongside and irrevocably linked to new theories about the mind and the origins of mental illness, came new methods of treatment.

A characteristic of psychoanalysis is the very firm link between theory and practice. New theories widen the field of observation, which in turn makes it possible for new data to emerge. With every step forward, however, come new obstacles to understanding, demanding further questioning of assumptions and refinement of technique.

In psychoanalysis this has been going on since Freud found with some of his early patients that his 'coercive' technique – based upon the theory that traumatic events which have been repressed are the cause of mental illness, and can be recalled with the aid of psychological pressure from the analyst – was often met with an equally powerful force opposed to remembering. This obstacle led him to conclude that those thoughts, feelings and memories whose recovery was resisted were in some way unacceptable to the patient, either because they were too painful, too embarrassing, or in conflict with the moral standards of the individual.

Thus, he discovered *resistance* – a cornerstone of psychoanalytic theory. Coercion was then useless, because it would always be met with resistance. The theory of resistance led to the new technique of *free association*, and the introduction of the fundamental rule – that the patient should speak without censorship of whatever was in his or her mind. The 'talking cure' was born.

Freud's friend and distinguished colleague Joseph Breuer found in his work with his patient, 'Anna O' (Breuer and Freud 1895) that if she could speak freely and in detail about the traumatic situations, and could relive the emotions attached to them in the presence of her physician, then she could achieve considerable relief from her symptoms.

But then, as is well known, a new problem arose. Anna O developed strong erotic feelings towards Breuer. He fled in distress from his patient, and from the implications of this phenomenon. The new discipline seemed to have met an insurmountable obstacle.

Freud too found that his patients developed strong feelings towards him, but had the extraordinary capacity to remain curious and interested. He came to recognise these feelings as belonging to the past and *transferred* on to the person of the analyst. Far from being an obstacle, transference now provided the key to deeper understanding. Thus, the analysis of the transference became the fundamental technique of psychoanalysis, and remains so to this day. The theory of transference led over time to a reformulation of ideas about the way the analytic relationship is conducted and profoundly affected the setting in which psychoanalysis could take place.

> Careful handling of the transference . . . is as a rule richly rewarded. If we succeed, as we usually can, in enlightening the patient on the true nature of the phenomena of transference, we shall have struck a powerful weapon out of the hand of his resistance and shall have converted dangers into gains. For a patient never forgets again what he has experienced in the form of transference; it carries a greater force of conviction than anything he can acquire in other ways.
>
> (Freud 1940: 177)

Psychoanalysis as we know it today was becoming recognisable, and new discoveries and refinements of technique multiplied. It is hardly surprising that important developments in psychoanalytic technique have arisen not from successful treatments, but from patients who presented difficulties in treatment, necessitating thinking things anew. It is that exploration of obstacles in treatment that has been characteristic of Betty Joseph's work, and has been so fruitful in developing her observational skill and the accompanying technique.

The contribution of Melanie Klein is, of course, central to the work of Betty Joseph, and to the authors of the chapters in this book. In her early work with children Klein observed that powerful persecutory and depressive states of a psychotic nature could be seen even in very young children, and this understanding laid the basis for her distinctive contribution to psychoanalytic theory and technique. What Freud had seen as the infantile neuroses Klein saw as the means adopted by the individual to work through or defend against the psychotic anxieties of the 'infantile paranoid-schizoid and depressive positions'. She used the term 'projective identification' to describe the key mental mechanism used to defend against and work through persecutory and depressive anxieties and the psychic pain of the depressive position.

> Klein uses the term 'projective identification' to describe a complex set of processes by which part of the self is split off and projected into an object to which the individual reacts as if the object were the self or the part of the self that has been projected into it. The individual who projects in this way will then in phantasy introject the object as coloured by what he has projected into it. It is through such constant interplay that the inner world of self and internal objects is built up. Splitting, projection, and introjection are the characteristic mental mechanisms of the paranoid-schizoid position, accompanied by idealisation, denigration, and denial.
>
> (Spillius 1994: 336)

Klein's technique, in accordance with her theories, began to differ considerably from that of her contemporaries. Even with very young children, she eschewed explanatory and educational techniques, believing that it was the interpretation of anxiety as it arises in the immediacy of the analytic session that produces relief and the possibility of insight. Her emphasis on the importance of the earliest relation to the breast, penis and the Oedipal couple, and the working through of paranoid-schizoid and depressive anxieties, led to her conviction that these very early anxieties must be explored at the deepest level if real insight and psychic change were to take place.

Before Klein, transference was thought of as referring to actual references by the patient to feelings and phantasies about the analyst. Klein widened and deepened this understanding, seeing the transference as comprising the 'total situation' (Klein 1952): that is, *everything* the patient brings to the session, including subtle non-verbal atmospheres and enactments of internal situations and relationships. This widening of the concepts of transference (and countertransference) has proved central to Betty Joseph's work.

Klein always used detailed clinical material both to illustrate and give evidence for her theoretical developments. This tradition has remained extremely important among her followers; pre-eminent in this tradition is Betty Joseph.

## On Betty Joseph's contribution

Within the Kleinian perspective, the work of Betty Joseph, along with that of W.R. Bion,[1] Rosenfeld and Segal, has profoundly, though in her case until recently rather quietly, influenced a new generation of psychoanalysts not only in Britain, but also worldwide. With them she has developed and extended Melanie Klein's concept of projective identification, and its implications for the analytic understanding of transference and countertransference in clinical practice.

Over a period of years Betty Joseph became interested in a particularly subtle set of obstacles – a constellation of puzzling clinical phenomena confronting the analyst with certain patients who seemed peculiarly stuck and inaccessible to ordinary analytic work. She noticed that many of these patients, although outwardly co-operative, attending regularly, bringing material, and apparently wanting to change, seemed to defeat her efforts to promote insight and psychic change. Even when the analysis seemed to progress and the patient reported change, Joseph felt there was no real emotional contact.

In her influential paper, 'The patient who is difficult to reach', Joseph (1975) brings to life the kind of bewildering predicament which will be familiar to most analysts and therapists, in which

> One finds oneself in a situation that looks exactly like an on-going analysis, with understanding, apparent contact, appreciation and even reported improvement. And yet one has a feeling of hollowness. If one considers one's counter transference, it may seem all a bit too easy, pleasant, unconflicted, or signs of conflict emerge but are somehow quickly dissipated.
>
> (Joseph 1975: 76)

Joseph's distinctive contribution lies in her unflinching openness to this daunting and apparently intractable clinical dilemma, and in her refinement of a technique which, she argues, offers the analyst a greater possibility of making meaningful contact with the patient.

In the introduction to Joseph's collected papers (Joseph 1989), the editors trace the development of her ideas and identify the major themes which constitute her unique contribution to modern psychoanalytic practice. These are

- the patient's need to maintain his or her existing psychic equilibrium, despite the conscious wish to change
- psychic change and the forces which promote or militate against it
- the evolution of a technique which takes account of the above, drawing particularly upon Melanie Klein's concept of the total transference situation, and later developments of the idea of projective identification and the use of countertransference
- an emphasis on remaining with the alive and immediate experience in the session, and the avoidance of sterile 'knowledge about'.

In her earliest papers Joseph (1959, 1960) drew attention to a way in which patients with apparently quite different psychopathologies showed at a deeper level a need to maintain their psychic equilibrium at all costs despite the conscious wish to change. She identified systems of defences based on the subtle and complex interweaving of projective and introjective identification, idealisation, splitting and omnipotence, which these patients used to prevent the disturbance of their established psychic balance.

Betty Joseph continued to develop her ideas about the various forces which promote or prevent psychic change and began to elucidate the distinctive technique that was to become her hallmark. This technique is characterised by close observation of the most minute shifts, changes in atmosphere, actions and pressures experienced in the to and fro of the session, and their interplay in the transference and countertransference.

Joseph explored the ways in which the analyst could be drawn into collusion with an apparently co-operative part of the patient, this collusion however serving not development, but the maintenance of the defensive structure, while the more needy and potentially responsive parts of the patient remained out of reach. Always with illuminating clinical material she looked at the many subtle means by which patients unconsciously perpetuate this state of affairs, not so much by what they say, but by how they act on the analyst through their communications – putting subtle pressure on the analyst to join them in enactments, thus living out aspects of themselves and their inner world.

She suggests that the analyst cannot remain untouched by these pressures from the patient, but an awareness of their significance as potential communication can lead to the analyst's regaining his or her analytic stance and to further understanding. But this awareness must remain problematic since so much of the analyst's countertransference is essentially unconscious. In these situations analysts may need help from colleagues in order to disentangle themselves from the countertransference enactment, and this understanding is the basis of the workshop.

When discussing how the analyst actually approaches the material, Joseph tries to start from a sense of what is going on in the room, in the relationship between patient and analyst and on the whole making links with the patient's past only as these links emerge in her own or the patient's mind, arising from what is currently going on. She feels that starting from history or being drawn into making premature links with the patient's past tends to lead to evasion of the immediacy of what is going on in the transference: evasion by patient, by analyst or both.

Transference is viewed by Joseph in the broadest sense, as including

> everything the patient brings into the relationship. What he brings in . . . can best be gauged by our focusing our attention on what is going on in the relationship, how he is using the analyst, alongside and beyond what he is saying. Much of our understanding of the transference comes through our understanding of how our patients act on us to feel things . . . how they try to draw us into their defensive systems; how they unconsciously act out with us in the transference, trying to get us to act out with them; how they convey aspects of their inner world built up from infancy – elaborated in childhood and adulthood, experiences often beyond the use of words, which we can

> often only capture through the feelings aroused in us, through our countertransference, used in the broad sense of the word.
>
> (Joseph 1985: 157)

Betty Joseph does not use the word 'courage' in relation to her work, although her great gift is found in her determination to remain curious and open-minded in the face of the patient's apparent emotional inaccessibility and failure to progress. Her work provides the analyst or therapist with a way of thinking that offers hope and the possibility of promoting real psychic change.

## The workshop

The workshop originated in 1962 as one of several postgraduate clinical seminars for qualified analysts interested in the ideas of Melanie Klein. The following is part of a document from 1963 signed by Dr Dugmore Hunter, chairman of the organising committee, outlining the purpose, organisation and content of the seminars:

> Kleinian Post-Graduate Education
>
> In January 1962, an experiment in post-graduate education for analysts interested in Mrs. Klein's work was organised by a committee consisting of Dr. Hunter, Chairman; Dr. D Meltzer, Secretary; Miss Menzies, Dr. Klein, Dr. Sohn, together with Miss Joseph (ex-officio).
>
> It was planned that the seminars should be re-formed annually, so that participants would have opportunities to move on to other events. A minor reorganisation took place in January 1963, and plans are now being made for 1964.
>
> At present there are two clinical seminars on Neurotic and Borderline Cases (Dr. Segal and Miss Joseph); one seminar on Psychotic Cases (Dr. Rosenfeld); one on Infant Observation (Mrs. Bick); and a group studying 'The Narrative' with Dr. Meltzer.
>
> The aim has been to keep clinical seminars small, with 4–6 members. Fees are paid; two guineas to the most senior analysts and one guinea to others.

Betty Joseph's seminar thus started life as a traditional teaching seminar. Around the late 1970s an unobserved change began to take place as the analysts in the group became more senior and experienced in their work. The group transformed itself into a 'workshop', namely a joint enterprise in which all kinds of puzzling or apparently intractable clinical phenomena could be openly explored.

Since the late 1980s the membership of the workshop has remained stable at about fifteen members. Over two consecutive fortnightly meetings, a member presents a piece of clinical work in detail. The patients discussed tend to be those who are 'difficult to reach', entrenched in pathological organisations (Steiner 1993), keeping the analysis stuck and the analyst caught up in repeated enactments and often in despair. The same patients are presented over a period of years, so that the group comes to know the particular clinical problems in depth, combining both the detail of the here-and-now with the long-term perspective. There is by no means unanimity of opinion among the members of the workshop, and discussion is lively and forthright.

When the editors discussed with her the characteristics of the workshop, Betty Joseph emphasised the importance of the cross-fertilisation of thinking between all the members, who, although united by a broadly shared theoretical framework, brought their own individual approach. She thought that one of the most important aspects of a stable group of this type is that the members come to trust and respect each other and tolerate each other's foibles, and thus feel able to present material freely and comfortably.

> It is after all recognised [she commented] that the very nature of the analytic work means that often the analyst cannot but be drawn into some kind of acting in, however subtle, with the patient. And perhaps one of the most important functions of the group is not only to help understand material but in standing outside the relationship between analyst and patient, to help the analyst visualise how he or she may be being caught up in some unconscious enactment.

Joseph believes that the very important function of the group is found in the capacity of members to help each other to contain the anxiety, sense of frustration and professional inadequacy that the work inevitably entails and make use of the awareness of these issues to further understanding of the patient's anxiety, defensive manoeuvres and sense of impasse that otherwise can prevent true psychic change.

The editors had hoped to include comments on each of the chapters by other members of the workshop, in order to try to capture the atmosphere of discussion in the group. With written contributions, however, this proved difficult, and the written commentaries are inevitably more formal than they would be in a discussion. We have, nevertheless, included these interesting commentaries following each chapter.

## The book

In June 1998, a day of lectures was held in celebration of Betty Joseph's eightieth birthday, and her contribution to psychoanalysis. From this came the idea of a book of papers which would try to convey the way in which the various members of the workshop have combined Betty Joseph's (and each other's) ideas within their own unique ways of working, always reaching towards a better understanding of their patients and constantly refining their technique.

With differing styles and with some different theoretical emphases all the contributors to this book illustrate, through the eleven chapters and a sample of comments from past and present members of the group, the spirit of inquiry in the workshop. The intention of the book is not to propound a 'correct' technique of psychoanalysis, but to illustrate how each writer deals with the struggle to understand the 'patient who is difficult to reach' and to keep psychoanalytic curiosity alive. This psychoanalytic curiosity is not a given; it is lost and must be rediscovered again and again in the interaction between patient and analyst.

We believe that the problems and patients described in the book will be familiar to every clinician, and it is our hope that the questions raised will stimulate readers, whatever their theoretical orientation, to further thought and questioning of their own way of working.

## The contributions

In his chapter, first given on the day of lectures in celebration of Betty Joseph's eightieth birthday, Michael Feldman explores the complexities of her theory of psychic change – what enables psychic change to take place and what militates against it – that is so central to her work. He also explores Joseph's formulations on technique. Using clinical material both of his own and from Joseph herself, he sets out many of the clinical preoccupations of the workshop which will be further explored by all the authors in the book.

As Feldman puts it,

> Joseph elaborates her understanding of these drives towards or away from development, by means of her study of the use the patient makes of the analyst and her interpretations on the one hand, and her own mental capacities, on the other. These capacities are sometimes used constructively, but the patient will also misuse understanding in a defensive way – to attack herself or her objects, to create a false compliance or collusion, or to whip up sado-masochistic excitement.

In addition to the patient's misuse of understanding, the analyst's own capacity to understand and interpret what is going on in the transference may also become distorted. Induced by unconscious pressures from the patient or from within him or herself, the analyst may rush into giving over-long explanatory interpretations containing what Feldman calls a 'because clause' which may cloud the issue, or might rush into premature interpretation of underlying unconscious phantasies and connections to the past that can lead to a cul-de-sac and reinforce the system of defences.

The first of the two clinical examples refers to a patient of his who, having missed sessions and been frequently late, defined his own behaviour as a healthy progress and reinforced this view with further associations. The analyst was alerted by the response to his interpretation and especially by the tone of the patient's voice that, by projective identification, he was identified with a particular version of his analyst.

The patient, however, perceived his analyst as trying to undermine his healthy state. The perception of his analyst corresponded to an archaic figure projected on to the analyst. Feldman describes how he felt drawn into interpreting in a way which confirmed the patient's view of him as critical and undermining, and how he took some time to recognise this. Such enactments, when they are understood, provide a useful insight into what is going on in the patient and the analyst. Although Feldman and the other authors do not refer explicitly to the workshop in their chapters, it is in precisely this kind of situation that he might have used the help of trusted colleagues in the workshop and of Joseph herself to step back and see more clearly what he had been caught up in. Often the enactments described are reflected in the various responses of members of the workshop. But familiarity with each other's ways of thinking and working and a common emphasis on the importance of understanding enactment and countertransference phenomena makes possible a greater understanding of the stalemate.

The second example comes from a paper by Joseph. Her patient, an adolescent girl, uses 'insight' as a weapon to create a sadomasochistic 'drama'. Painstaking analysis of these drama/enactments and the ability of her analyst and her father to withstand her outbursts facilitated real development. In both examples he notes that considerable analytic work is required before a patient can hear and use an interpretation as an interpretation.

In Chapter 2, John Steiner describes two patients in whom ordinary communication was disrupted by the use of primitive projective mechanisms. It is a chapter about pathological projective identification, the pressure on the analyst towards enactment, and about countertransference in the broadest sense. Steiner describes situations in which the analyst becomes aware of what is going on only *after* he has enacted the role or situation ascribed to him by his patient.

In Patient A, thinking was fragmented and intolerable feelings, desires and states of mind were projected into the analyst. In Patient B there was dissociation between language and affect, and disturbing affect was projected into the analyst. In both, the analyst was sometimes able to contain, understand and interpret the unbearable internal situation which the patients sought to avoid through their projections, but at others he found himself drawn into an enactment in which he felt induced to work very hard to supply the missing meaning or affect.

(Members of the workshop too might find themselves drawn into working very hard along with the analyst presenting, bringing contradictory interpretations and theoretical constructions in order to find respite from the pain and frustration and to avoid the unbearable sense of meaninglessness.)

In the latter case, the analyst (through the enactments) enabled the patient to remain comfortable, protected from his own destructiveness and states of meaninglessness and despair, thus becoming a part of the patient's defensive *psychic retreat* and maintaining his *pathological organisation of the personality* (Steiner 1993). Steiner suggests, however, that enactment is not only defensive. If analysts are able eventually to stand back and observe what is going on, they can use their observation to further their understanding of their patients' internal situation, and what is being evaded by the enactment.

Steiner integrates the ideas of Klein, Bion, Rosenfeld and Betty Joseph along with his own contributions – the 'psychic retreat' and the 'pathological organisation of the personality'. Steiner's original formulation of the psychic retreat has influenced Joseph's own thinking, and that of all members of the workshop, and the reader will note its use vividly exemplified in many of the chapters in the book. He discusses the need to be aware of the total situation, including non-verbal pressures and cues, and the inevitability of being drawn into enactments which avoid hated psychic reality and sustain the patient's *psychic status quo*. In order that such enactments can be thought about, the analyst needs to scrutinise his or her countertransference and thus try to understand the internal situation that is being projected and why the patient finds it so hard to tolerate it.

The way of working illustrated in Steiner's chapter describes the clinical approach that informs the workshop, and links can be seen with all the other contributions, which in their different ways also address the obstacles to understanding posed by the disruption of communication through the 'massive use of projective identification'.

This theme is further developed in Chapter 3 by Ignes Sodré, who explores a particular type of pathological projective identification colloquially referred to as 'the subject being in a state of massive projective identification with the object', and other less extreme uses of projective identification.

Sodré notes that what characterises what is described as a state of massive projective identification is that subjects not only project their personality, affects and their mode of functioning into the object, but also introject it in a cannibalistic way. She observes that manic phantasies of triumph over the object are a significant component of these states of pathological projective identification and introjection. She is concerned with the disturbances of patients' sense of identity and the technical difficulties when analysts are caught up in these projections, and their own sense of identity is affected.

Sodré's patient, Mr A, on entering the session, tells her with a sense of superiority that he had noticed that she is shortsighted and vain because she does not wear glasses. She interprets that there is probably an underlying reason why he perceives that she cannot see properly. He reacts with rage; *his* vision is 100 per cent. An impasse develops, in which the patient is triumphantly certain that he is the one whose vision is perfect, and the analyst finds herself trying to convince an impermeable, blind object that she can see. Movement from the impasse is resisted by the patient, who is committed to maintaining his pathological psychic equilibrium (Joseph 1988) through a firm identification with an idealised bad object.

Only when the analyst manages to regain a contact with a helpful internal object is she able to begin to see who is who in the interaction and what is being enacted in the transference–countertransference. This is of paramount importance in helping the analyst to regain her analytic stance and to unlock the impasse.

Feldman's, Steiner's and Sodré's contributions represent the kinds of clinical problems brought to the workshop, in which patients strive to maintain their psychic equilibrium through the use of projective mechanisms, and how the analyst's interpretations may be felt to threaten this balance. The workshop may function as the good object that can help the analyst disentangle who is who.

Ronald Britton, in a contribution originally presented on the Betty Joseph day of lectures, also discusses forms of projective identification and enactment, but describes a different kind of interaction. He comments that his Chapter 4 draws on two of Joseph's central ideas – the total transference situation as the most informative aspect of analysis, and the relationship between psychic equilibrium and psychic change.

He focuses on a group of patients similar to those described by Joseph as 'difficult to reach', who evoke in the analyst a particular countertransference – a complacent unconscious assumption that 'one need not worry about these patients, in contrast to others who prey on the analyst's mind'. As Joseph teaches, Britton continues, the unconscious assumption occurs not only in the mind of the patient, but also in the analyst's countertransference feelings and actions. The analyst must be able to look at *what is going on*, i.e. 'what is the role assigned to the analyst that is likely to be enacted by him or her?' Ingeniously contrasting Joseph's approach to that of Pangloss ('all is for the best'), in Voltaire's *Candide* (1759) Britton draws on Joseph's emphasis on the importance of the constant questioning of appearances – the need to observe the *total transference situation*, and not just the content of the patient's communications, in order to understand the patients particular 'constellations of object relations, anxieties and defences'.

The patients Britton discusses often occupy a position as the healthiest member of the family, as well as the patient one need not worry about, but the complacency is interrupted intermittently by

> brief glimpses of terrifying ideas about the analyst or untethered images of a frightening or horrifying kind attached to nothing in particular. These

transient incursions of archaic beliefs do not find a settled home in the transference and are rapidly dispelled by the reassuring familiarity of the analytic relationship.

Thus, these patients find a position in which the analysis itself enables them to disbelieve their own frightening thoughts. They retreat to comfortable complacency, seemingly participating co-operatively in an analysis to which they are in many ways impervious.

Britton also discusses another means of retreat from psychic reality: '"talking *about*" things as a means of joint disposal'.

Priscilla Roth discusses in Chapter 5 with thorough theoretical insight beneath the pragmatic approach, how we choose when and what we interpret to our patients. She 'maps out' a mental landscape comprising the different levels at which the patient's communications can be understood and interpreted.

At *level 1* the material is interpreted as being 'about' a figure in the patient's external or internal world. At *level 2* the interpretation is of the transference on to the analyst of specific qualities, dealt with at a distance. A *level 3* interpretation might be described as a total transference interpretation, including, for example, the ways in which the patient exerts pressure on the analyst to join in an enactment of an internal situation in order to maintain his or her psychic equilibrium. A *level 4* interpretation is the analyst's interpretation to him or herself about his or her own anxieties and defences, stirred by the patient's communications, which might make the analyst more susceptible to actually acting in with the patient. Roth painstakingly illustrates her thinking in her clinical material, as well as in the close examination of a vignette quoted from the work of Peter Giovacchini.

Where Betty Joseph in her technique might focus mainly on *level 3* and *level 4*, Roth suggests that while the analyst always aims at these, he or she must keep the entire landscape in mind, and must choose the most appropriate level at which to intervene, depending on what the patient is able to use at any given moment.

In Chapter 6 Patricia Daniel describes a patient whose analysis is dominated by an unconscious phantasy of having murdered his brother. This terrifying phantasy results in the development of a narcissistic defensive organisation which serves to protect him from persecutory anxiety and any awareness of guilt.

For the first few years of the analysis, Mr M was the kind of patient Joseph describes as 'difficult to reach', in that he came regularly, appeared polite and co-operative, and showed some genuine improvement in his work and personal life outside the analysis. In the analysis, however, he maintained a flat, deadened contact in which little resonated, leading Daniel to believe that any liveliness was equated with murderous violence.

Although Daniel knew of the birth of Mr M's younger brother when he was 14 months old from the initial interview, we learn with astonishment that he had not once mentioned the brother during the first five years of analysis. 'It was this striking omission,' Daniel comments, 'which led me to believe that the phantasied murder was of the only sibling.'

Daniel shows how the phantasy pervaded the analytic process, leading to repetitive enactments into which the analyst is drawn, in which the patient's capacity for liveliness and the analyst's capacity to think and interpret are obliterated, and a sense of despair and impasse ensues.

When the analyst attempted to describe the situation, the patient's passivity and deadening grip increased, leaving the analyst feeling alternately irritated, bored, despairing and desperate. The almost unbearable countertransference led Daniel at times into enactments in which she felt she colluded with the patient to murder liveliness, movement and understanding, and about which she found herself feeling inordinately guilty. Once again we can see in Daniel's work the kind of impasse from which workshop colleagues might have helped extricate the analyst.

As the analysis progressed, Daniel noticed that something more cruel and sadomasochistic was emerging, while guilt and despair were projected into the analyst. The chapter illustrates how the defensive organisation of the patient's personality maintained his *psychic equilibrium*, on a borderline between both paranoid anxiety and depressive pain, and shows the enormous difficulty the patient faces if he is to emerge from his 'psychic retreat'. The influence of Steiner's (1993) work on borderline states and pathological organisations of the personality, as well as that of Joseph, is evident in Daniel's contribution.

Gigliola Fornari Spoto describes in Chapter 7 the challenge posed by the analysis of a patient with a perverse pathological organisation. The patient's expression 'having his head stuck up his arse' describes his absorption with faeces and sexual phantasies, and is a prediction of the difficulties the analyst will encounter in reaching him.

The expression, coined by her patient, C, describes

> a state of extreme self-absorption, stillness and withdrawal from reality, where he loses contact with the world and becomes intensely preoccupied with sexual fantasies about bottoms and faeces. . . . It's a highly desirable state: his bottom is idealised as a narcissistic retreat, the comforting source of every good experience. His intense concentration on the bodily experience takes over his mind: the sought after mental torpor, which he reaches, is sexualised and makes him feel powerful and superior to me. My attempts to talk to him can be perceived as rather feeble and uninspiring, compared to the intense pleasure derived from the way he challenges me with his non-thinking.

Fornari Spoto suggests that her patient uses this psychic retreat to deal with persecutory Oedipal anxieties, difficulties related to breaks, the passage of time, and his separateness from the analyst. By sticking his head up his arse he can make himself unreachable and can project his need for contact into his analyst.

Like Daniel's patient, C is also passive, and responds to interpretations with a kind of agreement that signals that he is not emotionally engaged, and does not want to go any further with it, or by merging with the analyst in a 'state of blissful anti-thinking togetherness. . . . His aim becomes, to use his words, to "luxuriate in stupefaction".'

> 'Luxuriate in stupefaction' is an insider's succinct description of what perversions aim to achieve and why they are so compelling and addictive: the attack on reality and thinking, the making oneself stupid, torpid, dazed so that perception of reality is altered and distorted, is sexualised and used as a drug. 'Stupefaction' can be almost thought of as a layman's term for disavowal, the mechanism Freud saw as central to fetishism.

The author shows how essential is the close observation of the counter-transference, and what the patient is *doing*, when quite often, what the patient is *saying* aims at entangling the analyst in his perverse web.

David Taylor's Chapter 8 explores difficulties in learning and especially learning from the *analytic* experience. He discusses the complex and uncomfortable relationship that both patient and analyst can have with the professed analytic aim of 'knowing thyself':

> Since the analytic relationship is supposed to be based upon the idea of getting insight, it follows that it is a threat to patients whose defences are more than usually based upon not knowing. . . . an open attitude in analysis, and therefore to learning, is still a complicated business, even for relatively well-balanced individuals. In anyone, any new knowledge or position involves some disturbance arising, in part, from our ambivalence towards knowledge.

Taylor reviews the ideas of Freud, Ferenczi, Klein and Bion on the capacity to *learn* and to *know*. He is particularly influenced (as of course is Joseph herself) by Bion, and in this chapter focuses on his concepts of *maternal reverie* and *containment* (Bion 1962a). Taylor describes how the infant's capacity to tolerate frustration and the development of the individual's ability to bear mental experience may be harmed if the mother is not able to think about and contain the infant's projections of intolerable mental contents.

The first patient discussed, Mr G, had come into analysis because of a profound loss of interest in his scientific work, and a loss of enjoyment of life in general. Mr G exercised a powerful, sustained form of control on what could be experienced or meaningfully addressed in the analysis. Taylor attempts to demonstrate, in detailed clinical material, how (and why) this control was exercised, and why it could not be relinquished by Mr G.

> In the analytic situation this patient's defences took the form of a pervasive acting in whose purpose was to obviate, or fend off, the possibility of knowledge and insight. Verbal, apparently symbolic forms of communication in fact turned out to be concrete operations – actions upon the other – subtly disguised or not, as the case might be. These manipulations were intended, among other things, to keep underlying issues meaningless.

The second patient, Miss A, is less ill, and the clinical material serves to demonstrate how complex defences against knowledge may arise in all of us. Miss A becomes confused and angry in a session when the analyst interrupts her with an interpretation about her emerging feelings of desire, and her experience of the analyst as a separate person with a life and relationships outside the consulting room. Taylor observes that the confusion functions as a powerful defence against the emerging feelings and observations, but finds that Miss A can be helped in ensuing sessions to become freer and more openly curious.

Taylor emphasises the centrality of the Oedipus complex in the psychoanalytic inquiry into the emergence of knowledge, and the problems of bearing that knowledge, and relates this to the difficulties of both Miss A and Mr G. He quotes Bion's suggestion that the various *dramatis personae* in the Oedipus myth can be seen as personifications of functions of the mind, e.g. the conflict between Oedipus and the blind seer Tiresias as to whether to know or not to know. 'Looked at in this way, the Oedipus configuration is a part of the emotional/cognitive apparatus essential for knowing and learning, just as eyes and visual pathways are crucial to the processes of seeing.'

Athol Hughes' Chapter 9 is taken from her work with a 7-year-old boy who feared that talking would make him feel things he did not want to feel. Using material from this child and two adults, Hughes attempts to show how 'a certain type of patient empties verbal communication of meaning', fearing unconsciously that genuine communication will lead to intolerable psychic pain. By using projective identification, for example, to evacuate unwanted mental contents, to obliterate separateness and loss, or to omnipotently control or to act on the analyst, the patient 'can be seen to pervert the medium through which psychoanalysis is carried out: verbalised thought'.

Hughes draws on the history of psychoanalytic ideas about the use of verbal communication – from Anna O's loss of the capacity to speak when, as Breuer suggested, there was something she did not wish to say, through the contributions of Freud, Klein, Segal and Bion on symbolisation and the capacity to put thoughts into words. From Bion she takes the idea that certain patients fear that verbal communication not only is *not* helpful, but will also lead to what he called '*nameless dread*', and links this to Betty Joseph's thoughts on such patients' need to avoid psychic pain and to preserve their psychic equilibrium at all costs.

In her clinical material Hughes makes use of Joseph's ideas in order to illustrate how certain patients use words as actions in the service of primitive projective processes – to intrude into and act on the analyst's mind, thus subverting the communicative process and substituting enactment for creative thought which might lead to insight. Members of the workshop, like all analysts, need the help of colleagues in order to step back from such enactments and to regain their capacity to think.

In Chapter 10, Edna O'Shaughnessy, an early member of the workshop, uses moving material from the analysis some forty years ago of a very ill boy of 12 who, after making some movement towards attachment to the analyst and recognition of need and dependence, retreated into a psychotic identification with a cruel, all-powerful Frankenstein figure, in order to escape from intolerable psychic pain.

Hugh came into analysis in a broken down state, unable to attend school or to be alone, tyrannically ruling the household, and living in a bizarre world filled with psychotic anxieties. After about a year of painstaking work Hugh acknowledged a fragile development – a more alive, dependent, co-operative relationship with the analyst and his analysis – his 'two-way traffic'.

After only a few months, however, following the next analytic break, Hugh brought to his session for the first time a mask he had made of Frankenstein. From then on the mask came to every session, and eventually travelled everywhere with Hugh in a suitcase. In his defensive identification with the Frankenstein myth:

> He was describing a Promethean act of self-creation, a transmuting of dead bits and pieces into a being whose birth and care was not owed to parents and whose current better state was not owed to analysis. On the mask he often restitched the wound 'where Frankenstein got hit with a chair' to close the wounds of separation through which he disintegrates. By making an ever-present artefact which he could get into and get out of, one that was a victim of rejection and maltreatment, Hugh, in his omnipotent phantasies, freed himself from dependence on, confusion with, and fear, guilt and envy of, his ambiguous objects.

After three years Hugh, with the agreement of his parents, insistently brought the analysis to an end. Still in his projective identification with Frankenstein, he was, nevertheless, able to resume his education and to function somewhat better in life. In her chapter, O'Shaughnessy asks questions about the nature of Hugh's recovery, and about psychic limits. She suggests that while the 'two-way traffic' of the analysis enabled Hugh to recover to some extent, this recovery presented him with an impossible dilemma. To proceed with the recognition of his psychic reality – his dependence, his neediness, his inability to bear frustration or separation, his vulnerability to breakdown and fragmentation, guilt, and the nature of his own damaged self and that of his objects – threatened Hugh with catastrophic breakdown and madness.

Eventually, although the author reflects seriously upon her own limitations as an analyst, and on the limitations of psychoanalysis itself, she comes to believe that Hugh felt, possibly rightly, that proceeding further with the task of facing and working through his reality – internal and external – was too much, 'too big' for him. She wonders whether perhaps Hugh knew his own psychic limits, and 'stopped while the going was good'.

Martha Papadakis uses Joseph Conrad's novel *Victory* to explore a particular manifestation of envy in Chapter 11. As she puts it: 'While the sour grapes of envy may make their presence felt in crude and even violent ways, envy may also express itself with more subtlety – for instance in the ubiquitous affliction of doubt'. Confidence, trust, certainty are overthrown by confusion and hesitation under the dominance of doubt. In insidious and subtle ways the trust in one's good objects is attacked; undermined by envy; the eroding work of doubt and self-doubt wears down the capacity to love.

Axel Heyst, the protagonist of the novel, is haunted by his father's deathbed dictum: that Heyst should have a relationship with life in which he must 'look on [and] make no sound'. This curse, to be a passive observer in life, undermines Heyst's strengths and convictions. As the plot unfolds, Papadakis shows how Heyst's projective identification with his bad object – the life denying father – undermines his good objects. He becomes suspicious of the good faithful objects who had helped him to have a better connection to life. When the good new life Heyst has found is threatened, and he must fight to protect it, he is unable to do so, destroyed by doubt of the goodness of his internal object, and therefore, of himself.

Predicaments such as that of Axel Heyst may be encountered in patients who cannot tolerate the analyst's good qualities, as in Sodré's patient, who attacks the analyst's capacity to see. Envious attacks can manifest themselves in subtle and insidious ways, throwing the analyst into doubt and confusion and undermining the possibility of change.

The attention paid by the workshop to the emotional tone of the material, and its effect on the analyst's mind provides clues as to what is going on in the transference/countertransference. Influenced by Joseph's ideas and those of each other, the workshop looks at the various ways that the analyst's capacity to understand is eroded and the analytic process is undermined. It is as if the workshop becomes an auxiliary good object, helping the analyst to regain his or her analytic stance.

## Notes

1 Although it may not be immediately apparent, it is important to stress the strong connection between the work of Betty Joseph and the contributions of Bion, who emphasises the importance of the abandonment of memory, desire and understanding (Bion 1967: 18) as an optimum state of mind for the analyst to be able to explore the patient's experience unencumbered by pressures that derive either from within him or herself or from the patient. The former can manifest itself, for example, in the analyst's trying too hard to understand, or becoming excessively anxious to cure or bring relief.

This perspective underlies Joseph's work and has been developed particularly in her contribution on those patients who are 'difficult to reach'.

Bion strives to bring to light the differentiation between mental states which might, on the surface, appear to be similar. Such distinctions, although often subtle, have profound implications.

Bion (1962b) discussed how in certain situations words may be used less for communication than for their value as vehicles for ridding the mind of unwanted mental contents.

Similarly, Joseph's development of Klein's view of the transference as a 'total situation' emphasises that the patient's words taken in themselves are a very poor guide to the actual level of the patient's emotional experience. The patient's verbal communications can be fully understood only when they are taken as part of the total situation – that is, taking into account what is going on in the consulting room at that particular moment – the emotional atmosphere between analyst and patient, and the dominant anxieties and defences prevalent at the time.

Joseph (1988) also shows how words can function as a vehicle for projection which can have a powerful effect upon the mind of the analyst. 'I think that this process is so powerful, and yet so subtle that it makes it essential for the analyst in his work first of all to focus his attention on what is going on in the room, on the nature of his relationship, an issue vividly described by Bion (1963).' (p. 206) The influence of Bion's ideas will be apparent and in some cases central in the chapters in this book.

## References

Bion, W.R. (1962a) *Learning from Experience*, Maresfield Reprints, London: Karnac (1984).

—— (1962b) 'A theory of thinking', *Second Thoughts: Selected Papers on Psycho-Analysis*, New York: Jason Aronson (1967). First published in *International Journal of Psychoanalysis*, Volume 43, Parts 4–5.

—— (1963) *Elements of Psycho-Analysis*, London: Heinemann, reprinted in paperback, Maresfield Reprints, London: Karnac (1984).

—— (1967) 'Notes on memory and desire', *Melanie Klein Today: Developments in Theory and Practice*, Vol. 2, *Mainly Practice*, Elizabeth Bott Spillius (ed.), London: Routledge (1988) First published in *The Psychoanalytic Forum*, 2: 272–3, 279–80.

—— (1977) *Seven Servants: Four Works by Wilfred R. Bion*, New York: Jason Aronson.

Breuer, J. and Freud, S. (1895) 'Fräulein Anna O', *Studies on Hysteria, The Standard Edition of the Complete Works of Sigmund Freud* (SE), London: Hogarth Press (1950–1974), SE 2: 21–47.

Freud, S. (1940) 'An outline of psychoanalysis', SE 23:141–194.

Joseph, B. (1959) 'An aspect of the repetition compulsion', *Psychic Equilibrium and Psychic Change: Selected Papers of Betty Joseph*, M. Feldman and E. Bott Spillius (eds), London: Routledge (1989).

—— (1960) 'Some characteristics of the psychopathic personality', *Psychic Equilibrium and Psychic Change: Selected Papers of Betty Joseph*, M. Feldman and E. Bott Spillius (eds), London: Routledge (1989).

—— (1975) 'The patient who is difficult to reach', *Tactics and Techniques in Psycho-analytic Therapy*, vol. II, Countertransference, P.L. Giovacchini (ed.), New York: Jason Aronson; reprinted in *Psychic Equilibrium and Psychic Change: Selected Papers of Betty Joseph*, M. Feldman and E. Bott Spillius (eds), London: Routledge (1989).

—— (1985) 'Transference: the total situation', *Psychic Equilibrium and Psychic Change: Selected Papers of Betty Joseph*, M. Feldman and E. Bott Spillius (eds), London: Routledge (1989).

—— (1988) 'Object relations in clinical practice', *Psychic Equilibrium and Psychic Change: Selected Papers of Betty Joseph*, M. Feldman and E. Bott Spillius (eds), London: Routledge (1989).

—— (1989) *Psychic Equilibrium and Psychic Change: Selected Papers of Betty Joseph*, M. Feldman and E. Bott Spillius (eds), London: Routledge

Klein, M. (1952) 'The origins of transference', *The Writings of Melanie Klein*, vol. 3, *Envy and Gratitude and Other Works*, London: Hogarth Press (1975).

Spillius, E. Bott. (1994) 'Developments in Kleinian thought: overview and personal view', *Psychoanalytic Inquiry*, 14(3), *Contemporary Kleinian Psychoanalysis*, 324–364.

Steiner, J. (1993) *Psychic Retreats: Pathological Organizations of the Personality in Psychotic, Neurotic, and Borderline Patients*, London: Routledge.

# 1

# SUPPORTING PSYCHIC CHANGE: BETTY JOSEPH

*Michael Feldman*

James Strachey (1934) wrote his great paper on the therapeutic action of psychoanalysis at a time when many of Freud's fundamental ideas had already become established, and Klein's further research work was emerging. He quotes the passage from Freud's introductory lecture (published in 1917) where Freud suggests that psychic change

> is made possible by the alteration of the ego which is accomplished under the influence of the doctor's suggestion. By means of the work of interpretation, which transforms what is unconscious into what is conscious, the ego is enlarged at the cost of this unconscious; by means of instruction, it is made conciliatory towards the libido and inclined to grant it some satisfaction, and its repugnance to the claims of the libido is diminished. . . . The more closely events in the treatment coincide with this ideal description, the greater will be the success of the psycho-analytic therapy.
>
> (Freud 1917: 455)

Strachey observed that in the seventeen years since he wrote that passage, Freud produced very little that bears directly on the subject, and that little goes to show that he had not altered his views of the main principles involved.

Many of the subsequent formulations concerning psychic change incorporate two of the elements Freud presented in 1917. First, the 'geographical' model – the notion of the ego being enlarged, or more recently the notion of lost parts of the ego being recovered, reincorporated. Second, he considers the development of a different relationship between two parts of the psyche – the ego becoming more accepting of the claims of the libido. Sandler and Sandler (1994) formulate this in a more contemporary form as follows:

> We aim at freeing what has become, during the course of development, *unacceptable* in the present, in such a way that it is not acted out but is tolerated within the patient's psychic life without having to be defended against, by virtue of being viewed from a more mature and tolerant perspective.
>
> (Sandler and Sandler 1994: 438, original emphasis)

However, in 1933 Freud offered a formulation of the intentions of the therapeutic efforts of psychoanalysis that I find subtly different, stronger and more interesting. He said 'Its intention is, indeed, to strengthen the ego, to make it more independent of the super-ego, to widen its field of perception and enlarge its organisation', although he did add that this was 'So that it can appropriate fresh portions of the id' (Freud 1933: 80). Freud (1937) returned to some of these issues in 'Analysis terminable and interminable'. He was primarily interested in those factors which influenced the success or otherwise of analytic treatment, and identified the effects of trauma, and the role of the constitutional strength of the instincts. He also argued that the outcome of treatment depended on the extent to which the ego of the person under treatment was able to form a co-operative alliance with the analyst, in order to subdue portions of his id which are uncontrolled – that is to say to include them in the synthesis of his ego. In a schematic description of the process of treatment, he referred to the therapeutic work constantly swinging backwards and forwards like a pendulum, between a piece of id-analysis and a piece of ego-analysis. In the one case we want to make something from the id conscious, in the other we want to correct something in the ego. Finally, as is well known, in this paper he addresses the fact that in the course of the work of analysis, one may become aware of 'a force which is defending itself by every possible means against recovery and which is absolutely resolved to hold on to illness and suffering' (Freud 1937: 238). He concluded that the phenomena of masochism, the negative therapeutic reaction and the sense of guilt provide unmistakable indications of the presence of a power in mental life which could be described as the instinct of destruction.

Returning for a moment to Strachey's (1934) paper, the issue he raises is that in contrast to the rich and powerful model of the mental apparatus, the understanding of the neuroses, of defences and resistances which had been developed, the explanatory descriptions or theories concerning the actual process of therapeutic change, and how the analyst's interventions can promote such change seemed limited and unsatisfactory. He then tried to address some of the crucial issues himself – what kinds of interpretations promote psychic change, through what mechanisms do they operate, what is their impact on the patient, and what difficulties does the analyst have in making such mutative interventions? In the model he proposed, he not only recognised the way the analyst became identified with elements of the archaic object projected into him, but also suggested that therapeutic change comes about when the patient is able to re-introject the archaic superego, modified by the analyst's understanding.

I want to focus on that aspect of Joseph's (1989) work that follows directly in this fascinating, difficult and important tradition. Her thinking clearly embodies the theoretical and clinical model which Klein developed, elaborated and enriched by Rosenfeld, Segal and Bion. Her outstanding contribution lies in her capacity to focus sensitively and thoughtfully on fine clinical and technical issues. Thus, embedded in Joseph's work, is a complex and subtle theory of psychic change, which I propose to explore.

In a recent example of her work which I am going to examine in some detail, Joseph elaborates her understanding of these drives towards or away from development, by means of her study of the use the patient makes of the analyst and her interpretations on the one hand, and her own mental capacities, on the other. These capacities are sometimes used constructively, but the patient will also misuse understanding in a defensive way – to attack herself or her objects, to create a false compliance or collusion, or to whip up sadomasochistic excitement. Joseph illustrates the importance of attending not only to the symbolic content of the patient's communications, but also to the tone, the atmosphere that is created, and the responses elicited in the analyst. The patient not only uses projection into the analyst in phantasy, but also uses language and non-verbal behaviour to have an actual effect on the analyst, who may become drawn into various defensive enactments. By giving detailed attention to these processes in patients, in him or herself, and the interaction between them, the analyst can begin to build up a sense of the way that patients are using their own mind and the analyst's interpretations. Joseph refers to the way in which the analyst can thus, over time, build up a picture of the patients' inner worlds. What I wish to focus on is the fact that embedded in Joseph's understanding of these processes, and the use she makes of this understanding, lies a complex and subtle theory of psychic change.

In an unpublished paper 'The pursuit of insight and psychic change' Joseph (1997) begins with Freud's dictum 'Where id was ego shall be', which, she suggests, takes us to the core of our problem, namely 'Psychic structure and its inner objects and their possibility of change'. Our aim, she says, is to enable the personality to contain and be responsible for more aspects of itself, thus enlarging the ego and modifying its structure, and to increase its capacity for thinking, reality testing etc. As a step towards achieving this, she emphasises the need to attend closely to the way that patients hear the analyst's interpretations at a given moment, and to try to discover how they use them. The *way* that patients use the relationship with the analyst, and specifically their interpretation, provides us with crucial information about the internal dynamics of our patients' minds. We need to follow not only what happens to the interpretation itself, but also what has happened to that part of the personality that may, however briefly, have had insight. Does it, for example, get swallowed up or attacked by another part; does it arouse too much anxiety, become split off and projected into the analyst?

This perspective leads Joseph to focus not only her observations but also her interpretations on the way that patients are using their own mind, their own understanding and insight, how an interpretation was experienced, and what they have done with it. She stresses the importance of concentrating these observations on the manifestations of these processes in the detailed interactions of the session, generally avoiding interpretations that refer to phenomena that are not immediately accessible to the patient. She also believes it is important to avoid attaching explanatory or causal formulations to the interpretation before the patient has been able to recognise what it is that one is attempting to account for.

The theory of projective identification implicit in this perspective has been elaborated by Rosenfeld, Segal and others, and Bion has described his model of the way the patient's projections are received and modified by the analyst's capacity to tolerate and eventually to understand their contents. While Joseph also emphasises the need for the analyst to be able to cope with periods of anxiety, uncertainty and not-understanding, one of her distinctive contributions has been to recognise the way the patient's projections constitute a constant pressure towards enactment by the analyst in the session. Her recognition of the presence of this force, and the way it affects the analyst in the session leads her also to focus very closely on the analyst's experience, and the complex interactions which occur from moment to moment, which are an important source of understanding of the patient's internal world, as well as the basis for interpretations of such processes, which the analyst hopes will promote greater insight and psychic change.

This is then part of the process, which Joseph describes, of 'enlarging the ego' increasing its capacity for thinking, reality testing, etc. She argues that this is brought about in part through helping patients to internalise and identify with the analyst's thoughtful and containing functions, and their capacity to face reality, so that patients come to be able to observe and interest themselves more in the workings of their own minds. This is facilitated through the analyst's continuing efforts to clarify and formulate the experience that is actually available to patients at that moment, which they can recognise and acknowledge. Such clarification may, of course, involve the recognition of mechanisms that interfere with understanding. It is often necessary to go over this process repeatedly, taking into account the nature of the patient's responses to the analyst's interventions, in order for the analyst to clarify and refine the understanding of the situation both for him or herself and for the patient. Joseph argues that only when this vital descriptive and containing step has been achieved, is it useful to move to the gradual elucidation of the motives or reasons, continuing to focus mainly on the way these express themselves in the interaction in the session. If the analyst makes a more complex interpretation, which includes both the description and an explanatory formulation, the patient is liable, for defensive reasons, to lose contact with the reality of what is immediately present and available, and focus instead on the 'explanation' offered. It is sometimes evident that premature, broad explanatory interpretations are given partly to relieve anxiety both in the analyst and the patient, since the attempt really to clarify and to understand the immediate processes and interactions imposes considerable demands on both.

While formulations such as expanding or strengthening the ego provide a broad explanatory formulation, we still have to refine our understanding of the way in which the analyst's understanding and clarification contributes to the therapeutic process. We do, of course, encounter patients who seem to be capable of observing the workings of their own minds (as well as the analyst's) in a way that is not helpful. In these cases, we find the motivation for such observation is primarily envious or rivalrous, to demonstrate superiority and defend against any dependency. Thus although there may be partial understanding, there is also a powerful enactment of an omnipotent, narcissistic process which is hostile to any constructive interaction. On the contrary, the analyst's role in this process is attacked, devalued or ignored. There must therefore be other aspects of introjective identification which do truly contribute to the 'enlargement of the ego', the capacity to tolerate anxiety and conflict, etc. I hope the more detailed discussion of clinical material that follows may throw some light on these difficult issues.

We assume that the patient's experience of the analyst and the analyst's interpretations evokes an unconscious phantasy in the patient, based upon an archaic object relationship. Although the analyst may know this theoretically, it is often difficult to recognise the particular phantasy evoked in the patient at a given point in the session. On the contrary, the way the analyst addresses the patient is influenced by the analyst's assumptions about the patient's state of mind at that moment. These assumptions are, of course, subject to distortions based on the limitations of the analyst's understanding, and the way the patient's projections resonate with unconscious anxieties and needs. However, if the analyst is able to pay close attention to the patient's responses to his or her intervention they can alert the analyst to the nature of the object relationship which is actually present and alive, the unconscious phantasy which it embodies, and the meaning that the intervention had for the patient. This may then enable the analyst (at the time, or subsequently) to focus more directly on the patient's actual phantasies and experience, which can be taken account of in subsequent interpretations.

To give a brief example of my own, a patient who had been missing sessions and coming late to others began a session speaking in a fluent, assertive way, insisting that the fact that he had missed sessions was *not* an attack on the analysis. *He* thought it was an expression of his needs and his problems, which he went on to elaborate in a familiar way. After a pause, he said he didn't want to do anything he was supposed to do, including an important project at work. In part he took this as a good sign: he hoped he was less compliant, and a healthy rebelliousness was emerging. Later in the session he said he and his girlfriend had started eating special healthy foods, and had taken up Tai-chi. He actually felt very healthy at the moment, and indeed he sounded vigorous and alert.

The patient thus presents himself as a vigorous, healthy person, with his own understanding of the nature of his problems, and his own methods of treatment. Although he alluded to needs and problems, and I recognised elements of my own formulations in his explanations, he seemed neither in touch with these, nor any discomfort, guilt or concern about his lateness and the missed sessions. From my knowledge of this patient's propensity to identify with and take possession of his objects, as well as the way he actually conducted himself in this session, I attempted to describe the situation, in particular the way he seemed to have assumed the role and functions of the analyst. The patient disagreed immediately, with some vehemence. He said that on the contrary, he felt he was speaking for himself, expressing his own views, which he often finds difficult to do, and he was pleased about that.

What became evident was that the patient had not experienced my intervention as a description or interpretation which enabled him to recognise or understand something more about his own mind and the way it worked, or as the basis for further exploration or clarification. The interpretation thus did not provide him with anything he might use to think about or with. On the contrary, he construed the intervention primarily as the expression of an object relationship embodying his archaic experiences, to which he responded in a characteristic fashion. He assumed that the analyst was trying to undermine his confidence and health, and wanted a compliant, dependent patient. I was aware of this patient's insubstantial sense of his own personality, and how prone he was both to use and suffer from invasive and seductive invasions. On this occasion, I had failed to register properly the significance of his emphasis on what *he* thought, how *he* understood the situation, his concern with being less compliant. My interpretation, and the unconscious phantasy it evoked, was evidently felt as a threat to rob him of this achievement, and assert that he had merely assumed my role and function. He believed my main purpose in speaking to him was to try to reclaim the functions I had been robbed of, reverse the situation, and reduce him to a pathetic and dependent figure. His only way of countering this, as ever, was to assert himself in an angry, argumentative fashion, demonstrating the failure and inadequacy of my intervention.

In this example, in addition to my conscious attempt at descriptive explanation, I may well have felt it necessary to assert myself in a way which the patient was very sensitive to, and which he immediately responded to. It often only seems possible to recognise and understand these complex interactions after we have been drawn into such misunderstandings, or enactments. Joseph's work has helped to alert us to these recurrent situations, the necessity to recognise and recover from them, and in due course to show the patient some elements of what one comes to recognise has been going on. Thus once I could realise what I had not properly attended to, and the extent to which I might in fact have felt driven to try to reassert my role, I could perhaps provide the patient with a more accurate description of his experience, and interpret the way he had perceived my response. Furthermore, if I had sufficiently understood the responses the patient had evoked in me, and considered perhaps why he might need to evoke such responses, I might also have been able to make such an interpretation with less need unconsciously to assert myself.

One of the fundamental aims which Joseph articulates is to enable the patient increasingly to hear our interpretations as interpretations, as the communication of understanding. This must involve the diminution in the extent and force of the projective identification which the patient needs to employ, as Segal (1957, 1977) has described, so the interpretations can acquire new symbolic meaning, and are not primarily experienced as concrete manifestations of earlier object relationships. The crucial question which Joseph tries to address is how we can achieve this aim. One familiar way of enlarging the capacities and functions of the ego is of course to make interpretations which attempt to demonstrate the (unconscious) links between the patient's responses to the analyst, and his early object relationships. I believe Joseph has come to believe that while the analyst's recognition and understanding of such links in their broader historical context remains crucial, it is more therapeutically valuable to focus on the detailed *expression* of these underlying phantasies in the analytic session. They express themselves in the way the patient experiences and uses the analyst on the one hand, and the conscious and unconscious responses that are evoked in him, what he is drawn into feeling and enacting, on the other.

In the unpublished paper I have referred to, Joseph (1997) describes the early phase of the analysis of an adolescent girl, who came into analysis with a vague feeling of dissatisfaction with her life, a lack of confidence, uncertain what she wanted to do in the future. She came to recognise, with a sense of shock, that she actually had almost no interest in her work or in her life outside and that in some way she was different from the other girls at her school. The patient had thus been enabled to expand her awareness of herself, albeit in a very uncomfortable way; to recognise the existence of a problem in herself. Joseph then describes a session that took place while the patient's mother was away. The previous evening she had got into a panic about her school work and her future, feeling that no one would help her. When her father responded to her expression of despair, the patient shouted at him that he didn't understand, *she didn't have any interests*, and the two of them had a row. She did calm down, however, and asked her father where the family would be in a year or so. He explained some of the possibilities to her, including his concern that she should be settled, even though he and her mother might have to move. The patient remarked that she was glad they had had a fight, it was a revelation, usually there is a scene and she behaves as though she can't do anything about it, but this time her father knew she was creating a drama. Joseph's initial interpretative intervention focused on the fact that the patient had, in earlier sessions, recognised that this way of creating a drama prevented her from having to face the reality either of her real possibilities and capacities or of her limitations. The patient replied that it was funny, she knew, but she didn't know.

Joseph suggests that when the patient is confronted with the anxiety connected with her growing awareness of her difficulties, and their implications for her future, instead of being able to make any constructive use of what she had recognised in the previous session, her 'insight' is used instead as a kind of weapon against her father (and her analyst), to provoke and attack.

However, the father *was* able to recover, and reassured her that he wanted to see her settled. The patient was, in turn, able to calm down, and Joseph suggests this reflects the patient's capacity to discover, and make use of a good and helpful internal object. The corollary to this is that if either the patient or her object (or both) are unable to resist continuing the fight, perhaps because it is a source of too much gratification, it may be difficult or impossible for the patient to locate or engage with this good object. The other implication is that in some patients, of course, such an object does not exist or cannot be recovered. With my own patient whom I referred to earlier, although his primary objects appear to want to help, they are almost entirely experienced as seductive and invasive, with no real understanding or concern for him. With that patient, whenever a violent or excited interaction was replaced by a calmer and apparently more thoughtful atmosphere, it usually emerged that this was based on compliance and propitiation which is not strengthening, but confirms his despair.

With Joseph's patient, by contrast, she points out how, as the patient talks, she seems able to relate to an object, her father and her analyst, who can listen and tolerate her outburst. This rediscovery of a good internal object serves, in turn, to strengthen her ego, 'the thinking part of her personality', that leads to further brief movement in the session. Later in the session, we find another example, where the patient said she realised that she likes to make her grandmother sorry for her for having to come to analysis. When her grandmother asked why she came to analysis *four* times a week, the patient portrayed herself saying in a rather bland way, 'Well I have a lot to solve'. Joseph describes the way the tone and manner the patient adopts in the session serves to disown and project into the analyst the knowledge that she wants help, does indeed have a lot to solve, and needs a good deal of time in analysis for this. Thus once again she does not use the insight she had gained to further her knowledge and understanding, but in an active way to provoke and attack, apparently leaving herself in a rather bland and indifferent state.

In her work, Joseph repeatedly draws our attention to the importance of the analyst being sensitive to the tone and manner as well as the contents of the communication, and aware of the responses these evoke in the analyst. When the patient later says, for example, 'I suppose I should feel you are important and that I am lucky to come, I should treasure it, but I feel it as a burden', and then describes a schoolfriend who is *devoted* to her therapist, the analyst may become drawn into believing the patient has real insight, real regret about some response which is missing in her. Alternately, of course, the analyst might feel doubtful about the reality of the patient's insight or provoked and mocked by her manner of speaking. In either case, the analyst's understanding of the situation will be temporarily limited or distorted. Thus while the patient's projection of her uncomfortable awareness of her needs may take place in phantasy alone, Joseph's way of attending to the patient's communications enables us to follow the *means* by which, for example, real concern is projected into the analyst and disowned or mocked, engendering in the analyst an experience of frustration and exasperation. Joseph further suggests that, 'By now the insight, the capacity to value is no longer just denied and projected; it is used in a perverse way against real insight and against me'.

Near the end of the session, the patient brought a dream, in which she and her father were supposed to go to a dinner arranged at the school, but her father said they were sorry they couldn't come. The teacher was angry and bossy, but when they explained they had a prior engagement, she said OK. In her discussion of the dream, Joseph suggests that there are indications of the patient's insight into a number of related issues: the existence of the parental couple, represented by the father and the teacher, or analyst getting together to share a meal, or to share some understanding. There is some recognition of the value of the meal that is available, and perhaps some inklings of her own rivalry, jealousy and envy. One can then follow some of the mechanisms that protect the patient from the uncomfortable awareness of these issues. First, the projection of the part of her that wants or values into the teacher/analyst, who becomes angry and bossy when what she offers is rejected, and who has to be placated by the patient and her father, who have now become the central couple. The patient seems to have dealt with any anxiety and guilt about rejecting what the mother offers, and taking possession of the father by a mixture of projection and compliant appeasement, which Joseph then proceeds to investigate further.

While Joseph evidently has a model in her mind both of the patient's difficulties in her relationship to the breast and to the Oedipal couple, it is important to note that she does not, at this point, describe any interpretations of the underlying Oedipal phantasies. I hope to return to this issue. It is linked with Joseph's assumption that real psychic change is more likely to be promoted by the detailed description of how the patient is using the analyst, using interpretations, or using her own mind in a given session, and *then* to move to the analysis of the way the patient's history, and unconscious phantasies express themselves in the immediacy of the processes and interactions in the session. Although more explicit links, say, to the patient's relation to her primary objects might seem to be an alternative method of 'enlarging the ego', and such formulations remain of fundamental importance in the analyst's thinking, Joseph cautions that interpretations along these lines may represent a subtle form of defensive enactment by the analyst. To the extent that this is the case, such interventions are liable to be used by the patient for defensive purposes, rather than facilitating real psychic change.

In her analysis of the patient's dream Joseph describes the central importance for this patient of a form of compliance as a defence against insight. She had pointed out to the patient that the moment she made an interpretation, the patient immediately felt criticised. I presume the purpose of making this observation is to invite the patient to recognise the fact, and to begin to explore the reasons for the perceptions and distortions that might have led to this. The patient responded to her comment by agreeing, and giving a similar example in relation to a teacher. Joseph observes:

> By the time she had finished the description any interest in her own upset or the teacher's or my assumed criticism had disappeared and her main concern seemed to be in confirming my interpretation and then in giving further examples to show how right I was.

The analyst interpreted that they could see how when a conflict arose she tended to accept the viewpoint of whoever she was with at the moment, fitting in with each. The patient responded to this interpretation with immediate agreement, and gave examples of how she did exactly this with her grandmother. The analyst showed the patient how this was again presented as if to be in perfect agreement with her, fitting in until the two of them were 'mentally hand in hand'.

Joseph gives several illustrations of the way the patient often responded to particular anxieties or disturbance by withdrawing in just this way, attempting to draw her object into a state of total agreement, where there is little differentiation between herself and her object. 'Any contact with insight and understanding appears to be lost but it is more than lost it is actually annihilated and then she cannot use her mind properly, she "goes stupid" but feels safe'. If the analyst is able to recognise the process that is taking place, without becoming drawn into collusive agreement, and tries to speak about it, the patient does not necessarily feel understood or supported. On the contrary, she may experience the analyst's non-compliance as a threat to her equilibrium.

I should like to return to the point I touched on earlier, namely the use the analyst makes of his or her understanding of the underlying unconscious phantasies and their origins in the patient's history, using the material above to illustrate the issues. When Joseph describes the patient's propensity to fit in, to try to create an illusion of perfect agreement, one can see the way this may protect the patient against certain kinds of anxiety, conflict and guilt, but should we also be considering the 'underlying' phantasies – either the desired ones or the feared ones? For example, is the phantasy of perfect agreement a manifestation of Oedipal triumph over the excluded parent, or over the analyst him or herself? Does it represent a denial of differences, a defence against envy? Or is it a defence against the phantasy of some catastrophic consequences – in relation to her mother (who was away), her father, or the analyst? How useful is it to explore these underlying phantasies in an explicit way with the patient? I believe these and other possibilities form part of the framework of Joseph's conceptual model, but she has argued that it is important for analysts to keep them at the back of their mind, not to allow them to obtrude, as they may interfere with their capacity to be open to the impact and meaning of what is taking place in the session. I think she believes that we often make interpretations relating to our patients' history, their broader motives, and the underlying phantasies prematurely, responding defensively to the anxieties which are inevitably stirred up in the analyst, in an attempt to 'make sense' of what is happening. (I believe this is a similar issue to that addressed by Bion (1967) in his remarks about memory and desire.) I think she also believes that attempts to formulate such interpretations are often premature from the *patient's* point of view, and may reinforce his or her defensive structure. It must be said, however, that it is difficult to find the balance between the recognition of the potential for interpretations to be used defensively by analysts and patients, and the situation in which analysts may avoid making more direct interpretations relating to their patients' underlying phantasies, either in response to their own anxieties, or those which they are made consciously or unconsciously aware of in their patients.

The phantasies that Joseph does refer to are closely related to the processes that can be observed in the session – in particular the patient's difficulties with mental differentiation and separation. Although there are glimpses of the patient's interest in development, and her constructive desire for change, the anxieties which are elicited when her equilibrium is threatened lead to the re-emergence of primitive defensive mechanisms. For example, the patient felt uncomfortable in relation to a male cousin, and felt pressure to adopt the clothes and manners appropriate to a young woman. This challenged her habitual way of making herself comfortable by getting into a shirt and old pair of shorts of her father's. The anxieties aroused by the situation with the young man and the phantasies that were evoked increased the pull to get into and become identified with a familiar and comfortable object.

Joseph's view of the patient's current anxieties and defences is enriched by her reconstruction of the early infantile processes they partly recapitulate. She suggests that the pattern of responses to the threat of loss or change which she observed in the session may have been expressed by the infant clinging desperately to the breast, or becoming totally identified with the breast. She thus has great difficulty in being able to derive nourishment from an object recognised as separate, which enables her to develop a sense of structure and meaning, and finds herself in a state of confusion.

Joseph's (1997) paper serves to illustrate the particular focus of her work, and the implicit theory of psychic change which it embodies. While taking account of the material concerning the patient's current life, and making inferences concerning the patient's early infantile and childhood experience, her orientation is primarily towards the pattern of anxieties and defences to the fore at any moment in the session. For example, the patient's communication about her inclination to get into her father's old and comfortable shorts, particularly when she felt threatened by the pressure for development, facilitates the analyst's recognition of the patient's propensity to get comfortably into the analyst's words, or into her mind, rather than having to cope with the stress of relating to the analyst as a separate figure, trying to think and understand.

The work of Joseph and a number of colleagues is extending and developing Freud's familiar but profound formulation concerning transference.

> This struggle between the doctor and the patient, between intellect and instinctual life, between understanding and seeking to act, is played out almost exclusively in the phenomena of transference. It is on that field that the victory must be won. . . .

He goes on to say that the phenomena of transference

> do us the inestimable service of making the patient's hidden and forgotten erotic impulses immediate and manifest. For when all is said and done, it is impossible to destroy anyone *in absentia* or *in effigie*.
>
> (Freud 1912: 108)

While Joseph remains very concerned about the struggle between patient and analyst, and between understanding and seeking to act, she extends the focus beyond the patient's 'erotic impulses'. She emphasises the unique opportunity the analyst has of understanding not only the patient's needs and desires, but also the pattern of anxieties and defences through the way these are lived out in the session. She illustrates how this can be seen in the way the patient uses her mind, the way she responds to interpretations, and particularly the way she needs to use the analyst. Furthermore, Joseph argues that this is not only the most vivid and profound basis for understanding the patient, but also the field in which to address interpretations that are most likely to promote psychic change.

We seem more easily able to elucidate the forces that militate *against* change, than to elaborate on those that promote change. Joseph refers several times to the importance of the patient rediscovering a good object that exists, which could, for a while, be experienced as benign and supportive, and help her to face her psychic reality. However, Joseph then elaborates the point that at depth the patient seemed to believe that she was not actually tolerated, understood or loved, but was really hated by her important objects, including her analyst. 'So she has to fit in and go along with them – act what they want – not believing in any real understanding and being identified with an object that has given up trying to understand and make sense of anything'. The problem we all face, which I think Strachey (1934) was attempting to address, and which Joseph

(1997) spells out with great clarity, is that the analyst's interventions are likely to be experienced as emanating from such an unsupportive, non-understanding archaic object in different degrees. They are liable to be experienced as threats, intrusions or demands for compliance, rather than expressions of real concern, or attempts at real understanding. They then provoke the patient into the kinds of clinging or invasive responses Joseph describes, which result in a form of identification that goes even further towards obliterating the analyst as a separate, supportive object. In a closely analogous way, the patient's capacity for thinking and understanding are obliterated by her invasive occupation of the analyst's mind, and she then has no capacity to respond to interpretations with understanding. The great question which I think Strachey raised, and which Joseph's work continues to address, is how we break out of this vicious circle.

I do not believe there are any easy or clear answers to this. However, I think Joseph's approach offers us an important model. The first point is that she draws attention to the need to be aware of the pressures on the analyst (emanating from the patient, and from within the analyst) towards forms of compliance and enactment which support or even reinforce the pathological situation. Certain kinds of interpretations that may be gratifying or relieving for the analyst become readily incorporated into the patient's defensive system, or provide further gratification of a perverse and destructive force.

Although we talk, for convenience, of archaic internal objects as if they were fixed structures, I believe it may be more useful to see them as dynamic structures whose qualities and functions are maintained by the way they are treated, and what is projected into them. Their apparent stability derives from the continuity of the psychic needs they are required to fulfil, and the anxieties and defences to which they, in turn, give rise. If the analyst is able to follow with sufficient clarity what the patient does with him or her, externally and internally, and thus how the patient comes to see and experience the analyst, and if the analyst is able to share his or her understanding with the patient without becoming drawn too much into familiar pathological patterns, this can provide the patient with a sense of reassurance and containment. Such a sense of immediate contact with an understanding object may in turn diminish the pressure to maintain the pathological, archaic objects and object relationships which have proved necessary and/or gratifying to the patient. This seems to me to open up the prospect of simultaneous change in the quality of the patient's internal objects, and change in the way the analyst is experienced. The demands on the analyst for constraint, for understanding and containment, however, are considerable, and will usually be incompletely met.

In the paper I have been discussing, Joseph (1997) reveals the theoretical framework of her thinking. She speaks, for example, of the parts of the patient's personality that have been projected into her father, her teacher or her analyst. At other points she describes the patient's attempts to withdraw into an enclave in which she creates a paralysing compliant relationship with her object, or alternately the patient's more forceful projections of her whole personality – expressed as her getting into her father's clothes, into an identification with a falsely reassuring object. She describes the infantile paradigm that underlies the patient's propensity to cling desperately to her object, or concretely to her object's words. Thus the analyst is very aware of some of the unconscious phantasies which pervade the session, in particular the phantasies which these defensive movements embody. However, I think Joseph believes that while it is important for analysts to evolve such a theoretical and conceptual understanding of their patients, their inner worlds and their object relations in particular, this structure should not intrude into analysts' thinking in the session, but remain somehow at the back of their mind. It can be argued that this may lead to analysts restricting their interpretations too closely, and perhaps not making use of the therapeutic value that may lie in extending patients' understanding of themselves in relation to their history, and more complex, structured unconscious phantasies involving their primary objects.

Close attention to the way that patients are functioning within the session, how they use their own mind and their own experience, as well as the analyst's interventions, can enable the analyst to build up a picture of the forces within their patients which lead them to act upon, and thus to perceive their external and internal objects in accordance with archaic needs and anxieties. The analyst can, for example, become aware of the pressures on him or her to conform to repetitive patterns, and the intense anxiety and hostility aroused if the analyst does not so conform. If the analyst *is* able to recognise and bear the way he or she is being acted upon and reconstructed according to their patients' needs, and thus how the analyst is being experienced, and to speak to the patient about what is going on, without being driven to act in corresponding ways, this seems to provide the patient with an important experience of being understood, and an experience of relief. This in turn diminishes the force with which the archaic versions of the patient's objects (internal and external) have to be maintained. I believe this is an essential element for achieving psychic change, and it is this approach that is embodied in Joseph's work.

You may recall the quotation from Freud (1937), where he speaks of the therapeutic work constantly swinging backwards and forwards like a pendulum between a piece of id-analysis and a piece of ego-analysis. Many analysts will feel that this describes what they aim to achieve in their work. Joseph has, however, evolved a more specific and detailed theory of this therapeutic process. She stresses the importance first, of clarifying, with the patient, some limited aspect of his thinking, understanding, misunderstanding, the way he is using the analyst. This must be done in small steps, and be very much located in the present experience of the session, and it is only then of real therapeutic value to move to what could be described as a piece of 'id-analysis'. This involves the examination of the impulses, desires and motives that lead the patient to function in the way that has just been described.

These efforts can be successful only to the extent to which they do not, in any important way, represent analysts enacting their frustration, their own narcissistic or defensive needs (including their needs to cure their patients), or analysts' enactment of some role required of them by their patients. These are complex and difficult demands, and will always be met to varying degrees, and for varying periods of time. Such interventions, freed from overt theoretical, historical or explanatory contents, are very difficult to achieve, and to sustain, partly because they are also frightening for the analyst. It is striking that Strachey (1934) recognised this as well. He wrote:

> Behind this there is sometimes a lurking difficulty in the actual giving of the interpretation, for there seems to be a constant temptation for the analyst to do something else instead. He may ask questions, or he may give reassurances or advice or discourses upon theory, or he may give interpretations – but interpretations that are not mutative, extra-transference interpretations, interpretations that are non-immediate, or ambiguous, or inexact – or he may give two or more alternative interpretations simultaneously, or he may give interpretations and at the same time show his own scepticism about them. All of this strongly suggests that the giving of a mutative interpretation is a crucial act for the analyst as well as for the patient, and that he is exposing himself to some great danger in doing so.
>
> (Strachey 1934: 291)

What such interventions aim to achieve is very well illustrated in Joseph's work. I think she aims to strengthen the patient's capacity to observe, to recognise, to understand, particularly what goes on in his or her own mind within the fabric of the session, and in the patient's interaction with the analyst. I believe this is what Freud may have been referring to in his 1933 lecture, when he spoke of strengthening the ego, widening its field of perception and enlarging its organisation. I think this is a central aspect of what Strachey was seeking to achieve with a mutative interpretation – to enable the patient to recognise, to think, to understand, and partially to free himself from the domination of archaic object relationships.

## References


Bion, W.R. (1967) 'Notes on memory and desire', *The Psychoanalytic Forum*, 2: 272–273, 279–280; reprinted in *Melanie Klein Today: Developments in Theory and Practice*, vol. 2, *Mainly Practice*, E. Bott Spillius (ed.), London: Routledge (1988).

Freud, S. (1917) 'Introductory lectures: analytic therapy', SE 15: 455.

—— (1933) 'New introductory lectures: dissection of the personality', SE 22: 80.

——- (1937) 'Analysis terminable and interminable', SE 23: 209–253.

Joseph, B. (1989) *Psychic Equilibrium and Psychic Change: Selected Papers of Betty Joseph*, M. Feldman and E. Bott Spillius (eds), London: Routledge.

—— (1997) 'The pursuit of insight and psychic change', paper given to conference on Psychic Structure and Psychic Change: Therapeutic Factors in Psychoanalysis, University College London.

Sandler, J. and Sandler, A.M. (1994) 'Theoretical and technical comments on regression and anti-regression', *International Journal of Psychoanalysis*, 75: 431–439.

Segal, H. (1957) 'Notes on symbol formation', *International Journal of Psychoanalysis*, 38: 391–397; reprinted in *The Work of Hanna Segal*, New York: Jason Aronson (1981).

—— (1977) 'Psychoanalysis and freedom of thought', inaugural lecture, Freud Memorial Visiting Professor of Psychoanalysis, University College London, 1977–1978, published by H.K. Lewis, London; also in *The Work of Hanna Segal*, New York: Jason Aronson (1981); reprinted in paperback, London: Free Association Books (1986).

Strachey, J. (1934) 'The nature of the therapeutic action of psychoanalysis', *International Journal of Psychoanalysis*, 15:127–159; reprinted in *International Journal of Psychoanalysis*, 50: 275–291 (1969).

# DISCUSSION OF MICHAEL FELDMAN'S CHAPTER

## *Ignes Sodré*

Nothing could be more important for a working psychoanalyst than her concept of psychic change: what it constitutes, how it can be achieved, and the extent to which it is possible to realise it. Michael, in his usual lucid and precise way, studies Betty Joseph's work in depth to distil from it the theoretical and technical ideas that inform and determine her concept of psychic change.

As is well known, Betty Joseph's most original contribution to psychoanalytic technique is the particular emphasis on close attention to the minute detail of the relationship taking place in the here and now of the session – she is the master of particularity and specificity. What Michael describes, using clinical material of his own, but mainly focusing on some unpublished material of Joseph's, is how she believes that Psychic Change (in capital letters, as it were) can best be achieved through the investigation of the minute changes in the patient's unconscious behaviour in relation to the analyst, especially following an interpretation; for she believes (convincingly to us) that the response to the analyst's activity – the analyst's move towards the patient, and attempt to offer her own observation of his state of mind to him – creates a shift which reflects the deep layers of the archaic object relationship that is alive in the patient at that precise moment. So it is not the transference 'in general', to be found 'in the material' at large which is the focus of attention and descriptive comment, but the transformations in the movements (towards, away, to the surface, to the depth, lighter, darker, more or less intense) of the subtle choreography between subject and object, in the patient's mind, acted in within the relationship with the analyst. (Since the analyst herself is an active participant in this relationship, her mind has of course also to be subjected to constant close scrutiny.)

The central theoretical belief is that the archaic relationship is to be found embedded in these interchanges, and that ultimately this has to be the main object of the interventions – which she aims to make as clear and simple as possible, avoiding 'becauses' and reconstruction until a much later time when there has been clear psychological development and when the transference is more solidly understood – she believes that she must offer as little as possible which could (and almost certainly would) be used defensively.

Borrowing from economics, one could say that the publication in the session of the moment-to-moment results of the in-depth research into the dynamics of the 'micro' changes in the object relationship is what will eventually lead to the desired 'macro' changes. In this clear and informative contribution, one particular sentence strikes me as absolutely crucial to remember: 'Although we talk, for convenience, of archaic internal objects as if they were fixed structures,

I believe it may be more useful to see them as dynamic structures whose qualities and functions are maintained by the way they are treated, and what is projected into them.' This is essentially what makes psychoanalysis so difficult, often so deeply disturbing, and yet, always such a fascinating endeavour; and, more importantly, on this fact (of the fluidity, or at least potential fluidity, of primitive object relationships) we base our hope of therapeutic efficacy.

# 2

# CONTAINMENT, ENACTMENT AND COMMUNICATION

*John Steiner*

It has long been recognised that language can lead to proper communication only if analysts attend not simply to their patients' words but to their context and to the non-verbal cues that accompany them. It is now equally clear that analysts must attend to their own reactions, to the countertransference in the broadest sense, and this includes not just their emotional state but also their thoughts and their actions. We have learned that internal conflicts in patients become externalised in the transference and elements from patients' internal worlds are projected into their analysts. Feelings are created in analysts through projective identification that lead them to act so that they find themselves playing roles ascribed to them by their patients. An important possibility for communication emerges if analysts can contain their propensity to action, since they can then look at the pressures put on them and the feelings aroused in them as a part of the situation that needs to be understood. The period after giving an interpretation is also very important, and it is often only after analysts have been drawn into an enactment that they can become aware of what has happened. The patient's reactions to what has happened can be monitored and used to test and then modify the interpretation, which, as a result, will normally become more precise and gradually more comprehensible to the patient.[1] Analysts therefore have to integrate observations from different sources, indeed from all they can observe in the total situation of the transference, and also have to add something from their thinking and imagination before a meaningful understanding can be reached.

In many cases, the various elements the analyst observes are in harmony in the sense that they each make their own individual contribution to a coherent idea. The communication is then readily comprehensible and the task of interpretation can be fairly straightforward. Affect, context and countertransference combine to give depth and force to the verbal communication. At other times, however, integration is interfered with by processes either in the patient or in the analyst. Sometimes the material confronting the analyst is chaotic, and sometimes the elements the analyst is trying to integrate are in contradiction with each other. Splitting may lead to various types of dissociation, including that of affect from language, and when severe can lead to fragmentation of the patient's thinking and verbalising that may also disturb the analyst's capacity to observe and think. Clearly, obstacles to understanding arise as a result of such mechanisms that may leave the analyst in various states of confusion and helplessness. Nevertheless the potential to understand arises if the analyst recognises that the disturbance is itself a clue to what is happening.

Once recognised, chaos or contradiction in the patient's material or an upsurge of feeling on the part of the analyst may, for example, be used as markers that alert the analyst to the need to look in a different way at what is being communicated. There will always be doubt as to whether a new formulation represents a correct understanding or is the expression of a bias, a prejudice or an overvalued idea on the part of the analyst (Britton and Steiner 1994). Unconscious processes dominate the countertransference and it is easy for analysts to be misled if they give too much weight to observation. Segal (1977) has remarked that countertransference is the best of servants but the worst of masters.

The two patients I am going to describe created states of discord that left me confused and uncertain, and sometimes led me to try to provide meaning that would make sense of the confusion and reduce my anxiety. It was as if both patients came to count on me to work hard to supply the integration and meaning that they could not themselves provide. Once, when I interpreted this function to one of the patients, he replied: 'But isn't that your job?' and I could see that I had been enlisted to play a role in his mental equilibrium and become part of what I have previously described as a *pathological organisation of the personality*. Such organisations can provide a *psychic retreat* in which the patient can seek a refuge and which becomes an important part of the situation that needs to be understood (Steiner 1993).

The apparent inability of both patients to communicate in an ordinary way also made it difficult for me to get feedback as to whether my interpretations were correct or not. I found it important to address both the anxieties communicated to me by the splitting and fragmentation on the one hand and also the role I was induced to play when I functioned as the interpreter of meaning for the patients, on the other. Both had the potential to provide information about the patients and their object relations.

While they had much in common, the two patients were also very different. The first, Mr A, was mostly functioning at a psychotic level and his utterances were often fragmented, disjointed and enigmatic, so that it was difficult to know if anything meaningful was being communicated or not. The second patient, Mr B, was capable of greater integration and seemed to produce confusion of meaning by dissociating language and affect. He described extremely distressing scenes in a flat way, leaving me to feel the emotion they produced and the distress at his failure to be disturbed by it.

## Patient A

Mr A was a patient in his early forties, whose speech was broken up into short utterances that were very difficult to link together and to understand. His family was of English origin, but had business interests in a European country where they had mostly lived until recently, when they partially retired and moved to a small town north of London to help look after him. When this proved too difficult for them he was moved to a psychiatric hostel in London.

Early on in the analysis he had explained that his problems began from the moment in his fourth year when his mother pushed him out into an unbearable world of a kindergarten, which he described as 'chaos'. He did not connect this disaster with the fact that his younger brother was born at this time, but he could never forgive his mother for what happened. He was sent to a boarding school in England at the age of 11 and soon after had a breakdown in which he came to believe that everyone in the world was against him. This followed an act of betrayal by a schoolfriend, and when his parents failed to understand and did not take him out of the school, he responded by constructing a system that he called his visions into which he would escape when the ordinary world became unbearable.

The visions made up an idealised transcendental world in which he avoided the cruelties and injustices he had to suffer in what he called the 'world of mundane reality'. He was preoccupied with a fear of doing wrong, and often explained how much he suffered if he even inadvertently did something that made him guilty. In his visions, by contrast, he seemed free of guilt but he spoke of them with great caution, and he worried that I might view them as something mad that ought to be dismantled. It was striking that the visions contained buildings but were otherwise empty, as if all warmth, comfort, sexuality and liveliness had been stripped from them, leaving an idealised empty shell. He himself behaved as if he were a burnt-out case in which no living thoughts or feelings were to be found. He was dishevelled and usually came in looking like a tramp, sometimes walking through the rain or coping with train delays and taking pride at his stoicism.

The sessions contained long silences in which he lay motionless on the couch, giving the impression that he was barely alive, like a stone effigy. It was striking that, occasionally, watching him wasting his life and also wasting my work in his analysis, I felt a transient contact with a frightening destructiveness and cruelty that left me feeling rage and hatred for what he was doing. But this was difficult to sustain and was usually quickly replaced by pity and concern for his desperate state. These 'good' feelings towards him had what I later saw as a hollow ring and I wondered if I was not led to behave somehow like his mother did, who throughout his childhood felt very bad about his disturbance and had to appear loving and caring despite being extremely provoked by him.

After about six years of analysis the patient was considerably less frightened of me and spoke somewhat more freely. It had taken him about a year even to mention the visions, and he still withheld many of their details. A change in our relationship developed when his mother became seriously ill with a heart condition and he moved from the psychiatric hostel to live with his parents and help his father look after her. He presented the situation as one in which he had to reconcile two demands, to look after his mother on the one hand and to look after the analysis on the other. But he also admitted to feelings of excitement and power when he thought of nursing his mother as a reversal of the relationship they had when he was a small child. 'Now', he said, 'the boot was on the other foot'. I thought a similar excitement affected him when he was able to use his mother's illness as a justification for missing sessions and then for reducing his attendance from five to three sessions a week. He had always resented the way I determined holiday dates and structured the times of the sessions and he now felt justified and in control.

Later he increased again to four sessions a week but at the time of writing he was coming three times a week and travelling a long way to do so. In the week before this session he told me he could not come on the following Thursday. I pointed out that he had five sessions available and that he might wish to come on one of the other days instead. He was a bit taken aback but eventually said he would come on Tuesday.

### *First session*

He began this Tuesday session after about ten minutes' silence, saying, 'The visions are a suitable habitation for a control freak'.

His sessions were full of such enigmatic and disconnected remarks, which were followed by a silence as he waited for me to struggle with the question of their meaning. Although I was unsure what he meant, I knew from experience that I would not get further help from him, and what I did was to try to find meaning in his remark by using my intuition. I linked his remark to the fact that I had reminded him that he had five sessions available and I suggested that coming on a different day made him feel less in control.

He was silent for a while and then said, 'I have to accommodate to the real world so that I can stay alive'. I assumed that he meant that coming to the session had been an accommodation and that my comment on available sessions had been experienced as a demand that he come today. I suggested that he preferred the visions, where he was in control.

He said he would call them (the visions) dreams except that they are not when he is asleep; I enquired if he thought the visions were something like dreams. He said, 'Perhaps; there are bellows' and this led me to ask if the bellows were an element in the visions. After a pause he said, 'Like fanning a spark of life'. It was clear that there was a link to 'bellows' but I was not sure what this meant to him. I interpreted that he was implying that something inside him was being kept alive perhaps by my work, and I reminded him that mostly the visions seemed to be buildings empty of life and that was how he often presented himself.

He replied, 'You would call the fire brigade if the place caught fire'. I said that I thought he was now afraid that I was too interested in what was going on inside him so that he or I could get out of control. Perhaps that is why he needed to be a control freak. To this he said that he wished he had not mentioned the bellows. I interpreted that regretting mentioning the bellows was his way of dampening down his interest in my work by trying to remove what had come alive in the session. After a pause he said he had to turn to the visions when looking after his mother became too difficult, but the trouble was that in turning to the visions he can play God.

I said he was now letting me see that he was aware of an omnipotence that frightened him and I interpreted that he was angry that I had been able to use the imagery of the bellows to understand something about him. I thought he felt provoked by my work and was frightened by the power of his reactions. He interjected that he was not only afraid of being God but also of being the Devil. This led me to interpret that just now when something inside him was coming alive and was supported by my interpretations, he did not know if it was a good thing or a bad thing. Either seemed dangerous, because of the omnipotence that made him afraid he could get out of control.

In this session I thought the patient was able to communicate the fact that thoughts and feelings had come alive within him. He did this by using language in a highly idiosyncratic way so that to understand him I had to create a formulation that made use of my intuition as well as observations from within the sessions, from my knowledge of the patient's history and current life situation, from his previous accounts of his visions and attitudes to reality, and from an observation of my countertransference. I had to respond not just to his words and to the mood of the session but I also had to observe myself being drawn to make a series of interpretations about bellows, sparks and fire brigades, which were potentially meaningful but which also gave him a means by which he could feel in control and thus of supporting an omnipotence through which he could control the life and meaning in what I was saying.

### *Second session*

Some of these themes emerged again in a session that took place a few days later. He began saying, 'I wonder if you think I use my mother as a shield. You think it is convenient for me to look after her'.

I interpreted that he nearly always spoke about what I might think and that perhaps he recognised that he was using me as a shield, since in this way he did not have to think what his own views were.

His response was to say that what other people think was important in forming one's conscience. I interpreted that he was very concerned with conscience, which seemed to involve finding out what I thought was right. This was part of the shield that protected him from his own wishes. I thought he was unclear if he wanted a session today and if he used me in this way I was the one with desires and he had the conscience. As a result he was unable to consider what it was that he wanted.

He said, 'Yes, the forbidden fruit'. In a recent session he had described how caring for his mother involved a special feeling of intimacy that he thought of as similar to that which existed when she looked after him as a small child. I had asked if he and his mother did not feel embarrassed by such intimacy, and he had shrugged this off by explaining that he was simply doing his duty by caring for her. In the present session I interpreted that he felt drawn into a kind of intimacy with me like that which he described when nursing his mother, and that he had to deny that he had any desires or feelings towards me. Coming to his sessions was doing his duty but the reference to forbidden fruit seemed to suggest that he was aware of desires and feelings that he thought were forbidden. He responded by saying that the intimacy with his mother did not bother him at all. He was used to it.

I interpreted that the forbidden fruit was also a reference to *Paradise Lost* and I linked the experience of being sent to kindergarten with the expulsion from Paradise. I suggested that using his mother as a shield was connected in his mind with the situation before the fall when everything was perfect. If he used me to express his desires and feelings, he felt protected and was not bothered by the intimacy. I thought that this was what he tried to create in the visions, where there was no desire and no shame or embarrassment.

### *Discussion*

Looking back at these sessions it is clear that the communications from the patient left me in a dilemma. Should I try to make links and find meaning, or should I stay with the experience of fragmentation and discord, which gave the impression of a destroyed and meaningless internal world? The sense of deadness, emptiness and the despair they engendered were difficult to face, and the meanings I worked so hard to produce were likely to protect both patient and analyst from their full impact. The clues that the patient scattered in his material challenged me to find meaning and can be seen as part of his seduction of me into an enactment. In the course of his analysis I became increasingly aware of the role that I was led to adopt and increasingly to recognise how he depended on me to continue to try to construct something meaningful. In this way I was recruited into a pathological organisation of the personality, which played an important part in maintaining his equilibrium and in creating a *psychic retreat* in which his emptiness, deadness and despair could be evaded.

However, the clues he left and his reactions to my interpretations also raised the possibility that he was not as dead and empty as he appeared. Sometimes I said things that provoked him and led to a glimpse of a destructiveness and hatred that frightened him. When he could not damp down and control his reactions he became afraid that he could not cope, and resorted to his visions where he could reassert control through omnipotence. He seemed to recognise this omnipotence when he spoke about playing God and the Devil and I think it made him afraid that coming alive would reveal him as mad.

In relation to me in his analysis, I think that the patient's division of reality into two areas, the mundane, where he had to submit to authority, and the visionary, where he could create his own rules, was beginning to break down. Although he behaved as if he had to submit to my authority, he was also able to feel more free to come alive and even to protest when he felt under pressure to submit, for example, over conformity to the structure of the sessions. He remained afraid that such sparks of life arising in his relation to the analysis had to be attacked and controlled, but as a result of our work I think he was beginning to feel more free to protest and acknowledge the existence of feelings of his own. My efforts to find meaning were not only defensive and I think did allow us to make contact with his omnipotence and gradually to address his fear of madness.

## Patient B

The situation presented by Mr B was different and less chaotic. He had suffered a breakdown when he lost his job, and sought analysis in a state of acute anxiety and depression accompanied by severe obsessional indecision, concrete thinking, hypochondriasis and intractable back pains. He had made considerable progress over several years of analysis and was able to resume his work at a lower but still significant level of responsibility. His personal life, however, remained miserable and he clung on to relationships in a desperate and self-defeating way. He held on to an idealised fantasy of a family home where he could reside as a patriarch respected by wife and children, while in reality his demanding attitude led only to frustration in his relationships and a failure to develop his real capacities.

The sessions were marked by a peculiar type of superiority in which he repeatedly engaged in what seemed senseless and self-destructive acts, and he was proud of his capacity to suffer their consequences without anger or distress. Affect and language seemed to be split and he behaved as if he did not have access to emotional reactions in himself that would protect him from behaviour that was dangerous or destructive. In this situation I often became alarmed about his state of mind, particularly about a kind of mania in which his thoughts ran away from him in excitement. Themes that involved menace were frequently expressed, for example, as half-articulated threats that analysis was unscientific and even corrupt and that he was in a position to expose this to the public. I was not particularly threatened by him but I did sometimes find his superiority and denigration of psychoanalysis trying and at these times my irritation with him was difficult to contain. On the other hand he often convinced me that he was emotionally defective and that he could not use feelings of anxiety or guilt to regulate his thinking and behaviour. When this happened, instead of being aware of my anger towards him, I tended to feel and behave as if I should provide the emotion that was missing or even teach him how to recognise it in himself.

I will try to describe what I mean by presenting a session in which the patient arrived twenty minutes late. This was quite exceptional for him and he explained that either he had slept through the alarm or had forgotten to turn it on. He then described a dream in which *he was readdressing letter bombs. The writing had initially been done by someone else and he was pleased and proud that his writing was clearer. Then he had the thought that this was crazy, he was leaving finger prints on the letters and the police would be able to trace them back to him.* His associations were to the fact that he recently had seen police cars in my vicinity, which he assumed had something to do with a bomb scare. He then mentioned a recent bomb attack in Ireland in which three young children had been burned to death. Colleagues at work had been horrified but he had simply remarked, 'these things happen'.

It was this kind of dislocation between language and affect, created by the absence of human feeling to the stories of horror and violence, which made me feel transiently angry and then unsure of myself.

I interpreted that he seemed to wait for me to produce an emotional reaction to what had happened. It was most unusual for him to be late but he felt no alarm, as if to say, 'these things happen', and his dream seemed intended to provoke me, as if I were in danger. He replied only to say that he presumed I had in mind that the bombs would injure someone, but this had not entered the dream and he had no idea to whom the bombs were being addressed.

He seemed to be saying that I could be concerned with human suffering if I wanted, but that this was not anything which bothered him. I suggested that there might be a connection to recent material in which he had described attacks on psychoanalysis in newspapers that had disturbed and excited him.

He said he remembered a campaign he helped to organise as a student in which doctors were denounced because they helped to develop chemical weapons and did not think or care about ordinary people. Yesterday he had been asked to show a young student around the business and was moved by her enthusiasm. When he left university he had wanted to be a doctor because he thought it would help him get in touch with his feelings, and he often regretted that he had gone into industry.

I interpreted his wish to regain his capacity to be enthusiastic and enjoy things, including his analysis, but he also saw how he jumped at the chance if he could find fault with me and join in with those who denounce psychoanalysis. Although the connections I made seemed to be coherent and meaningful the interpretations did not lead to significant contact, and I thought that, once he had created the disturbing feelings in me, he disowned them just as he did when he had sent off the letter bombs in his dream. His only concern was that they should not be traced back to him, and he feared that this was exactly what I would do when I recognised the way he thought, which showed a pattern we were very familiar with.

Looking back on this session I think it is possible to see how the patient made use of my reactions to his material. Disturbing images, sleeping through the alarm, sending bombs, denouncing doctors seemed to coexist with memories of a youthful enthusiasm and a wish to be in touch with feelings. Once I became concerned and interested he saw me as enthusiastic in my efforts to find a response in him and this made him cold and superior. In fact he rejected the idea that anyone was in danger from his bomb-making and I think he was probably more concerned to torment and intimidate rather than destroy me with the attacks on psychoanalysis that he did nothing to curtail. One could say that he successfully projected his affects into me and got me to enact a role in which I became disturbed by his failure to take responsibility for his own feelings.

As long as I showed him through my responses that I was irritated, worried or concerned he could be reassured. In the dream he had been proud that his writing was so clear, and I think this was linked to the pleasure he got when he addressed the projections so clearly that they reached their mark. He was expert at evacuating those elements which disturbed him and he knew that when he remained undisturbed, saying, 'these things happen', I found it very difficult to bear. If I recognised his excitement at my distress he thought I would trace the sadism as coming from him. However, I often failed to do this and I think he believed that I was frightened of his anger so that an equilibrium was established in which he knew how to get into my mind and provoke a reaction he could cope with.

### The next session

He began the next session saying that he would visit his parents and meet his brother there at the weekend. He had not seen his brother for a long time and said he would like to talk to him about personal things but he knows that his brother would clam up if he tried, just as his mother did. He discussed the difficulty everyone in his family had in expressing feelings and described how all through his childhood his mother had tried to conceal his father's drinking. In fact all the children knew he was going through an alcoholic breakdown but they pretended that her disguise was successful. They saw that his mother could not admit that his father was out of control.

He proceeded to tell me a dream in which *he found himself in a 'Jewish Church', where food was being served, perhaps a slice of cake, and because he was hidden from view he felt comfortable. He was ashamed and guilty to find he had been in bed at the back of the church but the people there were friendly and offered him some of the food.*

His associations were to a cake shop near my consulting room where he occasionally goes to buy a croissant after a session. From the notices displayed he presumed the shop was orthodox Jewish and he was surprised to find they sold such sweet things. He is not Jewish but he assumed I was and certainly thought of psychoanalysis as something Jewish. I have little doubt that he knew that most people would use the term Synagogue rather than 'Jewish Church'.

I interpreted the dream to be another representation of the comfortable position he adopted, taking up residence in the analysis, feeling bad about it and then enjoying the sweet things offered here. As long as I kept the disturbed feelings to myself he could enjoy the atmosphere. But I also thought there was something menacing that was introduced by the 'Jewish Church' and the 'Jewish food'. I thought that his remarks were directed at me and that he assumed that I would be disturbed by them. When I struggled to find meaning in them the patient stepped back and said that it had nothing to do with him.

### Discussion

I think it is possible to see how I was led to endorse his comfortable view that he could avoid an awareness of his disturbance if he got me to experience the affect he was disconnected from. It remained unclear whether he truly knew nothing about these feelings and suffered from a kind of emotional defect state, or triumphantly cut himself off and enjoyed watching me struggle with the dislocations produced in me. I seemed transiently to express my irritation but had to suppress more violent rage.

It was difficult to know what the patient's own feelings were and how to address them. He seemed to anticipate my feelings very precisely and assumed that I expected him to be concerned about human feelings such as those that were connected with the weekend and, for example, his anticipated failure to make proper contact with his brother. The 'Jewish Church' with the Jewish sweet cakes seemed to represent a view of analysis as something desirable that he could appreciate. However, he was also conveying that it felt foreign to him; in his family he was unable to express his feelings and he did not know the right language to use. He felt like an intruder and expected me to try to catch him out and expel him. The menacing elements seemed to threaten his position but were also designed to evoke reactions in me. Analysis was being attacked, doctors and Jews were in danger of being denounced and all this, like his father's drinking, was being concealed as if I had to present a picture of myself as warm and permissive and under control. I was able to interpret some of this but I did not comment on his use of the term 'Jewish Church' instead of Synagogue. I think he felt this confirmed that his attitude to analysis and to things Jewish was too disturbing for me to tackle and that I would feel too guilty about my view of him as an intruder. He pretended not to know the term Synagogue, just as he did not know to whom the bombs were being addressed. I was allowed to be irritated with him, but his real fear that he would be expelled was not tackled. If he could get me to make interpretations that were right in a general way but which avoided what he was really afraid of he could feel clever and successful, but without ever feeling secure and truly accepted.

## Conclusion

My understanding of what was going on in these patients was clearly influenced by Klein's theories of projective identification (Klein 1946), and by Bion's description of the containing functions of objects (Bion 1962). These served as an aid to my efforts at integrating the various elements that made up the patient's communications and helped me to formulate the idea that in the course of trying to make myself open and receptive to the projective identifications of the patients I was in danger of allowing myself to be taken over and led to play a role that served to sustain rather than to understand what was going on. Gradually I came to see how each patient in a different way manoeuvred me to help him avoid facing an unacceptable reality.

When I could examine my own responses it was possible to see how the role I was led to play was, at one level, a way of evading the internal situation which the patients individually communicated through the evocation of states of fragmentation or dissonance. I was instrumental in sustaining a *psychic retreat* that helped them to avoid contact with reality and interfered with their development. However, recognising the role could also advance the understanding of the nature of the retreat and of the *pathological organisation of the personality* that sustained it.

In the case of Mr A, fragmented thoughts were brought with an expectation that I would provide linkage, continuity and meaning. As long as I was prepared to carry out this function for him he did not need to face the state of disintegration of his internal world. Nor did we have to face the question of the destructiveness that led to the fragmentation. Because of the role the analyst played, a psychic retreat was created that offered a kind of respite from a reality that was difficult for both analyst and patient to face. The retreat thus not only represented an evasion of psychic reality but also provided a means of understanding the patient's need to recruit objects to take on this role. With the collaboration of the analyst, a side of the patient remained alive in a projected form where it was able to counteract the despair, fragmentation and lack of meaning. These more alive aspects were threatening if they were felt to belong to the patient and were either disowned by projection into the analyst or controlled and dampened down if they became a threat.

In the case of Mr B the dissociation seemed to be more between affect and language. His analysis came to represent a place where he made himself comfortable, but where he was unable to develop an interest in his subjective experience. He wanted to be in the church and fed by it but not to join it. He was particularly frightened of being seen to be emotionally involved in his analysis both as an object of hatred and as something he cared about and valued. Any such feelings were projected and my role in sustaining this mechanism was to respond emotionally as if on his behalf.

In both patients language was either fragmented or divorced from affect, so that the ordinary methods of communication that require a capacity to integrate were not available. The state of mind produced in the analyst was partly an evacuation of states that the patients could not cope with, but it also represented a means of enlisting me to carry out functions that they could not or would not tolerate. An understanding of these mechanisms provided information about the pattern of object relations that the patients were trapped in.

## Acknowledgements

This article was published in the *International Journal of Psychoanalysis*, 81(2) (April 2000), and was based on a presentation given at the 41st Congress of the International Psychoanalytical Association, Santiago, Chile, 29 July 1999.

## Notes

1 This approach begins with Klein's description of projective identification and Bion's extension of it in his work on container/contained (Klein 1946; Bion 1962). Rosenfeld (1971) described various functions of projective identification including

that of serving as a primitive form of communication. Heimann (1950) drew attention to the link between projective identification and countertransference and Sandler (1976, 1977) formulated the idea of the 'actualisation' of an object-relationship in the transference and suggested that the analyst must have a free-floating responsiveness as well as a free-floating attention. Joseph (1989) has provided detailed descriptions of the way in which incipient enactments can serve as a communication.

## References

Bion, W.R. (1962) *Learning from Experience*, London: Heinemann.

Britton, R. and Steiner, J. (1994) 'Interpretation: selected fact or overvalued idea?', *International Journal of Psychoanalysis*, 75: 1069–1078.

Heimann, P. (1950) 'On countertransference', *International Journal of Psychoanalysis*, 31: 81–84.

Joseph, B. (1989) *Psychic Equilibrium and Psychic Change: Selected Papers of Betty Joseph*, M. Feldman and E. Bott Spillius (eds), London: Routledge.

Klein, M. (1946) 'Notes on some schizoid mechanisms', *International Journal of Psychoanalysis*, 27: 99–110, reprinted in *The Writings of Melanie Klein*, vol. 3, *Envy and Gratitude and Other Works*, London: Hogarth Press (1975).

Rosenfeld, H. (1971) 'Contributions to the psychopathology of psychotic patients: the importance of projective identification in the ego structure and object relations of the psychotic patient', *Problems of Psychosis*, P. Doucet and C. Laurin (eds), Amsterdam: Excerpta Medica; reprinted in *Melanie Klein Today: Developments in Theory and Practice*, vol. 1, *Mainly Theory*, E. Bott Spillius (ed.), London: Routledge (1998).

Sandler, J. (1976) 'Countertransference and role responsiveness', *International Review of Psychoanalysis*, 3: 43–47.

—— (1977) 'Actualisation and object relationships', *Journal of Philadelphia Association of Psychoanalysis*, 50: 79–90.

Segal, H. (1977) 'Countertransference', *International Journal of Psychoanalytic Psychotherapy*, 6: 31–37; reprinted in *The Work of Hanna Segal*, New York: Jason Aronson (1981).

Steiner, J. (1993) *Psychic Retreats: Pathological Organizations of the Personality in Psychotic, Neurotic, and Borderline Patients*, London: Routledge.

# DISCUSSION OF JOHN STEINER'S CHAPTER

## *Arturo Varchevker*

It is in the nature of the psychoanalytic process that communication and comprehension between patient and analyst is affected and disturbed by the exploration of the patient's unconscious and activation of past and present conflicts. When obstacles encountered are understood and overcome there is a leap forward in the analysis. John's contribution is especially helpful as it addresses to a greater or a lesser degree situations that analysts are likely to encounter when treating patients with very entrenched or severe pathology. He describes how the psychoanalyst is pushed out of his psychoanalytic stance by the pressures exercised on him by the patient's projections and finds himself recruited into playing a particular role in the patient's internal scenario.

John illustrates how in certain situations where the obstacle is not overcome and insight is not available, it is the enactment by the analyst that works like a 'compass'. This enactment is what orientates the analyst and it emerges through a blend of questioning and intuition, at times difficult to activate when the need for certainty pushes the analyst in a different direction.

John uses clinical material from two patients whose communications are fragmented or dissociated of affect. The communication feels enigmatic or disturbed and makes it quite difficult for him to know if his attempts at understanding are successful. He describes two aspects: a defensive nature of this state of mind and the enactment as a form of communication.

Patient A finds a pathological containment for his anxieties in what he calls 'the visions'. On Tuesday the session starts with a ten-minute silence followed by a remark, 'the visions are a suitable habitation for a control freak'. John feels that the control freak relates to the patient's need to exercise tight control over his objects. He believes that the patient feels vulnerable when he makes a concession to avoid missing a session by having to come outside his usual time and day. While the patient inhabits his visions during the first ten minutes of silence, he is also aware that while he is silent, the analyst is looking for him.

The patient's response to John's interpretation and the patient's view of himself as a control freak strikes me as significant as this seems like an acknowledgement and a communication. The patient acknowledges John's interpretation by telling him where he is in his silence. As the patient says, this is a concession he has to make, the acknowledgement of external reality. The need for control and making concessions sets the tone of the analytic interaction. I think that the particular type of language used by the patient and the concession the patient makes is an expression of a pattern of relating where the patient is constantly negotiating in order to keep everything under his control and forces the analyst to stretch his intuition and imagination. The second session shows more clearly how the concessions aid his organised defences to ensure that he is not going to be ejected from his paradise, which connects him with his early experiences. John shows how the 'hard work' the analyst is forced or seduced to do is part of the perfect omnipotent fantasy. This perfect refuge, 'his visions', structures his mode of relating, and the enactment and subsequent interaction become the key to understanding and unlocking the established defensive pattern.

The clinical material from the second patient shows another manifestation of the analyst's enactment in which the patient manages by projective identification to create disturbing emotional reactions that he disowns, while at the same time becoming excited when he sees them in his analyst.

When the analyst is forced to enact an unwanted aspect of the patient's emotions and made to work hard, I can think of two or three things that might occur:

- The analyst becomes aware of this and tries to regain the reflective stance.
- The analyst is recruited and succumbs to the enactment without insight.
- The analyst responds in a punitive way to what is going on.

In relation to these three possibilities and the material discussed I thought that often this type of pathological organisation gives way to exploitative modes of relating. In analysis these patients tend to develop an accurate sensitivity to blind spots or weakness in the analyst. This offers the possibility of exploiting them and fuelling the patient's sense of omnipotent control, with the additional devilish satisfaction John has alluded to. I wonder whether this is an aspect that plays an important part in the enactment and in the patients' fears.

This is a valuable contribution to the understanding of a very troublesome aspect of countertransference.

# 3

# WHO'S WHO?

## Notes on pathological identifications

*Ignes Sodré*

Freud's (1917) discovery, in 'Mourning and melancholia', of the process through which the ego unconsciously identifies with the introjected bad object (the rejecting loved object) thus becoming a victim of its own superego, was one of the most important breakthroughs in psychoanalysis: perhaps as important as the discovery of the meaning of dreams and of the Oedipus complex. The idea that when individuals feel 'I am the worst person in the world', they may in fact be unconsciously accusing somebody else whose victim they feel they are, but who, through a pathological process of introjection and identification, they have 'become', was indeed a revolutionary one, and one which is still of tremendous clinical importance for us today.

Freud (1917) describes the establishing of what he calls a narcissistic identification with the abandoned object in two ways: as a passive taking in of the object – 'thus the shadow of the object fell upon the ego' (p. 249) – and as an active process in which 'the ego wants to incorporate this object into itself, and, in accordance with the oral or cannibalistic phase of libidinal development in which it is, it wants to do so by devouring it' (p. 249). He also describes the ego as being overwhelmed by the object. It would seem then that there is no differentiation between self and object at that point – the introjected object occupies the entire ego – except of course that this is not entirely true, since the ego has undergone a 'cleavage' and some of it has now become the 'special agency' that judges it (the ego who has become the object) so harshly. As we know, the superego was subsequently also seen by Freud as the product of introjections. In psychoanalytic theory, introjections leading to identifications with primary objects very soon became linked with normal development; but the kind of identification described in 'Mourning and melancholia' is a massive, pathological one, characterised by an extraordinary clinical event: the subject seems to have 'become' the object.

In his paper 'On the psychopathology of narcissism' Rosenfeld (1964) stated:

> Identification is an important factor in narcissistic object relations. It may take place by introjection or by projection. When the object is omnipotently incorporated, the self becomes so identified with the incorporated object that all separate identity or any boundary between self and object is denied. In projective identification parts of the self omnipotently enter an object, for example, the mother, to take over certain qualities which would be experienced as desirable, and therefore claim to be the object or part-object. Identification by introjection and by projection usually occur simultaneously.
>
> (Rosenfeld 1964: 170)

This is an extremely clear differentiation between two modes of identification; the first description corresponds to Freud's mechanism in melancholia, the second follows Klein's (1946) discovery of the mechanism of projective identification. But I think it is worth noticing that Freud's description of the more active (cannibalistic) form of incorporation is in fact similar to the description of projective identification. Rosenfeld (1964) stressed the omnipotent quality of this type of projective identification; Freud had, as we know, pointed out the hidden mania implied in melancholia. It seems to me that some states of massive projective identification are like a manic version of what Freud described as the melancholic's narcissistic identification with the (now externally annihilated) object.

In this chapter I shall focus mainly on the interaction of projections, introjections and manic mechanisms in the creation and perpetuation of those states of pathological identification which are usually described as 'the subject is in massive projective identification with the object', as opposed to states where the subject 'gets rid of something' or 'does something to the object' by the use of projective identification. You will have gathered from my title that I am concerned with exploring extreme shifts in a person's sense of identity. I will bring clinical examples to illustrate both the question of the loss of a sense of identity and the shift into a different identity through the use of excessive introjective and projective identification.

The sense of identity stems simultaneously from the differentiation of the self from its objects and from various identifications with different aspects of the objects. All object relations depend on the capacity to remain oneself while being able to shift temporarily into the other's point of view. Any meaningful interchange between two people involves of necessity an intricate process of projections, introjections and identifications. 'Projective identification' is an umbrella term which includes many different processes involving the operation of both projection and introjection; it is used to describe normal modes of communication as well as extremely pathological manoeuvres and even permanent pathological states which are at the root of some character traits.

One way of differentiating the complex processes involved in the various aspects of what is called 'projective identification' from 'classical' projection is that projective identification takes place in an object relationship and, therefore, necessarily affects both subject and object (in phantasy, but often in external reality too), whereas it should be at least possible, in theory, to conceive of projection as not necessarily related to a specific object into which something is being projected. But having said that, I must confess that I find it difficult to imagine a projection into outer space, or into something inanimate or abstract, without imagining too that whatever has been projected into has become personified in some way.

Projective identification as a defence mechanism has as its primary aim the wish to get rid of a particular experience; I do not think it is true to say that what characterises projective identification is that the subject (the 'projector', as it were) maintains links with the part of the self that is now felt to be inside the object, the 'receptor' (see for instance Ogden's (1979) discussion). This may occur, but the hallmark of projective identification – and especially of pathological projective identification – is the wish to sever contact with something that provokes pain, fear, discomfort; the word 'identification' should, in this particular instance, refer to the object's identification (in the subject's mind) with the projected experience, and not to the subject's identification with the object; as Sandler (1988) clearly pointed out, the self wants to disidentify with that which is projected.

Projective identification, by definition, affects the sense of self, since it involves getting rid of aspects of the personality through splitting them off and locating them in the object, so that in the subject's phantasy the identities of both subject and object are affected. It also may involve acquiring aspects of the object, in which case the identities are further modified. In her seminal papers where she first discovered and conceptualised projective identification, Klein (1946, 1955) described both archaic processes furthering communication and development (a concept developed and expanded by Bion (1962) in his theory of the container) and a pathological process leading to loss of contact with the self and aiming at omnipotent control of the object. Massive projective identification with the object implies a phantasy of 'becoming' the object or a particular aspect or version of the object (and here the word identification refers also to the subject's identification with aspects of the object) whereas the object 'becomes' the self, or personifies an unbearable aspect of the self (a process first described by Anna Freud (1937) as 'identification with the aggressor'). I will suggest that such states of pathological identification imply the excessive use not only of violent projections but also of concrete, pathological introjections and that this mode of functioning also relies for its 'success' on the massive use of manic defences.

Excessive use of projective identification can lead, on the one hand, to confusion and loss of a firm sense of self and, on the other, to an extreme rigidity in character, where artificial new boundaries are created between subject and object, but are then tenaciously adhered to. In this case, the new boundaries between what is 'me' and what is 'you' have to be maintained as a fortress against the threat of the return of the split-off projected parts of the self, which results not in confusion but in its extreme opposite, in an absolute certainty which has to be maintained at all costs, to the impoverishment of the personality and serious disturbance in the capacity for object relations. Arrogance as a character trait is, I think, a good example of this state of affairs; it is essentially a state of permanent projective identification with an idealised bad object. (I will explain what I mean by this later.)

Looking rather schematically into what happens in projective identification, one could say that from the point of view of the 'projector', a part of the self becomes in phantasy a part of the object through a complicated manoeuvre which, for the sake of simplicity, we could temporarily call 'projective dis-identification'; the projector is not consciously aware of that aspect of the self, since he believes that it belongs to the object. This process, which happens in unconscious phantasy, can of course have an effect on the object – the 'receptor' – in external reality (Sandler describes this as the 'actualisation' of the projective identification, whereas Spillius uses the term 'evocative'). If this is the case then, from the point of view of the 'receptor', there is an intrusion of something foreign into the self which causes a partial – or total – 'forced introjective identification'.

What the outcome of this situation will be will depend on the degree of intrusiveness and violence of the projection matched up with the 'receptor's' capacity (or lack thereof) to introject and partially identify with what has been introjected without losing the boundaries of the self. In other words a helpful 'receptor' should be able to function as a container (Bion) who can simultaneously experience what it is like to feel what the other person feels (for instance, a mother who can empathise with her baby) through introjecting what is being projected as the experience of an object. This experience is, in the inner world, incorporated into the picture of the internal object and not into that of the self. (It is obvious that if a mother felt totally identified with her distressed baby she would not be able to help the baby. For example, she has to take in her baby's fear of not surviving and to be able partially, and temporarily, also fear for its survival. But if she becomes so persecuted and overwhelmed by the baby's terrified crying to the point of feeling, 'I will not survive', then she will 'be' the baby and the baby will 'be' a persecutor; more like a bad mother to her. This then might lead to her emotionally abandoning or even attacking the baby.)

The central characteristic of the use of 'projective identification' is the creation in the subject of a state of mind in which the boundaries between self and object have shifted. This state can be more or less flexible, temporary or permanent. The motives for such unconscious manoeuvres are manifold, from the need to maintain psychic equilibrium and avoid pain, to the more intrusive ones of robbing and depleting the object. The object's perception of and method of dealing with what is being projected will also affect the development of the object relationship that is taking place at that moment.

Even though 'projective identification' is used to describe normal as well as pathological processes, I think that we tend to think of projective processes as more pathological than introjective ones. When we think of somebody being identified with somebody else, we tend to think rather loosely of introjective identification as healthier than projective identification. We visualise two very different object relationships: one in which the self receives something from the object, and the other in which there is massive intrusion into the object. And of course emotional development does depend essentially on taking in from our objects and identifying with them. But we can excessively polarise these different modes, seeing one as a peaceful welcoming of the object into the inner world, and the other as the warlike invasion of the object. In fact, as we know there is pathological introjection as much as pathological projection. Furthermore, projection and introjection are psychic mechanisms based on phantasies which are felt to have the power of concrete actions, and phantasies are totally coloured by affect and motive. If identification is based on the wish to become the object (and therefore to rob the object of its identity), as opposed to the wish to be like the object, therefore allowing the object to continue existing with its identity preserved – then this is pathological and destructive. And although it is important in analysis to investigate the unconscious phantasy manoeuvres used to achieve this taking over of the object – to differentiate what happens through concrete introjection from what happens through intrusive massive projection – the fundamental point is that the integrity of the object has been damaged or destroyed in this process. We are talking here of an 'imperialist' attitude towards the object and in this universe the different phantasies and mechanisms employed are simply tactical manoeuvres to defeat the enemy.

Pathological introjective identification implies a phantasy of concretely taking something in, whereas a normal identification with an internal object presupposes a capacity to introject symbolically while allowing the object to retain its separate identity. The same is true of normal projection, of course: when the ego is functioning in a depressive position mode, symbolic projection into the other's mind – being able to put oneself imaginatively in the other's place – helps us to understand who the other person is.

In his paper 'Remarks on the relation of male homosexuality to paranoia, paranoid anxiety and narcissism' Rosenfeld (1949) uses a very interesting dream from his patient to illustrate the origin of projective identification. I will quote it here because it is such a clear example of two points I want to stress: first, the fact that not only affects and parts of the personality are projected, but also modes of functioning; and second, the role of wholesale, concrete introjection of the object in states of pathological, massive identification.

Rosenfeld describes this patient as consciously afraid that the analyst will become too interested in him; he is therefore often silent when he has thoughts that he thinks are of special interest to the analyst.

> Dream: He saw a famous surgeon operating on a patient, who observed with great admiration the skill displayed by the surgeon, who seemed intensely concentrated on his work. Suddenly the surgeon lost his balance and fell right inside the patient, with whom he got so entangled that he could scarcely manage to free himself. He nearly choked, and only by administering an oxygen apparatus could he manage to revive himself.

Rosenfeld comments that the patient had paranoid fears of being controlled by the analyst from inside and that later on in the analysis he became more aware of his fear of falling inside the analyst and becoming entangled inside him.

This dream is a very striking example of how the whole process of projective identification is itself projected. The surgeon/analyst in the dream relates to the patient via intrusive projective identification: such is his curiosity that he gets concretely inside his patient. What is projected is not only curiosity but also a mode of functioning. You could say that this happens because this is the only mode of relating that the patient knows. This is a patient who thinks very concretely; but the fact that the surgeon 'administers to himself an oxygen apparatus' seems to me to indicate that the patient thinks that the analyst can save his own life – his separate identity – by recovering his capacity to function as an analyst. I think the fact that the word 'apparatus' appears in the dream text, rather than simply 'oxygen', reinforces this idea. I suspect that 'administering an oxygen apparatus' stands for a capacity of the analyst's that the patient has, in phantasy, robbed him of through the projection of his all encompassing infantile curiosity. In the dream this capacity is now available for reintegration into the patient's picture of the analyst. (In the patient's inner world, the analyst 'cures' himself by re-establishing himself as the analyst, with a separate identity and capacities.) This suggests that this patient is therefore capable of conceiving of such a function. I imagine also that this patient has already begun to find out, in his analysis, that massive projective identification is not a great method through which to live one's life! I think this dream is a rather beautiful metaphor for moments when the analyst feels entirely at the mercy of violent projections and then recovers his capacity to function.

I also wanted to use this dream to illustrate something else. What we have here is the patient ending up with the analyst in his belly, as opposed to ending up inside the analyst. He has power over the analyst because the analyst is inside him, not him inside the analyst. In other words, not only has he projected a whole way of functioning into the analyst, but also he has swallowed the analyst: a pathological massive introjection. There is an expression in Portuguese to describe somebody who feels he is superior to everybody else: 'He thinks he's got the king in his belly'. (So, through swallowing the king, he is superior even to the king.) An extremely complex interplay between projections and introjections takes place continuously to perpetuate this peculiar state of affairs, but I think it may be useful when describing states of massive projective identification - 'becoming' the object – to picture not only the patient inside the analyst (following Klein's description of the infantile impulses to invade the mother) but also the patient with the analyst inside (related to phantasies of primitive oral incorporation of the mother). Triumph in this case comes from having swallowed the whole object, thus totally controlling and owning its power and strength. Manic mechanisms are involved in this process by which the self becomes so much bigger than the object and so much more powerful.

I hope to illustrate with the following clinical example the interplay of projective and introjective mechanisms in massive projective identification, as well as the manic flavour of such operations.

## Mr A: 'Becoming' the idealised bad object

A narcissistic young man comes into the session and looks at me more closely than usual, staring intensely into my eyes in a way that feels uncomfortable, intrusive. He lies on the couch and, with a rather superior tone of voice, tells me that he can clearly see that I must be quite shortsighted, I have that kind of unfocused look in my eyes. It is ridiculous that I do not wear glasses but I am obviously too vain to do so. I say rather hesitantly that perhaps there is a reason why he feels today that I cannot see him properly and I get an absolutely furious, indignant and self-righteous response: I want everything to be his problem, I don't want to admit to my own failures, and I clearly suffer from an inferiority complex about my eyesight. He adds that he has had his eyes tested and has 100 per cent vision.

I think a very complex process of projections, introjections and identifications has occured to produce this state of affairs and I will now look in detail into what I think may have happened.

Something has obviously taken place that is connected to vision, specifically to do with seeing into the other person. He may have felt misunderstood in the previous session but I am more inclined to think that he felt understood in a way that was threatening to him. My capacity to see inside him made him too anxious, lest insight would threaten his pathological, but desperately needed, psychic equilibrium (Joseph 1989) or, perhaps, because he feels envious when he thinks I have better 'eyes' than he – probably both. I do not know what has happened, but I ask you to accept this as a working hypothesis so that this can be used as an example of the kind of process that can take place.

What gives him the absolute certainty that I am shortsighted and pathologically vain (preferring not to see than to wear glasses) is, I suspect, a projection of his fear of insight and of his narcissism. This is one aspect of his use of projective identification whereby I, his object, am now identified with unwanted aspects of himself. From his point of view, though, this could also be described as projective dis-identification, since through this process he loses part of his identity. He has lost contact with his narcissistic hurt, his fear of being inferior and despised etc.

Another aspect of projective identification, the phantasy of intrusively being able to get inside the object – is illustrated by his omnisciently 'knowing' what is in my mind: he 'knows' that I cannot see properly and he also 'knows' that this makes me feel inferior to him.

There is something else going on though, which I think has to do with pathological introjection rather than projection. How has he acquired these omniscient (100 per cent vision), malevolent eyes and whose eyes are they? I suggest that these were originally my perceptive and therefore threatening analytic eyes, inflated by idealisation. I am shortsighted not only because I now contain the projection of his lack of insight – and his narcissistic inability to see as far as the other person – but also that my eyes that could see into him have been concretely incorporated by him. In this defective, concrete introjection, if he has the 'analyst's eyes', then I obviously do not have them any more. In other words, if we assume that I made some interpretation yesterday that revealed something to him that he had not been able to see before, and by interpreting made him aware that I could 'see' (had good 'eyesight' and was interested in him), he perhaps did not take this in a healthy introjective way which would make it possible for both of us to see, but instead took over my function concretely. He acquired my capacity to describe some aspect of himself or some situation in his internal world, rather than taking in my description of what I thought I was observing in him, so that the interpretation couldn't be used to further his capacity to think about himself. Instead, he became the Me who can see into somebody else's mind.

(In normal identification, I introject your perceptive eyes, they are now felt to be symbolically in my mind and, through identification, I may then be able to see like you see, but you remain the owner of your eyes. And since this is a benign interchange, the relationship remains one of mutual co-operation. In pathological identification, not only do I become the sole possessor of the eyes because of a failure in symbolisation, but also the relationship is now dominated by a struggle for power in which omniscient knowledge acts as a barrier against insight.)

The person who arrives in the consulting room is now an 'analyst' (or rather, a caricature of one) whose primary concern is to look inside the other's mind and reveal what can be seen there to a disturbed 'patient' me, but in a cruel, humiliating way.

This is then what is described as 'being in massive projective identification with' the object. This cruel, self-righteous, omniscient person lying on my couch is my patient in a state of total projective identification with . . . me! A rather distorted (I hope!) version of his analyst. And this is what it feels like to be seen through 'my' eyes, which are now my patient's property: it is to be seen as inferior, vain, blind. If this is what has happened, then the analyst in my patient's mind is definitely a bad object and a very powerful one. I suggest that this particular brand of badness – cruel omniscience – is the product of an idealisation of a hated but also envied capacity of the object. The feared perceptive eyes are certainly a very desirable attribute, which is why they get stolen. No shame or guilt are apparent in this process, only manic triumph.

In other sessions, the process may happen slightly differently. An object with helpful eyes may be temporarily introjected – sometimes he can feel helped by an interpretation and feel some relief at being understood – but then the separation at the end of the session may cause an upsurge of hostility due to the pain of jealousy or envy or to an increase in persecutory anxiety. In his phantasy, if he takes in what I give him he will lose his defences, will become dangerously dependent, etc. (In this case there would be hostile projections into the internal object and the perceptive eyes, now transformed into cruel eyes, have to be stolen as if they were a weapon to be stolen from an enemy.)

## Miss B: the loss of parts of the self

I will now bring an example from a patient who can get into massive states of projective identification with a bad object, but who does so much more temporarily. She is a very fragile, borderline young woman, whose identifications shift rather quickly, producing a sense of fragmentation and of loss of a sense of identity (I am very grateful to Richard Rusbridger for allowing me to use his clinical material).

The previous weekend had been extremely distressing for Miss B. Her boyfriend, C, a pop star musician, had been on tour around the country for several weeks and was coming back to visit her. She had been waiting for his arrival in an eager but also rather desperate mood. He arrived in a manic state, very much the star, made absolutely no emotional contact with her, found it intolerable when she started clinging to him, and finally left with his friends for an excited, drunken night out, leaving her behind in a distraught condition. Throughout the following week Miss B was in a very bad state, on the brink of completely falling apart. What follows is a summary of the following Monday session.

She starts talking, hesitating, and in a very croaky voice, 'Last night I just cancelled everything, and went out and got drunk, and had quite a nice time, and at one point felt much better about everything in a drunken way, and kind of went round the place'. She then said, 'It was really strange, because I thought I would do some work, but . . .' and went on to describe meeting several people for drinks in what seemed to be a very excited, possibly dangerous, way which seemed to the analyst to be exactly how she had described her boyfriend's activities in the previous weekend. The narrative was punctuated with comments like, 'I've erased everything from my mind'. At some point in the session she exclaimed, 'I am not afraid of C [the boyfriend] any more!'

It seemed clear to her analyst that her way of 'cancelling everything' was via getting into a state of massive projective identification with the manic boyfriend (in the transference a cruel weekend analyst). The patient in the room seemed to have come out of that state, now felt to be in the past, so that she seemed able to listen to his interpretations. But there was an interesting misunderstanding at one point. The narrative about the night's events had started with her explaining that she 'had driven John, a boy I know, home to X' (a place quite far away); it ended with her driving around very late at night, until she was 'flagged down by two chaps' and she had driven one of them 'home'. The analyst asked her if she meant that she had driven the man to his home and she answered, as if it was obvious, that she meant her own home.

The analyst was rather alarmed at this, feeling that his patient had been putting herself through a really dangerous experience, and took this description of the end of her manic night out to mean her acting out an identification with an unfaithful, promiscuous boyfriend/analyst.

Miss B made it clear then that this was not the case at all, that she had recognised a friend, Paul, in the road and that it had been helpful to have him at home, had made it possible for her to sleep. She then explained that 'cancelling everything' had begun as trying to stop a terrible pain in her back, and then it had become exciting to feel so very strong; but at the end of the night she had felt terrible about 'total disengagement'. It became quite clear, then, that for this patient, the state of massive projective identification with a manic bad object starts with 'driving away' to some far away place some part of herself and that she can only come 'home' (to her house, to her own identity, and also to her session) if she takes back inside parts of herself that have been fragmented and spread 'around town', as it were. So whatever actually happened in the previous night in external reality, what we have in the session is a narrative that gives a particular shape and meaning to psychic events.

This patient is on some level able to communicate to her analyst the temporary loss of contact with essential parts of herself that have to be recovered so as to enable her to go 'home', that is to say, to recover some sense of who she is. Her state of projective identification with the manic object is only temporary and threatens her with a loss of her sense of identity. Ultimately she knows that this powerful manic person in the night is not her real self. This is a temporary state, a defence that becomes threatening. I am not suggesting, of course, that this patient is suddenly 'cured' of her need to relate to her object through pathological projective identification. For instance, I suspect that even though she could come to the session and take in her analyst's interpretations, which involves a relationship with a less malevolent object and some awareness of a need to be helped to be more in contact with herself, her dependency still resides partly in this other, more receptive object. She mentioned at some point how much time she spends looking after others and there was a distinct sense in the material that the analyst in the here-and-now of the session is 'flagging her down' with his attention and his comments and that her listening to him is probably coloured by her 'helpfulness' to him. But it is clear that the objects involved in this interchange are in fact kinder and saner, and that she is consciously aware of her need to be 'reconnected' again.

In my patient Mr A, who was also identified with a manic object, these states are much more inflexible. He is much more solidly identified with the idealised bad object and there is great commitment to keeping things this way. The equilibrium of the personality depends on maintaining this identification, and splitting mechanisms are constantly used to prevent any awareness of weaker, dependent parts. Mr A's pathological identification is more or less permanent and when this equilibrium is threatened his reaction is paranoid. Miss B's projective identification with the object, although extensive, is only temporary. She is much more fragile, her defensive solutions do not last and the state of 'becoming' the object very quickly becomes a threat in itself. It is as if Mr A is in possession of the object, has taken it over; whereas Miss B seems possessed by the manic object. She never entirely loses her awareness that she has been invaded by something alien to her. Or perhaps one could say that she does not idealise the bad object in the same way Mr A does, and her identifications shift. In the presence of her sensitive analyst she is also projectively identified with a helpful parent who picks people up, drives them home, etc.

⋆ ⋆ ⋆

I will now bring another example from Mr A to illustrate the technical difficulties the analyst may feel confronted with when an object relation that seems very fixed and unchangeable is dominating the transference. I find it useful to refer here to Joseph's careful exploration and development of Klein's concept of transference as a 'total situation'. I think this concept can help us to keep in mind the fact that a whole mode of functioning between two people is being repeated in the situation in the session. (I am of course taking it for granted that, as the analyst, one must always try to differentiate between what is being projected and the effect this has on oneself, which is due at least partly to one's own psychological make-up.)

Mr A, who is by profession a journalist, wrote a novel and sent it to a well-known publisher. He received a letter of rejection from one of the directors of the publishing house (a writer himself). His reaction in the session was one of moral indignation and contempt. It was absolutely clear that this director had been motivated in his action by envy of Mr A's superiority as a novelist. As soon as I took up what I thought was Mr A's terrible hurt and disappointment at this rejection he became enraged with me, clearly feeling that I was trying to project into him feelings that were absolutely not his. I seemed to have become the publisher who was rejecting (refusing to publish, as it were) his point of view. Soon an impasse was created in the session. I felt I had either to accept his version of the situation or I would become entirely identified with the publisher in his mind and not only suffer a barrage of hatred and contempt but also, as the 'enemy', be entirely unable to help my patient. I began to feel more and more trapped in a situation in which I had either to remain silent or agree with what seemed to me a rather mad version of events; that the only conceivable reason for being rejected is that one is far superior to the rejecting person. (As with the 'eyesight' situation in the first example, what seems so disturbing in these states is his certainty about the state of mind of the object.)

It would seem that Mr A has projected his envy of a creative parent who can produce a viable baby into the 'publisher', an aspect of me as a parent whom he sees as wanting to thwart his creativity: possibly of course an internal object created originally by introjecting a disturbed parent. But is this what happens in the session? I did not feel envious of my patient, I felt isolated as if I had lost any hope of ever getting through to him. It was impossible for me to 'publish' my thoughts (for instance, about the pain of being rejected, the defensive nature of his superiority, and his hatred of me as a cruel publisher trying to put him down).

Thinking about the session afterwards, though, I became aware that all the interpretations I could think of were really aiming at changing the situation by reversing it: either his version is published, or my version is. No wonder we didn't get anywhere!

These are really difficult situations to get out of and often only through thinking carefully about it afterwards can one begin to visualise what actually took place, without having to be either victim or aggressor, which is what one undoubtedly is (and not only in the patient's phantasy) when trying to deal with projections by (unconsciously) re-projecting them. What I am talking about is a necessary shift in the analyst to a position from which it would be possible to observe what is happening in the interaction between these two people in the session. From this position it becomes more possible to see who is who and what is the object relationship which is being enacted in the transference. In this case, this could be seen to be one between somebody who is trying to get something through, something that absolutely must be seen to be of value, and somebody else who is impenetrable, unreachable, who says 'No!' to any attempt at communication. (This experience links closely to what I have learned about Mr A's first two years of life, when his mother was severely depressed and withdrawn.)

Mr A's change of identity gives me first-hand experience, as it were, of contact with his internal object. By trying to visualise the total situation, I have some hope of understanding his underlying despair and of finding a way out of the impasse in which we could be trapped into only repeating and not working through.

## References

Bion, W.R. (1962) *Learning from Experience*, London: Heinemann.

Freud, A. (1937) *The Ego and the Mechanisms of Defence*, London: Hogarth Press and the Institute of Psychoanalysis.

Freud, S. (1917) 'Mourning and melancholia', SE 14: 237–258.

Joseph, B. (1989) *Psychic Equilibrium and Psychic Change: Selected Papers of Betty Joseph*, M. Feldman and E. Bott Spillius (eds), London: Routledge.

Klein, M. (1946) 'Notes on some schizoid mechanisms', *The Writings of Melanie Klein*, vol. 3, *Envy and Gratitude and Other Works*, London: Hogarth Press (1975).

—— (1955) 'On identification', *The Writings of Melanie Klein*, vol. 3, *Envy, Gratitude and Other Works*, London: Hogarth Press (1975).

Ogden, T. (1979) 'On projective identification', *International Journal of Psychoanalysis*, 60: 357–373.

Rosenfeld, H. (1949) 'Remarks on the relation of male homosexuality to paranoia, paranoid anxiety, and narcissism', *Psychotic States*, Maresfield Reprints, London: Hogarth Press and Karnac (1965).

—— (1964) 'On the psychopathology of narcissism: a clinical approach', *Psychotic States*, Maresfield Reprints, London: Hogarth Press and Karnac (1965).

Sandler, J. (1988) *Projection, Identification, Projective Identification*, London: Karnac.

## DISCUSSION OF IGNES SODRÉ'S CHAPTER

*Betty Joseph*

This paper makes a most valuable contribution to our understanding of the complexity and significance of projective identification. Of the many issues that it raises the one that I would particularly like to think about is that of the problem for the analyst in interpreting projective identification. Ignes raises this question of technique towards the end of the chapter when she returns to Mr A, but it of course is around in one's mind throughout the presentation of case material; how does one handle this?

I think that she raises a very important issue when she describes how when thinking after the session, she realised that a problem had arisen in that her interpretations were 'aiming at changing the situation'. (Isn't this a trap that we as analysts in our therapeutic zeal or our despair are constantly falling into?) She stresses the importance of the analyst being able to shift to a position from which it would be possible to observe what is happening between analyst and patient in the session. I suspect this means that the more concretely the patient is using projective identification at the moment, the greater is the importance for the analyst to attempt to register what is being enacted in the session, what is being stirred up in analyst as well as patient, and use this in formulating the interpretations. I suspect this often means our needing to let things really get into us, contain them, and then concentrate our interpretations on how our patient sees or feels us (an analyst-centred interpretation as John Steiner expresses it.) Any interpretation to push a projection back into the patient must, by definition, not only fail but provoke more anxiety, anger or compliance in the patient.

Ignes makes a further interesting aside when discussing Miss B, saying 'So whatever actually happened in the previous night in external reality, what we have in the session is a narrative that gives a particular shape and meaning to psychic events.' In this case Miss B is able to give an account of what happened which enables the analyst to see the patient's mental functioning and her capacity temporarily to recover contact with parts of herself. It seems that here, when there are moments of depressive position functioning, interpretations are able to be made to the patient about how her ego is dealing with aspects of the self and I believe it is most important then that such interpretations are made. Then we have real insight as for a moment the analyst is able to talk to and with Miss B about the patient's own self. I think the whole area of how to interpret projective identification and thus how to make useful contact with the patient is one which is going to need much more consideration and that this sensitive and clear chapter gives us real help in this direction.

# DISCUSSION OF IGNES SODRÉ'S CHAPTER

## *Priscilla Roth*

The two things I like most about this important chapter are, in the first place, the identification, description and delineation of the powerful mental mechanism that Ignes calls massive pathological introjective identification, and, in the second place, the clarifying and illuminating clinical material she uses to demonstrate how this mechanism works. I have one, rather long, question to ask.

In the material of Mr A: what is so fascinating in this material is the nature of the object Ignes' patient identifies with. She writes:'He acquired my capacity to describe some aspect of himself or some situation in his internal world, rather than taking in my description of what I thought I was observing in him, so that the interpretation couldn't be used to further his capacity to think about himself. Instead, he became the Me who can see into somebody else's mind.' And a little later she writes 'the relationship is now dominated by a struggle for power in which omniscient knowledge acts as a barrier against insight'. What Ignes is describing, obviously, is not that he acquired *her* capacity, as it actually is and as she actually makes use of it, but that he acquired *his view* of or *his take* on her capacity – he acquired her capacity as it appears to him. Seen through his eyes, this seems to be a capacity used solely to get and maintain power over another person, over him. This is felt to be its only function, its only purpose, and in this state of mind no other purpose is even conceivable – all talk of learning, growing, gaining insight, helping, being helped, sharing, – all such ideas are felt to be completely meaningless, utterly false and simply weapons in her battle to establish her superiority over him.

All of this Ignes describes very clearly. What I am wondering is: is it inevitably true that such massive introjective identification has this quality? My immediate thought is that it does that in so far as it primarily involves an illusion of the possession of the other person's qualities in a massive way, 'becoming' another person, even when it is not overtly aggressive and hostile, has to include an attack on the separateness of the other. The way in which the taken-over qualities are not quite copied, but seem rather to be caricatured, would support this idea – the caricature containing within it such an element of envious mockery and hatred invading the supposedly admired qualities. But I wonder if it is possible that sometimes, even over quite a long time (much longer, say, than the example of Miss B demonstrated) even fairly massive introjective identification can be made use of as part of a developmental process. What I am thinking of are children who for periods seem to take over the voices, mannerisms, prejudices of their parents, or adolescents who ape the behaviour and style of their most envied peers. At these times it often seems that the introjective identification, though strange and clearly not integrated, serves as a temporary crutch, or maybe a temporary psychic retreat. This can go on for months, but what is important is that it seems to me it often isn't simply a unidimensional co-opting of all the power. It seems to allow for other development to take place, which would suggest that only a part of the ego is so identified with the object, and that the process somehow protects the rest of the ego and allows it to develop independently until the individual becomes strong enough to let go of the identification. Perhaps this is very different. I would be very interested to know what Ignes thinks about this.

## 4

# COMPLACENCY IN ANALYSIS AND EVERYDAY LIFE

*Ronald Britton*

> One day everything will be well, that is our hope:
> Everything's fine today, that is our illusion.
> (Voltaire, *Poème sur le désastre de Lisbonne*, 1756)

These lines refer to the disastrous earthquake of Lisbon in 1756, which resulted in great destruction and the death of many thousands; the Inquisition followed it by burning a number of people to death, since the University of Coimbra knew this to be a reliable method of preventing earthquakes. Both events feature in Voltaire's tale of *Candide; or the Optimist* (Voltaire 1759). In that story they provide further tests of Dr Pangloss's indestructible belief that all is for the best in the best of all possible worlds; this belief also remains unchanged by Dr Pangloss's subsequent hanging, which, owing to his executioner's incompetence, leads to the initiation of a post-mortem while he is still alive. In Candide and Dr Pangloss we have a literary antecedent to the complaisant patient and the complacent analyst. Candide, the complaisant, is happy to accept his mentor's dictum and remain his most agreeable pupil, and Pangloss, the complacent, while he can continue to teach his metaphysico-theologo-cosmolo-nigology to such a receptive person remains through all adversity convinced that this is the best of all possible worlds. 'Observe, for instance,' he comments, 'the nose is formed for spectacles therefore we wear spectacles. The legs are visibly designed for stockings; accordingly we wear stockings' (Voltaire 1759: 108). We must note, however, that Dr Pangloss does not say that things are right or good, but only 'that they cannot be otherwise than they are', so 'they who assert that everything is right do not express themselves correctly; they should say, that everything is best' (Voltaire 1759: 108). In other words, it is not moral idealism but a theology of realism, a sort of ideal pragmatism or idealisation of adaptation.

In the face of the vicissitudes of analysis this shared optimistic stoicism is appealing, and it is not surprising that we as analysts might unknowingly accept the role of Dr Pangloss offered to us by some well-meaning patients. It is just such an analytic transference/countertransference situation that I want to discuss in this chapter. It is one in which the hardships of the depressive position *appear* to be suffered and acknowledged by the individual, but in truth they are tempered by the belief that he or she is more fortunate than others who are less able to come to terms with reality; analysis becomes the pursuit of moral excellence in the company of an approving parental figure and the 'depressive position' becomes a resting place rather than a staging post.

In contrast to the Panglossian approach, that of Betty Joseph has been to emphasise the need for constant questioning of appearance. This is crucial in learning how to work in such a way as to discover, not simply from the content but also from the mode and development of the analysis itself, the 'specific constellations of object relations, anxieties, and defences' (Joseph 1989b: 126). As Betty Joseph put it in her paper on 'Defence mechanisms and phantasy in the psychoanalytical process':

> We can observe phantasies being attached to the analyst, as if forcing him into a particular role as a constant process going on in the analytic situation; so that anxieties arise, defences are mobilised, and the analyst is in the mind of the patient drawn into the process, continually being used as part of his defensive system.
>
> (Joseph 1989b: 126)

This chapter draws on two of her central ideas in particular: her view of the total transference situation as the most informative aspect of analysis, and her notion of the relationship between psychic equilibrium and psychic change. I want to discuss a particular group of patients in these terms; in some ways they resemble those referred to in Betty Joseph's own paper 'The patient who is difficult to reach' (Joseph 1989a), but they are more able to participate in analysis than those described by Joseph. On a session-by-session basis it would not be true to say they are 'difficult to reach', but it is all too likely that the analyst would be in the position she describes, if at any time he reflected on the analysis as a whole. That is, to quote Betty Joseph:

> One finds oneself in a situation that looks exactly like an on-going analysis with understanding, apparent contact, appreciation, and even reported improvement. . . . And yet . . . If one considers one's own countertransference it may seem all a bit too easy, pleasant and unconflicted.
>
> (Joseph 1989a: 76)

The hallmark of the group of patients I want to consider, who differ in other ways, is in the countertransference. It is one in which there develops a complacent, unconscious assumption in the analyst that one need not worry about these patients, in contrast to others who prey on the analyst's mind.

It is not, I want to emphasise, that there is no suffering, self-examination and self-reproach taking place in such analyses, but there is an unspoken belief that this is the proper order of things and that 'these things are sent to try us'. What I have found to signal real change in analysis in these cases is the eruption of indignation – not simply anger but a sense of outrage. It occurs when a previously existing unspoken, and unclaimed, sense of entitlement is felt to have been breached. At that moment the previously complaisant patient becomes, however briefly, like his or her invisible, difficult twin, unreasonable and demanding.

I have already suggested that in these patients analysis is usually regarded as a privileged state; there is a sense of a moral quest which makes its hardships seem like part of an apprenticeship, with the analyst assumed to be a sort of master mason helping the patient to join the initiated. As quoted earlier, Betty Joseph (1989b: 126) said: 'The analyst is in the mind of the patient drawn into the process, continually being used as part of his defensive system'. As she taught us, this occurs not only in the mind of the patient, but also in practice in the analyst's unwitting countertransference action and attitude. The question to be asked, therefore, in considering analytic sessions is not simply what of the unconscious is discoverable in the patient's words, but also what is going on? That is, in the cases I am describing, what is the role assigned to the analyst that is likely to be enacted by him or her?

If you will allow another literary allegory and see the patient, not as Candide now but as Christian in Bunyan's (1684) *Pilgrim's Progress*, the analyst would at first appear to be Christian's companion, Faithful, and then after poor Faithful's execution he becomes his second fellow-traveller, Hopeful. In Bunyan's story the character concerned was made Hopeful by 'the beholding' of the good relationship that had existed between Christian and Faithful: 'Thus one died to bear testimony to the truth, and another rises from his ashes' (Bunyan 1684: 109). Having become Hopeful, Christian's optimistic companion continued with him on his pilgrimage to their next adventure, escaping from Doubting Castle, where they were imprisoned by the Giant Despair. Any further recollections of the trial, execution and loss of Faithful were superseded by this adventure. However, how Faithful came to be executed cannot be without relevance if we take him to be a representative of the analyst. It happened in this way: on arriving at the town of Vanity Fair, when asked what they would buy, they replied, 'We buy the truth'. This created a hubbub, which led to their arrest (Bunyan 1684: 102).

They were charged and found guilty of opposing the religion of Vanity Fair, and Faithful was buffeted, lanced, stoned and burnt to death. The Judge's name was Lord Hate-good. The prosecutor at his trial was Mr Envy, and the jury consisted of Mr Blind-man, Mr No-good, Mr Malice, Mr Love-lust, Mr

Live-loose, Mr Heady, Mr High-mind, Mr Enmity, Mr Liar, Mr Cruelty, Mr Hate-light and Mr Implacable (Bunyan 1684: 108). These are a prosecutor, judge, counsel and jury most analysts would recognise. I have felt myself, like Faithful, to be in the dock in such a court in a number of analytic sessions, but not with the patients to whom I am referring. In fact, and this I think is very relevant, they are the very antithesis of the patients who might induce such feelings in the analyst; they are not simply unlike them, but the very opposite of such characters.

However, there is almost always someone significant in the lives of my complaisant patients with such characteristics, who appears as a parent, sibling, spouse, lover, colleague or even as a child. Since people with such agreeable personalities often become analysts or psychotherapists, the dreaded antithetic twin is sometimes to be found among their own patients and, when they are in analysis themselves, to fill their own analytic sessions just as they haunt their minds. Before exploring the significance of this any further I need to give more clinical detail.

As previously stated, I have found in my own practice and even more in supervision, a number of cases where there is a tendency towards excessive reasonableness in the patient and, in concert with this, a degree of complacency in the analyst. Although the patients' characters and analyses vary and their temperaments are similar in certain respects, their transferences and counter-transference are, in a certain respect, the same. The patients' family histories vary in detail but contain a common factor: they are the healthiest members of their families. They have relatively equable temperaments and, in both life and analysis, they are easygoing. Although they often come for professional reasons, they see themselves as needing analysis and value it and their analysts, unlike more narcissistic patients. They think they need improving the better to help everybody else.

In other words, I am not suggesting such patients are self-satisfied but, rather, that they are unrealistically free of discontent. They are ready to be self-critical because of their failures to remedy difficult relationships and they are very ready to agree, if it is suggested, that they are unconsciously hostile, rivalrous or unloving towards others. If one interprets that the difficult or nasty person they are dealing with is really an aspect of the self denied and projected, they will agree with alacrity and with some relief. Analysts can provide such people with a great opportunity to blame themselves in a quiet way, which suits them very well. I say in a quiet way, because the attribution of blame and the acknowledgement of guilt do not, in these cases, do more than ripple the calm surface of their analysis and their relationship with their analysts. They are not insensitive; nor are they free of anxiety or depression, but they have a penchant for settling for relatively little and can make a feast of crumbs. Precisely what they are greedy for is at first hard to spot since it makes them ostensibly so undemanding. I think that they are greedy for virtue and covetous of innocence. I quoted

Voltaire earlier because these patients remind me of Candide, who personified unmodifiable, optimistic innocence, and as their analyst one is invited to become Dr Pangloss, whose fidelity to the philosophy of Leibniz transcended experience.

They do not see themselves as needing much care and often fail to protect themselves from exploitation in their personal lives. In analysis, unlike most of their analytic siblings, they rarely blame their analysts for anything and accept whatever comes their way. In a way it is hard to convey the atmosphere of analysis in such cases because to describe the complaisance of the patient as I am doing now is to draw attention to it as a problem, whereas in practice it is precisely because there does not appear to be anything problematic that the analyst becomes complacent. It requires an effort by the analyst to do anything other than be pleased with apparent progress and gratefully accept calm seas after the choppy waters experienced in most of the other sessions of the day.

For this reason, except for educational reasons these patients are not often brought for supervision, unlike those regarded as 'difficult' cases, who are brought in large numbers. However, I have been fortunate in running a postgraduate seminar overseas for some years, where analytic cases have been brought routinely, and in that and in other similar situations I have heard about the 'non-difficult' analyses. Not long ago, when I was acting as visiting supervisor in another country, an analyst brought me a case like this, which she selected simply because she wanted to bring a patient for whom she had not had any supervision. When, however, she prepared the case for presentation to me she started to worry for the first time about the analysis that had been taking place for a good many years. By the time she talked to me she began by saying:

> This is a patient whom I have never worried about before. The analysis seemed to be going along fine and we both seemed to be working quite well, but when I looked at it I realised that nothing much has changed and that, actually, though she doesn't complain, nothing has happened in her life that she hoped analysis would do for her. When she came initially, in part, it was to enable her to marry and have children. She has been in analysis for many years and neither of us has noticed the time passing, or that because of the biological clock this must have become quite urgent.

The patient was a psychotherapist and spent quite an amount of analytic time talking about her troubled and troublesome patients; she was very grateful, therefore, for her own analysis in helping her with her countertransference. The analyst was easily able to link these work problems with her patient's family origins and appropriate aspects of the transference relationship. They worked comfortably together as analyst and patient, in contradistinction to the situation the patient was in with her difficult cases.

What I noticed as I listened to the case was that this patient, who came from a very troubled family, from which she had partly rescued herself, did not appear to have a life of her own outside her work and her analysis. In symmetry with this, I noticed that, although the analyst often interpreted the patient's reactions to breaks and weekends, and although the patient clearly missed the analyst in her absence, there was no real recrimination or anything that would make the analyst feel bad about it. There was also nothing in the patient's material that suggested that the analyst ever did anything during breaks other than be absent from sessions. This required a considerable use of the 'blind eye' by the patient, since she had, in a relatively small community, access to the social circle of her analyst, who was an attractive married woman a few years older than her patient and with a successful husband, lively children and expensive house. Naturally, envy was spoken of and acknowledged in this analysis, and the patient's Oedipus complex interpreted where it was clear enough in her dreams to be made explicit. I was impressed by the analyst's grasp of the analytic material and her use of analytic ideas. So what is it that I think was missing? One thing that was missing was sustained discontent; another was animosity, and completely absent was any malevolence. How was it, if envy and jealousy were interpreted, felt and acknowledged, that their presence did no more than ruffle the surface of the analytic relationship? I think the answer to this lay in the shared assumption that these were feelings to be expected in an analysis, like a price worth paying for a privilege.

I do not wish to pursue further the details of that analysis and want to make just one point, which I will return to later. What I think sustained the patient in a state of relative contentment and complaisance was the *belief* that her analyst *did not want her to change in any fundamental way*. Another element in this was the patient's unspoken assumption that she was, unlike others, a support to her analyst in her difficult vocation. Linked to this was a belief that the analyst's work was the centre of her life, and that her relationship with her patients, and this one in particular, transcended everything else. Thus jealousy was evaded and, without jealousy, envy had no foothold. In her turn, the analyst did not think her patient was fulfilling herself as she would wish nor was she enamoured of her patient, but she did like her and appreciated her efforts, struggles and fortitude. Who would not?

What I think is interesting is that when the progress of the analysis was seriously questioned it became clear that the analyst thought it would be very cruel to want more of her patient or to allow any sense of dissatisfaction to colour her own countertransference. To question the patient's obvious efforts to do her best under difficult circumstances immediately felt heartless to her analyst. In parallel with this, the analyst herself, once she questioned the success of her own work with the patient, was exposed to a quite savage process of self-recrimination. Following the first of the series of supervision sessions with the analyst, I also began to feel uncomfortable with the thought that I had upset the apple cart. There was some support for this apprehension of mine since the analyst's patient was, for the first time, unable to restrain herself from making intrusive telephone calls to her analyst over the analytic weekend and developed a hypochondriacal panic. When the patient's complaisance was disrupted, giving way to a panicky sense of persecution, the analyst's and/or her supervisor's complacency was interrupted by a sense of panicky guilt. It was as if the genie had been let out of the bottle as a frightening moral force with destructive potential. Thanks to the faith of the analyst in the necessity of exposing and exploring the current analytic situation and her patient's actual resilience and responsiveness, their shared fears of imminent catastrophe proved groundless. The struggle then was to prevent this itself from becoming further grounds for complacency.

In order to describe what I think was the inner situation that produced this episode I would like to return to the court scene I described from *Pilgrim's Progress* (Bunyan 1684). Seriously questioning the calm mutual regard and the virtues of untroublesomeness releases a destructive force which purports to be a moral force. It has the judicial powers of conscience, with the punitive methods of the Inquisition. Like Bunyan's judge and jury it resembles a destructive, envious superego and supercontainer of dissatisfaction. By its intervention, faith in the analytic situation is quickly destroyed, and resort is taken to hope as a substitute for faith, optimism deputising for confidence. Faithful is executed and Hopeful takes his place. This harsh force of a quasi-judicial kind was never far away, but while the analytic pair could remain mutually hopeful it was believed that it could be kept at bay and never encountered. What was really needed for progress in the analysis was a long enough period imprisoned in Doubting Castle to explore it and not simply escape from it.

Like all the other patients of whom I am thinking in this chapter, this woman was the healthiest and most equable member of a troubled family. I would like to include only those aspects held in common by otherwise different patients with different histories, partly for reasons of confidentiality and partly to make a general point. The patient I describe, therefore, is a composite picture of a patient in analysis, although any material I give is obviously specific.

As I have already implied, such a patient is the untroublesome, relatively well child who has disturbed and disturbing siblings and parents, who have difficulties of their own. In analysis any picture of an untroubled past is soon dispelled and the forgotten anxieties experienced in childhood soon recalled and recounted. Psychosomatic problems, usually short-lived, have occurred in the course of analysis. Current emotional disturbance is most often manifested in hypochondriacal form, usually short-lived, but transiently very alarming and apt to lead to fear of imminent death. These fears are relatively easily surmounted. Because of the very unlikely nature of these hypochondriacal fears, and because of the readiness of the patient to see their unreality and to accept psychological explanation, the anxieties have little purchase on the analyst, who is therefore personally untouched by them. In childhood the patient kept to him or herself such fears and other anxieties or readily accepted the automatic reassurance of a parent, who conveyed in doing so that 'we don't need to worry about you'. In analysis the patient takes advantage of the opportunity to expose such anxieties, both past and present, and feels considerable benefit from doing so. I do not want to minimise the benefit of this; nor would I for a moment suggest to the patient that it had no value. However, we should keep in mind Betty Joseph's maxim that we must also recognise that we are not only interpreting the transference, but also living in it. While creating a situation in which the patient can explore a forgotten past of anxiety in the presence of a sympathetic listener, we are also in the process recreating a scene of an untroublesome child with an untroubled parent. It is what Freud (1913) would have called a transference cure.

It is characteristic of such patients that they have brief intrusive hypochondriacal fears and similarly fleeting disturbing transference thoughts, out of keeping with the ongoing mainstream current of belief that prevails in the transference. These thoughts are, to use Freud's word, *unheimlich* – translated by Strachey as 'uncanny', a word that does not really do justice to the German. *Unheimlich* means eerie, but it also means alien, and it is the antithesis of *heimisch*, meaning homely and familiar. Freud's explanation for the *unheimlich* experience is that one encounters something in the world that appears to reinstate a primitive belief which the individual had not eliminated but, in Freud's word, apparently *surmounted*. In his paper '*Das Unheimlich*' ('The uncanny', Freud 1919), written before 'The ego and the id'(Freud 1923) and therefore before he had available to him the concept of an unconscious ego, he distinguishes between repressed infantile complexes, which he sees as belonging to the *unconscious*, and *archaic beliefs*, which he sees as surmounted but capable of re-emerging if given apparent support in the external world. He distinguishes between a state in which beliefs, though surmounted, remain latent, always ready to give rise to *unheimlich* experiences, and a state in which they have been abolished. 'Conversely,' he wrote, 'anyone who has completely and finally rid himself of animistic beliefs will be insensible to this type of the *Unheimlich*' (Freud 1919: 248). I think this distinction is a most important one in analysis. I would make the distinction between beliefs that have merely been surmounted or apparently outgrown and those that have been worked through and relinquished. It is relinquishment that is necessary for psychic change, and this takes time, needs working through and entails mourning for a lost belief like mourning for a lost object. A belief that has been surmounted I regard as one simply overcome by another belief which itself remains dependent on the prevailing context. It is then like believing one thing when in company and in daylight and another when alone in the dark.

I think this is true of the patients of whom I am talking. They have surmounted certain beliefs but not relinquished or modified them; subsequently, they put in fleeting appearances as *unheimlich* thoughts, or 'weird ideas', as one of my patients put it. Instead of sustained anxieties tethered in the transference, there are brief glimpses of terrifying ideas about the analyst or untethered images of a frightening or horrifying kind attached to nothing in particular. These transient incursions of archaic beliefs do not find a settled home in the transference and are rapidly dispelled by the reassuring familiarity of the analytic relationship.

I would like to illustrate this by describing some clinical material from a session some years ago, which I used to illustrate what I called the willing suspension of belief in a paper on belief (Britton 1995: 20–21). With hindsight, I take a more critical view of my work in that session and I hope to make a point about this. The patient was a lecturer in philosophy in a prestigious university who should, by this time, have been a senior lecturer. His family came from a foreign country where they had suffered persecution, and they had come to London as refugees. He had two sisters, one of whom was now homosexual and alienated from the family and one of whom was alcoholic; both women, unlike the patient, created problems for their parents. At the time of this session he had a girlfriend who worked in a City stockbrokers' firm. They lived together but she would not commit herself to a mutually agreed long-term arrangement. He regarded her as emotionally dependent but difficult to satisfy and at times impossible to talk to.

He began by saying: 'When I came in I thought you looked fed up, not interested, hostile or cold.' He paused briefly and, as if beginning again, he said:

> It is very interesting; I used the toilet here for the first time. On my way here I felt I had to have a shit, but didn't want to be late so I didn't stop. But I didn't want to do it here. Anyway I came slightly early to do so. When I was in the car I thought 'I have to' and I had a pain. I thought of a condition I was told I had years ago – don't know if you know it – *proctalgia fugax*, fleeting pain in the anus.

By this time the patient had warmed to the subject, and talked of himself and his experiences in a steadily more expansive way. Clearly, he was now talking to someone he thought of as interested and friendly. However, the sense of something sudden, violent and sinister (like the pain of *proctalgia fugax*, a fleeting, stabbing, anal pain) remained in my mind as a disturbing image, but one that had vanished from his discourse, which was easy and relaxed.

I commented: 'You cannot direct your feelings towards me fully, and I think you dare not take your fleeting picture seriously, of me as hostile; so you have covered the picture with words.'

After a pause, he told me a story about himself and his girlfriend. It followed a pattern. Initially, his description of events gave a clear picture of her treating him badly and his withdrawing, but as the account went on their relative positions became obscure and, finally, he became objectively but unemotionally self-critical. He followed it with a story of an episode with colleagues at work which followed the same pattern. At first it seemed clear to him that he had been wronged; then, as he amplified it, what he really thought about it became obscure and the final version was one of theoretical self-criticism.

I remained silent, which he found uncomfortable, and he commented on it. He returned to talk of his girlfriend. With considerable feeling, he voiced his suspicion that when she received the substantial financial bonus due to her from her work she would keep it for herself, despite his investment of everything he had earned, and more, in their life together. He continued to describe his great relief and warm feelings when he next saw her, because, despite their earlier sharp words, she was friendly. I said:

> Here, also, you invest everything in me; that is, you credit me with more than you have in the way of a good opinion of me. When you idealise me like that, you feel favoured and welcome. This relieves you of your apprehensions about me and our relationship. When you lose the idea that I am good and you are well off, fortunate, and favoured, I think you are exposed to a sudden sharp discomfort, a fleeting painful doubt about me.

The patient was thoughtful, and then said he was thinking of the story of the students who died in their flat because of the landlord's negligence. They were poisoned by the gas fire due to his disregard of its defects. (I have a gas fire in my room.)

I commented that when he puts himself in my hands that aspect of him that should protect his vulnerable self and take seriously his misgivings about his treatment prefers to dismiss danger in order to get on well with me on a basis of mutual esteem. So he allows himself to be, in effect, poisoned or buggered.

There was an intense silence, after which he said:

> I thought last week when I spoke to you about my colleague's anal fissure and you said that it was an example of a condition that gets worse before it gets better [I had linked this with analysis] . . . I understood what you meant about dilatation as treatment but I thought you said it with [searching for a word] relish. I thought it showed your . . . um . . . can't think of the word . . .
>
> 'Sadism?' I suggested. 'You mean my sadism?'
>
> 'That's right,' he said, 'I thought you were sadistic.'

I described this session in an earlier paper, to make the point that until a patient discovers that he or she really believes an idea, its correspondence, or lack of it, to external reality is irrelevant. In other words, until the patient's psychic reality is fully exposed, its rebuttal or verification by reality testing is premature. The implication was that I thought that this had been accomplished in the session, that the patient knew by the end of it that he seriously entertained a persecutory belief that the analyst might be a dangerous, cruel figure, and that he had been attempting to evade this belief. However, I would now see it differently; I think the patient considered by the end of the session that he had entertained a wild idea that was interesting to both himself and his analyst, but that he would be crazy to believe it.

The way I see it now is that this patient momentarily believed that if he expelled things, like offensive words of real substance, in my direction it would precipitate a retaliatory sadistic anal attack from me in return. This belief, transiently conscious, was apparently surmounted by the rapid re-establishment of the belief that the analyst was a benign figure who was interested in the vagaries of his patient's thinking and who would be pleased to think he was getting in touch with the negative transference. This was so close to the reality of the situation that the patient's strong grasp of external reality could be recruited to reimpose this benign internal version of the analyst, and thereby to surmount the more archaic and fearful belief that momentarily surfaced, only to be dismissed as a 'weird idea'.

The technical problem arose because, however accurate the interpretation might have been in drawing attention to the transient emergence of an alarming belief about the analyst, the very process of communication followed by interpretation at that moment was itself enough to restore the status quo. The actual capacity of this patient to reflect on his own thoughts in the company of his analyst could be used to evade the sense of their subjective reality and hence of their emotional consequences. In 'Subjectivity, objectivity and triangular space' (Britton 1998: 41–58), I described the achievement of triangular space as a result of establishing a 'third position' so that individuals can think about themselves while being themselves. This is a position often lacking in borderline patients in analysis, who then remain marooned with their analyst in the sea of their own subjectivity. The patient I am describing did the opposite. In this session he used his ability to find a third position to provide himself with a place to escape to from the ineluctability of subjective belief. In other words, *he thought about himself in order to avoid being himself.*

The key, I think, lay in the phrase that I used, 'in the company of his analyst'. I think the recovery of equilibrium rested on the patient's basic assumption that the priority should be to re-establish a mutually thoughtful discourse in order to guarantee for both of us that all was for the best in the best of possible worlds. This, as both patient and analyst knew, was in marked contrast to what someone difficult, such as his girlfriend, would have done. She would have proceeded without question on the assumption that her ideas about the analyst's malign intentions were facts. We also both knew that, however professionally committed I might be, I would not actually anticipate an experience of that kind with pleasure. So at that moment if the patient exercised his capacity for reasonable thoughtfulness he had it in his power to spare me an unpleasant experience.

With hindsight, I think that, rather than pursue the interpretative line as I did, I could more profitably have commented on how keen he was to be a thoughtful person and how anxious he was to avoid being a difficult person, or a person with difficult ideas, like his girlfriend or some other, difficult patient of mine – just as in childhood when he did not want to be like his problematic sisters. If, unlike such difficult people, he could talk reasonably about these things it meant they need not be taken seriously any longer. In other words, we, unlike them, knew better than to believe such things.

This is what I think Freud's phrase 'surmounted (*überwunden*) belief' means. In this process a belief is not reality tested and finally relinquished, but temporarily overcome by the reassurance of the analytic situation itself. It is based on contrasting the world momentarily imagined and the one shared with the analyst. Like the eruption of a child's belief in monsters in the middle of the night, it is overcome by the reassuring presence of the parent for that night, but this lasts only until the next time. Some incarnation of the dreaded monster threatens to appear in the person of the analyst, but the process of the analysis itself becomes the means of banishing it. The analysis retains its *heimisch* (homely) qualities and the individual remains vulnerable to the intrusions of the *unheimlich*, the horrifying *known–unknown* or *unknown–known*. The analyst unwittingly functions like the poet Rilke's mother, whose presence banished his childhood night terrors without modifying them, as he wrote in the third of *The Duino Elegies* (Rilke 1912). What Rilke discovered, painfully and slowly, over the next years was that his infantile relationship with his mother was the source of those very night-time terrors from which her presence shielded him, as I describe in 'Existential anxiety: Rilke's *Duino Elegies*' (Britton 1998: 146–165)

To return to the clinical scene I was describing, I think we have a situation where the notion that 'we can talk about these things' is sufficient to distinguish it from another imagined possibility, where this would not be the case. While we can talk about it, all is for the best.

Recently a colleague brought a case for supervision which illustrated this. The analyst was sensitive, thoughtful and good at her job. She had, like the other analyst I referred to earlier, brought the case for discussion, not because she felt she needed help with it, but for educational reasons. Indeed, she commented that what she would like was the opportunity to talk to me separately about another patient who was 'really difficult'. I am struck that, once again, the agreeable patient about to be considered was coupled in the mind of the analyst with someone who, in contrast, was felt to be really difficult. Nevertheless she introduced the presentation by saying that although everything seemed to be going all right, she was concerned because there had been four years of analysis and nothing seemed to be happening. Nothing was changing in the analysis and nothing new was developing in the patient's life outside it. What I noticed particularly, listening to the sessions she described, was a characteristic, almost reflex response of the patient to any interpretations that opened up awareness of anxiety or potential conflict. This response was 'Yes, we talked about that'. I thought the implication was that anything that 'we' could 'talk about' was now included within a benign relationship, as if once something was part of an analytic discourse this was a guarantee that it could no longer give rise to anything really undesirable. 'Talking about' things was a means of joint disposal, and the unconscious assumption of the patient was that the underlying purpose of analysis was to dispose of all the disagreeable and alarming aspects of life by including them within the category of 'Yes, we know about that'. The superficial resemblance between this state of affairs and the notion of containment as a therapeutic function of analysis adds to the beguiling shared belief that things are taking their proper course and that development will follow.

It seems that only a view of what Betty Joseph (1989c) has referred to as the total transference will reveal this sort of situation, and this has to include the countertransference activities and propensities of the analyst as well. I think it means constantly reviewing the prevailing state of analysis and its course, and not simply its session-by-session existence. Betty Joseph has demonstrated many times how the essence of the transference object relationship can be found in microcosm within the detailed interaction of an individual session. She has argued that in such moments of emergence it can be captured and may be open to real understanding. It involves repeatedly taking a hard look at the countertransference activities and tendencies of the analyst in a particular case. This approach has been practised in the clinical workshop that she has presided over for many years. The belief in the fruitfulness of this approach rests on two convictions. One is that it is only in the minutiae of the analyst's functioning in a particular case that the unconscious aspects of the countertransference of that case can be revealed, and the other conviction is the inevitability that some attitude or behaviour of the analyst will be influenced by his or her unconscious countertransference, which can be revealed but not forestalled. This requires us to acknowledge that we operate within the prevailing transference/countertransference, which we cannot transcend, but can possibly become aware of and understand, thereby achieving at least a degree of freedom. In 'The analyst's intuition: selected fact or overvalued idea?' (Britton 1998: 97–108) I describe an application of this approach which is based on a paper written jointly with John Steiner (Britton and Steiner 1994).

I would like to summarise what I have been saying about complacency in the analytic situation. With some of our patients we are apt to form a pair, unknowingly, like Dr Pangloss and Candide, unconsciously believing that although things are not right they are all for the best. Candide remains hopeful while Dr Pangloss knows best. I have suggested that this banishment of discontent from analysis is achieved by the patient thinking that even though the analyst wants him or her to improve, the analyst does not really want the patient to change. Change, it is assumed, would mean transformation into the patient's invisible, antithetic twin, who would be as unreasonable as the patient is reasonable.

Likewise, the alternative to the cherished benign version of the analyst that is perpetuated is someone alien and potentially terrifying. External figures in the patient's past have made flesh these inner images and there are usually figures currently in the patient's life that have a similar antithetical twin role. Other patients, like imaginary siblings, are believed to be as disturbing to the analyst as the patient is undisturbing.

While the patient believes that he or she is the 'all right' patient jealousy in the transference is in abeyance, and hence so is envy. Hanna Segal recently commented (personal communication) that in some cases only the eruption of jealousy leads to the emergence of envy. I think that this is because a privileged relationship is believed to exist between analyst and patient that is thought to be profoundly enviable. There is, after all, no better defence against envy than being enviable. As a consequence of this the patients I have been describing, while cocooned in their privileged position, are often very afraid of evoking envy and tend to placate others by minimising their own accomplishments or even avoiding success.

The proximity of these unconscious beliefs to the actual situation in the analysis makes them particularly difficult to budge. Insight, once gained, can quickly generate the feeling that the patient is what the analyst wants, in contrast to other obviously less insightful people. The risk of chronicity is considerable. What seems to be required is the enhancement in both analyst and patient of a sensitivity to the presence of complacency, and the development of some degree of allergy to smugness.

## Acknowledgements

This chapter was first published in R. Britton (1998) *Belief and Imagination: Explorations in Psychoanalysis*, London: Routledge.

## References

Britton, R. (1995) 'Psychic reality and unconscious belief', *International Journal of Psychoanalysis*, 76(1): 19–24.

—— (1998) *Belief and Imagination: Explorations in Psychoanalysis*, London: Routledge.

Britton, R. and Steiner, J. (1994) 'Interpretation: selected fact or overvalued idea?', *International Journal of Psychoanalysis*, 75(5–6): 1069–1078.

Bunyan, J. (1684) *Pilgrim's Progress*, London: George Routledge and Sons (1864).

Freud, S. (1913) 'On beginning the treatment', SE 12: 123–144.

—— (1919) 'The uncanny', SE 17: 219–252.

—— (1923) 'The ego and the id', SE 19: 12–68.

Joseph, B. (1989a) 'The patient who is difficult to reach', *Psychic Equilibrium and Psychic Change: Selected Papers of Betty Joseph*, M. Feldman and E. Bott Spillius (eds), London: Routledge.

—— (1989b) 'Defence mechanisms and phantasy in the psychoanalytical process', *Psychic Equilibrium and Psychic Change: Selected Papers of Betty Joseph*, M. Feldman and E. Bott Spillius (eds), London: Routledge.

—— (1989c) 'Transference: the total situation', *Psychic Equilibrium and Psychic Change: Selected Papers of Betty Joseph*, M. Feldman and E. Bott Spillius (eds), London: Routledge.

Rilke, R.M. (1912) *The Duino Elegies*, in *The Selected Poetry of Rainer Maria Rilke*, S. Mitchell (ed. and trans.), London: Pan (1987).

Voltaire (1759) *Candide; or the Optimist,* in *Voltaire Candide and Other Tales*, Tobias Smollett (trans.), revised by J.C. Thornton, London: J.M. Dent (1937, reprinted 1982).

## DISCUSSION OF RONALD BRITTON'S CHAPTER

### *David Taylor*

I recognised Ron's description of people who make an 'idealisation of adaptation', seeing the best in any situation no matter what its true disastrousness. In the analytic situation he writes that this can be part of a bargain struck with the analyst where the patient provides a subtle support by being 'an untroublesome patient with an untroubled parent'.

Yet this is only the surface, for behind the patient's apparent 'greed for virtue and covetousness of innocence', there exists a potential for a mutually hostile and destructive relationship, should any member become free of the 'politically correct' stance. Here, the comparison of these patients with Candide and Pangloss breaks down. The optimism of Voltaire's characters is instructive precisely because it so grossly fails to recognise the misfortunes and wolf-strategy war perils suffered at that time. In contrast, the patients described, although they may have a difficult girlfriend or difficult parents, are in their own psyches, and in their analyses, relatively protected by their position from a direct encounter with the destructive relationships that they seem to dread.

These people do seem to dread these conflicts, perhaps because an encounter with them is believed to be only destructive. Perhaps, in their life history there are events, or inner experiences, giving real ground for pessimism. They believe, fundamentally, that these matters do not turn out well. I wonder too about the sensitivity to psychological pain and personal fragility which may be manifest in patients like these. Sometimes, it appears to be their own pain that is feared. At other times, the pain or fragility of the object seems uppermost. In this sense the 'untroubled analyst' is only an appearance of being untroubled. The underlying belief is of a much more vulnerable object which sometimes seems to be modelled upon a struggling, pained or persecuted parental figure.

I find Ron's emphasis upon what is believed to be a real step forward in analysing these situations. However, one pitfall is that the analyst, feeling uncomfortable about doing what he feels is bad or unproductive work might become too focused upon changing it by effort or force of interpretation. This only leads to the fundamental beliefs being further denied rather than understood and modified through understanding, as is the aim.

# 5

# MAPPING THE LANDSCAPE

## Levels of transference interpretation

*Priscilla Roth*

In *A Clinician's Guide to Reading Freud*, Peter Giovacchini (1982) gives some material from his practice, which I would like to borrow in order to discuss some interesting issues it raises:

> During analysis, a 27-year-old woman patient of mine dreamed that she was at a dance. The setting was hazy, but she was able to see the grey suit worn by a man who asked her to dance. They danced around the room, and suddenly her partner steered her to a corner and pressed himself against her. She could feel his erect penis. Inasmuch as I often wore grey suits and the transference was clearly erotic, I believed this dream was an obvious allusion to her sexual feelings towards me. I also knew she was struggling with and defending herself against her impulses. Wishing to pursue this theme, I asked her to free-associate to the dream because she was inclined to pursue other seemingly unrelated topics. She hesitantly considered some of the dream elements, such as its haziness. I then directed her attention to the man in the grey suit. She was silent for approximately a minute and then became, what seemed to me, tremendously anxious. She finally reported a sensation of intense dizziness, feeling that the couch was spinning furiously. Gradually these feelings subsided and she continued talking but made no reference whatsoever to the dream. I became immensely curious and had to interrupt her and ask her about the dream. She naively answered: 'What dream?' To my astonishment, she had forgotten it completely. I then repeated the dream to her and was able to help her remember it. Once again I brought her attention to the man in the grey suit, and once more she felt the couch spinning and totally wiped the dream from her memory. I tried a third time and with the same results. As she experienced these spinning sensations, she described a

> vortex that was sucking her thoughts into it. Certainly the memory of her dream seemed to be pulled into the hidden recesses of her mind.
>
> (Giovacchini 1982: 13)

Giovacchini uses this material to discuss (and reject) the concept of primal repression. I am making use of it now to raise a different issue: the question of how we choose what we interpret to our patients – what level we come in at or 'go for'. I chose this material because it is clear, vivid and direct, and not too complicated, and because it seems to me it can be understood in several different ways.

In the first place, it is, one suspects, 'about' the patient's father, possibly her actual, external father, but almost certainly her image of a father, her internal father. In this respect the vignette is reminiscent of Freud's Dora case: Herr K and Dora's father, pressing themselves upon her. Giovacchini doesn't, in this session, interpret this. 'Your dream is about your father; you are afraid to know you have these thoughts about your father' is an interpretation that one could imagine Freud, at the time of Dora, making to this patient. And it would probably be, in one sense, true.

Second, 'You are afraid of your dream because your dream is about me'. As I understand it, this is the level at which Giovacchini understood his patient's material. What he shows us is an analyst in session, trying to talk to his patient in the session, about thoughts she had about him in the middle of the night called a dream. 'I often wear grey suits – the man in the dream wore a grey suit – in the middle of the night you had this fantasy about me'.

This is an interpretation about the transference of specific qualities, somewhat isolated and discrete – and these are dealt with from a distance.

But there are other ways of looking at this material, of course. Other levels of meaning that in no way negate the meanings I've already mentioned, but add something else as well.

Third, one might, as the analyst, feel and say something like 'There is something going on in this session, now, in which I, interpreting to you, am being perceived as the man in the dream. It is as if the dream is repeating itself here'. In this case the woman in the session and the woman having the dream are one and the same person; as is the analyst. The dream itself might be seen as a picture of the patient's view of her relationship with her analyst: a picture of which she is not fully aware, but which emerges in the session as well as in the dream.

Fourth, and closely related, we might consider the ways in which some combination of the patient's pressure, and the difficulties this stirs up in the analyst, lead to an unconsidered response by the analyst to create this situation – an internal relationship is in fact being enacted within the session, an enactment in which both analyst and patient are taking part.

When this happens, as it does in every analysis, the most important interpretation the analyst will make is to himself; in the Giovacchini example, he might ask himself 'Why do I find myself repeatedly pushing the patient into a corner? Why am I pressing my questions on her?' Having dealt with that in his own mind, he is then much freer to consider how to address his patient. He might, for example, in some situations, say something like, 'We seem to have arrived at a situation in which I am repeatedly pursuing you, or pushing you into a corner in a way that frightens you, like in your dream'.

For the purposes of this chapter, I don't want to go into how such an impasse comes about, or whose fault it is. It is essential for every analyst to think about who is pulling whom into the action, but what I want to focus on here is the different levels that are operating simultaneously – because as analysts we have to choose the most useful place to intervene.

There are certainly moments in every analysis where one would say 'This is your father you are afraid of, and you feel that the man in the grey suit is your father' (a *level 1* interpretation). There are also times when there is a view of the analyst in a dream that is not at all ego-syntonic to the patient: it happens in the middle of the night, as it were, and the patient in the session has no knowledge or recognition of it. So that as the analyst in the session you are trying to introduce your patient to aspects of herself and her internal object relationships that she doesn't consciously experience or know about (*level 2*). And much of the day-to-day work in analysis also concerns the way in which patients feel we are enacting, and indeed pull us to enact in the session the scenarios of their inner world – in order to maintain an internal status quo, to reassure themselves about their view of the world, and so on (*level 3*). In fact, this enactment may sometimes, unfortunately, be necessary in order for us to be aware of what is going on, and as analysts we must be alert to the part played in this by our own anxieties and defence mechanisms (*level 4*). So we have to have this whole landscape in our mind, with all these levels of interaction, levels of internal and external reality. We have to be able to allow a kind of free-floating awareness of the different levels of our experience of our patients' experiences. Then we have to decide where it is most useful to intervene. But we must always remember that in choosing to focus our attention on one aspect of the patient's communication we must, in our minds, hold onto and be aware of the other aspects as well.

## Clinical material

At this point I will present some more extensive clinical material of my own, so that we can look at this process in further detail. My patient is a 35-year-old South American woman. She is tall and slim, and an outstanding feature is her great mass of curly red hair. As a small child she lived alone with her mother for several years while her father travelled on business. Her mother is described as gay, beautiful and Bohemian; her father, who lived with them more permanently from the time my patient was about 3 years old, was a steady older man who was referred to by the patient and her mother as 'our rock'. The patient is now married with three children – a daughter, A, a little boy, B, and a baby girl, C, now 8 months old.

She has her own small market research company and at the time I am reporting had been engaged in a new project that presented her with what looked like good opportunities for her future. Because this project was underfinanced and speculative, she was employing students and part-time temporary workers. Her husband was a successful businessman, but the financial circumstances of the family fluctuated wildly. This presented problems about paying my fees, and several months had passed without her paying me. She had good excuses, but at the same time, she seemed not to be taking the problem seriously. I found myself very uncertain about what to do: I knew this woman could be very disturbed and disturbing, and that she badly needed her analysis; experience had made me feel that her children were in some danger if her analysis ended. So I therefore let the situation continue for too long. Consciously I was worried about her state of mind and about her children. In retrospect, there must have been unconscious reasons, too, why I waited too long to be firm with her: wanting to be liked by my patient, being too content to be idealised and insufficiently suspicious of her seductiveness and so on. But she began to get into a manic state, and became more and more dictatorial, with me and at home, and I began to realise that my lack of firmness about the money was contributing to that. I was also increasingly aware of my resentment of her treatment of me. So I addressed what I thought was going on and became much firmer with her, referring to the dangerous effects on her of what she was doing to me by not paying me, and conveyed to her that it had to be taken seriously.

I want to present the Wednesday and Thursday sessions of a week shortly after this, but I will first give a brief summary of the Monday and Tuesday sessions as background.

### *Monday*

She told me that she had spent the weekend working on the project – she had a difficult meeting with her staff who complained she didn't let them do their jobs. She redid the questionnaires, changed all the arrangements – in her words 'rewrote the script' – in major ways. She had invited everyone to her country cottage for the weekend; she now thought this was a mistake as it had obviously made them envious, since they are mostly unemployed and she has a lovely house: her maid kept walking through, the children's nanny was there and the gardener. She said how difficult it must have been for these struggling people to have to observe all this.

The patient's tone of voice and manner of speaking was striking and conveyed a very particular attitude; she was speaking, as the French say, *de haut en bas*. I thought she was taking me on a kind of tour of her lovely, rich, full life and that I was meant to be full of admiration and envy.

Briefly, I suggested to her that as she was describing her weekend, I thought she felt me to be like the 'struggling staff', enviously watching her with all she had. I said I thought her need for this kind of situation between us had been particularly provoked by her realisation that she needed her analysis and therefore was going to have to pay me, and that her description of the weekend seemed to be her attempt to reverse what she might otherwise feel at the weekend: how determined she was that she be the enviable centre of everything, and how awful it would be for her to have to know about my centrality for her.

### *Tuesday*

She referred back to Monday's session and the interpretation I had made to her, and said that in fact there was something she hadn't said about the weekend; not just this weekend, but what happened at weekends: she went mad. This weekend she shouted and screamed at her husband for not being available to her, for always being at work, keeping her at a distance and being cut-off from her. She had screamed at him and she had hit him. The children were in the room – it often happened this way, she said, that the children were there while she and her husband had these violent fights. She had then decided that she simply 'had to' tell her oldest daughter how suspicious she was about her husband's business trips to Europe – she was 'sure' he was having an affair, and thought the daughter ought to know. The implication was that the daughter's father was doing something filthy, sexual and corrupt and the daughter ought to know.

I told her I thought she wanted me to know how she couldn't contain and hold inside herself her rage with me over the weekend – the real weekend experience as opposed to the reversed weekend experience she had told me about on Monday. I linked her attacks on her husband to this rage with me, for not being available. She was silent. I felt she was listening. I then said something more: I said that I thought her furious fights with her husband had to be observed by her children because they have to be the observers of the passion and violence of the sexual parents – a view of them originating in her own violent attacks on them.

I said that while she insisted that she felt nothing about my weekends: no disturbance, no curiosity – or about my relationship with the man who answered the telephone when she phoned at my home – she showed us that there was a child who was to be horrified and appalled and furious at what a parent was doing – but that it was not going to be her, it would be her children, especially her daughter. I said she made her daughter have these feelings which she felt were unbearable for her to have herself.

Comment: within the Monday session there is a description of the weekend, which I could interpret along the lines of 'When you say them you mean me.' I am 'them' (the poor eager-to-be employed workers) who are made envious by all her possessions. I though she was projecting envy into the employees, standing for me. At the same time, she treated me with contempt more directly by not paying me, and I thought that all of this behaviour served as a defence against her own envy, or a defence against acknowledging my importance as her analyst. She makes herself the centre of everything. In terms of Giovacchini's example, this is along the lines of: the man in the grey suit is me. The poor, envious employees on the weekend were me (*level 2*).

By the time I made this interpretation on Monday, I had worked through and overcome my sense of impotence about her not paying me; I was not angry with the patient, nor did I feel contemptible. I felt strong enough and confident enough about my positive feelings towards the patient to interpret to her in a way that was firm, but wouldn't put her down.

Interpreting in this way on the Monday enabled her to bring the really bad acting out – the real weekend experience – on the Tuesday. My interpretation of the Tuesday material (highly summarised) took as its focus what was going on 'out there' – at the weekend, with her family, but as an introduction to what was going on in here, in order to be able to elucidate her inner world:

> You have a kind of dream going on inside you in which I am engaged in being part of a couple, which makes you feel horribly jealous and which you violently attack in your jealous rage. Attacked, this couple becomes violent in nature and you act this out with your husband and make your children bear the distress of it.

This is a strong interpretation, and when making it I am counting on several things about her, but most importantly, what I know of her capacity to bear some guilt.

I have to wait until the following session to see how the patient deals with this interpretation. I will have more to say about these interactions, and how I understand them, at a later point in this chapter. The following two sessions I will look at in detail.

### *Wednesday*

She told me that she had been in a terrible panic; the night before she couldn't sleep because of it. She was absolutely panicking about pollution. (This was in July, and it was very hot.) She spoke for a long time; the radio reported how very high the pollution level was and she was terrified about it and what it would do to them all. She felt there was poison all around. She had closed all the windows, but you couldn't get away from it. She was clearly very anxious.

I thought that she was telling me what she had done with what I had said to her in the previous day's session. This had centred on her telling me about putting very painful, horrible feelings into her children, and today's session was about millions and millions of infinitesimally small particles that were poisoning her children, her husband and herself. I had to make the decision in my own mind whether she felt I had been poisoning her on the previous day, by saying things about her that were felt to be cruel and murderous, or whether she was primarily talking about what she had done with the threat of guilt from the previous day's session. My feeling was that it was the latter. I thought this was her way of dealing with the guilt she was threatened with experiencing when she began to see what she was doing to her children, and behind that, to me in her mind. She had projected the poison into the atmosphere, and it therefore was not experienced as coming from her, but as coming from outside; the guilt not experienced inside her mind causing her pain, but broken and fragmented into bits and then coming back at her from outside. I am aware that the brevity of my description of the Monday and Tuesday sessions may make it difficult for some readers to be convinced that the Wednesday material was in response to Tuesday's session. I was convinced both by the seriousness of the patient's response on the Tuesday and by the level of anxiety on the Wednesday that the 'pollution' she was afraid of on Wednesday was linked to the session on the Tuesday.

I felt what she needed me to do was to bring these confusing bits of her experience together, to show her how painful these feelings were, but to assume she could, with my help, know about and bear them.

I therefore reminded her about yesterday's session when she had told me about very poisonous feelings that she had pushed into all her children, and particularly her oldest daughter. I said she was afraid to know what she felt about me at the weekend, and about her parents in her mind, so she projects these feelings into her children. Then, because she also loved her children and didn't want to hurt them, she was in danger of feeling very guilty about this. Such guilt was too painful for her; therefore she expelled it, and the poison, the awful badness, was in the air around them all – not in her.

There was a sharp intake of breath, and then, after a moment, she said, 'It is awful. You know, if there was a fire, I'd lay my life on the line for my children. But I can do this'. She paused. Then: 'Isn't it terrible what we can do to those we love?'

I said how frightening it was to be aware of what she did to her children. And, after a moment, I said I thought she in fact couldn't bear to think about it, and so she had to change it, disperse it around the world to 'What we do to those we love' – to make it not so much her, and her children, but general, all over the place. She was thoughtful for a moment and then said, 'You mean I don't really take it on'.

Comment: at this moment in the session I am keeping her attention on what I think she needs to know about, and I am still directing myself to what happens between her and her children. I am not addressing what is happening here, between her and me. I am acutely aware that the epicentre of the difficulties she is talking about is in her relationship with me in the transference. The jealousy, the sense of abandonment, her anger have their source originally of course in her earliest object relations, and now in her ongoing phantasies about her and me. But the location of all these feelings has shifted, defensively, to what is going on with her family, and I do address what is going on in her family and how it seems to be affected by what has been going on inside her and between us.

In this sense I am still located in a *level 2* area of interpretation. I am interpreting in the transference, but in the transference as it manifests itself outside the immediate here-and-now of the session. I want to emphasise that I am talking about complex transference manifestations: the way in which the patient uses projective identification to rid herself of unbearable feelings and to maintain her sense of equilibrium, the effects such projective manoeuvres have on her, and so on.

But I am very aware that all the time she and I are there in the room talking about these things I have not suddenly become neutral to her. The transference relationship (what I referred to earlier as *level 3*) is going on all the time, and I am aware of it, and wait for the moment when I can address it with her. At this point in the session we still had about twenty minutes left, and I was reasonably comfortable about allowing the session to develop and the here-and-now relationship between us to become clearer.

After a few minutes she said she has been thinking about her father. He used to be quite nice to her, probably to please her mother, who adores her. (Her actual words were 'to keep mama sweet'.) But once when she was very little and her mother was out, she had fallen down and cut her forehead. And she had screamed and screamed. And her father had sat her on the kitchen table and washed off the cut and put a plaster on it and said to her, 'Now just stop all that wailing. Your mother's not here now'. She had thought that was tough and hard of him . . . calling her bluff.

I said I wondered if perhaps she felt me now to be like the father in the story. That when I insisted that she had to pay me, and when I make her face what she was doing to me and to her family, she felt that a nice, soft malleable me – like her mother who adored her – had gone away, and that she was left with a tougher, harder father – me, who she doesn't feel will be seduced by her cries. I said I think she thinks there is a seducible me – like her mother – who lets her get away with things, lets her get away with not paying me, for instance, and a tougher harder me who won't be seduced, and she's afraid she is now stuck alone with this father aspect of me.

I was now addressing a picture of what was going on between us. The underlying transference relationship seemed to me to be *level 3*.

She was quiet for a minute and started to speak about her baby girl: 'She won't be put down; you go to her, you leave her to cry for forty minutes, she won't stop, she just goes on and on and tries to burrow into your neck – she won't be put down. But she's so vulnerable, she's just a baby – so I can't leave her, I can't put her down'.

I said I thought this was a picture of a monster baby, not, I thought, a picture of C, except as she feels it at the moment, but a picture of herself who uses her vulnerability for absolute power.

She said 'What do you mean?'

I said I thought that it was very painful and hard for her to begin to be aware that she thought I was sometimes forced, by my fears for her very real vulnerability, to pay for her life (her analysis, her servants, etc.). When she didn't pay me, I was in fact, paying for her to live as she liked – and she felt I was unable to put her down.

She said 'Yes'. It was the end of the session.

Comment: in retrospect, I think I did not properly address in this session what had happened when the patient went from 'I can do this to my children' to 'Isn't it terrible what *we* can do to those *we* love?' While being aware of the denuding of meaning in this material, and of the use the patient made of her vulnerability outside the analysis, and how that affected my behaviour, I missed something very important about what was going on within the session: that her understanding of the interpretation ('I can do this to my children') quickly became an appeasement of me, a seduction of me – it's what she uses to keep me 'sweet'. To go from 'I' (what 'I do') back to 'we' (what 'we do'). In fact, I wasn't seduced – I showed her that she didn't take the interpretation in. But what I didn't see at that point was the degree to which her seductiveness pervaded the whole analysis. I think my not falling for it brought the father material – she now felt she had, for the moment at least, been abandoned by her adoring mother, and was with a firm, hard father. Following that she reminded me about the monster baby who would not be put down: who I think felt quite sure at that point about getting the adoring mother back again.

So I did not act-out with the patient; I was not seduced, but I hadn't really understood the subtleties and pervasiveness of the seduction that was going on. Like Dr Giovacchini interpreting his patient's dream, I was ignoring a way we were playing things out within the session.

### *Thursday*

She was several minutes late, was silent and then said she was so sleepy, so tired. 'I just can't engage', she said.

I said it was the end of the week, her last session for the week, and that earlier in the week she had warned us about what happened at weekends. 'The real madness is at weekends', she had said on Tuesday. But now she was dis-engaged.

Here I think I was trying to put her in touch with feelings she had been engaged with earlier in the week and to show her what she might be dis-engaged from.

'Mmmm.' Long silence.

> When you said yesterday, about my panic . . . when you explained it in terms of . . . you know, the pollution, when you talked in terms of an expression of resistance, to do with something else, the analysis . . . well, I was thinking . . . I often get a panicky feeling in aeroplanes too. I can't bear flying.

Then quite a long story about having to take the boat to the continent last year because she hated going on aeroplanes. 'I wondered about it . . . in relation to my preoccupation with the pollution.' There was a pause. She then started again:

> Your explanation about my panic had a kind of simple meaning . . . I've wondered why everyone isn't panicking about the pollution . . . and I thought, 'I am afraid to fly . . . she is right . . . I do organise my life, organise everything not to have to think'.

I felt very uneasy about this material. I didn't doubt that it was factually true; I knew, in fact, that she was afraid to travel by aeroplane. But I thought it was emotionally not what it was appearing to be – I thought she was still disengaged, but trying to seduce me by saying what she thought I would want to hear. So I said I thought there was something going on under the surface of her words now – that she seemed to me to be saying something like 'Why not have a conversation about my problems with air travel . . . we could extend yesterday's discussion to a related problem' – but that I thought that this was an invitation to a dishonest situation, a kind of make-believe analysis.

Comment: I think here I was aware of a quality in the session that I had missed on the previous day: the way the patient tried to, and sometimes actually could, seduce me into believing we were working, when in fact, what was going on was something else – a seductive, mutual-admiration society. On the previous day, I had seen how she had denuded the agreement ('I can do this to my children') of meaning. What I hadn't seen was how it was an attempt to appease and seduce me. With this Thursday session, the seduction had become clearer . . . or, at least, clearer to me. So that now the interpretation I made to her is a *level 3* and indeed *level 4* interpretation as well, because it is taking into account my recognition of my own strong feelings about what is going on between us. It is not addressing her words but it is addressing the woman who is presenting the words, and my feeling about the pressures in the session.

She grumbled for a moment: 'I'm tired, it's Thursday', and then, after a minute or two, suddenly said:

> I had a dream last night. *Yesterday I had gone to see Stephen to ask if we could use his sound studio to record in. In the dream I went to see Stephen and he asked me to be his assistant, give him some help on the project I am actually in charge of. I thought to myself 'I have moved beyond that'. In the dream I went to the toilet . . .*

At this point in the telling of the dream she broke off to add an association:

> Here in this building the first floor toilet is broken. There is a sign on the door telling you to use the ones on the other floors. But in fact it is not the toilet itself which is broken – only the handle of the door – the only problem is that the door doesn't lock. Somebody was in the other toilet yesterday morning and so I went to the one with the sign, the one saying, 'Don't use'. But only the door handle is broken so I took a chance and put my bag by the door.

Here the association ended and she went back to the dream.

> In the dream *I was in the loo. In a building. In a school or something. Stephen asked me to participate – I thought 'I am doing this because I am helping him out, assisting him. I'm not sure I want to be involved and anyway I really have moved on from this'. I was feeling very good – the kind of really good feeling I have about my project. Then there was a purple flex, like a light fixture, it was very unusual: very pretty and glittery and purple. I spun it round and twirled it; it was pretty. And then it began to unravel – with those horrid black wires you get inside . . . I saw they could split and were live, and I thought they must be dangerous.*

She paused. *'I was feeling very good in the dream. And I thought "I've moved on". I think that is what the dream was about.'*

I said I thought her dream was about the dangerous state of mind she is in. I said I think she feels I am like Stephen in her dream: asking her to participate in her analysis – while she feels so good and feels she has 'moved on' from being my patient who needs analysis to being the director, the producer and organiser. She will help me out, by paying me, and also, as I think she was doing earlier in the session, by seeming to pick up my interpretation, seeming to participate in her analysis – but it is a performance and she actually feels quite superior about it. I linked this to the toilet: the rules aren't for her. The no entry signs aren't for her. She tells herself it is because her need is so great – but I think it is her desperate need to feel that she can break all the rules, break all the boundaries. Which I think makes her think she actually unravels me.

She said, 'Oh'. And then, 'Yes'.

After a moment I pointed out the purple dress I was wearing.

She said, 'Were you wearing that dress yesterday?' When I answered yes, she said 'Well, the flex was just that colour purple'. I'll just point out here that we have come full circle back to Giovacchini's material: the man in the grey suit is me – the purple flex is me. I said I think when she feels she will help me out by paying me, by participating because I want her to, like earlier in the session, she feels she is making me in my purple dress twirl and dance about; that she can fiddle with me, saying isn't it pretty, seducing me to be pretty, to 'keep me sweet'. But that I thought some part of her at least in the dream seems to know there is something black and dark and ugly and dangerous around.

She was silent for a few minutes. Then she said:

> It is a relief. When I feel I am a special case . . . I always feel I am a special case, somehow . . . but that is never a relief. But when you say what you say . . . I suppose it must be being in touch . . . it is somehow a relief.

I felt there was a clear difference between this response and what she had been like at the beginning of the session, when I had felt she was trying to seduce me. Here I believed her. It was the end of the session.

In the example from Dr Giovacchini there is a dream, and there is what is going on in the session, and they appear to be two quite separate events. Here we can see the way in which the interaction within the transference, in the analysis, appears in the dream: in both the dream and the analytic sessions she can be full of 'good' feeling, but it is omnipotent feeling – it involves repeatedly engaging in projective manoeuvres in which somebody else (the workers on Monday, her children on Tuesday, the demanding baby on Wednesday, Stephen in the dream; and underlying it all, me in the analysis whenever she feels I can be seduced or managed or handled) has to feel the feelings she can't bear: jealousy, dependency, envy, being needy and therefore, she thinks, contemptible. In this sense the dream is a reflection of the relationship, and the relationship is a reflection of the dream. I believe she could tell me about the dream because sometimes she wants a real understanding, a real knowledge of herself, a real relationship with me, more than she wants to 'feel good', to be a 'special case'. In order to have the sense of really being known, by me and herself, she has to look at the black wires inside the prettiness – the danger inside the feel-good factor. Of course she only can look at this very briefly, and then she has to 'move on'.

## Conclusion

In his 1972 paper, 'A critical appreciation of James Strachey's paper on the nature of the therapeutic action of psychoanalysis', Herbert Rosenfeld discusses some aspects of Hanna Segal's 1961 paper, given to the Edinburgh Congress.

> She particularly stresses the importance of the analysis of processes of splitting and projection and omnipotence. She gives examples of analytic material

> where mutative transference interpretations were given. . . . She discusses a patient who complained of disturbances in his capacity to get on with his work. He had projected his greedy destructive dirty part into the analyst and then had denied and dispersed it into many objects in the outside world by whom he felt persecuted. Through a dream where the patient felt invaded and persecuted by smokers she was able to make a transference interpretation of the analyst as a persecutor who represented through projective identification the greedy destructive parts of the patient. Segal reports that through this analytic experience and similar situations the patient was able to make more contact with the aggressive parts of his self, which strengthened his ego. He also was more able to form a more real relationship to the analyst, which the split off persecutory object relationship had prevented. Segal's description illustrates how transference interpretations can set the mutative process in motion but that this has to be followed up by working-through periods so that the mutative development can continue and be strengthened. It is important here to be clear that both the detailed transference interpretation and the working through process includes not only the elaboration of the patient's phantasies and behaviour in the transference but links the patients conflicts in detail with his present life situation and the past.
>
> (Rosenfeld 1972: 456–457)

In the sessions I have presented, the real conviction about what was going on between the patient and me only came in the final session of the week, when the material in the dream, and our understanding of its enactment in the transference, came together. At this point the patient and I could fully focus on exploring the vicissitudes of the transference relationship and the interaction has important meaning for both of us. But to get to this point we have had to roam freely over the landscape of the patient's material. One way this could be described, would be to say that for a while I find I am largely making what I have called *level 2* interpretations, interpretations that aren't primarily focused on at-this-moment, in-this-room. But these, too, are complex, and are attempts to understand – to make a map of – what the patient does with difficult and even unbearable states of mind. When in the Tuesday session I spoke to her about what she had done to her children over the weekend, linking it with her own feelings of outrage about the weekend break from me, I was talking to her about a complicated series of splitting, projections and projective identifications, and then about the effects these projections and projective identifications had on her: how persecuted they make her, or how guilty. Some readers might feel that it would be better to have focused entirely on the projections into the children, and not to have linked these to what was going on in the transference. In fact, I felt convinced that sympathetically understanding her own feelings at being left out, and the jealousy and anger these feelings provoked within her, enabled her to understand why she felt compelled to project such feelings into her children; helped her, that is, to understand what otherwise might have seemed like her arbitrary cruelty. (Of course, I couldn't help but hope that in the end this would enable her not to have to project so massively into her children.)

My point is that in order to get her to moments when she could stop 'moving on' and look at what was inside, I had to be willing to follow her over quite a broad landscape of her experience. I had to be prepared to allow the different levels of her experience to make an impact on me, in order for me to map out the way her internal objects became projected into her family, her colleagues and, very powerfully, into me. In the end I had no doubt that it was in the elucidation of the ongoing transference relationship in the analysis that I could have any real impact on her. But I thought I could not know about this fully, with the sort of richness that reflects the patient's experience, without allowing myself and the patient to roam a bit over the wide territory of her life. So I did not, could not, interpret only at *level 3* and *level 4*, although I tried continually to make myself aware of, and come back to, what I thought was going on at these levels. My real conviction about the patient's internal world and relationship with her objects only really came about through experiences which enabled me to think and interpret at *levels 3* and *4*. But I could get to these experiences only by allowing the patient and myself to engage with a wide variety of her experiences.

When we are working well as analysts, we and our patients exist in a very particular emotional landscape. We are continually being used to communicate, enact and reveal the patient's internal dramas. These dramas are in some ways quite simple; their purpose is to maintain the patient's equilibrium, to protect him or her from overwhelming anxiety, to restore the patient's sense of being able to manage internal and external reality. But the manifold ways in which each patient – and each patient–analyst couple – play out the externalisation of these dramas are what define the richness and variety, the very liveliness, of each individual analysis. Our sense of conviction about our patient's internal world comes ultimately from our understanding of the here-and-now transference relationship between us – this is, as I have said, the epicentre of the emotional meaning of an analysis. And I think that as analysts we keep one part of our mind located at this level all the time – it is where we somehow always live within the session. This is what I have called *levels 3* and *4* of understanding and of interpretation. But I think that much of the filling in, the enrichment, the colour of analysis takes place at a different level, while we become familiar with the quality and variety of our particular patient's particular world.

## Acknowledgements

This paper was first presented to the 7th Symposium of the European Psychoanalytical Federation on The Different Levels of Interpretation in Belgium on 30 March 1996, and published in June 2001 in the *International Journal of Psychoanalysis*, 82(3): 533–543.

## References

Giovacchini, P. (1982) *A Clinician's Guide to Reading Freud*, New York: Jason Aronson.

Rosenfeld, H. (1972) 'A critical appreciation of James Strachey's paper on the nature of the therapeutic action of psychoanalysis', *International Journal of Psychoanalysis*, 53: 455–461.

Segal, H. [1961](1962) 'The curative factors in psychoanalysis', *International Journal of Psychoanalysis* 43: 212–17; reprinted in *The Work of Hanna Segal: A Kleinian Approach to Clinical Practice*, New York/London: Jason Aronson (1981) and in paperback, Maresfield Library, London: Free Association Books (1986).

## DISCUSSION OF PRISCILLA ROTH'S CHAPTER

### *Michael Feldman*

In this clear and beautifully written chapter, Priscilla Roth addresses the important question of how we listen to, process and make use of our patients' communications, and how we take into account their subtle effects on the analyst. Her chapter highlights the developments in psychoanalytic theory and technique, and the move towards addressing the subtle interactions taking place within the fabric of the session, which we have come to believe is more effective therapeutically.

This is, of course, a modern and radical extension of the point Freud made in his classic paper on transference where he recognised the value and importance of the patient's 'hidden and forgotten erotic impulses' being made 'immediate and manifest' in the transference.

Roth begins her chapter with a clinical illustration from another analyst, who made a correct-sounding, classical interpretation of his patient's dream. In the dream she was dancing with a man who steered her into a corner, pressing himself upon her in a sexual way. Seeing clear links between himself and the figure in the dream, the analyst tried to get the patient to recognise the connection, but she became anxious and dizzy in the session, and felt as if the couch was spinning. After a while, when the patient seemed to have completely lost contact with the dream, the analyst reminded her of it, and once again tried to make the link with himself, and the patient once more had the experience of spinning.

What Roth draws attention to is the way in which the dream is being relived, and indeed re-enacted by both participants in the analytic session. She argues that if this can be recognised, it can provide immediate access to 'the patient's hidden and forgotten erotic impulses' in the way Freud described. The further implication of his formulation is that it is only when these impulses (and one might add these anxieties and defences) are present and can be addressed in an immediate way in the session, is there the prospect of psychic change being brought about.

Reflecting the interesting and important developments in our understanding in this area since Freud, Roth takes this argument further, however. She raises the question of why the analyst felt compelled to function, or to react in a particular way to the patient in this particular session. Why were certain aspects of the situation overlooked, and others taken up in particular ways – the whole issue of 'enactment'. We have come to believe that the recognition of elements of the analyst's responses, the inevitable subtle or not-so-subtle forms of enactment give us indications of the patient's intrapsychic dynamics and in particular her use of projective identification. Thus the analyst's responses must be considered, at least in part, to reflect aspects of the patient's internal object relationships, made present and alive in her interaction with the analyst.

In addition to the more classical formulations of transference, Roth expands the 'landscape' to include

> the way in which patients feel we are enacting, and indeed pull us to enact in the session the scenarios of their inner world – in order to maintain an internal status quo, to reassure themselves about their view of the world, and so on (*level 3*). In fact, this enactment may sometimes, unfortunately, be necessary in order for us to be aware of what is going on, and as analysts we must be alert to the part played in this by our own anxieties and defence mechanisms (*level 4*).

Roth then describes her work with a patient of her own. She explores the complex and subtle ways in which the analyst listens to and responds to the patient's communications. At times, she takes the patient's references to her interaction with her objects as an expression of the dynamics of her relationship with the analyst. Thus when during a session on a Monday the patient referred to various figures who had felt controlled by her, and envious of her, the analyst interpreted the reversal that had taken place, with the analyst portrayed as struggling with feelings of exclusion and envy over the weekend. While the interpretation sounded valid, and the analyst had actually felt treated in a superior and dismissive way by the patient, Roth recognised that the interpretation lacked a sense of immediacy, as its validity did not derive from the present interaction with her patient, as in the example she had quoted from another analyst. Nevertheless, whether it was her understanding of the defence mechanisms the patient used, or the fact that the patient had the reassuring experience that the interpretation was in fact not emanating from someone who, at that point, felt undermined and envious, this session was followed by one in which the patient was able more freely to describe a much more disturbed version of her experience of the weekend.

The analyst then moved to make an interpretation that the violent, destructive and sexual material the patient had brought, manifestly relating to her family over the weekend, expressed the patient's internal relationship to the analyst that had been alive over the weekend, and that had led to her acting out. Rather than having to be the jealous and pained excluded child, the patient had become identified with a member of an excited and destructive couple, while the dismay, confusion and pain were projected into her children.

When the patient arrived for the next session and spoke about her panic over pollution, the analyst understood this as a manifestation of her defence against guilt – both towards her children and her analyst. Rather than being able to experience the guilt, her experiences were fragmented and projected, and thus became persecuting. The analyst interpreted that the patient was afraid to know what she felt about the analyst on the weekend, and about her parents in her mind, so she projected these feelings into her children. Then, because she also loved her children and didn't want to hurt them, she was in danger of feeling very guilty, which would be too painful for her. She thus expels the badness so that it is in the air around them all, but not in her.

In an interesting discussion, Roth argues that in order to engage the patient in the examination of what is going on inside her, the analyst first has 'to be willing to follow her over quite a broad landscape of her experience'. She has to be prepared to allow the different levels of the patient's experience to make an impact on the analyst, for the analyst to be able to map out the way the patient's internal objects become projected into her family, her colleagues, and her analyst. Roth sees this work as a necessary precondition for the elucidation of the ongoing transference relationship in the analysis, through which the analyst achieves the sense of conviction about the nature of the patient's inner world.

However, the clinical material and the discussion presented in this chapter illustrate how complex these issues are. There do seem to be points at which the analyst has a sense of conviction about what is going on in the patient in relation to her family or the analyst, based on her understanding of the patient's material, and what she knows of the patient's phantasies. Some of her interventions which are based on this understanding do seem to have an impact on the patient, and to lead to a shift in the nature of the patient's communication.

However, Roth describes a different type of contact with the patient at other points in the session, where she is able to come to an understanding of interactions, and responses that have an immediacy and directness that imbue them with a different kind of conviction. She illustrates this in the last session to which she refers, where she describes how she became aware of a quality in the session which reflected the patient's defensive and triumphant attempts to appease and seduce, while feeling disengaged and superior.

While the engagement with the patient at this level can carry a much greater sense of aliveness, and conviction, and may be the main basis for bringing about therapeutic change, there are some indications in this chapter of the anxieties and difficulties that militate against it. Some of the difficulties may relate, as Roth suggests, to the problem of engaging the patient who seems preoccupied with her family, for example. Others relate to the emotional demands on the analyst which make it difficult to recognise and acknowledge the seductive or threatening pressures he or she is being subjected to, the subtle forms of enactment that accompany these pressures, and from which it is difficult to extricate oneself. Roth's chapter gives a vivid illustration of how she was able to recognise these very pressures, and by addressing them, she seemed to engage in a different way with her patient.

The issue Roth is addressing is not only the different ways of conceptualising what is taking place within the patient, including the symbolic meaning, but also important questions of technique – how different ways of hearing and understanding the patient's communications entail different kinds of interventions, and which of these is more conducive to psychic change.

Finally, what emerge in this chapter are formulations about a different landscape, namely the landscape of the analyst's mind, as she listens to and engages with the patient. She gives a vivid example of the flexible way in which the analyst's focus, her thoughts and understanding of her patient move across this internal landscape. Roth describes some of the ways in which the analyst attends, for example, to the patient's descriptions of her external life and relationships. The different perspectives adopted by the analyst may result from decisions about what is vital for the patient at that moment, or may result from anxieties and defences evoked in the analyst. The recognition of these anxieties and defences, or the ways in which the analyst becomes drawn into various forms of enactment allow the analyst to achieve a further perspective in her mind regarding what is happening between the patient and the analyst. This can lead to interpretations based on a deeper and more useful understanding of the patient.

# DISCUSSION OF PRISCILLA ROTH'S CHAPTER

## *Arturo Varchevker*

This chapter, like the chapter by Steiner, addresses the importance of communication in analysis. Both authors emphasise the significance of enactment as the vehicle that could aid understanding and insight

Roth focuses on the difficulties involved in experiencing, understanding and interpreting. The clinical material she has chosen and her discussion of it highlights the vicissitudes of the interpretative activity. She describes four levels of transference interpretation and considers that the level of interpretative activity starts where patient and analyst are able to meet, which means making a meaningful contact. Roth shows in the clinical material she has chosen, that for reasons located in the analyst as well as in the patient, the initial meeting takes place at what she calls *level 1* or *2*. This transference interpretation does not make a direct reference to what is going on in the here-and-now between patient and analyst. Roth argues that at times to roam over a wider territory, *levels 1* and *2*, is necessary and enriching and leads towards *levels 3* and *4*, but she emphasises the importance of reaching *levels 3* and *4* in pursuit of 'psychic change'.

Roth has chosen two clinical examples to illustrate this. The first belongs to another analyst who follows a more classical approach and whose interpretations are mainly at *levels 1* and *2*. The other example is taken from her own clinical work. Roth shows in this second example the interplay of the four levels. She describes how her patient, in order to avoid neediness and envy, avoided genuine contact with the analyst's interpretations. The patient's dramatic style could be seen as having the effect of recruiting the analyst to be her audience, possibly mirroring the experience of the patient's children, who were often in the room when their mother had rows with her husband.

Roth acknowledges that she became desensitised to the absence of firm boundaries in her patient and she recognises that the interaction in the analysis may have contributed to or exacerbated the patient's manic and dictatorial behaviour. Roth uses this material to explore levels of understanding and levels of interpretation. I would like to underline some aspects of this extremely useful presentation and put forward some thoughts related to it.

In her account of the Monday session, Roth took the view that her patient inverted the situation, which means that by projective identification she got rid of her neediness and envy and placed it onto the 'analyst–workers'. This behaviour activated a fear of the 'workers'–analyst's envious reaction' when her wealth is exposed. Roth interpreted this as *level 2*. I would like to speculate on the possible presence of another active part of the patient that is engaged simultaneously in a provocative manic attitude. If this is the case, the tensions between the various active parts of the patient are present in parallel and would manifest at different levels concurrently in the transference interaction. What would follow from this is that, if the patient's projections activate the analyst to respond at the same time to different versions enacted in the transference, the analyst is placed in a very difficult situation. Whatever version she interprets, the other version would be left out. This reminds me of the example given by Bion of the patient who simultaneously presses the going up and going down buttons in the lift.

Following Roth's sensitive account of the laborious interaction of the Monday, Tuesday and Wednesday clinical material, we come to the point where the patient responded to Roth's interpretation with the exclamation 'It is awful. You know, if there was a fire, I'd lay my life on the line for my children. But I can do this'. The second statement was 'Isn't it terrible what we can do to those we love?' We know that the patient is in a state of panic because of the persecutory guilt that is threatening her and we may think that the analyst's interpretation clears the air. Roth, however, was sensitive to the fact that, what, on the surface seemed an insightful recognition by the patient was in fact an attempt by her to defuse the analyst's interpretation through a seductive remark.

When the patient brought the father material to the session, she described a situation when her mother was out, she had fallen down and cut her forehead and she was in the hands of her father, who was attending to her cut. This led me to speculate that maybe the patient had fallen down from her manic state of seduction and manic control of her analyst when the Oedipal couple came together. I thought that this was an acknowledgment that her analyst had already reunited in her mind the split-off couple, and her various countertransference responses, and enabled her to make a total transference interpretation.

I thought that this chapter highlights so vividly the difficulties of understanding, and the questions of why, what and when to interpret – especially when genuine panic and insight at one moment could mean something different in the next.

# 6

# A PHANTASY OF MURDER AND ITS CONSEQUENCES

*Patricia Daniel*

In this chapter I will describe a patient whose personality was structured around a primitive phantasy that he had murdered his little brother. His psychic life was dominated by this phantasy which was suffused with such hatred toward his sibling and held with such omnipotence that it had led to an unconscious belief that he had actually murdered him. As a consequence the patient unconsciously felt persecuted and paranoid since he believed himself to be accused of murder. This internal configuration terrorised him and had resulted in a narcissistic organisation which dealt with primitive destructive impulses by neutralising them; all liveliness was believed to be enmeshed with destructive impulses and since there was no differentiation between aggression and destruction, so no aliveness or vitality could be tolerated. Furthermore the organisation also defended the patient against awareness of guilt which was believed to be unbearable and synonymous with condemnation (Steiner 1990). In the analysis, as in his life, a deadening process had to be maintained to defend him from awareness of murderousness on the one hand and persecution and guilt on the other. I hope to show how any movement led to a particular kind of repetition which, in turn, resulted in a situation where patient and analyst became blocked, immobilised and repetitive and where for long periods the analytic process appeared to be stultified. Very gradually a shift occurred which led to the emergence of cruelty and the projection of guilt. I will consider the nature and force of the various role enactments that the analyst was drawn into and the problems that arose in the countertransference.

There are some patients, both adults and children, whose psychic structure seems to be organised around a primitive overarching phantasy. When they enter analysis the phantasy is re-enacted in such a way that it comes to pervade and dominate the entire analytic process and the analyst is drawn into it. When such a situation persists and the underlying phantasy remains unrecognised it can lead to an impasse, as described by Rosenfeld (1987).

In an early paper Joseph (1989a [1971]) considers the interrelationship between passivity and aggression and thinks that passivity is not only defensive but also destructive. She stresses the importance of the silent manifestations of aggression in the transference being analysed and worked through so that livelier aspects of the personality can emerge. Writing of the transference in the total situation she emphasises how patients' phantasies, impulses, defences and conflicts will be lived out in the transference, and she gives detailed descriptions of the subtle ways in which the analyst is drawn into enacting phantasied roles (Joseph 1989b [1981], 1989c [1985], 1989d). Her painstaking work has greatly increased our appreciation of the minute defensive manoeuvres and the perverse secondary gratification which may be obtained from them.

What concerns me here are the various role enactments which the analyst was drawn into. The analysis was dominated by a primitive phantasy of murder of a sibling; so pervasive was this unconscious belief that in the transference it led to a repetitious obliteration of the patient's capacity for liveliness and mobility and the analyst's capacity to think and to interpret. There was such persistence in these re-enactments that they re-enforced a sense of desperation and despair in the analytic pair. It seemed we were linked in an appalling situation which had a quality of neverendingness. Later in the analysis when the patient began to consciously recognise his unconscious belief, powerful defences were mobilised to protect him from the dread of depression and breakdown.

## The analysis

Mr M, in his early thirties, sought an analysis for what he felt was his lack of confidence in himself and a lack of interest in life. After university he had continued studying to gain a professional qualification but then found it difficult to decide what to do next. After several false starts he was now in business but had no satisfaction in his work. In the preliminary interview he told me life had been uneventful for himself and his brother, fourteen months younger. His father he described as having always been somewhat depressed and unsuccessful professionally while mother was energetic and the driving force in the family's life. Both were now retired, and his brother was married, with children and living in another country.

During the first year of analysis Mr M was pleasant, polite and anxious to be co-operative but all that he told me of himself and his life was neutralised by a film of blandness so that I felt I had a restricted, minimalist view of him. Mr M would describe his daily concerns matter-of-factly, and his lack of emotional resonance led me to think there must be some dangerous equation between liveliness and aggression. Both were conspicuously absent from his material and demeanour. For my part, I found myself assailed by waves of irritation and helplessness alternating with boredom during his sessions. He had told me that his mother was rather organising and I noticed I would endeavour to keep alive and alert by trying to organise Mr M's material into some sort of pattern in my mind. When I thought I had a sense of what Mr M felt or wanted and put it to him, there would usually be a long pause followed by 'perhaps' or 'maybe' said in a distant neutral tone of voice. Occasionally during the initial silence after an interpretation I would feel he was touched for he would wipe his eyes with his hand as if clearing away tears. If I commented on this he would revert to a remote silence or might say 'um . . . um' in a non-committal tone. We seemed to be locked in a deadening, despairing and desperate relation. When I tried to describe this situation to Mr M he might say he agreed, 'It did seem to be rather like that' and I then felt his passivity increased but was now laced with despair. I in turn would feel I was rubbing it in in a cruel way for I think he heard me as despairing of him.

While this stuck situation continued for some three years, Mr M attended regularly and spoke of his day-to-day life in his flat, depressed manner. He changed jobs twice with better prospects each time and he felt more interested in his work. He withdrew from a relationship with an apparently quite disturbed and manipulative girl, and after two further brief relationships with girls, he settled into a relationship with his future wife. Mr M attributed these developments to the help he felt analysis was giving him. I thought he experienced the analysis as providing an assurance of interest in him and an insurance against depression and despair, the latter being projected into his analyst. While he continued to maintain this deadening affective state in sessions, I felt the analysis and I were stuck.

Yet there were two lively events in Mr M's account of himself which remained vivid in my mind. One was that he had written poetry while at university, though he had never showed his poems to anyone feeling they would be judged 'no good'. The other was in the preliminary interview when he had recalled his earliest memory when about 3 years old. He remembered being so violently enraged with his mother that he turned his back on her and left the room – 'I walked out on her' he said. He had no idea what had so provoked him. Though said in a tone devoid of emotion, I had a powerful sense of his feeling he had committed a dreadful crime; I imagined a toddler who felt murderous but who exerted extraordinary control by leaving the room. I came to view this event as a screen memory behind which lay murderousness toward his sibling and toward mother for bringing his brother into the world, and 'walking out' on him. This was, I think, a psychic trauma for Mr M.

Occasionally Mr M showed some affective response when I talked to him about his fear that analysis might disturb some balance that he felt he had gained, that I might push him into a depressed state and linked this to his experience with his internal and actual depressed father. On one occasion he described how they used to work silently alongside in the garden, how he then felt he was helping his father but they didn't talk. When I suggested he felt something similar was happening here: that he felt he was trying to help his depressed self through analysis but he felt we, too, were unable to talk about it, he seemed touched.

As we approached the fifth year of analysis another phase was ushered in with Mr M's sessions becoming filled with his preoccupation with installing a new, more advanced computer system at work. He spoke at length and in great detail about the system: what the computer could do, the problems it could solve, the intricacies of installing it and the 'teething' problems for the staff in adapting to its use. I thought about Mr M's mother's becoming pregnant with his brother when he was 6–7 months old and teething himself. He had never once mentioned a sibling during the analysis and I had only known of his brother's existence through direct questioning in the preliminary interview. It was this striking omission which led me to believe that the phantasied murder was of the only sibling.

I also heard about Mr X, senior to Mr M in the firm, who took every opportunity to point out the deficiencies in the new system. When I used to speak to Mr M about how he felt this was how I was behaving toward him too, how he did feel he now needed a new system to protect him from the impact of the analysis and how he feared it as a threat to his control system, he either passed over what I had said or said, quite firmly for him, that he did not believe it. Thus he omnipotently obliterated the ideas I produced, as he must have obliterated his mother's pregnancy and the new baby, and maintained his superiority and triumph over an old fogy of an analyst who lacked knowledge of computers and whom he despised. In the same way he continued omnipotently to obliterate all references to the mother's pregnancy, and the sibling, in the analysis. These obsessive ruminations about the computer system continued for many months and it seemed Mr M was using these as his new defensive system within sessions in order to defend himself against guilt and anxiety and the fear of something dangerous for him. About this time it slipped out that Mr M had two job offers on hand: one, a move to a partnership in a small firm, and the other a promotion to a more senior position in his present company. While he procrastinated about the choice of jobs, I was suggesting he felt in a quandary in the analysis because he believed I wanted him to move on and he felt his problem was which way to go on. He could maintain the same position where he had to keep a tight control over his analyst and the analysis. The alternative, he felt, was to move to some new, unknown and unpredictable position which was frightening to him. I spoke to him about how I thought he felt under great pressure to maintain the status quo here because he believed any move to be extremely dangerous for him. I emphasised that he felt himself to be in a position now where he felt under pressure about having some choice himself in the situation, similar to the two job offers. Predictably he gave no indication that this line of interpretation was having any impact: he remained passive. He continued to speak of the computer system which by now had taken on a life of its own, and it seemed that the actual job offers were adding to his uncertainty and mounting anxiety.

Some weeks went by and then he told me he had accepted promotion in his company and turned down the partnership job in the small firm. I thought the two job offers represented a primitive part-object triangular situation and his dilemma as to whether to stay put within his present company, standing for his controlling the analytic situation and the analyst, or move on to an unknown object (the partnership in a new firm) which also represented, internally, the possibility of different relations to different aspects of himself and to different aspects of his internal objects.

### *Internal situation*

It was around this time that Mr M had two dreams which conveyed his internal predicament and which I shall consider in some detail. He started a session saying he had had a dream. In the first dream,

> *he and some others were making their way through open undulating country: they may have been escaped Prisoners of War* (POWs)*. Two or three menacing black helicopters flew overhead. Then they saw on a rise ahead tanks and soldiers drawn up, so they realised they were approaching the battlefront. The SS were after them too, so the patient led them to hide in a narrow ditch. As he was crawling along the ditch he met a woman with a child coming from the opposite end. The child looked oriental. Next they were hiding in a barn and some of the people were discovered and being questioned. One of them was about to give the patient's whereabouts away, believing they were all discovered, though the patient was still hidden. He managed to stop the others giving him away. He woke in great fear.*

Mr M went on thinking about his situation in the dream. He had thought if he hid high up in the rafters above he might be safer and also in a position to drop down onto the SS to attack them, if he were found. The rafters above would be safer than disguising himself by hiding in a sack – which he also had thought of – because he would then be trapped if found. The striking thing about this dream and the associations was the intensity of the persecution felt by Mr M, who awoke from it in great fear. The oriental child he associated to a Taiwanese firm with whom he was doing business, and he spoke of their illegal custom of killing girl infants by hiding them in rubbish dumps. Then, in an increasingly remote tone of voice, he went on to say that he thought the dream indicated he should not accept promotion, that he would be doing the wrong thing by leaving his present job, he felt the dream was telling him to stop. Finally he remarked, in a voice which sounded both neutral and contrived, that he may be approaching some psychological battle area.

In retrospect I think Mr M's proposition that the dream was against his moving jobs was a subtle invitation to get me to have a go at persecuting him.

It was his attempt to convert real and intense persecution into sadomasochism by omnipotent control of the persecution through ritualising its enactment between us. His final remark about approaching some psychological battle area was, I now think, in mockery. But at the time I was struck by the ambiguity in his final remarks and thought they were to distract us from more disturbing aspects of the dream. So I first spoke about his difficulty in deciding what to do at work, in the dream and at this moment in the session; I suggested he was also indicating the situation in the analysis. I waited to see if Mr M would respond but he said nothing though I thought he was attentive. So I went on to link the menacing helicopters overhead, the tanks and soldiers ahead to a terrifying situation in his mind which he feared the analysis and I, as the SS behind him and black helicopters overhead, would discover. He believed the analysis and I were pursuing him into what he believed to be a very dangerous situation. I put it to him that his feeling safer in the rafters 'above' was the position he believed himself to be in, lodged inside my mind, following and influencing my thoughts, and from that position he felt out of my SS reach and able to anticipate whatever he feared I might discover about him. So he had wanted me to tell him what I thought about his dream as I was now doing. There followed a long silence during which I had no sense of what he felt, or indeed where he might now be hiding.

Mr M broke the silence to say that he had had a second dream, which followed the one he had just told me and he added that it was about a man who had been his boss in his previous job. *This man was ill and depressed: he had left his job because he had murdered someone, so he could not get another job. In the dream Mr M felt sorry for this man.* The patient said that he felt this man was himself and he then fell into a sinking silence so that I felt I was losing contact with him and needed to draw him out. This was difficult but after a struggle it transpired that his former boss, who I thought stood for his former self, did not move on in the reorganisation of the firm. He had stayed put, lost his car, received no additional remuneration for the longer hours he worked and failed to manage his department; he was still stuck in the same job. Mr M then reminded me that he himself did move out and despite difficulties in finding a job he had done so, and had recently been promoted to another one with more money. He added that he felt it was all rather exciting – though this was said in his customary flat tone. He then suggested perhaps it was parts of himself which had been murdered. While I thought this was so, that he had to keep 'dead' lively aspects of himself, the manner in which he made this last remark had sounded provocative and false as if meant to draw me into sadistic activity by making a critical interpretation which would be false and perceived as such by him. So I said I thought it was exciting him to try to draw me into a cruel and phoney exchange, but I also thought it was meant to cover up his very real fear of depression and being stuck in it, as he felt his father had been. He was silent but I felt he was moved, so I continued that he felt that I, too, was stuck, despairing of him, for he believed no movement was possible because of some murder which he believed to have taken place. Again he fell into what I experienced as a sinking silence and when I remarked on it he responded with 'um, um'; I was unsure whether these sounds were defensive, affirmative, or wanting me to go on talking showing I was alive. I now think the flatness of tone when he said 'he felt it was all rather exciting' and the provocative quality in his remark that perhaps it was parts of him which had been murdered, were indicators that the defensive deadening process was already at work even as he spoke, flattening out and covering his genuine excitement with a layer of false provocation. Furthermore the process successfully lured me too, to only recognise and interpret one side and to fail to pick up his genuine movement – to which he drew my attention – and his excitement at it.

## Discussion

Freud (1911, 1916–1917) describes hallucinatory wish fulfilment as the mental activity of the infant in frustration and he differentiates such activity from the emergence of phantasy proper which he sees as arising with the development of the reality principle. Phantasising is a thought activity which splits off and develops separately as the demands of reality are introduced and it may be conscious or repressed. Sandler and Nagera (1963) integrate Freud's writings about phantasy with his structural theory and see the infant's hallucinatory gratification as a basic precursor of later phantasising. Sandler and Sandler (1994) have more recently elaborated this view of phantasy and related it to their ideas about present and past unconscious. They make a distinction between phantasies in the present unconscious, which exist in the here-and-now and include transference phantasies, and those in the past unconscious which the authors suggest are largely reconstructions of the analyst's theories of mental functioning and of child development. They stress the need in analytic work to focus on phantasies and associated conflicts in the present unconscious before attending to the reconstruction of the past.

Klein in her work with young children was particularly interested in phantasy life that was actually an accompaniment to reality orientated behaviour. She recognised the child's acute anxiety concerning horrific sadistic impulses expressed in oral and anal phantasies, especially about intercourse and reproduction. These discoveries led to the Kleinian expansion of the concept (Isaacs 1952 [1948]). According to this theory a rudimentary ego develops from birth and is capable of forming phantasies about the infant's subjective experiences: these are thought at the start to take the form of bodily sensations, Freud's body ego, but quite early on they become transposed into mental representations. Both Freud and Klein hypothesised innate phantasies: when these innate preconceptions meet with experiences with objects primitive phantasies are formed concerning breast and penis, intercourse and reproduction. For Kleinians phantasy forming and phantasy life are thought to start from birth and to continue throughout life. All the contents and structures of the unconscious mind are thought to be organised in the form of phantasies and so Kleinians give a central position to unconscious phantasy. In the mind of the infant and small child these phantasies are intensely felt and omnipotent in their consequences. Early primitive phantasies lay the foundations, and they provide the matrix out of which will evolve the structures which will determine the character of the personality; they can also lead to confusions and misperceptions instead of to increasing differentiation as in more healthy mental development. Bion follows Klein in thinking there is an *a priori* knowledge of both breast and penis. Birksted-Breen (1996) sees breast and penis as also representing different functions; she suggests the breast has to do with the function of 'being with' and refers to the link between self and other, the penis-as-link with the function of giving structure and refers to the link between the parents.

To return to Mr M and his two dreams. The contrast between the atmosphere in the dreams is striking: the first persecutory and the second depressive. I think the second dream was brought in the session, as it was dreamt in the night, as a continuation of the first. The fact that Mr M broke his passive, hiding silence to tell it to me was a move forward. So also was the content of the dream and Mr M recognising something of himself in the ill, depressed murderer. But the moment he verbally acknowledged his recognition he sunk back and I felt impelled to struggle to help him associate to the dream. Then he again manages to come to life with several thoughts about his former boss/self who doesn't move, who stays stuck. In associating he is momentarily more mobile as he contrasts the former boss with himself who has moved jobs, has bettered his position and was moving now in response to the analyst's efforts to encourage him to have thoughts about his dream. But even as he said it was 'all rather exciting', the flat, lifeless tone was back. Then I misperceived his movement as provocation and falsity. Why did I fail to spot the movement between Mr M's two states – both in the immediacy of the session and in his associations to the second dream? I think my analytic capacity was impaired by the fusion between my own and the patient's terror of violence associated with murderousness. The problem for both patient and analyst was that the enactment of murder was also a defence against murder and the terrifying violence associated with it which was so closely linked to sadism. When I interpreted Mr M's fear of being stuck in depression and linked it to his father the effect was to push him back into depression, even though it seemed to touch Mr M. In interpreting in this way I think I was identified at that moment with the patient's depressed father, as well as defending myself against the force of the projected murderous violence and deadness.

Next day's session was again dominated by Mr M's mechanical computer talk, although someone at work was raising objections. When I suggested he felt some objections within himself about his computer system for closing his mind and the session today, in contrast to yesterday, Mr M would have none of it. To defend against the shift toward mobility the previous day he went back to his controlling system, being like his former boss, not moving from it.

These two dreams reveal the ramifications of the primitive phantasy which dominates Mr M's psychic structure and his analysis, as well as his actual life. In the first dream he is surrounded by threatening figures – soldiers and tanks in front and the SS behind – he is being pursued by them and tries to hide by crawling along a ditch. In the ditch he meets a woman carrying an oriental-looking child which he associates with the Taiwanese practice of the murder of infant girls. This is the concrete bodily phantasy of mother carrying his baby brother, with father/penis barring his way – the tanks and soldiers. The patient attempts to escape from the psychic fact of mother's pregnancy by the phantasy of crawling back inside mother but once there he confronts his infant sibling and father obstructing his way. The patient's violence fuels the phantasy of the intrusion into the mother's body and the murderous attack on the sibling. In addition there was his fear of his own violence and consequent retaliation. These affects suffuse the first intensely persecutory dream. The same phantasy is enacted at the mental level in the analysis where, in the transference, he projects himself into the analyst's mind and from there believes he knows and controls his object. When the control fails he resorts to obliteration of the object and its attributes, as for example when he responds to interpretations by calmly saying that he doesn't believe them. When in that position he hears interpretations as trying to dislodge him, as in concrete bodily form the penis and the phantasied other siblings try to prevent him from returning to the womb. The other people with Mr M in the dream who were trying to escape and were being questioned, represent the other aspects of himself which engage in the analysis and are feared to give him away. The second dream reveals his 'final solution' to the threat – the murder of his sibling. So concrete, omnipotent and omniscient is the phantasy that he has done murder in his internal world, so intense is his fear of his own murderous impulses, so great is the horrendous burden of persecutory guilt and fear of retaliation, that he is driven to immobilise himself. In the second dream he could not get another job. One of Mr M's reasons for having an analysis was that he could not decide what sort of work he could do. But depressive concern was there too, for in the dream Mr M was sorry for this guilty, depressed man which in the session he recognises as himself.

Mr M has had to keep 'dead' all lively capacities in himself because he is consumed by guilt and fear of retaliation. He fears to know that he believes himself to be a murderer: that in his hatred of his only sibling, conceived when he was only 5 months old, and in his omnipotent murderous infantile wishes toward him he believes he murdered him.

Britton (1995, 1998) regards unconscious belief as the function which confers the status of reality onto phantasies, which gives the force of reality to that which is psychic. All his life Mr M has had to project murderous rage, violence and guilt, and in analysis he also has to defend himself from the conflict aroused by the possible awareness that this murderousness might originate within himself. This is the immediate threatening situation in the transference which was also represented in the first persecutory dream. The phantasised attack on the sibling is out of hatred, envy and jealousy but it also extends to the mother who created the situation. You recall Mr M's childhood memory of walking out on his mother in fury, though he had no idea what had provoked him. Something similar repeatedly occurred in the transference. I would convey my interest and ideas in interpretations, whereupon Mr M might withdraw into silence, make a non-committal comment or agree in a dismissive tone of voice. Thus he kept disappearing, 'walking out' on me and my interpretations and not allowing a contact, leaving his analyst thwarted and depressed. In this manner he murdered the contact and murdered his own receptivity. I think Mr M consciously sensed this immobilisation of himself and the analysis – which unconsciously he deeply feared would expose his murderous impulses.

The intensity of Mr M's violent impulses and his fear of them compounded the difficulties which led him to believe nothing could change. He believed himself condemned to a lifelong burden of unbearable guilt which he consciously felt as diffuse anxiety and hopelessness. In the analysis this had to be experienced in the countertransference, especially in the repeated 'murdering' of my capacity to analyse. When I felt imprisoned and gave up, the patient's phantasy of murder was confirmed. When I managed to recover and analyse, the patient's guilt at what he was doing to the analysis and to me was then re-enforced and believed to be too unbearable to face. In this manner I experienced Mr M's projected predicament. Riesenberg-Malcolm (1999) speaks of patients who feel they are being punished for what they believe is the destruction or damage they phantasise they have done to their objects. She describes the way they may organise their behaviour in analysis so as to create a static situation which consists of their own suffering and misery combined with the analyst's immobilisation.

## Emergence of cruelty and guilt

In the year following these two dreams there was a gradual diminution in these defences. The computer talk faded away and some flexibility developed within the analysis. This, in turn, brought other problems. The emergence of some liveliness took the form of repetitive cruelty perpetrated by Mr M, and guilt projected into me. He took to coming late to sessions, or staying away and not letting me know. Sometimes he would go away on business and tell me he had just remembered at the end of the session the day before he went off. In sessions his material became repetitive and obvious, which I experienced as provoking me to speak to him in a way which I felt was predictable and stale. I tried to draw his attention to what I thought was going on by describing the cruelty and how I thought he wanted me to feel provoked, to feel responsible and helpless, and to feel bad about having such feelings. Mr M would respond by saying calmly 'I suppose it's possible . . . I don't know' and then he would withdraw into silence. For example, one Wednesday Mr M arrived ten minutes late saying he felt so weird on the way that he had had to get out of his car and walk a bit; he had thought he was having a heart attack so he must return to swimming regularly. He then reported a dream from the previous night. *He had arrived late at school and there was this master walking up and down outside: he wasn't angry, more exasperated. There were some other children playing and the patient went and joined in.* Mr M's only association was that the children were about 11 or 12, rather uncoordinated as children were at that age – spotty and fat. I felt there was a teasing, provocative quality to this and to the silence into which Mr M then retreated. I put it to him that the same was happening in the session as happened in his dream. He knew he was playing about, being silent, being late and he believed (accurately) that I was exasperated with him, which secretly excited him. I then suggested that when he was returning here he did get frightened that I would get closer to something at the heart of him which he believed to be life threatening: he feared I would attack him because of it. His response was predictable but also, at another level, true too. He said he didn't know and lapsed into silence. Next day he was fifteen minutes late and announced he was going abroad on business for two weeks in a month's time. He described plans for his trip, how he would stop off for a three-day holiday and would miss his session on the day of his return. The provocation, cruelty and sense of power continued throughout the session.

During the early years of the analysis Mr M and I were bound together in his phantasised closed system where he was projectively lodged inside my mind. There he hid and from this position he believed he knew the contents of my mind and could control my thinking. When he felt this system to be failing his anxiety increased and his projections intensified so that their force would attack my capacity to think. This was the enactment in the analytic situation of the concrete phantasy of having intrusively entered the mother's body, as revealed in the first dream. In such a parasitic relation he lived off the analysis and was able to make moves in his outside life, such as improving his work prospects and getting married. The two dreams ushered in a very gradual movement and led to the emergence of repetitive cruelty which I have tried to describe. These cruel attacks were within an Oedipal configuration. They centred around lateness, absences and secrecy for I would be left waiting, expecting him, would not be told when he would be absent or late. Or I might be taunted in the manner in which I was being told, as perhaps as a toddler he had felt tormented by his parents' secret intercourse and knowledge of the pregnancy. Within sessions our interactions took on a similar pattern for during Mr M's provocative silences he and I were both waiting for each other's thoughts – the secret dialogue with a third. Now what he told me was suffused with affect as he subtly conveyed his interest was elsewhere, in his travels, in redecorating his house or what he and his wife did together. Aliveness conveyed possession and projected jealousy, threaded through with cruelty, all of which were in marked contrast to the previous years of deadening lack of affect.

## Problems in the countertransference

Hinshelwood (1999) presents an overview of the concept of countertransference, its expansion and elaboration since 1950. He describes the Kleinian view as based upon processes of introjective and projective identifications and as drawing upon Bion's model of 'container and contained'. This view also makes a distinction between normal countertransference when the analyst is able to make the distinction between his own disturbance and his patient's, in contrast to when the analyst is drawn into enactments, evasions or other defensive moves to change the relationship – rather than to articulate its qualities. O'Shaughnessy (1992) describes two deteriorations of the psychoanalytic situation which may arise when the analyst is drawn into excessive acting out. In one which she names *enclaves* the analyst may so respond to the patient that the analysis is turned into a refuge from disturbance for both patient and analyst. Alternatively the analyst may succumb to pressures from the patient who is in terror of knowing and desperate to take flight from contact. The analyst may then turn the analysis into a series of *excursions* from trying to know what is psychically urgent. Feldman (1997) describes some of the difficulties in attempting to understand and interpret due to the mutual projective and introjective identifications of patient and analyst. He suggests the interaction between the patient's and the analyst's needs may lead to a repetitive enactment in the analysis which serves a defensive function for both patient and analyst and defends against more disturbing phantasies. He thinks it can therefore be very difficult for the analyst to extricate himself or his patient from such an unproductive situation.

During both the phases I have described it was difficult to bear the countertransference and the pressure to react and thus 'act in' was considerable. In the first phase when Mr M was remote and apparently depressed yet without affect, there was, paradoxically, a driven quality to the deadness. When I would try to describe what I thought was going on, whether inside himself or between us, what he felt I was wanting from him or doing to him, he would appear to ignore what I had said and continue with his own line of thought. It was I who was disturbed by his persistent lack of response. I would feel remote and out of touch, as he seemed to be, and at other times I felt irritated, angry, and useless. I noticed that I would start to berate myself internally for not understanding our predicament and I became increasingly driven by omniscient expectations of myself. For example when I failed to recognise Mr M's movement between the two dreams, it became a disproportionate omission in my mind. As there were many such instances I came to think there was a countertransference element which led me to feel I had done something awful, when I hadn't. This may have been the patient's situation: unconsciously he believed he had murdered his brother when in fact he hadn't, for it seemed the brother was married with children and making his way in life. I felt a disproportionate degree of guilt too about the lack of development in the analysis.

These events happened sufficiently frequently in the transference that they could be thought of as resembling serial murders of understanding. It seems likely that both parties to the analysis were unconsciously frightened by the power of the mutual projections of murderous hatred, violence and cruelty. One consequence was that the analysis proceeded at a snail's pace. Another element was a persistent unforgiving quality toward his object which I think contributed to the prolongation of the cruelty which proved to be so central. Consciously he felt the analysis helped him but unconsciously an unrelenting resentment prevented him from fully turning to his objects. It seemed as though he felt he could never get over his mother's 'crime' in producing a new baby.

I became more and more driven to try to move him. This driven feeling within myself alternated with losing interest and, worst of all, having a compelling sense of paralysis which led me to give up on him out of helplessness and despair. When interpretations did make emotional contact, these threatened his omnipotent projective lodging in my mind and were experienced as deeply disturbing to his psychic equilibrium. The surface blandness served to neutralise their impact, as did a delayed reaction. Sometimes I noticed that after a while, in the same session or a few days later, there would be material which seemed to be confirmation of what had been interpreted. Mr M was unaware of this and appeared quietly unimpressed when I would try to draw his attention to his unconscious response. The only exceptions were his very occasional dreams which he took as omnipotent 'signs' and interpretations about them were received in a similar manner. There was a profound split between thinking and feeling and a rigid demarcation between conscious and unconscious. The analyst had to bear and hold onto the projected frustration Mr M felt when there could be no shift in the internal situation. It was very gradual, almost imperceptible, when a shift came about. The importance and the difficulty for the analyst was not to miss these shifts.

## References

Birksted-Breen, D. (1996) 'Phallus, penis and mental space', *International Journal of Psychoanalysis*, 77(4): 649–657.

Britton, R. (1995) 'Psychic reality and unconscious belief', *International Journal of Psychoanalysis*, 76(1): 19–24.

—— (1998) 'Belief and psychic reality', *Belief and Imagination: Explorations in Psychoanalysis*, London: Routledge.

Feldman, M. (1997) 'Projective identification: the analyst's involvement', *International Journal of Psychoanalysis*, 78(2): 227–240.

Freud, S. (1911) 'Attempts at interpretation', SE 12: 35–58.

—— (1916–1917) 'Introductory lectures on psycho-analysis (Part 3), SE 16.

Hinshelwood, R.D. (1999) 'Countertransference', *International Journal of Psychoanalysis*, 80: 797–818.

Isaacs, S. (1952) 'The nature and function of phantasy', *Developments in Psycho-Analysis*, M. Klein, P. Heimann, S. Isaacs and J. Riviere (eds), London: Hogarth Press (1970).

Joseph, B. (1989a) 'On passivity and aggression: their interrelationship', *Psychic Equilibrium and Psychic Change: Selected Papers of Betty Joseph*, M. Feldman and E. Bott Spillius (eds), London: Routledge.

—— (1989b) 'Defence mechanisms and phantasy in the psychoanalytical process', *Psychic Equilibrium and Psychic Change: Selected Papers of Betty Joseph*, M. Feldman and E. Bott Spillius (eds), London: Routledge.

—— (1998c) 'Transference: the total situation', *Psychic Equilibrium and Psychic Change: Selected Papers of Betty Joseph*, M. Feldman and E. Bott Spillius (eds), London: Routledge.

—— (1989d) 'Psychic change and the psychoanalytic process', *Psychic Equilibrium and Psychic Change: Selected Papers of Betty Joseph*, M. Feldman and E. Bott Spillius (eds), London: Routledge.

O'Shaughnessy, E. (1992) 'Enclaves and excursions', *International Journal of Psychoanalysis*, 73: 603–611.

Riesenberg-Malcolm, R. (1999) 'Self-punishment as defence', *On Bearing Unbearable States of Mind*, Priscilla Roth (ed.), London: Routledge.

Rosenfeld, H. (1987) 'Afterthought', *Impasse and Interpretation*, London: Tavistock.

Sandler, J. and Nagera, H. (1963) 'Aspects of the metapsychology of fantasy', *The Psychoanalytical Study of the Child*, 18: 159–194.

Sandler, J. and Sandler, A.M. (1994) 'Phantasy and its transformations: a contemporary Freudian view', *International Journal of Psychoanalysis*, 75: 387–393.

Steiner, J. (1990) 'Role of unbearable guilt' *International Journal of Psychoanalysis*, 71: 87–94.

## DISCUSSION OF PATRICIA DANIEL'S CHAPTER

*Betty Joseph*

For me what this interesting and vividly recounted contribution particularly shows is the analyst's unending struggle to hold in her mind and work the importance of the patient's infantile phantasies and yet to be constantly aware of his current impulses and anxieties as they are aroused. Paddy gives a very convincing picture of the kind of relationship the patient established, withdrawing, deadening etc. Sometimes I wondered whether she might not have made more explicit to us earlier on how much the passive, despairing behaviour, making the analyst feel so stuck – though mobilised by anxiety – was also actively aimed at spoiling and destroying the ongoing work. Later she does link this with his sadism. Do we see something similar in the first dream? What seems to emerge most strikingly is how difficult it must be for the analyst herself to emerge from the POW camp established by the controls of the ever watchful patient constantly trying to imprison her and her work. But she does seem to be emerging and helping the patient, despite his anxieties and his violence, to move towards more depressive functioning with some ability to face guilt and concern both for his restricted self and his objects.

# DISCUSSION OF PATRICIA DANIEL'S CHAPTER

## *Richard Lucas*

Patients who persistently neutralise and exclude the analyst's attempts to reach them, inevitably stimulate the analyst to search for theories that may aid with understanding, as well as giving careful consideration to technique.

In her chapter, Paddy describes how she was forced to examine her countertransference reactions, and the enactments into which she was constantly drawn. She vividly describes how the patient would repeatedly try to nudge her into a defensive sadomasochistic avoidance relationship, and the subtle movements from persecutory to more depressive states.

I wonder whether it would also be helpful to consider two separate parts of the patient. A non-psychotic part comes along with a desire for help in making progress in relationships and at work. The patient brings also a problematic psychotic part for the analyst to experience first hand through its powerfully neutralising activity. In the introduction, Paddy draws attention to the dominating phantasies of the psychotic part – namely that it has murderously attacked his younger brother, clearly representing the sane needy self, and turned its back on his mother. But, while Paddy usefully emphasises the patient's defensive need to deaden in order not to know about his murderousness, I would also consider it important to look at the role of the death instinct, and primal envy of the mother/analyst's liveliness and creativity. Hence aliveness and vitality could not be tolerated in the analysis. Progress in the analysis both on the relationship and job front had to go on initially in secret, and passivity and deadness prevailed.

Paddy demonstrates how useful dreams were in shedding light on this internal conflict in Mr M. While the first dream graphically describes the predicament of analyst and patient as prisoners of the psychotic part, the SS, the second dream led to momentary insight. Perhaps this leaves us with a challenge of how to talk to the non-psychotic part of the patient about his resentment of the mother/analyst's creativity (new baby), and how it continues to operate against the very progress he is making in his own analysis.

# 7

# LUXURIATING IN STUPEFACTION

## The analysis of a narcissistic fetish

*Gigliola Fornari Spoto*

It's Monday. C, as he always does, arrives early for his session and uses the toilet. When I collect him, he just glances in my direction, greeting me with his customary formal, but not unfriendly, reserve; before lying down, he quickly surveys, as usual, the space behind the couch, where my chair and my desk are, to reassure himself, I feel, that everything is as he left it, and also to ascertain that nothing unpredictable or dangerous could assail him from behind. This visual exploration seems very important to him, and I know how quick he is in picking up anything new or different, even if he never talks about it. He then lies very still, with his legs quite open, rigid and passive at the same time, a position he will keep to the end of the session. Despite several years of analysis and the carefully ritualised sameness of his entry into the session, meeting his object (especially after a separation) continues to produce a surge of anxiety which cannot be verbalised and is expressed instead at a bodily level. His first words seem to suggest a possible reason for this difficulty. A brief silence, then he says, half defiantly, half apologetically: 'I'm afraid I don't have much to say today' . . . Another pause . . . 'I have got my head stuck up my arse.'

I am familiar with this kind of beginning. It means: 'Sorry, but I can't be here with you; I am somewhere else, much more compelling. But let's see if you can reach me – get me out of there and touch me. The thinking and the initiative are all yours, but I am not going to do much.' He offers himself rather provocatively, just as his bodily posture seems to suggest, as an object of impenetrable passivity. I know that he derives a sense of gratification from it.

'Having his head stuck up his arse' is an expression coined by C to describe a state of extreme self-absorption, stillness and withdrawal from reality, where he loses contact with the world and becomes intensely preoccupied with sexual fantasies about bottoms and faeces, the same fantasies he acts out with prostitutes.

It's a highly desirable state: his bottom is idealised as a narcissistic retreat, the comforting source of every good experience. His intense concentration on the bodily experience takes over his mind: the sought after mental torpor, which he reaches, is sexualised and makes him feel powerful and superior to me. My attempts to talk to him can be perceived as rather feeble and uninspiring, compared to the intense pleasure derived from the way he challenges me with his non-thinking.

There are, I think, various links which could be made, just by focusing on the brief vignette which I have given you, with several themes central to his psychopathology. He has to deal with the separation of the weekend, which he finds difficult because it breaks the phantasised seamlessness of our relationship. Reassuring himself that his object is unchanged, when he checks if traces of my external life have contaminated the consulting room, suggests a need for stillness and sameness, denies the passing of time, and is related to Oedipal anxieties – has there been an intercourse? Is there a new baby?

You could argue it is pretty straightforward material, with a mixture of pre-Oedipal and Oedipal anxieties, the stuff every analysis is made of. Yet these anxieties have a very persecutory quality for C, who I think feels violently ejected, by the weekend separation, from a state where he feels projectively identified with his object in a narcissistic dyad, and in control. He deals with these preoccupations, by 'sticking his head up his arse' (by getting inside another narcissistic object), by not thinking, by denying the reality of our separateness and the meaning of our relationship, by making himself unreachable, and by projecting into me the need for contact. You remember, though, that he is also very passive: if I interpret to him along the lines sketched out (say his anxiety about the weekend separation and the way he defends against it), he'll probably agree with me, but he'll do so in a way which implies he is not really emotionally touched and doesn't want to go any further with it. He will signal, nevertheless, his readiness to be taken over by the analysis and by my thinking, so that he can ultimately 'stick his head up my head' (or my arse), creating a state of blissful anti-thinking togetherness, reversing the awareness of our separateness and reclaiming his projective place inside the object. Both the withdrawal into his arse and this passivity, are, as I described, sexualised defensive states, which conceal an active way of attacking and preventing a connection with the reality of his object and with thinking. His aim becomes, to use his words, to 'luxuriate in stupefaction'.

I have used this short vignette as a compact account of some of the defining features of perversions, as they are described in the vast literature about them: perversions are sexualised, narcissistic attacks on the reality of otherness and difference, driven by the intolerance of such difference, whose aim is to create an alternative reality (Chasseguet-Smirgel 1985; McDougall 1978, 1995; Stoller 1976, 1985).

'Luxuriate in stupefaction' is an insider's succinct description of what perversions aim to achieve and why they are so compelling and addictive: the attack on reality and thinking, the making oneself stupid, torpid, dazed so that perception of reality is altered and distorted, is sexualised and used as a drug. 'Stupefaction' can be almost thought of as a layman's term for disavowal, the mechanism Freud saw as central to fetishism.

In this chapter I want to describe some of the difficulties encountered in the analysis of a perverse patient, by trying to show how the perversion and the sexualisation of the attack on reality and thinking weren't just confined to his sexual activities, but also underpinned his character structure, were lived out in the transference and used as a barrier against contact and understanding.

C came to analysis in his early thirties. An only child, he had felt imprisoned in a symbiotic tie with an authoritarian mother, experienced by him as both intrusive and cold. He thought his father was peripheral and distant, and never rescued him from his mother. He maintained that both his parents, like a triumphant persecutory Oedipal pair intent on humiliating him, denied him the possibility of expressing his autonomy, his masculinity and his sexuality.

Since he was 11 he had locked himself in the bathroom, defecated and watched himself in a mirror, masturbated and smeared shit over his bottom and penis. The masturbatory fantasy was that he was watching a girl defecating. He was always aware that this was a violent act which gave him a great sense of release. The smearing of shit seemed to empower him: he became dirty, dangerous and wild and gained a sense of identity from it. Later, plagued by an absolute terror of relationships with women, whom he projectively saw as frigid and anti-men, he started acting out his coprophilic fantasies with prostitutes. When he began the analysis he had never had a relationship with a woman. The prostitute would defecate and he would watch her or vice versa, and then he would smear shit on her. He talked about his pleasure in 'shoving all the shit back in'. He required the woman to assume a certain position and then keep still. He was very particular about the shape of the woman's bottom, which had to meet certain specifications. His potency remained tied to violent fantasies based on anal supremacy. However, inside this fortress of shit and violence there was enormous despair and some longing for a different mode of relating; it was the despair that brought him to analysis.

C was so deeply barricaded in his bottom, that he lived a friendless, isolated life. His anxieties about contact with an object were expressed in the language of primitive orality. When he liked a woman he wanted to 'gobble her up', to possess her completely, only to feel very quickly smothered and suffocated. He once had a dream about a walrus who starts kissing a seal; to begin with, everything is fine, but then the kiss turns into a bite and the walrus eats the seal up. The expression 'the kiss that turns into a bite' was used by him to describe the impossibility of loving somebody. He felt that a form of devouring hatred was the prime mover for him, and would always contaminate his love. As soon as there was contact, he experienced that the person wanted something from him (largely a projection of his oral desires) so he'd rather 'bite their heads off first'. There was a defiant, self-aggrandising satisfaction when he described himself as full of hatred, which defended him very effectively against the disorganising anxieties produced by closeness.

Once in analysis, he defended against contact by misconstruing the analytical situation and its neutrality as a repeat of the dehumanised relationship with the prostitute: he came, did his business, offloaded something, paid me and went. The outright violence of the smearing fantasies was tamed and transformed into a sterilised interaction and into an obsessional undoing of the connections which were made, probably not dissimilar to the 'shoving it all back in' which he liked to do with the prostitute. If we had a session where I thought some work had been done, he regularly (and infuriatingly) came back saying something like 'I felt better after yesterday's session, but it didn't last, and after I thought what a lot of old tosh, what am I doing wasting all my money etc.'. This was meant to smear my interpretations, changing useful words into shit, and provocatively to engage me in some kind of scripted tussle where I was expected to chastise him for his attacks on the analysis and where sadomasochism was the preferred currency. I felt immobilised in a fixed position, like the prostitute. An added difficulty was that interpreting things in these terms was experienced by him as if I was actually 'doing' what I was talking about (words were actions for C) and thus very exciting to him. Needless to say, he came to his sessions religiously, in a compulsive way. Keeping a sense of conviction in my analytical voice wasn't easy; sometimes I feared that the analysis could turn into an interminable enactment of the perversion, as if his bottom fetish could become an addictive 'analysis fetish', where he could 'luxuriate in stupefaction' instead of doing analytical work.

I want now to give some material, in the form of a dream, which I think shows the kind of psychic reality which the sadomasochistic enactments or the passive symbiotic tie to the analysis were attempting to deny.

> *He goes to a concert. It should be in London, but in fact it's in D where his parents live. He is supposed to meet a woman friend but she doesn't show up. Instead he realises his parents are there. They begin to talk to one another and he cannot hear the music. The concert has started and he is furious. He tries to shut them up, without success. First he says shush, then he screams, but they just keep on talking. He is mad at them, stands up and shouts at the top of his voice 'Shut up'. They are unperturbed. All the people stand up in the theatre trying to silence the parents, to no avail.*

He was surprised to have a dream about his parents being together, and associated to a concert he went to with a woman friend, and to somebody behind them noisily unwrapping sweets, which had annoyed him. He said about his parents that 'they have the most annoying habit; they seem to be able to talk for hours about nothing'. It reminded him of how it drove him mad, when he was a child, to be sent to bed early, when it was still light, and he lay in bed, hearing the incessant talk of the parents downstairs, hating that 'they were having all the fun'.

I think the dream shows how persecutory the analysis becomes when it has an impact on him, and how much he needs to silence this impact. If I am not the girlfriend/prostitute with whom he can enact his fantasies, I am experienced as an overpowering Oedipal couple which prevents him from listening to 'his' superior brand of anal music. (C was a refined connoisseur of classical music.) The primal scene phantasy of an unstoppable oral/verbal intercourse between his parents suggests an awareness of a combined object, an awareness which is quickly denied by degrading the hated and excluding intercourse to inane chit-chat. There is a deadly competition for whose 'music' ought to be given centre stage, mine or his, whose version of reality, his, coloured by the grievances of his infantile self, or mine. C sticks to his unnegotiable version of the Oedipus complex, where the parents have sex against the child, so that he can fuel his hatred against them, and, in the transference, his hatred for the analysis represented by the parental intercourse. The voice of the parents, however, can't be silenced in the dream; there is a furious recognition that he cannot silence the voice of reality, the voice of the analyst, even if he tries his best to.

I could draw some hope from a dream such as this that my persistence wasn't in vain, and get some understanding of C's repetitive, addictive effort, through the perverse enactments in the transference, to transform my voice and our interaction into undifferentiated and meaningless chit-chat, but how to go beyond this remained the central struggle in the analysis.

I want to bring some more detailed clinical material to illustrate this struggle. First, some background information. In the course of the analysis C had met several women, but the relationships were very brief because he either became superior or felt ill treated. Eventually he met L, a rather inhibited but warm and intelligent woman. With some apprehension he asked her to marry him and she accepted. Getting married meant he would have to move outside London and probably stop the analysis. After the initial relief he became doubtful and started thinking of marriage as another 'raw deal', where he had to give without receiving anything back. After years of holding himself together with hatred and with so little belief in his capacity to love, he was very frightened of any sustained closeness. He now had an 'obligation', felt smothered and hooked. Until they got engaged he was in love; after the engagement he said he was 'in hate'.

He fuelled his hatred by ruminating about largely imaginary triangular situations with L featuring her friends, her parents, and her work, from which he felt excluded, and by brooding over vengeance. A curious splitting was operating; he used the analysis to detoxify or shit out his hatred, 'getting off' on these masturbatory sadomasochistic interactions with L, while in reality the relationship continued and he was able to sustain some warmth and closeness with her. I had interpreted that he was hooked on his picture of himself as the perennially ill-treated child (which he would play out in the 'virtual' reality of analysis) rather than dealing with the actual difficulties of his relationship with L and the possible end of the analysis.

The prospect of marrying and leaving the analysis seemed to have made this tension more acute, as if he felt under pressure to leave the fetish of analysis for the reality of real relationships, with closeness and loss at the centre of this reality. The material which I am briefly going to present precedes an analytical break.

On Wednesday he had spoken – something he had rarely done before – about his problems in the sexual relationship with L, who he maintained was against sex for religious reasons. He had compared sex with the prostitute with sex with L. Sex with the prostitute was erotic – he was always in control, sex was 'on tap'. In '"ordinary sex" you put yourself in somebody else's hands and lost control'. That was nice in a way, he added, because it was a bit like a relationship with a mother who does everything for you, but then it became like a dungeon with chains, from which he had to free himself. It felt like a man debasing himself. We were familiar with both kinds of 'sex' in the transference, but C seemed more interested and more in contact with how frightening the actual experience of sexual and emotional closeness was for him.

On Thursday he started the session by saying that he had been asked to chair a meeting at work. 'As you know', he added, 'I hate that. I just want to go to sleep.' He supposed he could get by by letting others say what they want and not paying attention. When others express their views he doesn't want to listen, he is not interested. He continued on in this vein. I said that he seemed to be wanting to chair the session with his passivity; he'll go to sleep, he'll let me speak and won't listen, but in fact he actively promotes a sense of futility about it. Perhaps he wanted me to go to sleep too, so that I wouldn't remember yesterday's session, where he was interested more in the chair, or notice that chairing a meeting is a new thing for him and he might in fact be quite pleased about it.

He said he remembered yesterday's session. (Silence.) It was probably the break that made him feel like this. (A pause.) He said he is either asleep or he gets into a raw deal (shorthand for sadomasochistic fantasies). After a pause he said that on Sunday, when he saw L, first it was OK, then he started feeling that it was unfair. She has to make up her mind. She wants him, then she doesn't want him any more, he feels she is dangling him on a string, he is not going to take it, etc. He could have spent the afternoon like this, listless and withdrawn. He then remembered there was an orchid exhibition at Kew and thought they might go and see it. They did and he felt better. While talking to her he realised that he has always used a word wrongly, or rather it is his mother's misuse of the word. The word is 'frowst'. He had said to L that instead of staying in and 'frowst' they could go to the exhibition. His mother's meaning for the word is moping. L didn't know the word so they looked it up in the dictionary and it said 'luxuriating in stupefaction'. He was really surprised about how much stronger and different the meaning of the word actually is. He thinks that this is what he does when there is a break. It's not really going to sleep; it's more like 'luxuriating in stupefaction'.

I was also surprised, because it was extremely rare for C to volunteer any kind of new or spontaneous thinking. I said that he was surprised to discover that he gets so much pleasure when he indulges in making himself or me stupid and torpid, luxuriating in imaginary 'raw deals' which make him lose sight of what's going on either here or when a break comes or with L.

'Yes', he says, 'that's about it'. (Silence.) But everything really feels so much of an effort, he really can't face the meeting, he doesn't want to go, he couldn't be bothered to come to the session, he doesn't want to see L this weekend. This, I felt, was said without real conviction.

After some silence, he spoke about L and the coming weekend, and about the fact that he is fed up that she keeps him waiting, saying that she has to do a lot of thinking, and he just feels like saying that he's going to drop her etc. (This has again the quality of distortion.)

I say that he has just done a bit of thinking about what happens when there is a break, when he has to wait, when he can't control the other person, but he's lost it. I also said that whereas his surprise earlier on seemed real to me, I thought he was now effortlessly slipping into a well-rehearsed performance, without much conviction, which allows him not to know what he actually feels about the break or what he is frightened of with L. It sounded very much like he's 'luxuriating' in it.

He said that he thought I was probably right but he feels he can come alive only if he has a raw deal. After a pause he said he was thinking of when he was 11 or 12. Everybody has sexual feelings at that age; the problem is how you are going to express them. At the time he didn't know anything else. He thought that smearing shit was sex, the only sex there was. He thought he could never have a possibility of anything else, no other contact. He didn't have a hope in the world that there could ever he anyone, so that smearing shit seemed to be the only alternative. He sounded more real here.

I interpreted that I felt now he was dangling me on a string, giving me something, his willingness to think differently, but then taking it back. First he says let's go together to the orchid exhibition and he knows he can feel better if he does that. Then he locks himself in the bathroom on his own, smearing shit, maintaining that he does it because there is no chance of any other relationship when in fact he has just had an experience of another relationship. I also added how far apart the orchids and the shit seemed to be. Perhaps he feels very confused about his feelings, like he did when he was 11: is it sex, is it violence, is it love, is it hatred? The session ended with C saying that he could recognise the confusion. 'It's a bit like the kiss that turns into a bite', he added, 'That's me'. His natural state is to be programmed to hate. He understood what

I meant, it made sense, but sometimes he felt that what he needed was an operation, where they removed his nut and gave him a new one.

The session begins with the familiar alternative between 'going to sleep' (head in his arse) and a prospect of sadomasochistic engagement with me. Surprisingly, though, C has some freely associated thoughts which, interestingly, are about difference from his mother and distortion of meaning. Although not exactly new (I have interpreted along similar lines before), they allow him to find *his* own description of what his passivity or invitations to sadomasochism are about and to realise how much pleasure he gets from it. Moreover, he can experience relief when he breaks the vicious circle. He reclaims his disowned and projected capacity to think, has a sense that he is different, separate from his mother, and he's free to be his adult self, and to go with L to the orchid exhibition. I think he also understands that he can blank out the experience of loss by reducing it to masochistic misery and indulging in it. What is puzzling is that, despite knowing that he can come alive and relate to his object, as he does in the session, with curiosity and willingness to understand, he tries to go back, although without much conviction, to the safety of what he calls raw deal, the spurious masturbatory aliveness which he gets from his ruminative hatred.

He has just processed something, then he undoes the processing, changing the feelings into raw, unmanageable stuff, which he can only shit out. To sustain contact is difficult for C, it requires real effort. It is confusing, perhaps because it moves between the opposites of idealisation and denigration (the orchids and the shit). I felt that his description of himself aged 11 conveyed something of the disorganising and contradictory intensity of adolescent emotions. In the session, having made contact with me, he then 'dangles me on a string', with some awareness that he is tormenting me. Analysis and the thinking it offers can't really touch him, he 'naturally' can't love, he needs surgery.

The reference to the 'kiss that turns into a bite', although relevant, can also be used as a defensive endorsement of his unchangeability. And of course 'dangling me on a string' is also how he controls the loss of his object, which is what he was trying to address in the earlier part of the session, when he spoke about 'luxuriating in stupefaction'.

On Friday he is silent for several minutes. 'I have got nothing to say.' Another long silence, then he says he had a dream, but it's not worth telling, it's so obvious. Silence again. He has spent a lot of time yesterday thinking that he cannot love L, because he feels that she wants something from him and she is not prepared to give him anything back; he's the one who will have to make all the changes.

I say that perhaps he wants to tell me about his dream, but in order to do so he needs to make me curious about it and create a situation where he imagines that I force him to give it to me. He says he's been lying here saying to himself, 'I'll be damned if I tell you about it, but I might just as well spill the beans. Anyway here it is.' (This felt a bit contrived. I felt he really wanted to tell me the dream.)

In the dream he is with a woman. They have an active interaction – he can't remember what it is, something to do with history. Then, what he can remember is that he touches the woman's head and face in a very affectionate way. 'It's very obvious isn't it? The woman must be you.' He thought that the popular view of psychoanalysis is that you fall in love with your analyst, and Bingo, there you have it. He laughs. It's very difficult for me to respond to this. I think that the dream seems to contain some real warmth (which after all is so rare in C), but I also say to myself 'don't get excited about it'.

I say he's doing his best for us not to take his dream seriously, and treat it as a sort of cheap romantic caricature of analysis. Yesterday he was saying he can come alive only with hatred, today there is love. He trivialises into pop psychoanalysis his experience of yesterday's session. Perhaps he felt we had had an 'active interaction', as in the dream, which had made sense to him, and was relieved and warm about it.

He says that it would be certainly easier for him to talk about shit or have a dream where he sticks his dagger in me. It's just that it feels so tacky to have a dream where you love your analyst, it makes him feel small and weak, like a good boy. I say, 'Without your dagger?' (He used to say his mother wanted him as a 'good little boy, with a shiny face and a little tie'.)

He smiled and said 'Probably'. It makes him feel on the spot and he doesn't like it. I say that perhaps he feels some appreciation for me and the work we did yesterday. I thought it pleased him to have the dream, but as soon as he expresses this he persuades himself that he gives in to humiliating and infantilising submission. It's like what he was saying about 'ordinary' sex, which begins with trust and turns into debasement.

He is silent. Something else has happened, he says. On Wednesday he decided to phone L. He supposes he was luxuriating in stupefaction before that, having a go at her in his head for the usual things. But then he phoned her and there was a fault with the line, he couldn't hear properly. Actually it wasn't a fault with the line, it's his phone that is faulty. It's a very old phone. It's a BT phone, it must have been in the flat since it was built, about thirty years ago. Because it's old he could rent it at a very low price. He added, 'You know me, I'm a miser, and that's why I kept it for so long'. But he has decided that he needs to change the phone and he has arranged to get a new one. He supposes that he's telling me that he's not such a miser after all, the dream is also about being less of a miser with his feelings.

While he speaks I realise that thirty years, the age of the faulty phone, is the number of years which have passed since he was 11 or 12 and the beginning of the perverse activities. I draw his attention to this and to the fact that he had spoken about this period in the previous session, maintaining how raw and unprocessed it still was. I say that it's as if he's recognising that he has an old and cheap telephone which distorts communication between me and him, just as when he changes his feeling of appreciation for the analysis into a situation where he's being coerced into submission. These are old feelings and they come cheap, it's so easy to summon them. I add that the reference to history is both a reference to his insistence that it's his history which shaped him, but also to the fact that time has passed, the analysis has a history, and things can actually change and move.

He says yes, all his life he has been dreaming of having a proper woman, and now that he has one, it's ironic he spends his time thinking perhaps he's better off on his own. The session continued with a better sense of contact and my overall feeling is that the movement from Thursday continues.

The movement isn't linear, even if there is perhaps less 'shoving it all back'. The tension in the session is between a 'proper' relationship with his object and the anxieties which this entails, and a distorted one. The ordinary feelings of warmth and relief undergo various transformations, which carry an element of sexualised excitement, and ultimately avoid real contact. There is the persecutory 'don't let yourself love anybody, because they will suck you dry', the tacky and sugary 'falling in love with your analyst', the humiliating masochistic submission. The distortion also affects the way my interpretations are received, and I think is the equivalent of the smearing, where something good gets smeared and changed into something dirty. As the session progresses, though, C becomes aware of the distortion, and also of how easy and emotionally 'cheap' it is to use his old 'telephone' (a direct line to the grievances of his warped past) because it prevents proper understanding. I have presented these sessions not because they lead to a major breakthrough, but because they illustrate the painstaking and discontinuous nature of the work with this patient.

## Conclusion

Money-Kyrle (1971) sees perversions as deriving from the conflict between recognition and misrecognition of what he calls the facts of life. He talks about the essential link between the quality of the relationship with the breast and the successive capacity to recognise the goodness of parental intercourse. If the breast has been recognised as the supremely good object, it will be easier for the child 'to conceptualise his parents' intercourse as a supremely creative act', which in turn will mitigate the feelings of jealousy and exclusion of the Oedipus complex. Perversion, on the other hand (he uses here Meltzer's (1996) ideas) 'begins with the misrecognition of the baby's own bottom as the spurious substitute for the breasts, which have been forgotten'. This confusion of the baby's bottom with the mother's breast can become a substitute not only for the lost relationship with the breast but also for parental intercourse. It is the mechanism of projective identification which leads to this confusion, short-circuiting problems of loss and separateness and the possibility of working them through in the depressive position. Money-Kyrle's concept of misrecognition, as a central mechanism in perversion, is related, as Steiner (1993) points out, to the Freudian (1927), notion of disavowal which allows the fetishist to hold two contradictory versions of reality, as a way of defending from the anxiety of castration, and, as the recent literature on fetishism (Greenacre 1970) points out, from anxieties about the relationship with and separation from the primary object. It could be said that C turned to his bottom as a narcissistic fetish, a spurious substitute for the lost good object, into which he could withdraw to avoid the difficult reality of relationships, attacking the existence of a good parental intercourse, and claiming the superiority of the substitute. The narcissistic nature of the bottom fetish is well described by the 'head up his arse' image with its physically impossible contortionism, which I think evokes the primitive, omnipotent connotations of the idealised anal sphincter, the closed magic ring described by Glover (1938) and Shengold (1988, 1995).

I have tried to show how C used analysis in a fetishistic way to protect himself from the reality of his relationship to his analyst and his objects and from the thinking about these relationships. Since the fetish was used to misrepresent the psychic reality of difference and separateness it was difficult for C to have an analysis which generated new meaning and easier for him to rely on the fixed, repetitive narcissistic closure of his anality, which transformed meaning into an undifferentiated mass. I have focused on the nature of the attack on meaning, the smearing and its sexualisation, as it unfolded in the transference, and I have used my patient's words, luxuriating in stupefaction, to describe the addictive quality of this process.

I hope I have also been able to show how it was possible to break through the rigidity and the addictiveness of the perverse organisation and its reliance on sexualised hatred. When this happened, as I have shown with the material from the two sessions, the anal sterility gave way to a different kind of connection, and C regained access to his humanity and his capacity to love.

By focusing on the clinical interaction and on how the perversion came alive in the character structure and in the transference, I haven't been able to discuss the many theoretical contributions which are relevant to my topic. A question which also remains to be addressed is why C chose a spurious substitute. I think C had a mother who probably could not contain the frightening, fragmenting intensity which emotions carried for him, and who used C as an object of her projections. On the other hand, there was, on C's part, a hateful intolerance of situations of need, separateness, dependence, which meant that he could only exist inside his object, and real contact with an object separate from himself remained so intensely persecutory that it had to be abolished.

C used to say, 'I am all right with people as long as they are not there', as long, that is, as he could, ensconced in his omnipotent anal refuge, control and abolish the reality of otherness. To help him to be 'all right with people when they are there' remains the unfinished task of his analysis.

## References


Chasseguet-Smirgel, J. (1985) *Creativity and Perversion*, London: Free Association Books.

Freud, S. (1927) 'Fetishism', SE 21: 149–157.

Glover, E. (1938) 'A note on idealisation', *On the Early Development of the Mind*, London: Imago (1956).

Greenacre, P. (1970) 'Fetishism', *Sexual Deviation*, 3rd edn, I. Rosen (ed.), Oxford: Oxford University Press (1996).

McDougall, J. (1978) *Plea for a Measure of Abnormality*, New York: International Universities Press, revised edition, New York: Brunner/Mazel (1992).

—— (1995) *The Many Faces of Eros*, London: Free Association Books.

Meltzer, D. (1996) 'The relationship of anal masturbation to projective identification', *International Journal of Psychoanalysis*, 47: 335–342.

Money-Kyrle, R. (1971) 'The aim of psychoanalysis', *International Journal of Psychoanalysis*, 52: 103–106; reprinted in *The Collected Papers of Roger Money-Kyrle*, Perthshire: Clunie Press (1978).

Shengold, L. (1988) *Halo in the Sky Defence: Observation on Anality and Defence*, New Haven, CT: Yale University Press (1992).

—— (1995 ) 'The ring of the narcissist', *International Journal of Psychoanalysis*, 76: 1205–1213.

Steiner, J. (1993) *Psychic Retreats: Pathological Organizations in Psychotic, Neurotic and Borderline Patients*, London: Routledge.

Stoller, R. (1976) *Perversion: The Erotic Form of Hatred*, New York: Pantheon.

—— (1985) *Observing the Erotic Imagination*, New Haven, CT: Yale University Press.

# DISCUSSION OF GIGLIOLA FORNARI SPOTO'S CHAPTER

*Martha Papadakis*

Gigliola describes beautifully and with compassion in her introduction a patient presenting himself as if he is in love with his bottom at the moment he returns to his much needed analyst after the weekend absence. At the same time he makes a parody of his analyst full of herself like a bottom and purveys the two of them as such a couple of buttocks infatuated with each other. Gigliola is struggling with the mindless fusion he is trying by this means to attain and the perverse function it has. This is a man without friends, denuded of sexual experience, locked in an internal sadomasochistic faecal couple (the walrus consuming the seal), who has an analyst bringing this to light and understanding for the first time.

In the first dream I agree with Gigliola, the patient is conveying a hopeful view of the transference and the parental couple. Maybe more could be made of the unconscious insight in the patient contained in his description. Apparently this concert should have been in London (an interminable analysis?), but actually no, it takes place where he came from and his parents live and this is also linked to the fact that his new relationship is facing C with quitting London and losing the analysis. He is mad with fury (the violent 'shut up' in the dream) at the parents talking, but undeterred by the different parts of him represented by 'all the people in the hall', they continue their talk and this must also stand for a stronger internal couple in C. This creative couple is surely the basis of his development in his analysis, despite the subsequent attempt he makes to derogate the analytic currency of talking into chit-chat and shit-shat consequent upon his envy.

Important and central in this relationship is the great improvement which is taking place as a result of analysis and C is frightened. Gigliola attends to the claustrophobic aspect of his being trapped in the dungeon of a raw deal; maybe a sort of heterosexual rough trade, in the marriage he is contemplating in which his underlying fear is not having changed enough. His 'stupidity' actively restricts and distracts him, I thought, from the recognition of his destructiveness that his improvement makes him cognisant of and fragmentation seems to be the manner by which this is attained. He has done bad things and can do them again to parents; women, men and children must come into this too. 'Sexual' (life) feelings everybody has but as he says 'the problem is how you are going to express them', whether you are 11 or 41 years old. Orchids are, in every sense, symbolic of something precious and fragile in the good contact of people with each other which can be destroyed.

This analysis may appear effortlessly to be transforming C from walrus to human being but much work is going into the shift from an anal fixation in dominance and control to the genitality of sexuality and loss and all the associated emotions. I think the patient knows this and is frightened of what in himself attacks 'the painstaking and discontinuous work' of the analyst that makes real demands in the countertransference to compensate for and repair the deficit in the mother's original capacity to introject beside the contributions of C.

The narrative of a succeeding analysis brings the inevitable problem of the creativity of the analyst for the patient. A problem the patient is confronted with when the object is there and allowed to be, and presumably does not have when they are not as C cheerfully remarks saying he is all right when people are not there. I think presence of the object brings with it awareness of what envy and possessiveness can do. It is a poignant discovery for C that finding a greater capacity to love also means leaving, and losing the analysis for a real marriage in a real world; a tender and painful negotiation that C, with the help of his analyst, is finding he can make.

## 8

# BEYOND LEARNING THEORY

*David Taylor*

> What kind of fool are you? Do you realise that by your violent and unphilosophical kicking of the door you have precipitated the abortion of a discovery?' [A student's voice from an upper-storey window of the Thinking Shop to the man knocking rudely below]
>
> (Aristophanes, *The Clouds*)

In 'Three essays on the theory of sexuality' Freud used a quotation from Goethe's Faust, 'From Heaven, across the world, to Hell' to convey how the highest and the lowest motives closely accompany each other in the sphere of sexuality. The same is true of the contradictions in our motives and attitudes to learning. It is not uncommon for a person to have the deepest and most extreme hatred or fear of knowledge and learning while still loving them for their own sakes. Indeed this coexistence is to be expected as a relatively usual state of affairs. Unfortunately, the potential for these contradictions can lead on to difficulties with learning, especially with new learning from experience.

It is well known, for example, that in some borderline patients, difficulties with learning from experience can be especially marked. In their lives there is always the potential for a bind because the underlying anxieties are often unmentalisable and, at the same time, what is needed for recognising and investigating them isn't functioning too well, either. In their treatments borderline patients can become very dependent upon various forms of acting in which they employ in order to feel contained, supported or liked. When these defences become strained the ensuing disturbance is often externalised and what was acted in gets acted out. The way that the anxieties and feelings which lie behind these behaviours cannot be experienced in terms of thought or feeling can seem strange or eerie. It is as if there is to be known a mental state with an undeniable substantiality but with few identifying features. Instead the individual after due pause responds with some – often repetitive – evacuative action.

There have been many important contributions to the psychoanalytic understanding of this well-recognised phenomenon. Bion argues that when the mother fails (i.e. her reverie fails) then the infant's capacity for tolerating frustration is being doubly stressed. The breakdown of the mental link with the mother means that the infant has to tolerate a greater amount of frustration because its needs are unmet. But at the same time the infant's capacity to tolerate the frustration of its belief in thought as a means of maintaining its link with an object is also being deeply tested. Clinically, it does often seem as if, in respect of certain areas of mental life, the test arising from internal and external sources has been too great for the infantile ego, and the capacity for tolerating mental experience hasn't been able to develop.

Difficulties with knowledge and learning are present to some extent in everyone. Understanding these sometimes subtle manifestations in patients in general will be helpful, as well as contributing to our comprehension of the difficulties encountered with more borderline patients. In this chapter I will be discussing two patients to illuminate the way in which obstacles to new learning can be expressed in the analytic situation. Appreciating the nature of the patient's current ability to learn from experience in this way may also prove helpful diagnostically and in understanding the nature of the therapeutic work likely to be required.

The two cases described are contrasted. In many respects neither of the patients was ill. In one the need to control what could be experienced, what could happen or be meaningfully addressed in the analytic situation was very sustained and organised. I will try to show how this control operated and something of its significance, and to indicate why its relinquishment or alteration was so difficult for the patient. In the analytic situation this patient's defences took the form of a pervasive acting in whose purpose was to obviate, or fend off, the possibility of knowledge and insight. Verbal, apparently symbolic forms of communication in fact turned out to be concrete operations – actions upon the other – subtly disguised or not, as the case might be. These manipulations were intended, among other things, to keep underlying issues meaningless.

Considering patients' communications in this way provides a means of discerning the uncomfortable and complicated relationship they (and often we) have with the professed analytic aim of 'knowing thyself' and with learning from analytic experience. Since the analytic relationship is supposed to be based upon the idea of getting insight, it follows that it is a threat to patients whose defences are more than usually based upon not knowing. However, the material from the second patient indicates how an open attitude in analysis, and therefore to learning, is still a complicated business, even for relatively well-balanced individuals. In anyone, any new knowledge or position involves some disturbance arising, in part, from our ambivalence towards knowledge.

## Conceptual background

Insight and awareness have always been central to psychoanalysis. Freud and Breuer's original idea about the cure of hysterical symptoms was that by becoming aware of certain pathogenic experiences and affects, the somatisation that was expressed in the symptoms would no longer be necessary. From the beginning they encountered strong resistances to free association, and therefore to enlightenment. Freud returned again and again to these resistances and his ultimate conclusions concerned the deepest layers of motivation. The observation that the compulsion to repeat so frequently overrode the individual's efforts to learn and change made a deep impression upon Freud. Instead of learning or developing we repeat and we undo.

In spite of the range and penetration of Freud's work, ideas about knowledge and learning still remained marginal to the main theories of psychoanalysis. Ferenczi (1913, 1926) partly remedied this position in two important papers. He likened the reality principle, the ego's capacity to delay the resort to immediate gratification, to the then modern invention of the reckoning machine, trying to suggest how the ego needs to recognise, to grapple and struggle with, to come to terms with the various situations of reality – to reach a reckoning with them. However, reaching a reckoning with internal and external realities is easier said than done

In the 1920s, at around the same time as Ferenczi's second paper, Klein (who was much influenced by Ferenczi's ideas) came, through her analyses of young children, to the view that the mother's person and her body are the primary focus for the infant's most powerful instinctual desires. Among these she included a primary impulse to know: the epistemophilic instinct. In 'The early stages of the Oedipus complex' (Klein 1928), she described the child as experiencing this intense wish to know at a time when the fruits of knowing are, as she puts it, 'an onrush of problems and questions' resulting in

> One of the most bitter grievances we come across in the unconscious . . . [which] is that these many overwhelming questions, which are apparently only partly conscious and even when conscious cannot yet be expressed in words remain unanswered. Another reproach follows hard upon this, namely, that the child could not understand words and speech. Thus his first questions go back beyond the beginnings of his understanding of speech. In analysis both these grievances give rise to an enormous amount of hate.
>
> (Klein 1928: 188)

This situation, with its intense sense of injury and rivalry stimulated by the growing knowledge of the mother, by her body, by her possession of the father and his penis, and by the babies in fantasy or in reality growing inside her, is revived by the analytic situation. This understanding helps us to appreciate why, in spite of all our best intentions, hatred and sadism are often very close and menacing companions to knowledge and why they so often arise when we need to be able to tolerate not already knowing and having to learn instead.

As the title *Learning from Experience* indicates, Bion (1962) placed thinking and learning processes as central, while the developmental role of concern about the effects of the instincts receded into the background. Klein investigated the relations between love, hate and reparation whereas Bion investigated those between love, hate and knowledge. He suggested the term 'beta elements' to describe mental contents not amenable for dream thought (and therefore not for general thought or learning either). Although beta elements may arise in the course of development because of external or traumatic happenings it is essential to appreciate that they are mental objects. They are unprocessed internal psychological reaction states which are experienced as indigestible, but real. Less advanced than repressed memories, they can only be used for a primitive kind of thinking consisting of a manipulation of things. Projective identification lends itself as a way of dealing with these objects because it permits their evacuation rather than there being a need for a symbolic or conceptual apparatus in the mind of the subject using words and thoughts. Such concrete operations can serve to rid the individual of 'accretions of stimuli' which are thereby kept meaningless.

Bion's understanding was based on patients who were psychotic, confused or thought disordered, but its relevance to the psychotic part of the normal personality and to human psychology in general was clear. His understanding of certain types of actions (he compared them to scowls) as a means used by the psychotic part of the personality to get rid of something can be linked to Joseph's (1983) influential developments of technique. Her extension of the notion of acting in involves the analyst's paying attention to the nuances of the patient–analyst relationship in order to appreciate the significance of the many ways in which the analysand 'nudges' or 'manipulates' the analyst to take up this or that position. This technical development, and Joseph's associated understanding, has become a powerful analytic tool for enabling patients to contact primitive anxieties which are often dealt with by action-based ways of relating and communicating. Subsequently, a whole tradition of analysts have used these ideas of Bion and Joseph in the further working out of psychotic and borderline states or areas of the personality (see for example, Britton *et al.* 1989; Feldman and Spillius 1989; O'Shaughnessy 1992, 1993; Steiner 1993; Segal 1981; Anderson 1992). Riesenberg-Malcolm (1993), in a paper on *As-If* states has explicitly linked this way of operating in an analysis with a failure to learn.

In his original paper, Ferenczi (1926) had commented upon the disparity which then existed between the abundance of psychoanalytic theories about instinctual life and the relative lack of attention to the phenomena of intellectual functioning and judgement. One of the reasons for this was the then predominant psychoanalytic view that instincts and their conflicts were the really decisive issues in the personality. But we should recollect that the attempt to link two main strands of psychological life, the physical and the mental – no less than the difficult task of reconciling them in life itself – has been a major problem in philosophy and the natural sciences. Psychoanalysis is no exception. Naturally so, since these problems with integrating reason and passion are ubiquitous and versions of them are often central to the treatment situation.

For instance, an understanding intervention by an analyst may serve to remind a patient of good feelings towards the analyst when the patient is also angry and attacking because of a forthcoming break. Such an intervention may lead the patient towards concern for the analyst (and for what he represents for the patient). Interpretations of this sort may be felt by patients as expressing the analyst's attitude towards them. At the infantile level they may be felt to correspond to parental care giving – feeding, cleaning, holding and loving – or, on other occasions, to seducing, being angry, neglecting, or indeed to the entire relationship to the parental figure. When viewed in such a light, the specific meaningful content of interpretations may be much less important to the patient than the relationship which the manner of interpretation is evoking. For analytic work in this mode to be effective we are relying upon the patient's capacity for symbolism to realise that at some level the psychoanalytic relationship is not the wished-for care one hopefully receives as a child, nor the wished relationship itself, while it may need to be reminiscent of that care to be able to do its job.

However, there are other times in analyses when the content of the understanding, the knowledge, the facts of the matter, the reality – even when unpleasant – are what have become important to the patient rather than these sensuous evocations of certain analytic exchanges. At these times it is likely that the personality will be divided by emotional forces marshalled for and against further understanding. The reason for this is that something has been realised or recognised.

## Clinical material

The first patient, a man in his early forties, was rather happily married with three teenage children. He had sought analysis as he felt there were serious and worsening problems in his work as a scientist. He felt a gradually growing loss of interest in his investigations, along with a lack of enjoyment in life generally. While he had no major obsessional symptoms, there was a sense of his increasing constriction and adherence to the ordinary routine and this did have an obsessional feel to it. His working class family had had a difficult time during his early years, but they were also caring and closely identified with each other. At first sight his mother was the somewhat steadier character, while his father seemed more obviously vulnerable and emotionally precarious. When the patient was a teenager, his father suffered a breakdown from which he only partially recovered. As a young man Mr G was obviously intelligent and creative but a little unsettled. In his early twenties while doing a research doctorate he met and married his Argentine wife, who worked in a similar field.

A few months after starting his analysis Mr G revealed that many years before he entered analysis, he had gone through a period of acting out which had involved a series of minor thefts. This behaviour – not subsequently repeated – had nevertheless continued to trouble him and it contributed to a general feeling of unease that he had about himself. It seemed to have been a response to a time in his life when he had felt on the verge of abandonment.

At the time he first told me of the stealing it was a relief to me, because of the way it threw light upon a disturbing pattern which had already become established within his treatment. Gradually I came to realise that this pattern was of great importance even though I was often invited or pressurised to disregard it. The pattern was that Mr G could seldom let a session pass without saying things which were intentionally either consciously or unconsciously incomplete. Also it seemed important that I should realise, but with uncertainty, that this was so. Often these matters would concern triangular situations. For instance, he would invite me to make some comment about a third person, at times putting considerable pressure upon me to do so. Or they would involve his reporting some contact with another person where he would not reveal to me all that he knew, or all that had gone on. Every time I was to know, or rather half-know, that this was so. The knot was made tighter and more complicated because I felt that if I spoke of these issues he would feel triumphantly that his secret communication and control had, in fact, worked. On the other hand if I did not speak of these matters the cagey atmosphere created would become the proof of his successful control. Quite often I would feel caught up in these procedures. More often than not I felt in danger of being tricked into losing my analytic balance upon the tightrope he had set up, and I had to be especially careful about my phrasing to avoid falling.

In the construction of these situations it seemed that Mr G always needed to be playing the part of the person who was in control of the other and the one who knew more. He often tried to make me curious. I was to be the one who felt the need for the resolution of these tantalising uncertainties. He placed himself in positions of unavailability designed to capture my interest in him. He avoided like the plague any analytic situations where he did not know in advance what I might say or think.

However, in one session he had spoken with more freedom and seriousness than usual about how awkward he felt about his tendency to be uninvolved in family matters. In particular, his middle son, a rather troubled and sometimes depressed 12 year old, difficult to approach and talk to, is a source of worry in the family. Mr G told me in a very different way than usual of a conversation he'd had with his son, who had told him that he had realised that he (the son) is easily upset by some of his friends whenever he is going to have to do something that's making him anxious. I had been impressed by Mr G's thoughtful ability to be more open to his son's difficulties and more genuinely involved in taking steps to help him sort them out. Although he hadn't commented upon this altered stance, when I directed our attention to it he readily agreed that it was so. His different, more robust, more empirical capacity had stayed quite vividly in my mind and I felt it had made an impression upon him too.

The next day he began the session saying that he had come from a meeting with a consultant whom he and his wife had seen to discuss some possible therapy for his son. He went on to talk about how he had spoken with his wife about money, another area in which he keeps himself uninvolved. They want their son to have therapy. However, since they already had financial difficulties, how on earth were they going to manage it?

The patient had started speaking in a flat, restrained way, and as he continued his voice had taken on a self-satisfied quality, one which always made me feel that he wasn't being entirely straightforward. I became increasingly struck by the combination of the flatness with a kind of manipulative passivity, which made me think that the patient knew a bit more than he was saying. For instance, the problems about money that he referred to were well known to both of us; there was something almost ostentatious about the way he cast himself in the role of the one who neglected taking responsibility for attending to finances. I felt that he already knew that what was required from him was taking more responsibility for his son's difficulties as he had seemed to do the day before. I repeatedly feel acted upon in ways like this by Mr G and believe that he is occupying, and 'knowingly' so, a position where he can provoke reactions in me about which I can do nothing. With this manoeuvre he seems to feel that he is at the centre of my attention. If he loses this position he is prey to the kinds of anxieties which led to the acting out he'd done when he was younger.

In this particular session I stayed relatively quiet for a while and I thought that Mr G began to sense that I wasn't rising to the bait. He said it had become obvious to him too that something was going on and he said that he wasn't entirely 'in' what he was saying and he wondered if he was doing something tricky. While this seemed true it also felt like a way of reaching a compromise with me and what work might be done in the session. I drew his attention to the mixed way in which he was speaking, trying to emphasise the flatness as something that we hadn't previously looked at or formulated. I reminded him of how we both knew that when he had been to visit a potential therapist for his son that he had been more genuinely active in his enquiries, and he knew that this type of attitude was what was required. I thought he also knew that he was capable of it but the problem was that to have this capacity out in the open here involved him in relinquishing this belief that he could control a place in my mind with behaviour he described as tricky. Mr G then said that he hated the fact that his son needed help. I thought that he did really mind about his son and so I agreed with him, and said that he also hated the need to open things up within himself in his analysis. Again I reminded Mr G of his talk with his son, how it reflected an alive and elucidating attitude, quite impressive between a father and son, but that nothing was to be made of this.

Some real shift gradually took place in Mr G's analysis but always in the face of a powerful tendency to re-establish the previous controlling operations. Then my comments would once again be evidence of my complicity or as unconvincing denials rather than interpretations.

At this time Mr G was still trying to continue a situation where a kind of self-satisfaction was dominant rather than the more active empirical learning that he had begun to be capable of. This background sense of unjustified self-satisfaction is, I think, something that comes from an area of omnipotence in his personality. It is linked to his understandable wish that things can be easily put right.

This narcissistic self-satisfaction was dependent upon his achieving a place in the centre of my mind. It always required a lot of analytic work for me to free myself sufficiently to achieve a position of genuine equipoise, from which real interpretations could be formulated. Often my efforts would lead to long, stubborn or stuporose silences from him. If pushed, he would sometimes openly express a hostile contemptuous attitude in which he would seek to diminish me and deride what had been realised about him. Typically, after some kind of face-off he would bring powerful dreams full of violent but telling imagery, but often the opportunity they appeared to offer to deepen understanding would be used as a bait to trick me and buy me off. It is hard for me to overstate the extent of the sustained and organised methods used by Mr G to oppose or undermine our analytic endeavours. Some of his more attacking responses were aimed at the emerging anxiety, pain and conflict previously defended against while others seemed to be more aimed at the knowledge itself : what he had realised, his knowing and being different as well as my knowing and being different.

Gradually, it became possible to build up a picture of what had prompted this powerful defence against the analytic method, and indeed against any new learning in general. It seemed to me that in a restricted area, Mr G behaved like a tantalising, withholding and rather tormenting parent. He aimed to be the one in control, the one who was needed rather than needing, the manipulator of the Oedipal triangle, while I, and many others, would be the frustrated or excited and curious children whose unlawful, humiliating needs and desires were always on the edge of exposure. Whenever Mr G lost his hold on the position he tried to maintain in the analysis he would be precipitated into a resentful disturbance consisting of intense jealousy and a fear that the child he had now become would be neglected in an unendurable way. It became increasingly clear that this fear stemmed in part from both parents' disturbance. Not just his father's, but something about his mother which had also become more evident: she had many tantalising, disturbing qualities. Mention of these did not form part of the day-to-day currency of the sessions but they gradually became clear, and it seemed possible that as an infant Mr G had been exposed to many unbearably difficult emotional situations. As soon as he had become psychologically capable of doing so he seemed to have projected this vulnerability into his younger siblings rather in the way he sought to do in the analysis. It should not be forgotten, however, that Mr G was also ambitious, envious and jealous and it was always hard to sort out whether these qualities were the primary causes of his difficulties or secondarily magnified in reaction to the parents' tantalising qualities.

There are other analyses where defences against the ordinary shifts and alterations arising out of analytic work are less organised and obtrusive. In these it is possible to see clearly both some of the structure of the still strong reactions that are encountered, as well as some of the ego capacities that begin to develop as new awareness becomes possible. For example, Miss A, a lawyer in her late twenties, the child of religious and restrictive parents, had had trouble with a number of unintegrated feelings. As her experience of the treatment deepened, more openly possessive wishes emerged. These feelings had a sexual component which was very embarrassing to Miss A, but to me they seemed to originate at least as much from infantile yearnings previously held at arm's length by her rather correct restrained manner. One day Miss A was particularly embarrassed and very stirred up by having had an explicitly sexual dream in which she was in bed lying next to a thinly disguised version of her analyst.

I interpreted that she must feel that I was being inconsistent in a contradictory way, simultaneously keeping at a distance and stirring-up, while not properly appreciating her growing involvement, susceptibility and vulnerability to the analysis in which she wants more, but in confused ways and where she cannot have what she wants completely. For the first three-quarters of the following day's session the patient made no mention of any of this, although I knew she had been very agitated by it. Towards the end she mentioned a file she'd been looking at which contained allegations relating to the misconduct of a barrister colleague remotely known to her. Struck by the way she quickly passed over the reference to the file, I interrupted her and said that I thought the file had brought up the awkward and confused issue of sexual wishes which had so bothered her yesterday, and that she wished to close that file.

Uncharacteristically, and in a way that I didn't expect, Miss A reacted strongly to my statement. She objected that I'd interrupted her and then, paying no attention to the content of what I'd said, she became very upset, and was silent for quite a long time. Then she said she didn't know what I was saying and why I'd interrupted her. She said she felt confused and that she didn't know what was going on. She felt tied up in a corner. Her reaction was very intense and she conveyed vividly the impression of someone perplexed, troubled and injured. I was puzzled because I didn't feel I'd interrupted in an unkind or unfriendly way but I began to wonder if I'd misread the situation. I made a number of interpretations suggesting that she'd taken up an injured, masochistic position which meant that any guilt or embarrassment she had previously been feeling could now instead be left with me who had injured her. However these and other comments seemed only to deepen the hole that had been dug and the patient left the session at the end unhappily and without any resolution.

The following day Miss A told me that she'd felt terribly troubled after the session. She still didn't know or understand what had happened. However, she now felt a little bit better because she'd taken the morning off and had been able to treat herself by going to one of her sister's restaurants and having a nice meal. For the first time, although still only half audibly, she mentioned the name of the chain of restaurants, which her sister owned and had very successfully built up. Previously, in the analysis it had been noticeable how she had avoided naming this.

I thought that something of my interpretations of the previous day had, in fact, been heard by Miss A. This and the passage of time had freed her sufficiently to be able to go into a previously forbidden territory, namely, the analyst's possible interest in her successful sister and her restaurants. There was some dream material to confirm this idea. In one part of the dream, the analyst was angry with Miss A for making claims and 'didn't like the fact that she noticed absolutely everything'. I thought that this patient's confusion following my interruption had functioned to prevent her from tolerating her emerging feelings of desire. (In the dream there were also images of much desired strawberries and cream.) I had emerged out of her confusion no longer as an object of desire but as an accusing and attacking superego figure. She felt my interruption to be evidence of my inability to tolerate her capacity to notice everything, or of my inability to bear guilt or responsibility, instead projecting it into her with my subsequent interpreting. In the session it was possible to work with this. Her first, open use of the name of the sister's restaurants could be acknowledged. This could lead on to naming her more realistic awareness of the analyst as someone who also had a life outside the consulting room. The patient was able to be a little freer and more openly curious as a result.

## Conclusion

In any psychoanalytic inquiry into knowledge and learning the Oedipus complex is going to be central. The power of the myth's thematic content is interwoven with the emergence of knowledge and the problems of bearing that knowledge. The rivalry for the possession of the mother between Oedipus and Laius is paralleled by conflict over whether to know or not to know between Oedipus and the blind seer, Tiresias.

The Oedipus complex is generally thought of in terms of its characteristic phantasies, conflicts and object relations forming part of the contents of the mind, but when Bion (1963) considered the Oedipus myth he suggested that some of its *dramatis personae* can be seen as personifications of functions of the mind. Tiresias can be viewed as representing intuition and percipience. Oedipus is self-righteous, proud and hubristically curious. Furthermore, the Oedipus configuration, by representing, organising and motivating key mental functions and capacities, can be seen as one of the ego's means of understanding and of inquiry. It is a dynamic template through which the ego engages with itself and with the world. Looked at in this way, the Oedipus configuration is a part of the emotional/cognitive apparatus essential for knowing and learning, just as eyes and visual pathways are crucial to the processes of seeing.

It is not that we walk around with a copy of Sophocles' text installed in the brain. We all have a personal and individual myth with certain general commonalties and this arises out of our early experiences, internal and external. The individual ego with its survival driven aim of developing some kind of functioning apparatus grows out of responses to these experiences. How this functioning apparatus ends up will vary greatly from individual to individual, but becoming social necessarily involves correlating or reconciling these personal myths with the social myth of the group.

In the clinical material I have described just a few of the many issues involved in achieving a discovering and knowing function. With Miss A, the second patient, being able to contain elements of an Oedipus configuration is connected with the development of some ability to know and learn, even though the exercise of this often leads to difficulty. Her step in the direction of greater acknowledgement of her wishes and desires is followed by an attack on her new insight, in which she becomes confused and perplexed. In the session she felt that the problem came from the analyst who had interrupted her. In her dream, she wonders if the analyst figure was threatened by the fact that she notices everything and thinks that he doesn't want her to claim any rights of possession.

It is true to some extent that parents are threatened by the curiosity of their child. The dawning realisation that they have a life, and a sexual life, beyond the knowledge and permission of the child can lead directly to the conviction or suspicion that they have committed an offence, or a crime, or that they have let one down and they are now seen for what they truly are – intrinsically unsound and unreliable. Many of us start our Oedipal investigations like this, with the assumption that our parents are guilty until proved innocent. Of course, the generosity of spirit with which different personalities approach these investigations varies. There are also variations in the degree to which these initial assumptions of trust or suspicion can be corrected in the light of actual evidence.

Another developmentally important capacity connected with the recognition of the relationship between the parents is the ability to recognise the independence of other people's thought. They think and realise without our consent or knowledge and they engage with matters that we haven't conceived or dreamt of. The older generation says to the younger 'before you were thought of', when they talk about something that happened before the child was born. They thought of you, not you of them. And what we uncover in our Oedipal investigations existed without requiring our discovery: discovery is not the same as creation. Bion spelt out that this also operates at the level of our experience of thought itself, where the idea is that thoughts come before our thinking of them. A thought coming to us without our explicitly wishing it is very similar to a discovery in or about the external world. Using Ferenczi's analogy, we have to develop something like a reckoning machine in order to deal with our thoughts as well as our discoveries.

In contrast to Miss A, the other patient, Mr G, was not able to contain an Oedipal configuration. He was holding on to the position of being one of the primary, parental objects while the analyst had Mr G's repudiated experience of being the watching and acted-upon child. As a consequence Mr G not only had little real interest in investigating anything which might disturb him, he also had little capacity to do so. In their place was a self-satisfaction associated with his identification with the parent, a self-satisfaction derived from his assumption of a spurious form of carnal knowledge. More generally, he had a tendency to promote a kind of sensuality, putting it forward as a superior rival, falsely opposed to the inherent awkwardness of learning. This was a narcissistic state in which there was no need for any development. Prototypically, the wish of the narcissist is to look the same as they did at an ideal time. Appearances should be kept the same and unchanging. Mr G was trying to maintain his objects on an artificially repaired basis.

Any learning which did take place constituted a threat to Mr G's narcissism because it revealed him as a being with wishes and needs. In the analysis, a situation was established which was permitted to alter only superficially. The analyst and patient could sometimes play alternate parts, but it was always as actors in the same play. Whenever something did disturb the status quo, steps were rapidly taken to nullify this. Mr G often behaved in ways which suggested that he really hoped to be able to maintain his position until he died. Then things could change, but he wouldn't have to be around to survive the turbulence.

What lay behind Mr G's defensive organisation? Rosenfeld (1971) showed how these narcissistic structures are often a defence against powerful destructive forces within the personality and there was much of this in Mr G. Changes in his defensive organisation released much more open expressions of aggression, envy, jealousy and rivalry. He also feared the pain connected with the realisation that his infantile suffering had actually happened, and with this came anxieties connected with accepting the reality of his parents and their problems.

Some of this Mr G could get in touch with, but to a large extent he could not know what his feared experiences were, nor how they could be endured or modified. Mr G's forms of acting in, his apparently verbal, apparently conceptually based communications seemed to deal with a set of primitive feelings that he could not know, holding them at bay by evacuating them into his objects.

These states could be regarded as beta-elements. In my view, unmentalised and unmentalisable psychological states lie behind the kind of continuous acting in encountered in such patients.

Understanding and appreciating the nature of the stresses to which the infantile capacity for thought has been exposed, combined with an awareness of the individual's current valency towards thought itself, are important aspects of any modifying process. For instance, in borderline patients, where these states are common, we know that many will have experienced traumatic or disorganised upbringings and that there is a high incidence of generational and boundary confusions, including incestuous family relationships, or sexual or physical abuse. Mental illness in the parents, loss through murder or suicide, or less overt difficulties with parents whose particular disharmonious qualities pose especial problems, can also be important factors causing 'unmentalisable' states. The mother who betrays motherhood in some way, or the father who betrays fatherhood, often lead to the failure or confusion of natural categories of expectation because they have been met by an experience that can only be called anti-good.

Obviously, the internal objects connected with these gross adversities do not lend themselves to differentiating between good and bad experiences, or good and bad objects, and they present major problems for the development of thought. They make it more likely that the individual will have unmentalised and unmentalisable states and anxieties. In these situations there is the likelihood of a bind. The underlying anxieties are unmentalised and unmentalisable, but, at the same time, what is needed for recognising and investigating them, including the Oedipus configuration, isn't functional as a means of investigation. The individual concerned seems to feel – if at this level they can be said to 'feel' at all – that the continued operation of experience only results in something that seems to be beyond endurable experience.

Although these predicaments are the rule in borderline patients, perhaps they are present in a less extreme form in most of us. They arise out of experiences that have presented issues that are insoluble in the person's development, but it is only partly because of that that it is not possible for them to be fully experienced, borne, put into words and worked through. In addition, the forces which have been organised against thinking, knowing and learning mean that the individual has been unable to develop the ego equipment required to be able to experience, investigate and learn. Being sensitive to the acting in which holds at bay these primitive forms of mental life is essential to enable the patient to make contact with them so that development can occur.

## References


Anderson, R. (ed.) (1992) *Clinical Lectures on Klein and Bion*, London: Routledge.

Bion, W.R. (1962) *Learning from Experience*, Maresfield Reprints, London: Karnac (1984).

—— (1963) *Elements of Psychoanalysis*, London: Heinemann, reprinted by Karnac.

Britton, R.S., Feldman, M. and O'Shaughnessy, E. (1989) *The Oedipus Complex Today*, London: Karnac.

Feldman, M. and Spillius, E.Bott. (1989) Introductions, *Psychic Equilibrium and Psychic Change: Selected Papers of Betty Joseph*, M. Feldman and E. Bott Spillius (eds), London: Routledge.

Ferenczi, S. (1913) 'Stages in the development of the sense of reality', *First Contributions to Psychoanalysis*, London: Hogarth Press (1952).

—— (1926) 'The problem of the acceptance of unpleasant ideas: advances in knowledge of the sense of reality', *International Journal of Psychoanalysis*, 7: 312–323; reprinted in *Further Contributions to Psychoanalysis*, London: Hogarth Press (1950).

Freud, S. (1905) 'Three essays on the theory of sexuality', SE 7.

Joseph, B. (1983) 'On understanding and not understanding: some technical issues', *International Journal of Psychoanalysis*, 64: 291–298; reprinted in *Psychic Equilibrium and Psychic Change: Selected Papers of Betty Joseph*, M. Feldman and E. Bott Spillius (eds), London: Routledge.

Klein, M. (1928) 'The early stages of the Oedipus complex', *The Writings of Melanie Klein*, vol. 1, *Love, Guilt and Reparation and Other Works*, London: Hogarth Press (1975).

O'Shaughnessy, E. (1992) 'Psychosis: not thinking in a bizarre world', *Clinical Lectures on Klein and Bion*, R. Anderson (ed.), London: Routledge (1992).

—— (1993) 'Enclaves and excursions', *International Journal of Psychoanalysis*, 73: 603–611.

Riesenberg-Malcolm, R. (1993) 'As-if: the phenomenon of not learning', *International Journal of Psychoanalysis*, 71: 385–392; reprinted in *On Bearing Unbearable States of Mind*, London: Routledge (1999).

Rosenfeld, H. (1971) 'A clinical approach to the psychoanalytic theory of the life and death instincts: an investigation of the aggressive aspects of narcissism', *International Journal of Psychoanalysis*, 52: 169–178.

Segal, H. (1981) *The Work of Hanna Segal*, New Library of Psychoanalysis, London: Tavistock.

Steiner, J. (1993) *Psychic Retreats: Pathological Organizations of the Personality in Psychotic, Neurotic, and Borderline Patients*, London: Routledge.

## DISCUSSION OF DAVID TAYLOR'S CHAPTER

*Patricia Daniel*

This is a very interesting and carefully worked out clinical elaboration of Bion's idea of the Oedipus complex as a personification of functions of the mind.

Miss A's capacity for tolerating the frustration of thought may be further stressed by the parameters of the analytic situation, with the analyst's stance being, at some level, experienced as restricting and controlling of Miss A's emotional life, especially curiosity and libidinal desires. (Her parents are described as religious and emotionally restricting.)

I wonder if these are represented by the sister's chain of restaurants? Hence her secretiveness about the name of the chain, for to reveal the name might be tantamount to revealing her desires – including for the analysis.

# DISCUSSION OF DAVID TAYLOR'S CHAPTER

## *Priscilla Roth*

This chapter provides a richly textured examination of the difficulties of not-knowing – as these are projected into and experienced by the analyst, and as they are dealt with by the patient. I particularly like David's description of the experience of being Mr G's analyst, repetitively pushed and manipulated into a position in which the patient can feel – indeed can be – in control of him. I thought David's remark early on in the clinical section of the chapter that he had had a feeling of 'relief' when his patient told him about the stealing episodes in his history because it 'threw some light' on a disturbing pattern in the treatment, was telling. The experience of not-knowing is uncomfortable and we are always relieved when we can move out of it, into a position where we think we can 'know' something. This point is described in the later material.

I had some particular thoughts in response to David's comment that 'hatred and sadism are often very close and menacing companions to knowledge and . . . often arise when we need to be able to tolerate not *already* knowing and having to learn instead' (my italics). I have italicised 'already' because its use here implies that eventually one can know, and that the only problem is the pain of waiting in a state of not-yet-knowing and having to learn. But of course one of the most painful situations patients have to face is that they can't ever completely know their object. This is implicit in the chapter, but I thought it worth emphasising – that learning is only ever partial, and particularly learning about another person. What the patient has to bear is not simply that learning takes time, but that it is always partial and incomplete.

As David also suggests, there is always a powerful relationship between the wish to know and the wish to possess, which ultimately means to destroy. At best we can eventually know *about* our objects; we can never fully know them, and this creates painful states of envy and jealousy and the use of defensive manoeuvres to change the situation. Borderline patients often 'know' all sorts of empty things; they often present with a strangely impenetrable knowingness and inadequate curiosity in order never to have to be aware of how partial and incomplete knowing actually is.

Mr G creates a situation in which he controls all his analyst's options. David can do either 'A' or 'B': he can speak about how Mr G leaves him (David) 'half-knowing', or he can not speak about it. There are no other options. The patient knows all the possible places the analyst can be in his mind and the limits of the analyst's possible behaviour and he acts in such a way as to imprison the analyst within the confines of what he (Mr G) can predict. I understand this to be what David means when he writes that the patient controls him. It is by these means that Mr G creates a situation in which he can believe that he completely 'knows' his analyst.

One possibility, as David says, is that Mr G is envious and jealous; for example, he hates it that his son, and he, need help. But, again as David says, it is not hard to get the feeling that in his early life not enough was in his control and what was not controllable threatened him with mental chaos.

Miss A's material also brought interesting thoughts. David very meaningfully interprets that what is confusing and painful for her is that she cannot completely have what she wants. In this context, I wondered whether the increasing closeness of the analytic relationship, particularly manifested in the compassionate and containing interpretation David made about what she must feel was her analyst's inconsistency in stirring up her desires and at the same time keeping her at a distance, led Miss A defensively to project her sexual wishes into him so that the file about the misconduct of the barrister referred at that moment not to her sexual wishes but to what she now thought were his. This alternative view – that the analyst was at that moment felt to contain the forbidden and embarrassing sexual wishes – would explain her strong reaction to his interruption: her complaint that she felt the analyst was tying her up in a corner. It seems right to understand that her sexual wishes were very bound up with infantile yearnings, and were unintegrated. Could it be that she couldn't (maybe yet) identify and keep these separate in herself, and that as soon as she felt in touch with an awareness of longing, these feelings became sexualised and then had to be immediately projected? I thoroughly enjoyed reading and thinking about this chapter.

# 9

# TALKING MAKES THINGS HAPPEN

## A contribution to the understanding of patients' use of speech in the clinical situation

*Athol Hughes*

A 7-year-old boy in analysis asked me, 'Do your joints fall off when you have leprosy?' To my request that he tell me what he thought leprosy was, he replied, 'When you don't feel anything'. He was expressing quite clearly the idea that the lack of feelings leads to atrophy of 'joints that fall off'. Such joints are not available for movement; lack of movement is related 'to not feeling anything'. To this boy, a disease that leads to physical atrophy and that is connected to lack of feeling, finds its counterpart in the emotional world where lack of feeling leads to atrophy of movement, to no change and no development.

In this chapter I am going to consider ways that some patients in psychoanalysis can use speech to stop movement and change. Betty Joseph has emphasised how, although speech can be used to communicate feelings, it can also be used to avoid significant communications. I want to show how a certain type of patient empties verbal communication of meaning, in an effort to avoid the outcome of its use. The patient's unconscious fear is that genuine communication will lead to intolerable psychic pain. In her clinical work Betty Joseph has shown with great clarity how certain patients resort to primitive mechanisms such as projective identification, projecting unwanted feelings into their object, in order to avoid genuine communication. In using projective identification the patient can be seen to pervert the medium through which psychoanalysis is carried out: verbalised thought.

Freud placed particular emphasis on the importance of verbal communication. He considered that in the unconscious, the presentation (representation) is of the 'thing' alone, which leads to concrete thinking. In other words, in the unconscious, the representation remains a 'thing' and so does not become an 'idea', the product of abstract thinking. However, in the preconscious, the thing-presentation is replaced by presentation of the word belonging to it. The 'thing' is then linked to the word. If a representation of a 'thing is not put into words which will describe it, the situation pertaining to it, remains in the unconscious in a state of repression' (Freud 1915: 202). It is not in a state for thinking. Through the use of words the unconscious becomes conscious. Freud considers that there is a mental process whereby in the beginning is the thought, then the words to speak of it. Words make 'becoming conscious' possible. In 'The ego and the id' Freud (1923: 21) says that thinking in pictures is an incomplete form of becoming conscious. It is nearer to the unconscious than thinking in words. It is older than the latter ontogenetically and phylogenetically and certainly can seem to be a more primitive form of internal communication than the more abstract use of words.

It is interesting to note that the woman who first recognised the importance of verbalisation in the dialogue between patient and analyst, had difficulty in speaking, even under hypnosis. At the start of her illness, Anna O 'was at a loss to find words and this difficulty gradually increased' (Breuer and Freud 1895: 25). She lost her command of grammar and syntax and 'in the process of time she became almost completely deprived of words'. For two weeks she spoke not at all. When Breuer recognised and told her that there was something she did not want to say, her symptoms were ameliorated and her disturbance of speech was 'talked away'. She could speak then, but only in English, although she did not know that she was doing so. She could not understand what was said to her in German, her native tongue. However, she was able to read French and Italian. If she was required to read aloud in one of these languages, she produced 'with extraordinary fluency, an admirable extempore English translation' (Breuer and Freud 1895: 26). It is interesting to speculate why she would not speak in her mother tongue and yet could communicate correctly in a foreign one. There is little reference to her mother in the account of Breuer's treatment of Anna O, so we do not know the part played by her relationship to her mother in the development of her hysteria. No doubt it was significant.

Freud was interested in the symbolic meaning of the patient's communications and its relationship to sublimation. The work of Melanie Klein shows how all activity has symbolic significance; to her, the primary sublimation is 'speech and pleasure in movement' (1923: 73). The capacities to work through and contain anxieties that are related to aggression and hostility are fundamental in fostering the development of symbols and the capacity to communicate by means of speech. Klein expands Freud's ideas about the formation of thought by exploring the meaning of children's play, which she sees as representing the child's phantasies about its inner world and that of the mother. The play itself is of great significance in terms of symbolic value. It shows in a powerful and dynamic manner the vividness of the inner world of the child who projects onto objects in the external world ideas about its organs and their functions. She shows how all aspects of development contribute to the process of modifying anxiety. This includes the development of speech, beginning with the imitation of sounds, which 'brings the child nearer to people he loves and enables him to find new objects' (Klein 1952: 112).

In her therapeutic work with children, Klein was the first to stress the importance of play as a medium of symbolisation; she also stresses the importance of words. In an early short paper called 'The importance of words in early analysis' Klein (1927b) discusses the part played by words in symbolisation. She shows how a child of 5, when encouraged to use words in his play, was able to understand the significance of the names he attributed to his objects. The words the child used were, according to Klein, 'a bridge to reality which the child avoids as long as he brings forth his phantasies only by playing'. She concludes, 'It always means progress when the child has to acknowledge the reality of the object through his own words' (Klein 1927b: 314).

Klein explains how when pre-verbal feelings and phantasies are revived in the analysis, they appear as 'memories of feelings' and are put into words with the help of the analyst. It is necessary to use words to describe phenomena belonging to the earliest stages of development. 'We cannot translate the language of the unconscious into consciousness without lending it words from our conscious realm' (Klein 1957: 180, footnote). In considering her views of child analysis she reiterates that she does not regard any child analysis as finished unless the work can be expressed in speech, to the extent to which the child is capable, and as such it is linked to reality (Klein 1927a: 150). Her work on identification and particularly on the concept of projective identification enlarges our views about the difficulties that can arise in the use of abstract, verbal communication.

Hanna Segal has contributed much to our understanding of how excessive use of projective identification, for whatever reason, inhibits the development of verbal capacities. Concrete symbolism is connected to the use of projective identification. In the process of projecting unwanted parts of the self into the object, an identification with the object takes place that seeks to obliterate the differences between the self and the outside world. Part of the ego is confused with the object. Segal's (1991: 40) work illustrates the gradual change in the formation and use of symbols in the depressive position. In working through the depressive position, during which the loss of the object can be experienced and tolerated, projective identifications are gradually withdrawn and the individual's separateness and knowledge of him or herself is gradually established. The internal is distinguished from the external. (The feelings of ambivalence, guilt and regret become bearable.) Prior to the depressive position, feelings related to the paranoid-schizoid position give rise, not to symbolic function, but to a 'symbolic equation' where the absence of the idealised object is denied. There is a gradual change in the formation and use of symbols in the depressive position. The capacity to communicate with oneself and with one's own unconscious is closely related to the use of symbols particularly verbal ones. Segal

(1957: 58) says 'not all internal communication is verbal thinking but all verbal thinking is an internal communication by means of symbols – words'.

Bion's (1962) work contributes a great deal to our understanding of symbolic processes, including the development of speech. To the frightened infant in the patient, movement in the analysis can produce what Bion called 'nameless dread'. If that is the case then the psychoanalyst is seen as forcing an intolerable situation on the patient. Bion considers that individuals who suffer 'nameless dread' are those whose mothers were unable to accept their infant's projections of terror and fear of dying. In introjecting the mother's non-acceptance of terror, these infants are left, not with a fear of dying, but with a nameless dread.

I suggest that some patients who have difficulty in using words for symbolic function feel that their first communications were not received and their reintrojection of a non-communicating object leads to an expectation that this process will be repeated in the analysis. These patients compulsively repeat the same pattern of avoidance, of non-communication, not only in the analytic work, but also in their external lives, to the detriment of their social, sexual and occupational achievements. They repeat familiar patterns of behaviour to deal with the primary trauma: the experience of having a non-responsive mother whom they see as having abandoned them to a dread that is so terrible that it cannot be talked about, it cannot be named. They fear that the analysis will lead them, once more, to the same terrifying situation.

As Eskelinen de Folch (1987) asks, can we not help such patients to have contact with these terrifying objects in less extreme situations? She suggests that we can, through psychoanalysis, but then raises the question of whether the process of psychoanalysis is really a less extreme situation than the original archaic trauma? To some patients it would seem that it is just as terrible; psychoanalysis means facing terrifying objects and fears of death and dying. We have to reach what she calls 'the concealed nuclei of the personality' which contain the fear of death and dying by verbal communication in the analysis. Then the fear of dying can be turned into a situation that can be understood and projections become reversible.

The work of Betty Joseph gives us clear insights into how patients avoid verbal communications by trying to intrude into the psychoanalyst's mind and thinking to stop the communicative processes, fostered by the use of words. Spillius and Feldman (1989), in their comprehensive introductions to Joseph's papers, describe how she sees the analyst needing to attend, not only to the verbal content of the patient's communications, but to how words can be used to affect the analyst's state of mind. In such instances speech is used as a form of acting out. As Feldman and Spillius say, the analyst focuses 'on what the patient is *doing* through his words and through his silences' (Feldman and Spillius 1989: 49).

With reference to this point, Joseph says: 'What the patient says is in itself of course extremely important but it has to be seen within the framework of what he does' (Joseph 1989: 206). The interaction in the transference and the countertransference is of particular importance and this where non-verbal communications play such a vital part. Speech implies separateness of subject and object who need to communicate their thoughts to each other. Projective identification, on the other hand, is often used to convince the subject that he or she is one with the object, that there is no difference in ways of thinking, or even in ways of being. If, on the other hand, individuals are helped to see that they and their object are different and separate one from the other, the knowledge can impart a devastatingly painful blow to their narcissistic omnipotence, through which he seeks to eliminate such differences.

In discussing the difficulties that patients experience in tolerating psychic pain, Joseph describes how at times they find verbal understanding and the expression of thought through interpretations of little use. For such patients words are not used to express insight and abstract ideas, but are used to give concrete evidence of their analysts' involvement in their day-to-day troubles which they want sorted out as a mother is expected to handle a child's needs.

In an interesting clinical example Joseph (1998) describes an adolescent girl's use of verbal communications. The girl considered that the analyst's speech 'took her over' while she herself had an empty way of talking designed to placate the analyst, to keep her quiet. This type of interchange was devoid of significance, while to the patient, action, such as staying away from sessions, was the only valid communication.

Non-verbal communications are of prime importance in helping us understand our patients. However, I want to stress here that it is only when the patients are able to use words to show they understand, and can integrate the understanding, that the interpretations become 'mutative', as Strachey (1934) in his classic paper describes it. Speech becomes imbued with meaning through a recognition and acceptance of the emotions that it arouses.

I should like now to give some clinical examples of the use and the non-use of verbal communications. I shall start with a vignette from the analysis of the 7-year-old child quoted at the start of this chapter. Peter was referred for analysis because his parents were concerned about the ways in which he seemed cut off from his feelings, and although not autistic by any means, he showed a lack of responsiveness to people that was distressing. Furthermore he was not learning at school and his verbal capacities were deficient.

In the session in which he asked me whether joints fell off as a result of leprosy, he told me how his very disturbed older sister was afraid of talking. He went on to say, 'Talking makes things happen, I don't talk I just do things', and he ran the toy car he was playing with around and around in circles. In speaking of his sister's fear of talking he was speaking of his own. 'Talking makes things happen' so he fears that speech will make him 'feel' something. Communicating with another person can lead to change, particularly in the inner world, and so can lead to psychic movement. By trying to stop such movement Peter imposes atrophy on his emotional world and on his learning.

Peter had told me in a previous session how his sister was so terrified of movement that she would not stay in a parked car without a driver. She feared that the car would start moving spontaneously and she would be killed in the ensuing crash. He said that she did not believe her parents' explanation of how the brakes work. She and he (since he was speaking of his own fears, in telling those of his sister's) had their own reality that defied the known world of physical forces. Peter's fear of spontaneous physical movement expressed his fear of spontaneous emotional involvement that could result from verbal communication. 'Talking makes things happen' and the happenings that Peter feared were something out of his control that would lead to disaster, a 'nameless dread'.

Through the work of the psychoanalysis pre-verbal emotions and phantasies are roused and these can be given verbal significance. However, certain patients, and among them I include Peter, dread the return of the pre-verbal phantasies; they do all that they can to stop the process. Speech makes connections between the known of the conscious and the unknown of the unconscious. These patients do not want to know the content of the latter, and prefer to keep it unknown. The aim of psychoanalysis is to show that verbal communication can lead to understanding that things 'need not happen'; that patients such as Peter can understand themselves and their impulses through talking about them without acting them out. Emotionally charged material can find expression through words. The individual sees that the internal world of phantasy is separate and different from the external world of activity. However, before the differentiation can take place, the primitive phantasies related to omnipotence need to be examined and understood in the context of the narcissism of the infant. In the more archaic part of his mind, Peter attributes omnipotent magic power to wishes, thoughts and words; to speak of a thing is to make it happen.

Verbal meaning is avoided to keep the unconscious at bay. It is only when the powerful uses of primary process thinking and projective identifications are abandoned as the work of the analysis progresses, that the patient acknowledges his or her separateness and that of the analyst so that the stage is set in which words can become the medium of communication.

Often in the five years of analytic work Peter would stop communicating through words and resort to activity. The following incident illustrates his way of trying to handle a highly emotionally charged event in his life. He could not tolerate the feelings that talking about the event aroused, and he changed the verbal communication into one of action.

In a session in which he had been able to speak of his fears concerning his grandfather, who was seriously ill, and might soon die, Peter understood that talking was helpful, and its helpfulness did 'make things happen'. What happened was that he faced his anxiety about death and the feelings of helplessness that speaking of death aroused in him. Not only was he facing the fact that his grandfather might soon die, but also he was facing the fact that death exists. It could be talked about and seen in relation to him and to me. It was the first time that he had been able to put such overwhelming feelings into words, and he was very upset. The impending death of his grandfather brought up anxieties about me as well. He was concerned about my survival in the face of the attacks he had made on me over the years of analytic work. He looked as if he were about to cry, something he had done very little in his analysis. However, in a way that had become repetitive in the work, he reverted to his more usual form of manic denial and said that he would be glad when his grandfather died – he and his family would all get something left to them on his death. In his flight to mania, Peter triumphed over his fears about death, over concerns for his grandfather, and anxiety about loss and parting. He obliterated these fears with thought of material gain.

In a matter of seconds, Peter's verbal communication changed to activity. He excitedly spilled water on the playroom floor while apparently ignoring everything I said. I spoke of how he was trying to wash away his understanding of his fears and worries about death. I said that he was terrified of saying goodbye to his grandfather so instead of being worried and upset, he told himself he would gain from his death.

In slopping water around, Peter suddenly slipped on the wet floor, and fell with a thud that must have caused him pain, although he did not say so. His fall took him completely by surprise and he looked shocked as well as pained.

In reverting to activity, Peter showed that he could not deal with the emotions that talking had aroused. By spilling water around on the floor, he showed how he wanted to wash away his fears of death and dying. He punished himself for trying to escape from the unexpected upset that our conversation had aroused in him by his fall. It shocked him. His powerful superego punished him painfully for his aggressive denial of concern and for his repudiation of fears.

After I spoke of the source of his fears and anxieties, he recovered his equilibrium in a matter of seconds and in a manic controlling way he spilled more water on the floor and deliberately took a run to slide in it and to fall. This time he was in control. There were no surprises and no further damage to his omnipotent sense that he could, and would, obliterate feelings of fear, anxiety and concern. He had been shocked and pained to find that talking to me about his worries about his grandfather's illness, meant that he was not the leper 'who does not feel anything'. He had to escape from his fears as well as from his recognition of his need for help to deal with them. He became manically triumphant over his upset self who had wanted to talk, and over me, in the analytic situation, who wanted to understand him through our talking and to help him to understand himself.

Manic triumph over pain lead him to repeat the fall to show that he was not surprised nor pained by insight. Our conversation had resulted in some understanding of his fears, and insight into his sense of terror about loss. He tried to show that he could omnipotently stop feelings of concern by turning to the idea of material gain, but he punished himself for that with his fall. Rather than acknowledge his hurt, he repeated the activity that had lead to the pain and shock, in an attempt to control it.

To Greenacre (1952) the tendency to act out can be related to distortion in speech and verbal thought arising from disturbance in the first year of life. The disturbance can result in an omnipotent reliance on magic, with a faulty development in the reality sense. She saw the children she studied as emphasising the visual and showing a tendency to dramatisation. To enact a situation in a dramatic or imitative way, in the eyes of some children, is to make it look as if it were true, which is the same as making it actually be true. Greenacre emphasises orality, and shows how the orally frustrated child expresses distress through heightened motility and speech difficulties. This seemed characteristic of Peter, who showed a tendency to demonstrate that what he suffered was manageable by dramatic activity rather than by speech.

Throughout the analytic work with Peter it was apparent that he had overwhelming anxiety about the loss of his object. He dramatised his efforts to deny and control this by activity. This vignette illustrates how his fear and the recognition of his need for help to deal with loss had momentarily disturbed his equilibrium. He tried to regain it by denial of his concern and by resorting to frantic activity.

An incident from the analytic work with a woman patient gives a dramatic illustration of how verbal communication can be seen as making unpleasant things happen. The woman, Miss B, explained in a session which followed one in which she had been absent (with no reason given to the therapist), that she had not come to her session the previous day because she had an appointment with the dentist after it. She had a severe and tenacious fear of dentistry. She said that if she had come to the session she would have had to talk about her fear, whereas by not coming to it before the dental appointment, she avoided realising until the dental treatment was half-way through, that she was in the chair and that she was panicking. By absenting herself from the session and the discussion of her fear, she considered that she absented herself from a portion of the panic. Talking about fears does not reduce them, absence does.

Miss B had told of how as a child important emotional situations were not talked about in her family. She was often told not to upset herself by talking about anxiety producing events. The most extreme example of this was her mother saying to Miss B that she must not upset herself by talking and crying, on the day Miss B said goodbye to her mother as the latter lay dying in hospital. Talking about sadness, loss and the ultimate loss, death, leads only to 'upset', not to empathy, sympathy and comfort. 'Upset' must be avoided at all cost, both to Miss B and to her mother. Pain cannot be tolerated and suffered in the mourning process; it must be bypassed, as if, if it is ignored, it will go away. To the patient the best way to avoid pain is to absent oneself from occasions where it would be discussed. One could hypothesise that Miss B's mother was not one who could tolerate infantile distress and mitigate it by talking to her distressed infant.

Miss B often found that talking about feelings resulted in upset. As a consequence, as well as absenting herself *from* sessions, she absented herself *within* sessions by introducing a tremendous confusion. The confusion would nullify whatever her therapist was saying, and result in a lack of differentiation between subject and object; it was difficult to know of whom or to whom she was speaking. Words were deprived of meaning.

A male patient, whom I shall call Mr G, characteristically reverted to a previous state when he recognised some new insight that illustrated shifts in his internal world. The communication between us had resulted in what he identified as 'feeling out of control' and he experienced panic, verging on terror. Change was terrifying to him, it was bound to be for the worse – it could not represent improvement. When new understanding showed that he had used help, his psychic equilibrium was toppled, much in the same way as Peter's had been. He had once told me that on these occasions he had a momentary feeling that he was crazy. His feeling of craziness was related to a sense of an appalling loss of identity. Sometimes at the end of a session during which understanding had lead to a change in his perspective, he experienced a physical disequilibrium on standing to leave. It was not dizziness, but it was as if he were going to lose his balance and fall.

A dream he reported illustrates how his balance became upset when he acknowledged insight and help received in the analytic work. He reported the dream in a session that followed one in which he had gained understanding of ways in which his needs for closeness and warmth could be met. He had made an important professional contribution in his work the day before the dream. His contribution pleased him, but he complained that it was not all that it might have been. In discussing his disillusionment about the differences between actuality and phantasy he began to understand how necessary it was that he give up his narcissistic ideals of perfection and settle for what was 'good enough'. He needed to do this in terms of what he expected of himself and also in terms of what he expected from others. In acknowledging this he said he felt closer and warmer to his girlfriend and also to me, the parental representative in the analytic work.

He had the dream the night after his important professional contribution. He dreamed that he was in bed and a man grabbed him by the wrists and said 'I want to talk to you'. Mr G said that he was terrified and unable to speak – he had no words. He was in a panic, and had to act to free himself from this paralysing situation. He did not know what he did but he succeeded in getting free. He was then outside in an area surrounded on all sides, like a square. Again the man came to grab him, but he managed to get free, because, he said, 'the man thrust me away from him'.

This is an illuminating description of how the patient avoids involvement and dependency in all areas of his life. There are undercurrents of homosexual excitement in the dream: he is in bed and is grabbed as if were to be a rape. The day before Mr G had expressed appreciation of warmth and closeness while speaking of the help he had had in analysis that had promoted his professional competence. But he experiences the consequences of our verbal interchanges as a form of homosexual rape, an overwhelming violation of his sense of self.

At this time in the analysis we had done considerable work on the way that Mr G repeatedly erotises the analytic situation, and the excited homosexual communication was not lost on either of us. But the important communication in the dream that I am investigating here, is his conviction that speaking of warm feelings and appreciation is like a rape and leads to a dangerous situation that paralyses him. From the start of his analysis Mr G nullified communication in the sessions by projective identification. When the man grabs him a second time, he frees himself by projecting his own rejecting self. The man thrusts him from him and Mr G attains freedom from his object, and from the pain and concern that such an object aroused in him.

This is a familiar mechanism of Mr G's. Throughout his life he has escaped awareness of his hatred, and awareness of how he repudiates need of others, by the projection of his rejecting self. He had been grabbed by insight that allowed him to be in touch with his need for warmth and acceptance. In the dream he is 'inside' in bed, that is in the session, in analysis. Then he is 'outside', although still surrounded, this time by buildings. Rey (1979, quoted by Steiner 1993) describes a borderline type of patient who is neither inside nor yet outside, but who exists in a borderline area which Steiner calls a psychic retreat. Mr G repeatedly retreats from closeness, involvement and dependency by developing a situation in the analysis in which he attempts to involve the analyst in an enactment of rejection. The action is a form of 'acting in'. Joseph (1989: 82) has convincingly described this type of manoeuvre, in which the analyst can unwittingly be caught up in an enactment.

Mr G frequently reports dreams but he has shown that he wants little contact with their content. At the start of the analysis he ventured few associations. In their visual impact his dreams carry more feeling than much of the verbal communication with which he complies because he sees the analytic process as demanding it. His differentiation of internal and external was precarious. He says at times that words are 'written in stone' – as such they are ever enduring; what is said cannot be unsaid. Words do not represent, they *are*. At the same time he often considers that speech is a medium of competition, and as such, conversation is not to be used to exchange ideas but is a battle between rivals, in which one or other of the two combatants is victorious.

Bion (1962) describes in 'A theory of thinking' how thoughts arise from the mating of a pre-concept with a frustration, while conceptual thinking arises from the pre-concept's conjunction with a satisfactory emotional experience. Mr G's evasion of frustration by silence does not result in modification of frustration that can lead to conceptual thinking. He frees himself by destroying the progress he has made – by losing his words. By so doing he destroys the possibilities of conceptual thinking, thinking that is linked to the idea of a good object and a satisfactory emotional experience. He does not introject an object, the analyst, who helps him to think about his experiences and so helps him to develop an interchange between his conscious and his unconscious mind. The situation becomes a nightmare in which he has evacuated understanding and warmth and his appreciation of what is good and productive in himself.

Mr G is searching endlessly for a type of mental umbilical cord that would provide a blissful connection with an ideal object for life: that would be always available, without expectation of contribution from him, verbal or otherwise. Many attempts to find a woman who would fulfil these requirements have met with disappointment and bitterness.

The panic that Mr G feels when there is contact is similar to the panic that he experiences when he is subject to restrictions or frustrations of any kind. Such impositions threaten his omnipotence and call out deathly hatred in him. He often projects the hatred and in the transference I am often experienced by him as an uncontrollable malignant object out to do him damage. His withdrawal into a paralysed state is closely connected to his hatred of life and movement. When he feels the stirrings of life in himself as a consequence of our verbal interchange, he strives to free himself by imposing a death-like silence.

A fear of death and dying has dominated Mr G's life. He was referred for analysis after he had what was thought at first to be a heart attack. His symptoms, which included severe pain, indicated a heart attack, but no physical cause was ascertained. It became clear in the analysis that the symptoms were related to fears of dependency and abandonment. The day before the symptoms, he had been told by his girlfriend that she was leaving him. By the end of a long analysis, Mr G was more able to tolerate the feelings aroused by loss. He was able to verbally work through his understanding that loss was not an abandonment that would lead to death. He found that being able to introject his good experiences could lead to love and appreciation, that sustain him even in loss. Words had enriched his life. As O'Shaughnessy (1988: 149) shows in her paper 'Words and working through', 'change only comes with the active functioning of the patient's ego in working through in words'.

Klein (1946) elaborates the struggle within the individual to destroy his objects, as at the same time he wants to preserve them. She describes how anxiety is aroused by the operation of the death instinct within the individual, which is expressed as a fear of annihilation. The extreme terror 'aroused by intrusion of dangers threatening from the deep layers of the unconscious is to some extent constant' and she goes on to say that it is part of the instability of the neurotic and psychotic individual (Klein 1958: 243).

To Freud, too, progress in the analysis arouses anxieties that threaten the internal stability of the individual. In 'Analysis terminable and interminable' Freud (1937) shows how resistance in analysis illustrates the force of the death instinct which 'is defending itself by every possible means against recovery and which is absolutely resolved to hold onto illness and suffering'. Recovery and living lead to guilt, pain and conflict, while to the patient caught in the throes of the death instinct, death leads to oblivion and apparent peace with cessation of pain.

I have discussed and given clinical examples in this chapter to illustrate how patients caught up in despair that verbal communication cannot express their terror, resort to activity of one type or another, to repetition and to paralysis of movement and development. I have used concepts relative to communication that have been elucidated by Betty Joseph, who has shown how verbal interchange in psychoanalysis can be used either to foster development or to prevent it. Many investigators since Freud and Klein have shown that a necessary condition for emotional growth is that experience be given substance through speech. Some patients do great damage to their development and to their contact with their inner and outer worlds by the obliteration of verbal contact.

It is only when patients can tolerate their fears of where the verbal communications in the analysis are taking them, that they can see that in the real world they are not infants who fear archaic terrors that paralyse them. The psychoanalytic process is not leading them to a situation of 'nameless dread'. It is leading them to a situation where their feelings and terrors can be given names, talked about and understood in the context of the present day and present situation. It is through such identification of experience and tolerance of anxiety that verbal communication can lead to psychic growth and development.

## References

Bion, W.R. (1962) 'A theory of thinking', *International Journal of Psychoanalysis*, 43: 306–310; reprinted in W.R. Bion, *Second Thoughts*, New York: Jason Aronson (1967), and in E. Bott Spillius (ed.) *Melanie Klein Today: Developments in Theory and Practice*, Vol. 1, *Mainly Theory*, London: Routledge (1988).

Breuer, J. and Freud, S. (1895) 'Fräulein Anna O', *Studies on Hysteria*, SE 2: 21–47.

Eskelinen de Folch, T. (1987) 'The obstacles to analytic cure: comments on "Analysis terminable and interminable"', *IPA Educational Monographs*, no.1, J. Sandler (ed.).

Feldman, M. and Spillius, E. (1989) Introduction to Part 2, *Psychic Equilibrium and Psychic Change: Selected Papers of Betty Joseph*, M. Feldman and E. Bott Spillius (eds), London: Routledge (1989).

Freud, S. (1915) 'The unconscious', SE 14: 159–209.

—— (1923) 'The ego and the id', SE 19: 12–68.

—— (1937) 'Analysis terminable and interminable', SE 23: 209–253.

Greenacre, P. (1952) *Trauma, Growth and Personality*, New York: International Universities Press.

Joseph, B. (1975) 'The patient who is difficult to reach'. In P.L. Giovacchini (ed.) *Tactics and Techniques in Psychoanalytic Therapy*, vol. 2 *Countertransference*, New York: Jason Aronson; reprinted in *Psychic Equilibrium and Psychic Change: Selected Papers of Betty Joseph*, M. Feldman and E. Bott Spillius (eds), London: Routledge (1989).

—— (1988) 'Object relations in clinical practice', *The Psychoanalytic Quarterly* 57f (October) part IV; reprinted in *Psychic Equilibrium and Psychic Change: Selected Papers of Betty Joseph*, M. Feldman and E. Bott Spillius (eds), London: Routledge (1989).

—— (1998) 'Aggressiveness as an obstacle', unpublished paper, *Bulletin of the British Psycho-Analytical Society*, 34(9).

Klein, M. (1923) 'The role of the school in the libidinal development of the child', *The Writings of Melanie Klein*, vol. 1, *Love, Guilt and Reparation and Other Works*, London: Hogarth Press (1975).

—— (1927a) 'Symposium on child analysis', *The Writings of Melanie Klein*, vol. 1, *Love, Guilt and Reparation and Other Works*, London: Hogarth Press (1975).

—— (1927b) 'The importance of words in early analysis', *The Writings of Melanie Klein*, vol. 3, *Envy and Gratitude and Other Works*, London: Hogarth Press (1975).

—— (1946) 'Notes on some schizoid mechanisms', *The Writings of Melanie Klein*, vol. 3, *Envy and Gratitude and Other Works,* London: Hogarth Press (1975).

—— (1952) 'On observing the behaviour of young infants', *The Writings of Melanie Klein*, vol. 3, *Envy and Gratitude and Other Works*, London: Hogarth Press (1975).

—— (1957) 'Envy and gratitude', *The Writings of Melanie Klein*, vol. 3, *Envy and Gratitude and Other Works*, London: Hogarth Press (1975).

—— (1958) 'On the development of mental functioning', *The Writings of Melanie Klein*, vol. 3, *Envy and Gratitude and Other Works*, London: Hogarth Press (1975).

O'Shaughnessy, E. (1988) 'Words and working through', *Melanie Klein Today, Developments in Theory and Practice*, vol. 2, *Mainly Practice*, E. Bott Spillius (ed.), London: Routledge.

Rey, H. (1979) 'Schizoid phenomena in the borderline', *Advances in Psychotherapy of the Borderline Patient*, J. LeBoit and A.Capponi (eds), New York: Jason Aronson.

Segal, H. (1957) 'Notes on symbol formation', *The Work of Hanna Segal*, New York: Jason Aronson (1981).

—— (1991) *Dreams, Phantasy and Art*, London: Routledge.

Spillius, E.B. and Feldman, M. (1989) 'General introduction', *Psychic Equilibrium and Psychic Change: Selected Papers of Betty Joseph*, M. Feldman and E. Bott Spillius (eds), London: Routledge.

Steiner, J. (1993) *Psychic Retreats: Pathological Organizations of the Personality in Psychotic, Neurotic, and Borderline Patients*, London: Routledge.

Strachey, J. (1934) 'The nature of the therapeutic action of psychoanalysis', *International Journal of Psychoanalysis*, 15: 127–159.

## DISCUSSION OF ATHOL HUGHES'S CHAPTER

*Patricia Daniel*

Athol has chosen an interesting topic in her chapter: the contradiction between the classical psychoanalytic notion that making the unconscious conscious implies the capacity for verbalisation, and is therefore a 'good thing', leading to psychic change, and the conviction of many patients that it is precisely this which makes it a 'bad thing', leading to catastrophic disturbance. The chapter stimulated a few questions in my mind.

Where Peter repeats his fall in a manic controlling way – was the motivation primarily to defend against the shock and pain of his awareness of what he felt, and had briefly faced, or might the repetition also have been to manage the dosage – to gain mastery in a developmental way?

Did he feel exposed at being seen to fall/fail at not managing to face his anxieties for very long? And might he have feared that his analyst expected him to face and bear more than he could at that point in the session. Alternatively, was the motivation behind the repetition to stop, divert or pervert his moment of genuine shock and pain?

In the example of Mr G's dream of being in bed and a man grabbing him by the wrists, saying he wanted to talk to him I was reminded of Birksted-Breen's idea of penis as link. The dream could be seen as representing the masculine aspect of the analytic function, the talking/interpreting, from which the patient tries to free himself. The function is disguised, or maybe mocked, as an eroticised scene between patient and analyst.

# DISCUSSION OF ATHOL HUGHES'S CHAPTER

## *Jane Temperley*

Psychoanalysis is conducted through the medium of speech. Even with children, where play is often the major form of communication, Hughes restates the importance of understanding that it is mediated in words and thereby rendered capable of being thought about. Her chapter illustrates how threatening this understanding can be and how speech itself can be used to mask and attack meaning.

In the 'total situation' it is not only the patient who can use words defensively: so too may the analyst. The mother who responds to her infant or child's anxiety with words is not necessarily as containing as a less verbal mother whose inner security (her relation to her internal objects) is experienced as holding. In the analytic situation the analyst's voice and manner of speaking may give a message at variance with her words, however appropriate these are. What words can make possible is that an inarticulate experience can be known and thought about.

Athol's three patients illustrate different varieties of defensiveness about articulation of feelings into words and different reactions to being helped by the analyst's understanding to know and to bear what otherwise might be evacuated in activity or avoided by projective identification. I think that when her child patient Peter momentarily experiences a range of feelings toward his dying grandfather – feelings of loss and concern that belong to the depressive position – he retreats into manic activity to counteract the depressive pain which with his analyst's help he had just been able to put into words and to know.

The woman patient Miss B shows the effect of a very uncontaining mother; she lacked the experience of being helped by another person to face pain. As a result she had a very reduced capacity to think. Freud described thinking as the ability to use bound mental samples of unpleasant experience in order to relate more effectively to reality. Far from being helped by her mother to do this, she had been urged to eschew it.

These two patients found that insight caused them pain – the boy retreated from the possibility of grief and the woman from the prospect of anxiety she could not imagine might be contained. With the third case matters are more complex. Mr G's analyst's interventions caused him to feel more hopeful, closer to her and more effective at work. His negative reaction in the dream seems to arise more from an affront to his sense of self-sufficiency or to the eruption of claustrophobic/agoraphobic anxieties.

# 10

# A PROJECTIVE IDENTIFICATION WITH FRANKENSTEIN

## Some questions about psychic limits

*Edna O'Shaughnessy*

I am looking back at an analysis of some forty years ago. A 12-year-old boy came mentally broken down and left at his urgent insistence after three years, able to resume his life and his education, while maintaining a projective identification with Frankenstein.

I present this as a case study in order to ask questions about psychic limits. What was the nature of my patient's recovery? What impelled his identification with Frankenstein? Were there inherent limits in his psyche requiring some such outcome? And my limitations? Would a different or better analysis have enabled a different type of outcome?

### Clinical material

As told by his parents, Hugh was their youngest child, born when his mother was stressed by having to run a too-large house. At six weeks their housekeeper thought Hugh screamed because he needed a bottle to supplement breast feeding, but Hugh still screamed. Later, Hugh disliked and did little and poor work in a succession of schools and his education finally ceased when Father brought him home weeping and panic-stricken from a weekly boarding school. From then on Hugh stayed at home, unable to be alone, go out, or let his parents be out together. They told me he ruled the household. He had what they called 'habits', his chief one being collecting and keeping rubbish. His parents also told me that an elder son had been born with a physical disability and that, in regard to Hugh, they were desperate that he obtain a good education. They were angry with Hugh (especially Mother) and frightened, as well as concerned and worried that they demanded too much of him.

Father brought Hugh to the first session. I saw a beautiful boy with a nice smile, rigid and sad, clinging to father. In the playroom Hugh was terrified and clung to a small chair. He gazed out of the window to empty his mind or looked, not at me or the furniture, but at the spaces between.

From his hovering gaze I could tell that these spaces seemed to him to be full of particles. He also showed feelings of curiosity about the open drawer of playthings, of contempt and expectation of my contempt that he was interested. Unspontaneously – he needed the prompt of a question from me – he spoke a few words, while rubbing finger and thumb together. I spoke to him about all he had let me observe.

On the second day Hugh came with two books and a newspaper (the start of a characteristic way of communicating). On the cover of *More about Paddington* was a picture of a small bear on a cushion, which I took as offering a picture of himself and his new analysis. Hugh stared anxiously at the wall, minutely rubbing his belt, eventually telling me he was watching a hand pointing a finger. He moved the book aside to reveal headlines on the newspaper: 'BOY FRIEND, EXTRA'. I interpreted that he felt frightened and pointed at, accused of masturbation, and he wanted me to know that his penis was like an extra, a boyfriend to hold on to in a frightening world.

Hugh felt himself to be in a space of small particles and over-sized looming things, another of which was a watching eye on the latch of the window. The little chair he held onto, like his penis, father, and later myself, signified the real world that stopped him from succumbing to a psychotic panic in a menacing space of fragments and bizarre objects (Bion 1957). Though terrified and placatory, he was grateful and gained relief from having his terror and the nature of his threatening world recognised. He often made an affirmatory 'Mmmm'. He communicated through morsels of sometimes confused speech, body movements, pictures and headlines in newspapers. When he was able to sit down, he played a little with toys and paper. Mostly he made vivid drawings for which he had a gift.

He began to carry everywhere a transparent bag with a book in it called *A Creepy World*. I understood this as his ideograph (Money-Kyrle 1965) for his belief that, like the book inside the bag, he was with his creepy world inside the analysis. Some days he lost his capacity to distinguish the real world from his psychotic world, which was always there. Then, with finger movements, or the flicker of an eye muscle, or the grinding of a top tooth on a bottom tooth, he launched attacks on enemies in order to survive. Pulverising persecutors made him fear a return attack from small things; any slight noise or movement made him rigid with fear. He drew bits, pieces and vague trailing shapes, and I came to know what he already knew, that he felt in danger of bits from his self and his objects seeping out in his breath and speech or his hands as he drew and getting confused with me and the room. To staunch and to recoup his losses he had to be sparing of movement and words, take his drawings home, and whenever he saw a piece of fluff or speck of dirt he put it in his pocket: 'One of my habits', he told me tonelessly.

In a needed omnipotent phantasy, Hugh felt me as continuously with and around him until I told him about the Easter break. He swung round and stared at me, his face wide in a shock of disbelief. The next day he came bearing a drawing of misaligned concentric circles with a sunken gap. He said accusingly, 'England and France were once joined. Then a volcano came and they got separated. The middle bit got sunk and now they are like this', pointing to the mismatching, the sunken bit and the gap. I said he was showing me what I had done to him. He no longer felt as he had before, that, whether we were near or far, we were joined and I was around him. My holiday words had pushed into him and sunk him in his middle. Hugh drew a moon with four (he had four sessions) rockets round it which he said dropped darts of air onto the moon and then there would be enough air to live. He made smell after smell, frantic when he could not stop. He drew an earth and a distant moon with craters which the four rockets were leaving. In sum, Hugh responded to the first separation with elemental intensity, a characteristic of psychotic children described by many authors (e.g. Winnicott 1945; Mahler 1961; Tustin 1972). The shock of my withdrawal left Hugh sunk and angry, his orifices open and incontinent; he accused me of failing to match his unlimited need of me to be always round him and to breathe life into him. He is left like a dead moon, marked by craters of my and his violence.

After this first break Hugh's beauty vanished. He returned with sores and pimples round his mouth, a cut on his thumb, dirty and dim looking, like a too-long-neglected infant. With trembling hands he took from his drawer a paint box he had not touched before. He drew it from its wrappings and grew calm as he gazed at the colours. I spoke to him about his feeling in the holiday that he and I were dead and how seeing the colours meant there still was life here. But life had changed.

Instead of his *Creepy World* book in the transparent bag, Hugh brought a flicker booklet. By flickering its pages he made a 'film' of a figure jumping up from the end of a seesaw so that the figure on the other end was shot into space and the two figures changed places in the air and landed on the opposite end of the seesaw. Hugh often anxiously halted the film with a figure stranded in the air to picture his chronic anxiety that at any moment I could get up and go, and hurtle him into space. He could, and did, reverse our places and make me know and endure his position by keeping me stranded in silent horrific dead hours. Hugh brought a cloth cap with a 'popper' on its 'flap' and pressed the popper in and out, to show me his repeated attempts to pop into objects, who keep pushing him out, to escape his flap, i.e. his anxiety. Rosenfeld (1965) emphasises that this is central to psychotic object relations. In this battling hostile world, very much also the situation with his parents who were trying to get him out and moving, he showed me his subtle methods of entry and control. He made paper squirrels and frogs with extending tails and tongues, and drew eyes on stalks. Specific omnipotent phantasies emerged about how the flatus from his tail, or his spittle, or his tongue, indeed any organ or body product, could dart out to bridge the gap between himself and an object, enter it and control it. In consequence, his world is threatening and eerie: invisible threads and wires connect him to objects.

He also brought two boomerangs, which he threw repeatedly towards the wall, saying despondently, 'They never go anywhere, they just come back to me', which I understood as his showing me how his signals were not received. He conveyed intense despair, still feeling in himself a neglected baby, now a youth, whose parents (as I could currently observe for myself) did not comprehend the enormity of his mental handicap, distress and anxiety. He represented them by circles with swastikas, and as devils with horns. These they were not; these were Hugh's distortions. Hugh was excited by, and admiring of, his 'opposite of the ordinary' ways, as he called them, his omnipotent masturbation phantasies (such as his secret methods of entry and control) that, for him, were concretely realised. Indeed, his contemptuous refusal at home even to try 'ordinary' ways was one of the many sources of his parents' resentment.

With analysis Hugh's bizarre world and psychotic anxieties receded. He perceived again, in his fashion, the ordinary world and took from it the minimal necessary for survival by a process I thought of as accretion; e.g. when he saw me he squeezed the muscles round one eye so it flickered like a camera eye and 'took' me. In this way he accumulated picture slices. I think all his senses were impaired and had become mechanical collectors of sights, noises, words, etc., acquiring not vital introjects but concrete bits and pieces.

At home he became able to stay by himself, at first for brief periods. Then he made expeditions on his own to his local town. In my notes of that time, I record that he was much less anxious and more alive. Hugh started lessons again with a private tutor. His parents were enormously relieved. They soon insisted, in my view prematurely, that he make the journey to his sessions, by country bus, train and London underground, alone. Except for one or two days when they yielded to his entreaties to be brought by car, Hugh came on his own, sometimes suffering horrendous levels of fear, which his parents, recognising that he needed to be pushed out, and persecuted by their bondage to him, could not allow themselves to know.

Hugh had been in analysis for a year. He made a declaration: 'I can now see two-way traffic; last term in the road there was only one-way traffic. But now there are some road-works at the top of the hill.' It was his acknowledgement of a two-way interchange of work between him and me. That evening his mother telephoned to complain she was unbearably depressed, Hugh was impossible and she could not stand it, and the next day Hugh cancelled his appreciation of the day before, saying, 'Why do I have to come? I don't find you do anything', after which he collapsed into worrying about 'bits of dirt shining in the sun', the rubble of our two-way work. Here was a first glimpse of how the recognition of helpful object relations precipitates an unbearable depression which he at once projects, after which he destroys the self and object that are helpfully linked (cf. Segal's (1957) account of depression in the schizophrenic).

Nevertheless, a new era had begun. Over the next months, though short-lived, there were sequences of acknowledged two-way endeavours between him and me, the most intense occurring when his parents went away for two weeks on their first holiday in years. Alone, Hugh made the long journeys to and from his sessions. He felt his parents had been torn out of him, leaving a hole from which more and more of him was lost daily. He stood at the window watching leaves being blown by the wind and told me in a voice choked with fear that there was a tree without any leaves on it. This was his ultimate dread: he would fall to pieces, be dispersed like leaves in the wind and cease to exist. By the end of the fortnight he had dwindled to a standstill.

His crisis in his parents' absence repeats his traumatised reaction to the first analytic break, but with a difference: he now had an object to come to. Afterwards he was movingly grateful. During the next weeks our relations were more alive, and full of contradictions. Hugh felt needy, grateful, resentful of his dependence, and hated all these feelings. He made a puppet of paper and string, explaining that the strings went into the puppet and held its bits together and that the strings pulled the puppet along and made it walk. The puppet expressed the truth of his invaded and controlled world of omnipotent psychotic phantasy, but, as a model, it negated all the human side of our link that was also present.

In the next analytic break Hugh's experiences again had more human elements. On the Monday of his return he spoke of a Morse code buzzer with a missing part, of its needing to be picked up and wanting to send messages, and of being recharged when the two parts were fitted together. But by Thursday Hugh had turned sullen. He saw me as a 'Snow-white' who made him one of her inferior dwarves. He had brought with him 'a green man tied by strings to a parachute' and he dropped the green man repeatedly onto the table so that it pulled the parachute down. Concentrated and thoughtful, he said, 'The green man is too big for the parachute'. On the Friday, Hugh came for the first time with his Frankenstein mask, and a newspaper.

He placed the mask of papier mâché on the newspaper saying, 'It's a mask I made of Frankenstein; it's Frankenstein's monster, but I call it Frankenstein'. He made a speech. 'Frankenstein is human, not a robot. There' and he indicated the wound with stitches he had drawn on the forehead – 'he got hit with a chair when he went mad and broke the wires that held him. There should be a bolt' – he meant the bolt at the monster's neck – 'but I did not put it in'. He rubbed the back of the mask where there was an opening, saying, 'I cut it down the back'. Then he moved the mask aside to reveal an advertisement in the newspaper: 'LONDON PRIDE – BEAUTY IN BLOUSES', after which he completely ignored me and gave all his attention to Frankenstein. I said he had turned away from me whom he today saw as full of pride in tying him to the analysis like a bottle puppet, so that he missed it in the holidays and wanted it like a breast, the beauty in blouses. I said he was wanting me to understand he had human feelings: like the green man he felt too big to be tied to me. Later Hugh said: 'The monster is grey-green, hard and not soft, and the professor made him from old things dug up from graves'. I spoke about how he was losing his new worrying mixed feelings about me by breaking his ties and digging up old things and being like Frankenstein. As the session neared its close Hugh grew dead-looking. I said that hardening and escaping from being what he calls 'a bottle puppet' deadened his feeling of being alive and there being colour.

From then on Hugh always brought the mask. He remodelled it or sat with his head in it. He related over and over Frankenstein's story as if it were his story. Hugh knew the story not from Mary Shelley's book *Frankenstein, or The Modern Prometheus* (1818) but from James Whale's 1931 film in which Boris Karloff plays the monster. In the film, Frankenstein the scientist transgresses the limits of nature and makes a living creature who is a monster whom he then rejects. The appeal to Hugh of this story was very great. It expressed his deep sense of rejection by his objects and his painful feeling of being different from others, and because Frankenstein is monstrous only from rejection and being misunderstood, it freed him from the anxiety and depression of being 'a green man', whose narcissism and envy pull his objects down. With each element of the tale Hugh claimed an affinity. He would tell me how Frankenstein was not born but built bigger than normal by science from old things dug up from graves, pointing out that he had made his papier-mâché monster from bits of old newspaper and glue. He was describing a Promethean act of self-creation, a transmuting of dead bits and pieces into a being whose birth and care was not owed to parents and whose current better state was not owed to analysis. On the mask he often restitched the wound 'where Frankenstein got hit with a chair' to close the wounds of separation through which he disintegrates. By making an ever-present artefact which he could get into and get out of, one that was a victim of rejection and maltreatment, Hugh, in his omnipotent phantasies, freed himself from dependence on, confusion with, and fear, guilt and envy of, his ambiguous objects.

Hugh put his Frankenstein mask in a suitcase and carried it everywhere. He made a drawing of 'a framed picture of Frankenstein'. Frankenstein occupied the entire picture. Outside the frame was a small pudgy face, about which Hugh said contemptuously: 'It is ordinary, it has a low forehead, it is not intelligent'. He continued: 'The monster has a high brow and is intelligent, and there is more of him'. This mental state, in which Hugh projected himself into and identified with Frankenstein, was never, except fleetingly, undone in the analysis.

For reasons of space I omit the details of the period in which I struggled with a patient mostly little available. Sometimes Hugh played or acted being Frankenstein, sometimes Frankenstein was a mask behind and in which he could hide. Often Hugh felt changed; he was Frankenstein. There were cycles when his contempt for me and his excitement escalated and he grew alarmingly mad and manic, followed after a while by a collapse when, with pain and despair, he would say something like, 'Shadows are real' and be, in his way, more in contact for a few sessions. Nevertheless, Hugh did not wish to relinquish his Frankenstein; his aim, it emerged, was to learn how to avoid madness, mania or despair and he secretly listened to what I said for this purpose.

Though his 'habits' continued, e.g. his collecting bits of rubbish, which for Hugh was the retrieval of lost fragments of self and objects, at home and school there was ongoing improvement. In analysis Hugh became more split and projected into me all opposition to his Frankenstein state of mind. He brought a gadget with a skinny hand that shot out to snatch away money and maintained this was what I was: a robber stealing money from his parents, and more immediately, aiming to steal his Frankenstein away. For the first time since the start of treatment he began to nag his parents to stop. He found them willing allies. Enthusiastic about his improvement (he was now attending a crammer and coping with larger groups of children and several teachers) they felt all energies should be directed to placing him in a good school.

Very occasionally his lost self returned in horror. He would say, 'Frankenstein is not real' or 'Frankenstein is a kind of dead thing'. Even if relieved for a while, despair, anxiety and suspicion of me drove him back to idealising Frankenstein who brought him another sort of relief by shedding anxiety and despair, gaining a feeling of all problems solved, plus excitement and energy at his triumph over me with his 'opposite of the ordinary' solution by means of the monster.

Hugh was in earnest to hunt the analysis down. He took a Judo course and did menacing karate cuts in the session, saying he could smash the table in half. He met interpretations with hostile silence or a loud, 'Stupid!', 'No!', 'Wrong!' At home he insisted he wanted no educational arrangements that would allow him to continue coming for analysis. His parents entered him at a public school for the following academic year, at which point Hugh spoke of Judo tricks and a film in which a ruler was setting himself up as a god and that it was a bit mad to do that. This was his moment of fear that his parents and I were being ruled by his mad tricks into ending his analysis. His parents came to see me. I told them my opinion that Hugh needed to continue his analysis. They acknowledged there was 'some very odd behaviour indeed', but could not let themselves see more than that and so we agreed a date for termination.

The end was approaching. Hugh said one day that he had been thrown in Judo and had hurt his foot. He then talked of an old programme, *Top Cat*, the one where the alley cat saw an abandoned baby in a park. I said he saw the ending of the analysis as his parents and myself abandoning a baby. He said he was tired and had been working at his history last night. He rubbed his fingers backwards and forwards saying, 'Crooked, not straight', and spoke about vampires, werewolves, and then, with an arch intonation, Poe's *Tales of Mystery and*

*Imagination*. I thought he was pointing out that while he had his stories, the grown-ups had Poe, which he thought had a rude meaning, so the grown-ups too had their unreal lavatory phantasies and were not really straight. I said he was in despair about his analysis stopping. It seemed to prove I was crooked: how else could I abandon him?

Hugh could feel despair for a moment only. To his last session he brought two books and laid them on the table. One was his Judo book with the cover of the Judo expert pulling his opponent down. The other was called *Frankenstein's Revenge*. These were the high and powerfully controlling images through which we were both meant to see the ending.

I was left pulled down, anxious about my patient and anxious about my work.

I had two later communications from Hugh: a letter telling me he had passed his school exams, and a few years after that, a coloured postcard of a peacock fanning its tail, on the other side of which Hugh wrote to say he had finished his course of study and obtained his diploma.

## Discussion

Hugh's identification with Frankenstein, as an outcome of a psychoanalysis, is perturbing. Yet, he started broken down and when he left his analysis he could function. How shall we understand this?

As I see it, because I recognised he was broken down and struggling with psychotic panics in a bizarre universe that was his mental world outside of him, Hugh could expose more of his condition to me and feel it was known. And because I spoke in an analytic way, he felt I was not submerged by his psychosis and so he could hold on to me, even though, as we have seen, he tied himself to me in an intrusive and abnormal way. Our 'two-way traffic', the analytic work, enabled Hugh to recover.

This recovery put him in a predicament, which he saw as 'too big', i.e. beyond the limits of himself and his objects to resolve. You will recall Hugh's recognition of being helped, of need, of feeling more alive when with the analyst, but dwarfed and humiliated, believing the analyst to be full of pride, purifying herself to Snow-white, disavowing both her own deficiencies in understanding him, and also, that although he was better, his vulnerability to disintegration on separation and the envious 'green man' in him who deadens and fragments were still uncured.

Fearing breakdown again, he sees it as 'more intelligent' to break his ties and project himself into a new identity, the hard impervious Frankenstein monster, a second skin as described by Bick (1968), an identificate as described by Sohn (1985). Monstrous, with a justified black and distorted vision, ingratitude and unreality, and carrying dangers of madness and mania, Frankenstein, even so, rendered Hugh many services: he appeared to integrate Hugh's fragmented mind into a coherent identity, he was not humiliated but bigger than normal, and he disposed of fear and guilt. Moreover, he is always there and so closes the wounds of separation through which Hugh disintegrates.

Very near the end, using again the phrase 'too big', Hugh said, 'The rest is too big', and a few days later he related the first and only dreams of the analysis:

> I had three dreams. In the first dream I was emptying bits from my pockets and my mother was crying. I went up to her to put my arms around her

He started laughing.

> Oh, and my mother turned round and said, 'Don't worry; I am going to kill you'.

I interrupted to remark that he was laughing because his dream is frightening. He said dismissively, 'It was scaring in the night' and continued telling his first dream:

> I woke up and I must have turned round because I went to sleep with my blanket round me and my arm under it, and when I woke up –

his voice was throttled by anxiety

> – I was round the other way and my arm was out. I got out and ran away.

I asked if he knew why he went to his mother in the dream. He answered, 'Because I was sorry'. I then spoke to him about his deep unhappiness; he was sorry his habits upset his mother and he wanted her to know he was sorry. Yet he was terrified of turning round and reaching towards her, because, as he saw her in his dream, she would not accept his sorry – the mother in his mind is murderously revengeful.

There was a long pause. Then Hugh said bleakly:

> In the second dream you pursued me to my home and whichever way I ran, you caught me.

I spoke to him about how he was appealing to me to understand that he felt it was impossible for him to stay in analysis or to admit being sorry about ending it, because, as he sees me, I pursue him to rob him of the home and blanket around him that Frankenstein is for him. After a pause he said:

> In the third dream there was a great hunt and I was with the great hunter. I was looking at a picture where guns were hidden.

This third dream is Hugh's tragic answer to the monsters in his inner world: they are deadened into being merely pictures and he joins the hunters, his murderous superego and pursuing analyst, and becomes himself the hunter Frankenstein.

We can now see more fully Hugh's plight and his limits. He has monstrous objects, cruelly unaccepting and vengeful, which in external reality to some extent they are, though it is by no means all they are; these monsters are full of his deadly projections. Hugh functions with a preponderance of death instincts and registers few benign experiences, e.g. he deadens even the small event of an analyst recognising he laughs from terror when he tells his dream of the murderous mother. His narcissism is at variance with his unlimited dependence, and his intolerance of frustration is at variance with reality. In omnipotent phantasies he intrudes into his objects and hates and fears return invasions from anything alive, and he fragments and deadens experience (see Feldman 2000). Hugh knows he does this and he is sorry that he does.

But working through, the binding and modifying of conflicts and feelings, is beyond the limits of the ties that exist between him and his objects. Indeed, any further evolution of their relations, Hugh believes, will threaten him with paranoid and/or depressive breakdown. In despair, he breaks away from his objects, and like a modern Prometheus aims to construct an artefact,[1] and by intrusion into it to gain a new existence and identity. It is important to mention that near the end, as Hugh remodelled the mask, in some sessions it more and more took on the look of his mother. For Hugh these were moments of horror, when he recognised he had not after all made a transcendental escape, but that his 'new' identity was an old maternal monster.

Hugh is limited, on the one side, by objects with whom there can be little working through and who threaten deterioration, and on the other, by the limits to his belief in his artefact: total belief will make him mad and manic, but if he does not believe enough, he will know it for a fraud, or feel that after all he has not escaped but is imprisoned inside his old monstrous object. Hugh has to maintain a position between psychotic breakdown at the one end and madness at the other. He must aim for a mental state with a projective identification with a 'new' object that serves as his container and a protective hard mask, while hedging – often by means of jokiness – his knowledge of what is real and what is unreal, as cycles of deadening, fragmenting and ejecting continue, along with some live, though aberrant, mental activity. In some such way Hugh can ward off both breakdown and madness, and can manage to function.

Is it right though to try to describe Hugh's psychic limits without bringing in my limits as his analyst? Is not such a one-sided approach even outrageous? My work certainly had its limitations. There are things I would now do differently. To mention only two. There is the question of language. Especially at first, I used too much part-object body language. This language was also mistaken in another and more seriously misunderstanding way. Hugh's parts, like his wholes, were not natural kinds like breast or penis or person; they were bizarre bits and entities. I conflated my world and his world, and Hugh did not forget or forgive this error: remember how on the day he first brought the Frankenstein mask, he brought also the newspaper advertisement: 'LONDON PRIDE – BEAUTY IN BLOUSES'. I also worry that later in the analysis I was too much controlled into fitting in with his Hugh–Frankenstein world.

I do not wish to say Hugh could not have had a different or a better analysis. Even so, I submit, for consideration, the contention that with any analyst Hugh will have some such limited and quasi-delusional outcome. Freud (1911: 71) expressed it thus about Schreber: 'The delusional formation which we take to be the pathological product, is in reality an attempt at recovery'.

Had Hugh stayed longer, what might one hope for? Not for normal progress, the integration of split and projected parts of the self, mourning or Oedipal resolutions (see Steiner 1996). Psychoanalysis is no modern Prometheus. As Bion (1957) observed, the psychotic personality does not become non-psychotic, but has its own aberrant evolution. I would hope Hugh might have been able to find a less bizarre object as his identificate. I would also hope, when I think of the world of monsters which he briefly let come alive in his three dreams, that more analysis would lessen his horrific anxieties about a murderous superego and a relentless analyst. However, it may not have been possible, given our problems with two-way traffic, and the confusion and anxiety that follows upon any good development, for Hugh to acknowledge that I could come to know his and my limits and not demand he be other than he is, without his being precipitated into a deep, even suicidal depression.

The questions I ask in this chapter about limits are the questions I ask myself when I look back and try to understand my disturbance and anxiety. What were Hugh's psychic limits? What were the limitations of my work then? And my limitations when compared with other colleagues? What might be the limits now, when there have been advances in psychoanalytic understanding and I am more experienced? What are the limits of any psychoanalysis? And finally, when I think of the urgency of his insistence that the analysis end, I think that perhaps Hugh knew his limits and stopped while the going was good.

## Acknowledgements

I am grateful to Dr Ron Britton for insightful comments on an earlier paper about this patient given to the BP-AS (*Bulletin* 1975) and for his encouragement to explore again its Promethean theme.

## Note

1 Hugh's Frankenstein has affinities, which reflect the overlap and the difference between psychosis and autism, with Tustin's (1986) autistic objects in that it is self-generated, idiosyncratic, hard and serves some of the same psychic functions e.g. protects from separateness, but it is unlike them in not being a sensation object. For Hugh, Frankenstein was mainly an object of omnipotent thought and phantasy. Anxious about destabilising him, I did not find a way of really addressing, in addition to its defensive services against multiple anxieties, either the distortion and deadening of which this dominating vision was the concrete end result, or his attachment to me which was also 'somewhere' unavailably there. And colleagues will surely have criticisms of my understanding and work with this case and suggestions to make.

## References


Bick, E. (1968) 'The experience of the skin in early object relations', *International Journal of Psychoanalysis*, 49: 484–486; reprinted in *Melanie Klein Today, Developments in Theory and Practice*, vol. 1, *Mainly Theory*, E. Bott Spillius (ed.), London: Routledge (1998).

Bion, W.R. (1957) 'Differentiation of the psychotic from the non-psychotic personalities', *International Journal of Psychoanalysis*, 38: 266–275; reprinted in *Second Thoughts*, London: Heinemann (1967).

Britton, R. (1998) *Belief and Imagination: Explorations in Psychoanalysis*, London: Routledge.

Feldman, M. (2000) 'Some views on the manifestation of the death instinct in clinical work', *International Journal of Psychoanalysis*, 81: 53–66.

Freud, S. (1911) 'Psycho-analytic notes upon an autobiographical account of a case of paranoia', SE 12: 3–82.

Mahler, M. (1961) 'On sadness and grief in infancy and childhood: loss and restoration of the symbiotic love object', *The Psychoanalytic Study of the Child*, 16: 332–351.

Money-Kyrle, R. (1965) 'Success and failure in mental maturation', *The Collected Papers of Roger Money-Kyrle*, D. Meltzer (ed.), Perthshire: Clunie Press (1978).

Rosenfeld, H. (1965) *Psychotic States: A Psychoanalytical Approach*, London: Hogarth Press.

Segal, H. (1957) 'Depression in the schizophrenic', *International Journal of Psychoanalysis*, 37: 339–343; reprinted in *Melanie Klein Today, Developments in Theory and Practice*, vol. 1, *Mainly Theory*, E. Bott Spillius (ed.), London: Routledge (1998).

Shelley, M. (1818) *Frankenstein, or The Modern Prometheus*, M. Joseph (ed.), London: Oxford University Press (1969).

Sohn, L. (1985) 'Narcissistic organisation, projective identification and the formation of the identificate', *International Journal of Psychoanalysis*, 66: 201–213; reprinted in *Melanie Klein Today*, vol. 1, *Mainly Theory*, E. Bott Spillius (ed.), London: Routledge (1998).

Steiner, J. (1996) 'The aim of psychoanalysis in theory and practice', *International Journal of Psychoanalysis*, 77: 1073–1085.

Tustin, F. (1972) *Autism and Child Psychosis*, London: Hogarth Press.

—— (1986) *Autistic Barriers in Neurotic Patients*, London: Karnac.
Winnicott, D.W. (1945) 'Primitive emotional development', *International Journal of Psychoanalysis*, 26: 137–143.

# DISCUSSION OF EDNA O'SHAUGHNESSY'S CHAPTER

*Irma Brenman Pick*

When this valuable and courageous paper was presented at a Scientific Meeting of the British Psychoanalytic Society, I was struck by the fact that although many interesting points were raised, for example about outcome studies, the effect of a handicapped sibling on the patient, and about adolescence, we seemed to avoid addressing the real issue which Red raised – i.e. what are the limits of what can be achieved? Rather there was, as always, in discussion of clinical material, an implication that had the analyst addressed or focused on X, Y, or Z a better result may have been achieved. Yet she raised a very important issue, which it seemed we were reluctant to consider.

I believe that we were optimistic forty years ago about the possibilities of 'curing' psychotic patients. The view, then, might have been that had the patient been able to receive the kind of understanding that Red so ably provided, significant changes might be hoped for. Of course, the work with her enabled him to move back to school, and that was undoubtedly of great importance, but the question she asks is: what are the limits of what can be achieved with such a damaged young person?

Awed as we were forty years ago by the amazing new discoveries and understandings in relation to psychotic thinking, I believe that we did not take fully on board the limitations that what is available 4 or even 5 hours per week, even at its best, may not be enough to equip the patient for the other 164 hours in the week; how is he to survive? Red's patient vividly demonstrates that his mask can be with him at all times; from his point of view, this feature makes it a preferable alternative.

This mask, possibly representing a parodied version of his (masked) mother, may perhaps have been all he had as an infant, and all he has to go home to at the end of the session. Within such a mask his mother was able to function. The alternative might, perhaps, have been (for her) a catastrophic breakdown. There are suggestions of this in her inability to cope when, for example, he became more depressed. To some extent, we all depend on masks to allow us to function; in this boy's case it seemed to be all he had; it seems he hates it, clings to it and uses it to triumph over his analyst and the analysis she offers.

In his projective identification with this feature in his mother, he failed/fails to build up a more robust and real internal object. While the analysis offers him this possibility, it also confronts him with problems of separateness, dependency, jealousy and envy. It threatens to remove the 'mask' that all the problems reside in the other/mother. Is there sufficient sanity/strength in him to support him, together with his analyst, to bear the pain of the damage he has done, and does, to himself and his object, and to bear the pain of looking at his actually damaged self, as well as his damaged object?

Red asks – did the patient 'know' to get out while the going was good? Was the alternative to limited functioning within the mask, catastrophic breakdown? To some extent we are mindful of this question when we do assessments. If the now 55-year-old patient, or his mother, functioning within her mask, presented, we might well think it best, as Freud said in 'Analysis terminable and interminable', to let sleeping dogs lie.

But the difficult question is one that is with us also in our work with more ordinary patients. It might be argued that such judgements are made every time we offer an interpretation; and surely in relation to decisions about termination. The case Red presents is stark, and the patient and his parents made the decision to end. Yet, whenever the issue of termination arises there is a question to be addressed, a judgement to be made. When is one engaged in a collusion in respecting the defence, and when is this appropriate? Certainly, in my experience, the question about when to terminate is always difficult. Do we sell the patient short by agreeing (prematurely) to terminate, not supporting the realistically capable part of the patient against the pull to retaining the mask, or do we go on interminably or even dangerously, not accepting the limits of what can be achieved? Of course, the question is even more vexed when thinking about termination in the analyses of those who will become future psychoanalysts. Bion, tongue in cheek, spoke of the 'cure' by becoming a 'certified psychoanalyst'. I think that what we are dealing with, then, is not an issue of 'tact' but of judgements which have to be made, where the consequences may be grave, and where it may be extremely difficult to predict to what extent the patient has been able to internalise a more useful helpmate, and to what extent the analysis itself is used as a mask.

# DISCUSSION OF EDNA O'SHAUGHNESSY'S CHAPTER

*Robin Anderson*

Red's work even forty years ago has all the hallmarks we recognise in her: an ability to feel her way right into the heart of her patient's deepest fears and maddest states which she does with a lightness of touch and a compassion which one senses to be very relieving to her patients. This certainly was the case for Hugh, at least until he was well enough to decide to distance himself from these qualities in his analyst. Despite the fact that Red's analysis of Hugh took place all that time ago, Hugh's plight and indeed that of his analyst has a freshness that is both moving and disturbing.

This broken down psychotic boy tortured by a bizarre 'creepy' world brings to his second session a picture of Paddington Bear sitting on a cushion. I found myself thinking of the contrast between Paddington's arrival at the Browns' house in Westbourne Grove and Hugh's arrival into his family home. The settling in could not have been more different. Paddington seems to have an absolute confidence that he will be loved and accepted and that he is indeed worthy of such affection, which of course all the children who became so attached to him shared. When Hugh then shows his analyst the headline 'BOY FRIEND, EXTRA' was he conveying a hope, a longing, that he could be that kind of boy? Red interprets his penis as the only 'friend' he has, but I did wonder even at that stage if Hugh was impressed by the little bear's pluck and wished that he could find a home in his analysis and a friend in his analyst in a way that he had never been able to do as a screaming, terrified, hating and hateful baby arriving into a family who longed for a whole and undamaged child. Sadly he was not that kind of bear or boy. We all instinctively admired Paddington but sadly Hugh could not find it in himself to feel admirable like that and he quickly knew it. It seems that when he begins to have the space to see his analyst as a separate object and he can only do this when he has felt held and accepted for long enough by her – the creepy world in the transparent bag – he is faced with such a marked contrast between the two of them. He cannot keep his world alive without the air supply of his analyst yet she is still full of colour and life after that first break and he is so impressed by that. Later Red shows us how much hatred and envy this provokes in Hugh and now he is faced with a new set of anxieties which replace those of simply surviving.

Red reveals Hugh's state of mind and level of functioning when she describes how his insight that there is now two-way traffic gives rise to a depression which he can only project into his unwilling mother. Although there is further working through it could only be gruelling and difficult and indeed it was for the reasons that Red makes so clear. Too much recognition of his weakness provokes his hatred of his rescuer and too much addiction to his omnipotence renders him mad and unable to live in the world of other people which he does want to do.

Red wonders if it could have ended differently if she had been seeing Hugh today. All the work on pathological organisations following Rosenfeld's groundbreaking work on narcissism (Rosenfeld 1964, 1971) was still many years away when Hugh had his analysis and I would like to think that this body of knowledge and experience might help to hold the analyst's inevitable despair in facing a patient's cold rejection for so long. This might have happened but even if this was a factor in the outcome I think this analysis was faced with a problem which I fear is just as unsolved today as it was then. Not only is there Hugh's own attitude to help but also as with all children his analysis is a joint effort with his parents. Children come to analysis because they have parents who wish to bring them and yet we do not have the possibility of analysing the complex motives of the parents of children as we can in adult patients who are responsible for their own analyses. It is true that some children can be helped who would be very unlikely to seek help as adults, but conversely some children are not held in analysis beyond a certain point if their parents do not wish it. Although for understandable reasons of confidentiality we do not hear a great deal about the parents' motivation, what does seem to come through is that the parents long for a normal healthy boy and even if they didn't have that, at the point the analysis ended they did at least have a boy who could begin to thrive at school. The price for further help would have been to tolerate yet more disturbance and depression and perhaps that was a price too high for them as well as for Hugh.

There was some recovery. At least Hugh could have a life even if it would be restricted by his powerful defences against pain. Prior to achieving the 'borderline position' he seemed destined for a completely isolated life perhaps in an actual psychotic state. At the point that he finished he did seem to be able to have some kind of functioning life; perhaps some of it a bit of a dead life but he does carry in him an essential piece of insight which enables him to be less mad even if he can't allow himself to know it very much – that 'Frankenstein is not real'.

## References

Rosenfeld, H. (1964) 'On the psychopathology of narcissism: a clinical approach', *International Journal of Psychoanalysis*, 45: 332–337.

—— (1971) 'A clinical approach to the psychopathology of the life and death instincts: an investigation into the aggressive aspects of narcissism', *International Journal of Psychoanalysis*, 52: 169–178.

# 11

# TO DEFY THE FATES

## Doubt as an expression of envy

*Martha Papadakis*

In this chapter I will investigate the nature of envy as developed in the paper 'Envy in everyday life' by Betty Joseph (1986). In the character of Heyst in the novel of Joseph Conrad (1915), *Victory*, I want to examine how the presence of envy manifests itself as doubt, in particular self-doubt. This doubt differs from the obsessional sense of doubt versus certainty, or the creative doubt involved in the act of making something that must be divested of omnipotence, and concerns more fundamentally the inability to establish trust and confidence in the goodness of the object and therefore in the self. This is a consequence of the failure of the ego to cope with envy and paves the way instead for a collapse to take place in the internal world.

Fate, as proposed by the ancient Greek oracle, commonly concerns a destiny, ultimately the close ally of death, which the individual struggles to avert. In the great myths and stories of Adam and Eve, Oedipus, Orpheus and Eurydice, and Othello for example, is contained the unfolding of an inevitable tragedy based on the inability of humankind to refrain from attacking its good objects be it through disobedience, ignorance, doubt or jealousy, and therefore the human inability to protect those good objects adequately and preserve them from destruction. The tragic fate of humankind is *par excellence* consequent upon envy; envy is inevitable and in envying, it is the good things which are threatened with destruction. This is the human fate, a psychoanalytic understanding of which would involve the concept of the primitive superego. 'The world', wrote Joseph Conrad, 'is a bad dog and will bite you if you give it a chance'. This is reminiscent of those familiar sayings – the dog in the manger, or the impulse to bite the hand that feeds. And surely this 'world' that the author is alluding to, alas exists within us all.

There is irony in the realisation, most frequently coming too late and hence impregnated with regret, that a future foreseen could be a future averted (and that introduces another whole problem not relevant to this chapter). Consequently the knowledge of the self associated with this hindsight can be suffused with considerable mental pain, guilt and remorse. The anguish of this realisation is of the most acute kind, and indeed may be too much to bear, and leads to suicide, as with the hero of Conrad's novel *Victory*, written in 1915. Power accrues to this perspective all the more because 'fate' is associated with punishment, for sins consciously or unconsciously committed, that in their cruel turn exact a retribution; the basis of the concept of Talion Law.

When envy predominates there has been trouble in the earliest relationship to the object and that trouble lingers on in all that follows. The presence of envy signifies the absence of trust in another. It is the primary internal factor obviating against development and creativity and for good reason. For envy is above all a hatred of life and therefore a manifestation according to certain thinkers, of the death instinct (Freud 1920; Klein 1957; Joseph 1981). For while being destructive towards others, and what is admired in them, it is also inherently self-destructive. It is the intention to spoil which makes envy so troublesome, together with the intention to deprive another of what is desirable and take possession of it that takes precedence over the desire itself. This in turn can cause disturbance in taking in good things, as a result of the grievance that arises from the discovery of their origin in others as opposed to oneself and as a consequence of the resentment and mistrust that is generated. When the underlying state is an envious one other emotions will be saturated by the impulse to denigrate and to take away. Excessive use of defences against envy, such as omnipotence and splitting, can be a further source of trouble.

While the sour grapes of envy may make their presence felt in crude and even violent ways, envy may also express itself with more subtlety – for instance in the ubiquitous affliction of doubt. This is most striking when there is a predominance of doubt where confidence and conviction would be appropriate. Instead, occupying their place are hesitation, uncertainty and confusion. The doubting person asks 'Is this right?' 'Am I good?' 'Do I deserve this?' and so on, feeling that the deepest values that guide actions through life are in question, and is so 'lost' in thoughts that crucial judgements cannot be made. This kind of doubt is distinct from obsessional phenomena, for here an underlying attack is being made on what is good that puts that good up for ransom. This omnipotent persecutory doubt is not to be confused with creative doubts which arise from not knowing.

## The novel

Destructive envy is most powerfully described in *Victory*. It was written against the background of the First World War when Conrad was 57 years old. In this novel the author returns to the Malay Archipelago where his earlier hero *Lord Jim* (1899) had, like Axel Heyst in *Victory*, struggled to assert the lofty ideals which ultimately contained the seeds of his own destruction. Despite the cruel injunction of his dead father to remove himself from life, Heyst falls in love with an English Cockney girl from Giancomo's Travelling Ladies Orchestra and flees with her to the remote island of Samburan. However, this action incurs the wrath of his old enemy Schomberg who sends out a posse to murder Heyst and recapture the girl. Tragically in the ensuing struggle, while trying to protect her lover, the girl is accidentally shot dead and in utter despair Heyst takes his own life.

The story concentrates on the lonely and noble hero Axel Heyst, whom the reader meets as an orphan who lost his mother, as it were before the historic record of the novel began. All we know is that his father, on his deathbed, proclaims that his only son must have a relation with life in which he is 'to look on [and] make no sound', and thus cursed, to be forever a witness and not a participant. In accordance with this principle and in obedience to this father, Heyst duly leads a solitary and detached life; evidence of the absence of his mother, his submission to his father, and his evasion of any challenge to him. He prefers to be enthralled and dominated by this envious father with whom he has made a pact inside himself to be in an emasculated homosexual partnership that denies the loss of his mother.

However, his encounter with two people thrusts him into an involvement and a commitment to life that brings his 'drifting' to a halt. First, there is a man, Morrison, whom he cannot resist saving from financial ruin, though he cannot prevent his death, a death for which he is wracked by guilt, and then there is a woman, Lena, who he rescues from a dire personal situation and who falls in love with him. With her both great joy and tragedy unfold. She elopes with him to his island retreat, but they are pursued by a trinity of diabolical scoundrels, Pedro, Ricardo and Jones (like some malign split-off bits of the self that break through into consciousness). This pursuit is at the behest of the treacherous innkeeper who is infatuated with Lena, and hates Heyst with the venom born of the lover scorned. The innkeeper leads the trio to believe that Heyst has murdered the man who was his friend and plundered his treasure, and seduced Lena, whom the innkeeper sees as his possession. The innkeeper attributes to his mortal enemy Heyst all his bad intentions – to plunder, murder and rape. And indeed there is a treasure which Heyst has, in the love between himself and Lena. 'Every time she spoke she seemed to abandon to him something of herself . . . something excessively subtle and inexpressible to which he was infinitely sensible.'

Yet at the same time Heyst is gripped by a curious inertia, an inertia which ultimately proves fatal and in losing his love, he also loses his will to live and takes his own life. However, the victory of the title concerns the capacity in Lena, after 'doubt entered into him', to prove that indeed she so truly loves him that she is prepared to make the greatest sacrifice of all and lay down her life to save Heyst. His victory is learning, in turn, after her death and before taking his own life, a most painful truth.

'Woe to the man who has not learned while young to hope, to love – and to put his trust in life' and in this way freed himself from bondage to the past and to death. For Heyst this is the grip of his remote and judgemental father to whom he turns, after losing his beloved mother, and whom he is unable to overthrow until it is too late. This father 'looks on' and mocks life, and the entanglement his son has with him suggests an unresolved mourning for his mother.

It is this loss of love, the love he recovers in Lena, as a result of the inertia of the hero, and the doubt that underlies it, that I would like to explore further using this masterly novel as an illustration. In 'Envy in everyday life' Betty Joseph writes about

> Feelings of resentment at someone doing better . . . and vague hostility, rivalry and competitiveness . . . but when it is more powerful . . . trouble starts . . . carping criticism [that] always finds doubts . . . and the criticism and doubts can look real.
>
> (Joseph 1986: 182)

The doubts can look more real, as Betty Joseph explains, than anything positive. The positive becomes both unconvincing and ineffectual. For what is attacked at the centre is the faith and the trust a person has in their good objects and therefore, since these objects are also internal, what is of goodness in the self. It is a more formidable problem to resolve this if the attack is taking place from within the self.

Doubt gnaws into the quality of goodness and undermines it, making knowledge and the enlarging of experience, beyond Paradise, that is idealised, a poisoned thing that brings bitterness and despair and a 'vision of the world destroyed' as Conrad describes it. The danger of knowledge is central to the myth of Adam and Eve; the forbidden fruit is irresistible, but once consumed the knowledge it brings shatters Paradise. For Othello the destruction of paradise takes another route. Attention is focused on the workings of one of the seven deadly sins, envy, in the character of Iago who has the power to blind Othello to his love for Desdemona and render him deaf to hers for him. She is literally murdered by his doubt. To have knowledge, by implication, is to have innocence spoilt, though knowledge is attained through the loss of innocence, but not necessarily by the destruction of it.

The most intense and violent envy is directed against the sexual couple. In its possessiveness envy attempts to refute a triangular relationship and clings in the unconscious to the terrifying combined parental figure in which the parents in the primal scene are fused. In its more differentiated form the couple, enjoying the ultimate sexual pleasure, also personify creativity in the form of new life, internally in the development of the self and externally in the potential for a child. 'A fresh start' was how Conrad described the love between Lena and Heyst. Relationships of such importance always signify change and emotional growth for the self, and open up something infinite in the discovering of another person and in the recovering of the loved parental couple.

For the couple in *Victory* their contact brings about a transformation in their sense of themselves and their sense of isolation in the silent universe of 'no sound'. [Lena's] 'smile . . . conveyed warmth . . . an ardour to live . . . new to his [Heyst's] experience', and again Lena felt 'the impress of something most rare and precious – his embraces made her own by her courage in saving his life' or again 'her irresistible desire to give herself up' to her love for this man. While these references are sexual they simultaneously allude to the emotionally momentous. In this coupling a third can only be an intrusion, into the mutually gratifying exclusivity of the twosome and what they give each other. 'An island', a paradise of first love, or last love as it was for that couple, where 'we can safely defy the fates', declares Heyst idealistically, with the presumption of an Oedipus. In the mind there is such a place where it seems for a moment something perfect is possible, even, briefly, capable of being attained.

It is however from the point of view of the third, outside and looking on (which is also a universal experience), that envy of that sublime aspect of the couple is mobilised. Envy as an affective position is one that combines a sense of dispossession joined together with entitlement. It is in the failure of Heyst to deal with that position, in the form of the devilish trio that intrude into his paradise of love, and more seriously into 'his infernal mistrust of life', that his character comes unstuck, unleashing tragedy. In becoming vulnerable to his love for Lena, that revives the first loss of his mother, Heyst is also made vulnerable to the envy which attacks it that is central to the troubled relationship with his father inside himself and then 'life has him fairly by the throat'. Of all the sins envy, essentially malign in wanting bad for another, is closest to evil in its ruthless attack on goodness. Ricardo, like a splinter of the bad relation to his father, says, 'You are no more to me one way or another, than that fly there' referring to his object of desire, Lena, 'I do not care what I do'. He personifies amorality and callousness, in the face of which Heyst is helpless.

However, it is not care which weakens Heyst; he has a big heart and cares most deeply. Rather it is doubt as Betty Joseph describes it: 'The doubts that can look real'. It is a 'peculiar stagnation', which, like Hamlet in his dark ruminations, undermines Heyst, sapping his resolve and leaving him filled with apprehension. Heyst's doubt, arising from his hatred of his father, and homosexual submission to him, leads inevitably to his doubting Lena who in turn requires of him a potent rebellion against his castrating father. From the moment of the arrival of the trio on the island Heyst is aware that 'he has lost a sense of her [Lena's] existence' and indeed he is inexorably to lose her as he lost his mother. Their enchantment is broken. Belief and the associated conviction, based on trust in the primary good object and the antithesis of doubt, eludes him, and yet the loss began earlier, internally long before their arrival. From Lena Heyst learns, with astonishment, of the lies spread about him, that he robbed and murdered his dear friend Morrison and took advantage of her helplessness to seduce her. From then on he is wounded. It is as though he has discovered his own unconscious death wishes toward his father and attacks on his good mother, and these cause a crisis of confidence in himself and his goodness as a man.

The calumny opens up doubts and weakens his confidence in the goodness of what he has actually done to save his friend, and take care of his beloved. He is plunged into an abyss of confusion between good and bad and becomes a man who 'doubts his own love' (Freud 1909: 241). He doubts those who warrant his trust and are loyal to him; Lena and his faithful Chinese servant Wang, who ends up deserting him, seeing him as 'a doomed man'. Instead his melancholia draws him in the direction of self-devaluation, both to deny his own unconscious envy and punish himself for it at the same time. In this way Heyst sets about his own undoing and placates his aggressors, who plunge him back again into the old problems with his mother and father. His capacity to make judgements necessary for the survival of their love is lost in a world, as a consequence, now full of danger. The 'painful and ominous dream of separation' from which Lena wakes becomes, in time, the nightmare of their reality.

In contrast Lena's love strengthens 'the faith that had been born in her . . . in the man of her destiny' and enables her to act with clarity of mind and with bravery, her only doubt being her own strength, but utterly certain of her love for Heyst. However his servant thinks 'Number One is a doomed man', and increasingly, he acts like one. The scoundrels want his 'swag', his money, but for Heyst it is his love for Lena, she is his riches, but in having her he finds himself disarmed from defending her. It is this state of mind, in which the envious individual 'always finds doubts' as Betty Joseph describes (even if the envy is by one part of the self toward another), that afflicts Heyst, saps his strength and renders him impotent and helpless to defend what he most loves in the world. More and more he is dominated by an envious internal object that possesses his ego. The envy is not experienced as his own but as rather the take-over by this envious father who does not want him to have a life, but only look on. The troubles there duly come to haunt his love for Lena, his doubting of her brings guilt which then makes him doubt himself. Doubt envelops him and the doubt ultimately concerns himself. Never has he lifted 'his hand on a man'. He wants to refute the fact that he has to fight for his good objects and stand up to that which threatens to destroy them. In fact he is in a collusion with a bad object who is allowed to get away with murder of his good object; perhaps his own morbid theory of the death of his mother.

Three important factors contribute to this situation. In envy the components of idealisation as a defence against destructive feelings (death wishes) and the guilt feelings consequent upon such feelings are all interrelated. First, Heyst idealises a view of the world in which aggression, including his own, is absent. An idealisation reminiscent of Klein's description of 'the universal longing for the prenatal state', a state of fusion that can never be exactly reconstituted again. In this way Heyst is without means 'to defy the fates' and withstand the envious intruders on his island who come to plunder and murder him. 'I have refined everything away', says Heyst, leaving him literally without a weapon for the fray that confronts him. With this idealisation he attempts to ward off 'the world' of envy and persecution and establish a bulwark against them on the presumption that he can meet the world on his terms. It is clear that his paradise, like his innocence, has become appallingly vulnerable when that is called to account.

The enviable individual may be unfamiliar with envious feelings, and naive as to their potential for destruction, as is evident in Heyst's willingness to suspect those who are faithful good objects in lieu of his actual and undeniable enemies. His policy of appeasement of his tormentors marks a deterioration in his character. When he is put under pressure he relates to them, as to his father, by capitulation.

A second factor contributing to Heyst's fatalism is his fear of death, most striking in a man formerly so brave and fearless, 'I have lost all belief in realities', he tells Lena, by which he means courage and the conviction that he needs to arm himself against doubt and oppose evil. Are these his own death wishes he is powerless to oppose? Having found or rather re-found his 'rare and precious' object, he doubts his right to it and his capacity to repair it. He feels himself unworthy of it and suspects his own goodness when he has grounds to believe in it, as he has grounds to suspect the bad intentions of his enemies In his ruminations there is a kind of thinking, not as a 'trial form of action' as Freud (1911) defined it but as substitute for and alternative to action. The more Heyst thinks of how he will defend himself and Lena without a knife or a gun, the more paralysed he is in his predicament, as though mesmerised by doubt and enthralled with his own impending death, which he is actively seeking out. Others play out the denouement of the novel, determining its outcome, while Heyst becomes a pawn in his own destiny; a man without a proper part in his own drama.

A third component contributing to Heyst's inhibition is his sense of guilt. A guilt that is premature and excessive associated with the grief resulting from the early loss of his mother and the related internalisation of a punitive object. It condemns him before he is able to act, for wishes and thoughts he might have had or deeds he might have done and this saps the aggression he requires to defend himself against his attackers. The original situation in which the good maternal object succumbs and the bad paternal object triumphs is repeated and there is a lack of a good heterosexual alternative to that father. Guilt, so crucial in envy, results from the process of devaluation either of the self or others, so crucial in envy. The depth of Heyst's despair in failing to adequately protect his internal good mother, to whom there is not one reference in the novel (in contrast to the prominence of his father) is revived in the relationship to Lena, with whom his despair is precipitate. Before the fighting even starts he seems to have given up and resigned himself to fate, reflecting his paralysis in relation to his own feelings, particularly terror at his aggression.

As with Original Sin, premature guilt brings with it a sense of retribution, which may be for provoking envy or turning it around and projecting it. To arouse the evil eye is to incite trouble, and this sort of guilt quickly deteriorates into persecution. It is precisely this sort of trouble that makes relationships so important, as Lena explains to Heyst. This unconscious sense of guilt makes something purposeful of bad luck, and comes as 'a sort of punishment from an angry Heaven' for moral badness. It is related to feeling undeserving of happiness or good fortune. The punitive superego father (mixed up with aspects of the mother) of Heyst seems to glare down on the couple from a position of Schopenhauerian 'vision', detached and vengeful, proclaiming no hope, just futility. To have what is enviable (the love of Lena) is to incur his Oedipal father's wrath and revenge.

Freud declared that hate is older than love, and must be mitigated by it. Heyst after many years wandering trying to find his way on his own without the need to love, locked into his hatred of his father, discovered love much later in life and was less familiar with it. Conrad himself married when he was 39 years old. Both the hero and heroine of *Victory*, like Adam and Eve, felt undeserving of their happiness and love and explained their misfortune, their 'fate' on this basis. Indeed Heyst felt 'like a dead man already', marked, singled out or cast out, momentarily indistinguishable from his malevolent double Jones, who says 'I am the world itself come to pay you a visit . . . I am an outcast, almost an outlaw. I am a sort of fate – the retribution that waits its time'. This 'world', which is the malign relation with his father, consumes him and makes him doubt his love for Lena.

Heyst is also an outsider, aspiring to an absolute self-sufficiency, and this sets him apart and leaves him psychologically exposed in the face of threatening forces. 'The mood of grim doubt intruded on him only when he was alone', wrote Conrad. This mood was connected with his archaic picture of his dead father, a picture suffused with his own loss and maternal deprivation and in such contradiction with the one of warmth and growth with Lena. Heyst was a good man but one alone in the world, surely an outcast by his own father and behind that by his mother, something that is deeper and older.

This picture of a bad father, stern and cold, declaring 'look on – make no sound' was a 'father who had spent his life blowing blasts upon a terrible trumpet which had filled Heaven and Earth with ruins'. With such a bleak internal object, it is difficult for Heyst to fight his external enemies; the internal enemy has first to be fought. An object personifying the envious perspective, 'producing misfortune by his evil eye' (Cicero). Could it be that in Heyst's own forgotten past, who like Conrad himself lost his mother when he was 8 years old and his father when he was 12, there is a lost and longed for couple, the parents united in love and in their love for him, the child. As the villains look in, covetously, on his paradise so he looks in, from outside, on a lovely but lost world. A world now inaccessible to him, lost forever. The world he aspires to recreate anew with Lena, and Cassandra-like, helplessly foresees falling apart.

The eye features as an important agent of envy, for it is the eye, that window to the soul, which conveys the look within. The envious green-eyed look contains the two powerful components of envy; the sense of entitlement, with which grievance is so often associated the moment there is any frustration, and a sense of deprivation of what is so desired. Such a look features in *Chance* (1913), the novel Conrad wrote before *Victory*, in which another Oedipal tragedy is told. In this, the lonely bitter old father, recently released from prison, his own life in ruins, looks in such a way upon his daughter and her new life in the form of her love for another man. This father regards his child as his possession and yet he observes her loving another. What he sees evokes an emotion that is intolerable and he tries to poison her lover. The provocation of being denied what is passionately desired is too much and he is precipitated by the intensity of his feelings into attempting to commit murder.

It is only the love and therefore concern for another person that can stand between such a primitive enactment of envious feelings and the drawing back from it. It is also the love and concern for the other which releases us from being imprisoned in such intense and destructive emotion and therefore provides a possible resolution. In its most violent form, a form which greatly interested Conrad, envy disregards the object completely. 'The girl', sneers the innkeeper in *Victory*, 'means nothing to me'. His obsession with her governs his mind and at the same time what he says is true. To him she is of no consequence. His demands on her are absolute and ruthless; be mine, all mine and nothing of your own self. He has a right to her, that she loves another is simply unacceptable. If, at the same time, the girl is destroyed in the pursuit of his desire for her, well so be it. Self-doubt in no way afflicts this man as it does Heyst, and makes the innkeeper and his trio of henchmen efficient machines for killing.

Since envy addresses itself to the part and not the whole person it is made all the more potent by being founded on an illusion, in the same way as idealisation is. The part is not the whole. A sense of reality attempts to encompass that whole and recognises the partial nature of what is known and understood. There are moments of acute pleasure and well being that do exist as part of the rest of reality. However the illusions, in their perfection, may be very compelling, seizing hold of the individual with a tenacity that makes it impossible to relinquish them and tolerate reality. The innkeeper is possessed by just such an illusion about Lena. In *Victory*, on the one hand, there are the individuals who are the willing and unquestioning executors of destructive envy, the band of brigands that threaten the beautiful island Heyst has created, and on the other hand there is the inner torment and impotence of the hero himself, lost in an incestuous Oedipal configuration, and lost also in his doubts about the nature of humankind, and therefore himself, since he is also a man.

Conrad asks us, can he spend his life in paradise apart from 'the world' ('the bad dog that will bite you if you give it a chance')? The First World War precipitated the world into a convulsion of change through the intrusion of that 'world', at the very time when Conrad was writing his novel. That is the 'world' of bad forces that the intruders also represent. Inevitably these forces break through the defences against them and have to be accounted for; otherwise there is restriction and isolation. Conrad's answer to the question as to whether humans can live their lives in paradise is a resounding no. He tells us it is necessary to find a way to live in 'the world', and with human nature as it is, however unlike it is to how we might like it to be.

## Conclusion

In *Victory*, a tale of love lost, Conrad investigates the nature of love and the causes of its loss. His hero, bereft of conviction, in particular the conviction needed to contend with experiences of good and bad and learn which is which, together with the assertion of good experience over bad, drifts amidst a sea of doubts. He proclaims in identification with his dead father, 'the silenced destroyer of systems, of hopes, of beliefs' that 'he who forms a tie is lost', but Conrad shows us by the end of this novel that the opposite is true; he who does not form a tie is lost. For neither has he the consolation of others in his loneliness, nor does he achieve the confidence that accrues from surviving the vicissitudes of experience, to stand firm in the world of realities and fight for the good things when faced with the inevitable confrontation. Heyst is unable to overthrow his identification with the father and to defy the fates, until it is too late and he in turn is tragically cast out.

Envy is the major obstacle to the capacity to love and one way it may manifest its presence is in doubt. Evasion of envy, most potently of the sexual couple, brings unhappiness and mistrust. If things go well primitive destructive envy can evolve into a more realistic adult form that merges into constructive rivalry and jealousy. The capacity to love involves the recognition and tolerance of envy. Its location solely in the external world is a precarious solution that is restrictive to development as Heyst, in his exposed position, discovers.

> Woe to the man whose heart has not learnt while young to hope, to love – and to put its trust in life.

Heyst cries in anguish on the death of his beloved, in despair at losing her and shortly before taking his own life. Woe to the man who has not wrestled with the bitter grip of envy, in others but primarily in himself, the envy of the one excluded, the envy of the one without. By the same token, blessed is he who learns, as does Heyst, albeit tragically, 'to hope, to love – and to put its trust in life'. This after all is the achievement of humankind – to learn to love and to be loved.

## References

Conrad, J. (1915) *Victory*, Oxford: World Classics (1986).

Freud, S. (1909) 'Notes upon a case of obsessional neurosis', SE 10: 241. London: Hogarth Press (1955).

—— (1911) 'Formulations on the two principles of mental functioning', SE 12: 213.

Joseph, B. (1981) 'Addiction to near death', *Psychic Equilibrium and Psychic Change: Selected Papers of Betty Joseph*, M. Feldman and E. Bott Spillius (eds), London: Routledge (1989).

—— (1986) 'Envy in everyday life', *Psychic Equilibrium and Psychic Change: Selected Papers of Betty Joseph*, M. Feldman and E. Bott Spillius (eds), London: Routledge (1989).

Klein, M. (1957) 'Envy and gratitude', *The Writings of Melanie Klein*, vol. 3, *Envy and Gratitude and Other Works*, London: Hogarth Press (1975).

# DISCUSSION OF MARTHA PAPADAKIS' CHAPTER

## *Ignes Sodré*

In this chapter Martha illustrates Joseph's conceptualisation in her paper 'Envy in everyday life', in particular in relation to the envy which causes self-doubt in relation to the loved object, in connection with an important aspect of character development in Conrad's novel *Victory*. Her central point is that Conrad's main character, Heyst, although capable of real love, isn't strong enough to tolerate the attacks of persecuting, envious objects who exist in external reality, but who become of course the personification of internal objects, with whom destructive parts of the self identify. Faced with too much persecution, Heyst becomes Freud's 'man who doubts his own love' and is destroyed by this. Heyst's fear that his love is too weak is seen to derive not only from the early death of his mother, which brings doubt in 'destiny' – fate is a cruel, unloving superego – but also from serious depression in relation to the capacity to keep his object alive by loving it sufficiently. It seems to me that the cruel superego is formed by the introjection of a father who is hateful on two counts: because he was not capable of protecting and saving the mother (and therefore failed in his most important function) and because he is felt to be a 'third' in a jealous/envious position in relation to an idealised mother–baby couple – and therefore is accused of murder. There is much to be discussed in this rich contribution, but for me the most interesting issue is that of the connection between a *Paradise Lost/Paradise Regained* scenario and the destructive envy of the couple in the ideal situation. I think that Martha puts to very good use the connection between clinical and literary insights. She explores the connections with the melancholia of early loss and consequent lack of trust in love, and shows convincingly how the melancholic personality – be it in a real or in an imaginary human being – is weakened when confronted by simultaneous envious attacks from the superego and from the baby self. Heyst's father, in his deathbed, condemns his son to live the life of an observer; he must 'look on [and] make no sound' – in other words, he feels compelled to live his life in the emotional position of a baby looking at the primal scene, too guilty and too depressed, too afraid either to intrude or to separate and create a life of his own.

Pathological doubt, I think, always belongs to an internal configuration in which the existence of another (be it a separate being, or a different frame of mind, or the opposite affect) is what destroys the belief in the existence of a paradisical one-to-one, which in wishful phantasy should be a psychic space where the reality of the rest of the world and its intruding eyes is avoided. The problem of the 'paradise regained' configuration is not only that the reality of the third will inevitably intrude – ultimately, of course, reality *is* the third – but also that the idealised couple itself, as the author has so convincingly illustrated, constantly 'defies the Fates' by projecting envy.

Healthy doubt, the capacity to question and to be able to hold two different points of view simultaneously, should work towards the diminishing of idealisation, towards the acceptance of 'good enough' reality. Pathological doubt, which destroys rather than modifies, derives both from the fragility of the 'paradise' phantasy when confronted with realistic questioning, but also from the narcissistic rage at the impossibility of maintaining, of being in total possession of, that which is idealised – if the object (and/or self) isn't perfect, it might as well be dead. Clinically of course it is terribly important to differentiate which are the feelings that come from the melancholic 'my love is not enough', leading to despair, from those connected to the disillusionment coming from the narcissistic need for perfection. Envious self-doubting is presumably more narcissistic.

# EPILOGUE

## *Betty Joseph*

The editors suggested that I should write a note about what the workshop has meant to me since I am the only individual who has been in it since its inception. But this fact in itself causes problems, since the workshop has become so much part of my professional life that it is difficult to stand outside and comment. When this workshop – then a clinical seminar – began, more than forty years ago, we were a disparate group of people meeting to discuss cases. But soon it developed into one of a small number of teaching seminars in which I was the seminar leader, and from which members left when they became more senior and had their own teaching or administrative responsibilities. Then slowly we discovered that no one was leaving, we could include no new people and had become a consistent group meeting to discuss cases with absolute regularity. This very fact has meant that a bond of friendship and trust has been built up which has enabled us to share ideas, failings and achievements with a considerable degree of freedom and to exchange ideas, borrow from, differ with each other and slowly build up each his or her own approach. In addition it has helped the group to function in a particular way – that is to be able to recognise and verbalise ways in which a presenter may unconsciously be being caught up in some enactment, some unrecognised defensive manoeuvre or emotional attitude affecting his capacity to understand or interpret freely, and thus help him or her to clarify what is likely to be going on and to contain it. It may be that this is one of the most important functions of a group of this kind.

This is a very diverse group of people; all share the same basic theoretical approach, but each comes with his or her own personal slant or interest, so that there is constant stimulation and sharing and the original seminar has become, in truth, a workshop. Nowadays sometimes as the evening goes on, if a particularly difficult case is being discussed, many ideas may have been floated but we realise that we have only very partially come to some understanding and the evening ends with little clarification. At other times as the discussion continues out of a sense of incomprehension in the presenter and the group ideas start to come together and some real sense of understanding emerges.

It is hard work but enormously stimulating to have to struggle for understanding in this way but for me it has been and is a very important experience working with a group of people who can help each other to share their thinking, tolerate unclarity and uncertainty and learn together and I am very grateful for the opportunity.

# Index

# THE SHEFFIELD MURDERS 1865 to 1965

Printed & published by:
ALD Design & Print
279 Sharrow Vale Road
Sheffield S11 8ZF
Great Britain
Tel: 0114 267 9402
a.lofthouse@btinternet.com

First Published December 2003

ISBN 1-901587-37-1

# THE SHEFFIELD MURDERS 1865 to 1965

Being Volume Two of
*The Sheffield Hanged*

**David Bentley**

## *Other publications by the same Author*

Select Cases from the Twelve Judges' Notebooks

English Criminal Justice in the Nineteenth Century

Victorian Men of Law

The Sheffield Hanged, 1750-1864

## *About the Author*

David Bentley is a circuit judge. Born in Sheffield and educated at King Edward VII School, Sheffield, University College, London and the University of Sheffield, he practised at the bar in Sheffield from 1969 until his appointment to the bench in 1988. He took silk in 1984. He has a doctorate in nineteenth-century legal history and is the author of books and articles on the subject. He lives in Sheffield with his wife and two sons.

## *Other titles in the series:*

| | |
|---|---|
| Mi-Amigo - The Story of Sheffield's Flying Fortress, *David Harvey* | ISBN 1-901587-00-2 |
| Tales From a Peak District Bookshop, *Mike Smith* | ISBN 1-901587-01-0 |
| Tha' Don't look Proper, *Anne Hunt* | ISBN 1-901587-02-9 |
| Shiny Sheff - The Story of Sheffield's Fighting Ships, *Alistair Lofthouse* | ISBN 1-901587-03-7 |
| Doug's War - An Erksome Business, *Doug Sanderson* | ISBN 1-901587-04-5 |
| The Dramatic Story of The Sheffield Flood, *Peter Machan* | ISBN 1-901587-05-3 |
| Carl Wark - Peak District Fortress or Folly?, *Mick Savage* | ISBN 1-901587-06-1 |
| Then & Now - Sheffield, *Alistair Lofthouse* | ISBN 1-901587-07-X |
| Charlie Peace, The Banner Cross Murderer, *Peter Machan* | ISBN 1-901587-08-8 |
| Then & Now - The Sheffield Blitz, *Alistair Lofthouse* | ISBN 1-901587-09-6 |
| They Lived in Sharrow and Nether Edge, *Nether Edge Neighbourhood Group* | ISBN 1-901587-10-X |
| Discovering Derbyshire's White Peak, *Tom Bates* | ISBN 1-901587-11-8 |
| Lost Sheffield - Portrait of a Victorian City, *Peter Machan* | ISBN 1-901587-12-6 |
| The Sheffield Outrages, The Trade Union Scandals, *Peter Machan* | ISBN 1-901587-14-2 |
| A Layman's Look at the History, Industry, People and Places of Oughtibridge Worrall and Wharncliffe Side, *Doug Sanderson* | ISBN 1-901587-15-0 |
| Derbyshire in Old Photographs, *E Mottram & A Lofthouse* | ISBN 1-901587-16-9 |
| Weerz me dad? 40s & 50s Childhood Stories *Fred Pass* | ISBN 1-901587-17-7 |
| 'Orreight mi Ol?', *Don Alexander* | ISBN 1-901587-18-5 |
| More By Luck Than Judgement, *Prof. Roy Newton* | ISBN 1-901587-21-5 |
| Memories of the Workhouse & Hospital at Fir Vale, *Lyn Howsam* | ISBN 1-901587-22-3 |
| All Mine - Memories of a Bomb & Mine Disposal Officer, *Noel Cashford MBE* | ISBN 1-901587-23-1 |
| The Sheffield Hanged, *David Bentley* | ISBN 1-901587-24-X |
| Victorian Men of Law, *David Bentley* | ISBN 1-901587-90-8 |
| Tell It Agee'rn Fred, A compilation of Poems, *Fred Pass* | ISBN 1-901587-25-8 |
| Club 60 & The Esquire 1960-67 - Sounds of the 60s, *Don Hale/Terry Thornton* | ISBN 1-901587-26-6 |
| The Story of Sheffield's High Street, *Pat Dallman* | ISBN 1-902587-27-4 |
| The Lighter Side of War - 'England's Bilko', *Don Alexander* | ISBN 1-901587-28-2 |
| Return to the Beaches, *Jack Barker* | ISBN 1-901587-29-0 |
| Memories of Sheffield's King Mojo Club, *D Manvell & J Firminger* | ISBN 1-901587-30-4 |
| Then & Now - The Monsal Trail, *Alistair Lofthouse* | ISBN 1-901587-31-2 |
| Round & About Grenoside, *Grenoside &District Local History Group* | ISBN 1-901587-32-0 |
| South West Wings, *R Sutton* | ISBN 1-901587-33-9 |
| Wings over Wiltshire, *Rod Priddle* | ISBN 1-901587-34-7 |
| In Peace we train for War, *Trevor Diack* | ISBN 1-901587-35-5 |

# Contents

# *Foreword*

The history and pattern of murders in major English cities such as Birmingham, Leeds and Manchester is well documented.[1] When last year I wrote *The Sheffield Hanged* my purpose was to provide Sheffield with a similar record. That account stopped at 1864, the year in which Leeds was made an Assize town and Sheffield murderer, Joseph Myers was publicly executed outside its prison at Armley. This book takes the story down to 1965, the year in which capital punishment for murder was abolished.[2]

The list of those executed for Sheffield murders between 1865 and 1965 is not a long one. Just eighteen were put to death. Most were hanged at Armley Gaol including the infamous Charlie Peace and the Fowler brothers. The names of the others and the details of their crimes have, for the most part, been long since forgotten. But their cases excited huge local interest at the time and have lost none of their power to shock. They also bring home just how hard life was for the Sheffield poor in this era. When in 1884 Joseph Laycock's murdered family was laid to rest, it was in an unmarked pauper's grave; when Harry Hobson slew Ada Stothard in 1887 the anarchist journal *Freedom* was in no doubt that it was hopeless and grinding poverty which had driven him to do it; in the last week of her life Lizzie Lax (murdered in August, 1925) could see no future for herself and her children but the workhouse and when, earlier that year, Jock

---

[1] See John K Eddleston, *Murderous Birmingham, Murderous Leeds, Murderous Manchester*, Breedon Books, Derby, 1997,

[2] Only murders for which the capital penalty was exacted are included.

Plommer was murdered by the Fowlers his family was, at a stroke, rendered destitute.

I have tried to provide the reader with as much detail as possible about the location of the murders. Many of the buildings and streets referred to are no more but some have survived. It is still possible to call in for a drink at the *Banner Cross Hotel* where the inquest upon Arthur Dyson was opened. The concrete bases of the huts of the POW camp at Redmires are still there. So too is the building which once housed Highfields police station (I must have passed it hundreds of times over the years and yet never noticed it – but only for want of looking). When you are next in Crookes, pause for a moment outside the *Barnado's Charity Shop* at no. 231: it was here that Lee Doon murdered his employer and buried the body in the cellar, and in nearby School Lane you can see the surgery from which Dr John Blakely practised.

I am grateful to all who have encouraged and assisted me in the writing of this book and would like, in particular, to thank to thank the staff of the Sheffield Local Studies Library for all the help they have given me, the South Yorkshire police for permission to reproduce photographs of Charlie Peace, the Garvins and the Fowlers and lastly Patrick Robertshaw for suggesting improvements to the text.

# 1

## The Road to the Gallows

In 1865, the only crime for which men were still hanged in England was murder.

For Sheffield murderers the journey to the scaffold began at the Central Police Office cells in Castle Green, for it was there that those arrested for serious crime were lodged to await examination by a magistrate.

Sheffield's first police force, set up under a Town Improvement Act of 1818, had operated out of offices on the lower floor of the Town Hall in Castle Street, the building which housed the magistrates' courts. It soon outgrew this accommodation but for years the town turned a deaf ear to its demand for new premises. By 1860 the position was becoming desperate and in 1864 the Town Council, notorious for its reluctance to spend money, finally yielded and authorised the building of a new office at Castle Green. With a lofty stone front, built in the Italian style and extending back to Water Lane, it cost £15,102. It contained:

> *commodious offices for the Chief Constable, officers, clerks, detectives and charge officers, a large room for the meetings of the Watch Committee, 17 cells of very safe construction capable of holding about 70 prisoners and a large covered yard in which the whole police force [could] be paraded,*

with the cell area connected to the Town Hall by an underground passage. After the police moved out, the Town Hall was used exclusively as a court-house.

It was the duty of the police to bring those arrested for murder or other felony before a magistrate for preliminary examination as soon as reasonably practicable. The examination was not a trial (magistrates had no power to try murder or other grave felonies): its purpose was firstly to record the evidence against the accused and secondly, to determine whether that evidence was sufficient to justify sending him to the Assizes for trial. The witnesses in support of the charge were called by a solicitor instructed on behalf of the police and questioned on oath, the accused, or his lawyer (if he had one) having the right to cross-examine. The evidence of each was taken down in the form of a written deposition which he would be required to sign before leaving the witness box. Once the prosecution witnesses had been heard their depositions would be read over to the accused and he would be asked whether he wished to say anything in answer to the charge. The magistrate was obliged to caution him that he was not obliged to say anything and, in fact, few defendants did, preferring instead to 'reserve their defence.' As well as making his answer to the charge there and then, the accused could, if he chose, call witnesses and, after 1898, even give evidence on his own behalf.

Most prisoners, especially those represented by lawyers, preferred to keep their powder dry and to make no answer except to deny their guilt and state that they reserved their defence. The practice of reserved defences came under much criticism from Assize judges at the end of the nineteenth and in the early years of the twentieth century. It was, however, deeply ingrained and such strictures were ignored. Having listened to the accused's answer and witnesses, if any, the examining magistrate had to decide whether the evidence disclosed a *prima facie* case of guilt (that is one which called for an answer from the accused). If he concluded that it did, he would commit the accused in custody for trial at the next Assizes.

Preliminary examinations were normally held in the main court-room at Castle Street. During the period 1870-1914, when the town had a stipendiary magistrate, cases of murder were generally listed before him.

Upon the accused's first appearance before the examining magistrate, he would commonly be remanded in custody for seven days to enable the police to complete their inquiries. Murder cases inevitably attracted huge press interest and the evidence given at the committal hearing was always extensively reported in the local newspapers. Such reporting had an obvious potential for stirring up prejudice against a defendant in the minds of prospective jurors, but it was not until 1967 that the law stepped in to prohibit the publication of such reports.

In cases of homicide there would, in addition to the hearing in the magistrates' court, also be a coroner's inquest, the purpose of which was to establish the identity of the deceased and the cause of death. Depositions would be taken from all persons who had relevant evidence to give. The accused, if present, had the right to give evidence and might be permitted to put questions. If the inquest jury returned a verdict of murder or manslaughter against the accused the coroner would commit him for trial. In the 1860s, it was usual in cases of suspected homicide for the body to be taken to the nearest public house where a post-mortem would be carried out and the inquest opened. At the opening of the inquest, after the jury had viewed the body, the coroner would take evidence of identification and then adjourn the proceedings to be resumed on a later date at the

Town Hall. The use of public houses for inquests was discontinued in Sheffield following the building of a public mortuary and coroner's court in Plum Lane in 1884 (replaced in 1914 by a new building in Nursery Street and in 1977 by the present Medico-Legal Centre).

In homicide cases, the magistrates' preliminary examination and the coroner's inquest inevitably covered the same ground, with the same witnesses giving the same evidence at each. Often (especially after creation in 1879 of the office of Director of Public Prosecutions)[3] by the time the preliminary examination concluded the accused already stood committed for trial on a coroner's warrant. To avoid this duplication it was enacted in 1926 that where a coroner was informed that some person had been charged before examining justices with the murder, manslaughter or infanticide of a deceased person, he should, in the absence of reason to the contrary, adjourn the inquest into the death until after the conclusion of the criminal proceedings.

An accused committed for trial for murder would invariably be remanded in custody to one of the West Riding's two gaols, Armley Prison at Leeds or the Wakefield House of Correction to await the next sitting of the Assize judges in Leeds.

## Preparing for trial

The interval between committal and trial gave the prisoner and his lawyers (if he had any) an opportunity to consider what answer he should offer to the charge which he faced. By now he knew the case

3 The Director was charged with overseeing all murder prosecutions; the need to consult him inevitably slowed down the committal process.

he had to meet: he had heard the prosecution witnesses tell their story once, if not twice, and would have been supplied with a copy of their depositions.

In the nineteenth century, if, on a prosecution for murder, the Crown proved that the accused's hand had caused the deceased's death then the burden shifted to him to prove that the case was not one of murder. The defences available in law were accident (that death had been caused accidentally and not by a deliberate blow), self-defence (that the blow which caused death had been struck in defence of himself or another, no more force having been used than was reasonably necessary),[4] lack of intent (that when he struck the deceased it had not been his intention either to kill or to cause grievous bodily harm),[5] provocation (that he had been provoked to lose his self control by the conduct of the deceased)[6] and insanity (that at the time of the killing he was labouring under such a defect of reason from disease of the mind that he either did not know the nature of the act he was doing or, alternatively, did not know it was wrong, that is to say prohibited by law).[7] In the course of the twentieth century the law became by degrees more favourable to the accused. In a ground making ruling in 1937 the House of Lords held that, although the accused bore the burden of proof on insanity, in relation to all other defences such as self-defence and provocation it was not

---

4 Accident and self defence were defences which, if made out, resulted in the accused's complete acquittal.

5 A person who caused death by an unlawful blow struck without any intent either to kill or to cause grievous bodily harm to his victim was guilty of manslaughter only.

6 Provocation was a defence which the law sought to confine within very narrow bounds, insisting, in particular, that the killing should have followed immediately upon the provocation with no opportunity for cooling off. If made out it reduced the offence to manslaughter

7 This narrow definition of insanity had been laid down in *M'Naghten's Case*, 1843. Prisoners found to be guilty but insane were committed to a criminal lunatic asylum.

for him to prove them but for the prosecution to rule them out. Twenty years later the Homicide Act extended the law as to provocation and also introduced the defence of diminished responsibility.[8] It also abolished the harsh felony-murder rule under which a person who killed, even accidentally, in the course of committing a violent felony such as robbery was automatically guilty of murder.

## The Assizes

Those accused of murder took their trial in London at the Old Bailey and elsewhere at the Assize court for the county in which the crime had been committed

In 1865, England was for Assize purposes divided into seven circuits. Each spring and summer the fifteen common law judges (after 1875 judges of the High Court) would leave London to take the Assizes; two judges travelled each circuit, one to deliver the gaols (i.e. to try crime) the other to try civil causes. The counties within a circuit were visited in a fixed order the Assize sittings normally being held in the county town. Until 1864, York was the assize town for all Yorkshire. In that year, however, the West Riding was made a separate county for Assize purposes with Leeds as its county town. Henceforth all Sheffield murderers would take their trial there, instead of at York, and if convicted would be executed there. So far as Sheffield was concerned, the new Assize was less than popular. On

[8] The defence was available only in murder cases. If made out, and the burden of proving it lay with the defence, it had the effect of reducing what would otherwise have been murder to manslaughter. To establish the defence, the accused had to satisfy the jury that it was more probable than not that, at the time of the killing, he was suffering from a gross abnormality of mind which substantially impaired his mental responsibility for his acts.

the occasion of the execution of Myers and Sargisson at Armley in 1864 the *Sheffield Telegraph* commented sourly on Leeds' 'ambition to hang criminals.'

The following year, the Social Science Congress was held in Sheffield and, during one of the debates, local solicitor, Robert Gainsford, argued that Sheffield should have its own Assize. This was an ambitious proposal given that it did not even possess a court of Quarter Sessions. Nonetheless, the idea was taken up and, in 1867, the town council, promoted a Bill to make the borough an Assize town. To house the Assizes the council planned to erect a court building in Castle Street on the site of the existing court-house and the *Black Rock* public house. The cost was estimated at £30,000 and the Bill provided that the outlying towns and districts in the southern part of the West Riding, which would be served by the new Assize, should pay part of the cost. Their inhabitants were scandalized. Why should they pay for a new public building in Sheffield? Opposition was particularly fierce in Doncaster, whose council declared that it would oppose the Bill unless the clause was dropped. By the time Sheffield gave way on the point the damage had been done. The government, influenced in all probability by the hostility the scheme had aroused in the riding, declared that it was not willing to make Sheffield an Assize town, leaving the council no option but to withdraw the Bill. It could, however, console itself with the thought that it was not the only large manufacturing town without an Assize. Birmingham was in the same plight. But, whereas Birmingham would in 1884 finally be made an Assize town, Sheffield would have to wait until 1955.

The building in which the West Riding Assizes were held was Leeds Town Hall. Opened by Queen Victoria in 1858, it had cost £47,335 and represented an attempt by Leeds to outdo Bradford with its recently built St George's Hall. Like the Castle Street Town Hall, it was a multi-purpose building and was designed to house court rooms, municipal offices, a great hall and a council chamber. The courts used for the Assizes were on the ground floor and to the rear of the great hall 'Each 55' long by 67' wide and 56' in height; they rank with the best courts in the country' boasted a Leeds guide book. The great hall or Victoria Hall could accommodate 8,000 people and, in the twentieth century it would be used for concerts and dances. When the Assize court was sitting late it was not unknown for sentence of death to be passed to the accompaniment of the strains of dance music issuing from the Hall. On the same floor as the Hall and the Assize courts were the council chamber and borough court, the bar library, committee, judges,' barristers,' magistrates,' jury and waiting rooms, all connected with each other and with the entrance by a ten foot wide corridor which ran entirely around the Hall. On the first floor were a magistrates' court, the grand jury room and various municipal offices; in the basement the cell area and police offices.

During the 1870s legislation was passed requiring Assizes to be held four times a year. This gave rise to many problems and eventually the system was changed, the sitting pattern at large centres being a spring and summer Assize plus a winter gaol delivery, at which criminal, but not civil, work was taken.

## Trial

The first task of the judge at the start of a criminal Assize was to swear and charge the grand jury. In the twelfth century, the duty of the grand jury had been to present to the King's Justices the names of those suspected of crime. By the sixteenth-century, however, its role was scrutiny. A prisoner could only be put on trial at Assizes if the grand jury found an indictment against him, which they could not do unless satisfied that the evidence of the prosecutor and his witnesses sufficiently strong to call for an answer. The jury consisted of between twelve and 23 jurors, drawn mainly from the ranks of the county magistracy. It took evidence in private in the absence of the accused, reaching decisions by majority vote. In his charge the judge would give the jury legal directions about any case likely to cause difficulty, following which they would retire to their room. The witnesses in the various cases would then be sworn in open court and sent along to the grand jury room to wait their turn to be examined. If, in a case, the jury were satisfied that there was *prima facie* evidence of guilt, they would indorse the proposed indictment 'true bill' and it would be carried into court to be tried. If not so satisfied, they would indorse it 'no true bill' in which event the accused would, at the end of the Assize, be discharged 'by proclamation' (which would usually mean an end to the prosecution).

By the nineteenth century the grand jury was regarded as a costly and unnecessary anachronism. The evidence against those committed for trial had already been considered by an examining magistrate and, if the charge was homicide, by a coroner's jury as well. A further inquiry, which obliged all the witnesses in all cases to be present at the beginning of the Assize so that the grand jury could examine them, was, argued its critics, a waste of both time and money. Defended by the judges on the ground that it was a valuable constitutional safeguard for prisoners, the grand jury survived well into the twentieth century.

As soon as indictments began to emerge for the grand jury room, the court would begin to try them.

The first step in any trial, be it for murder or any other offence, was arraignment: the accused would be put in the dock, the indictment would be read to him and he would be called on to plead to it. If he pleaded not guilty, a jury[9] would be empanelled to try him. The jury which would be all male[10] was chosen by ballot from a panel summoned by the sheriff, the accused having the right to challenge up to twenty jurors without cause and an unlimited number for cause shown.

Although the accused had the right to be defended by counsel, if he could not afford to pay for a barrister, and most could not, he normally had to defend himself. In murder cases, however, an informal system of legal aid operated, it being customary where a prisoner, capitally charged, was unrepresented to ask one of the barristers present in court to undertake his defence, a request which was never refused. It was hardly a satisfactory system since the counsel assigned had little time either to familiarise himself with the case or take instructions from the prisoner, but it was better than nothing.

---

[9] Often referred to as the petty jury to distinguish it from the grand jury.
[10] Not until 1918 did women become eligible to serve on juries.

Once the jury had been sworn, prosecuting counsel would open (outline) the Crown case to them and then call his witnesses, with the prisoner or his counsel having the right to cross-examine. The prosecution witnesses having been heard, the accused had the right to call witnesses in his defence. He was not, however, permitted to give evidence himself nor might his wife be a witness for him. Lawyers offered two justifications for the rule; first, since he was personally interested in the outcome of the case, any evidence which he or his wife gave was likely to be biased and perjured; second, the rule protected him against self-incrimination; to abolish it would lead to the establishment of something akin to the disliked French form of procedure, with prisoners compelled by rigorous cross-examination to convict themselves out of their own mouths. The accused was, however, entitled to make an unsworn statement from the dock (upon which he could not be questioned), explaining as best he could his answer to the charge and attempting to point out the deficiencies in the prosecution case. After the defence case had closed, there would be closing speeches from counsel and the judge would sum the case up to the jury, telling them the law they needed to know to try it and reminding them of the evidence given. The jury would then consider their verdict which had to be unanimous. Once they had retired they would be denied food, drink and fire until they had brought back a verdict. Because juries in felony cases were forbidden to separate once the trial had begun, it was common for courts to sit late into the evening to spare them the hardship of being locked up overnight.

A prisoner who pleaded guilty to or was convicted by a jury of murder would be asked, before sentence of death was passed, if he had anything to say why sentence should not be passed upon him.

The purpose of the question was to enable him to raise any matter which might operate as a bar to his being sentenced or provide grounds for postponement of sentence. One such matter was pregnancy which, if established to the satisfaction a jury of twelve matrons, would normally result in a female murderess being reprieved. If no bar or ground for postponement was shown, the clerk of the court would call for silence, the black cap would be placed on the judge's head and he would proceed to sentence. In 1948 an alteration was made in the form of the death sentence, the words 'you will be hanged by the neck until you are dead' being replaced by the simpler form 'you will suffer death by hanging.'[11]

Against a conviction for murder (or any other felony), a prisoner had no right of appeal. If the trial judge felt doubt about some point of law which had arisen during the trial, it was open to him to refer the point to the Court for Crown Cases Reserved and to postpone execution until their decision was known, but it was entirely at his discretion whether he did so and very few cases were in fact reserved. It was also possible for the accused's friends or lawyers to petition the Crown that his life be spared. If they could lay before the Home Office new evidence or some compelling ground for intervention success was possible, if rare.

The period 1898 to 1907 saw major changes to the trial system. In 1898 the prohibition upon prisoners giving evidence, which had been eroded piecemeal over the previous 50 years, was abolished.

---

[11] Prior to 1948 the form of death sentence which judges were directed to use in all cases was 'The sentence of the Court upon you is, that you be taken from this place to a lawful prison and thence to a place of execution, and that you be there hanged until you are dead; and that your body be afterwards buried within the precincts of the prison in which you shall have last been confined before your execution. And may the Lord have mercy upon your soul.' As to the reason for the alteration, see the Report of the Royal Commission on Capital Punishment, 1949-53, 1953 Cmnd 8932, para 686.

Henceforth, any accused might if he wished give evidence on his own behalf or call his spouse to do so. The initial reception to the Act from defendants and their lawyers was unenthusiastic and, in the twelve months following its coming into force, the number who availed themselves of the new privilege was small. Over the next half-century what opponents of the reform had predicted came to pass. The right to give evidence quickly came to be seen as a mixed blessing: while every prisoner who went into the witness box hoped that his evidence would secure his acquittal, often its effect was simply to strengthen the case against him and contribute to his conviction.

In 1903 a Poor Prisoners' Defence Act was passed. This empowered a committing magistrate, who was satisfied that a prisoner lacked the means to pay for his own defence, to grant a defence certificate entitling the prisoner to the services of a solicitor and counsel paid for by the State.

In 1907 a Court of Criminal Appeal was established consisting of the Lord Chief Justice and the judges of the Queen's Bench Division of the High Court. To this new court any person convicted on indictment might, with the leave of one of the judges of the court, appeal against his conviction or sentence. The new court had powers to quash convictions and to reduce or increase sentence. It also had very limited powers to hear new evidence. It had no power to order a retrial and, as it made clear at its first sitting, it considered that its role was limited to reviewing not to rehearing cases afresh. It quickly earned a reputation for reluctance to intervene in capital cases.

## From conviction to Execution

After being sentenced to death a prisoner would be placed in one of the condemned cells at the prison where he had been confined immediately before his trial. He would be ministered to by the prison chaplain and carefully watched to see that he did not cheat the gallows by committing suicide.[12] He would also be allowed to receive visits from his family.

The normal interval between sentence and execution was three weeks (in 1902 the Home Office recommended that executions take place on any weekday but Monday, in the week following the third Sunday after sentence had been passed).[13]

In 1865 executions were still carried out in public, usually upon a temporary scaffold erected in front of the prison in which the accused had been held following his conviction.

The Capital Punishment Amendment Act, 1868 abolished public executions. Henceforth all executions were to be carried out within the walls of the prison where the condemned was confined and out of sight of the public. The reform was one which had long been urged.[14] One of the grounds on which it had been opposed was that it would undermine confidence in the criminal law. The masses, an 1863 royal commission was told, would never accept private executions which would give rise to ugly rumours and distortions; the poor would never believe that a member of the upper classes had been done to

---

[12] On the night of December 19, 1865 a condemned prisoner at Armley named Sykes managed to commit suicide by throwing himself over the balustrade of the second floor gallery onto a stone floor 30 feet below.

[13] The precise date was decided by the under-sheriff (who might fix it to suit his own convenience).

[14] It had been recommended by a House of Lords Select Committee in 1856 and ten years later by a Royal Commission on Capital Punishment.

death if the execution was carried out in private. In an attempt to allay such fears the Act required that immediately following an execution two notices should be posted at the prison gates: one signed by the under-sheriff and prison governor certifying that judgment of death had been carried out, the other by the prison surgeon certifying death. It also required that the coroner hold an inquest inside the prison, within 24 hours of the execution. Rules issued by the Home Office added yet further requirements: as the condemned man began his walk to the scaffold the prison bell must be rung and, after the execution, a black flag should be raised.[15] Under the Act the sheriff had power to admit such persons as to him seemed proper to witness the execution, and this power was generally exercised in favour of the press with the result that newspaper readers received as full a description of executions after the Act as before it.[16]

At first, private executions were carried out on portable scaffolds erected usually in the prison yard. This arrangement invariably involved the prisoner having to walk from cell to scaffold and then

---

[15] At Armley the flag was raised on the prison's central tower, at York on Clifford's Tower. Cf Thomas Hardy, *Tess of the Durbervilles*, Collins, London (1958 reprint), pp. 445-46. 'When [Angel and Lisa Lu reached the top of the great West Hill the clocks in the town struck eight. Each gave a start at the notes. The prospect from this summit was almost unlimited. In the valley beneath lay the city they had just left. In front of the other city edifices rose a large red bricked building with level grey roofs and rows of short barred windows bespeaking captivity. From the middle of the building an ugly flat topped octagonal tower ascended...Upon the cornice of this tower a tall staff ascended ...Their eyes were riveted upon it. A few minutes after the hour had struck something moved slowly up the staff and extended itself upon the breeze. It was a black flag. Justice was done and the President of the Immortals had ended his sport with Tess.'

[16] The reaction of the condemned to the presence of reporters varied considerably. When Henry Wainwright stepped onto the scaffold at Newgate in 1875 he turned to the watching pressmen and shouted 'You curs. Come to see a man die, have you?' Joseph Detheridge, hanged at Portland in 1869 for the murder of a warder made their presence an excuse for a joke : 'Who are these people?' he asked. 'Are they all come to save me?' William Horry executed at Lincoln in April 1872 took the opportunity to deliver a long harangue to them.

mount a set of steps to the gallows.[17]

By the twentieth century, however, many of the larger city prisons had self-contained execution blocks, with the condemned cell adjoining the execution chamber.[18]

The 1870s saw the introduction of a new technique of execution - 'the long drop.' First used in Ireland and said to derive from advice from the Irish College of Surgeons, the long drop sought, by use of a much longer length of rope than had hitherto normally been employed in hangings, to subject the condemned man to a blow to the neck of sufficient force to dislocate one of more of the cervical vertebrae. 'Such a dislocation,' explained the Report of Royal Commission on Capital Punishment, 1949-53, 'causes immediate unconsciousness and there is no chance of later recovery of consciousness, since breathing is no longer possible.' The new method was undoubtedly an improvement upon traditional hanging technique which produced death by slow strangulation, but it was not risk free. If too long a drop was given the noose might rip the condemned man's head from his shoulders. This actually happened twice in 1885[19] and again in August 1891.[20]

Nor was decapitation the only type of mishap which could occur. During the execution of Burton at Durham in 1883, when the trap fell

---

[17] At some prisons the walk was very long indeed: at Maidstone, for example, 'a condemned prisoner had to walk the whole length of two long halls and at least 50 yards in the open air to reach the scaffold': J. Atholl, The *Shadow of the Gallows*, John Long Ltd, London 1954, p. 97.

[18] See the Report of the Royal Commission on Capital Punishment, 1949-53 (Cmnd 8931), para 711: 'in most of the English prisons equipped for executions the execution chamber adjoins the condemned cell.'

[19] At the execution of Shrimpton at Worcester on May 25 and Goodale at Norwich on November 30, 1886.

[20] At the execution of Conway at Kirkdale on August 1891 (carried out after the publication of the table of drops recommended by the Aberdare Committee and, unfortunately for the authorities, in front of reporters).

the rope caught under the elbow of the condemned man, who had to be drawn up alive and turned off again. Roberts, executed at Cardiff in 1885, slowly strangled to death, having been given so short a drop that his head could still be seen protruding above the floor of the scaffold after the trap had fallen. In 1884 Binns, the Newgate executioner, gave every appearance of being drunk during a hanging at Walton Gaol. Although reporters were, by now, usually refused admission to executions[21] news of such incidents still got out and, in 1886, the Home Secretary appointed a Departmental Committee under Lord Aberdare:

> *to inquire into the existing practice as to the carrying out of sentences of death and the causes which in several recent cases have led either to failure or to unseemly occurrences and to consider what arrangements may be adopted (without altering the existing law) to ensure that all executions may be carried out in a becoming manner without risk of failure or miscarriage in any respect'*

Its report, published two years later, stressed the critical importance of getting the length of the drop right. If the drop was too short the victim would suffocate slowly, if too long decapitation could result which, though a revolting prospect, was in its opinion the lesser of the two evils. In order to minimise the risk of mishap it recommended the adoption of a uniform design of scaffold, a standard length and thickness of rope, a method of securing the slack and most important of all that hangmen should use the table of drops

[21] Some prisons were excluding reporters as early as 1879 but not until 1883 did the practice become general. At Durham the press were still being admitted to executions as late as 1916, but this was very much an exception to normal practice. (A Pierrepoint, *Executioner Pierrepoint*, Coronet Books, London 1977, p 70). The last execution which reporters are known to have attended was that of Parker and Probert at Wandsworth on May 4, 1934 (Harry Potter, *Hanging in Judgment* (SCM Press, London, 1993), p 236, n. 41). Pierrepoint, op. cit., p 69 suggests that 'the presence of newspaper representatives at executions was ... discouraged lest they should report the truth too accurately.'

which it appended to the report.[22] If these measures were adopted, accidents would still occur[23] but 'this shock to public opinion [would] be of extreme rarity.' The report was speedily acted upon by the Home Office which also wrote to sheriffs recommending that from now on the executioners should reside in the prison itself on the eve of an execution, and the amount of drink they be allowed should be limited to a pint of ale at dinner and supper and a quarter of a pint of spirits.

In 1901 the Home Office issued instructions that the prison bell should no longer be tolled at executions and two years later the practice of raising the black flag was also discontinued. As the external publicity given to executions diminished so the Home Office policy of releasing as little information to the press as possible took even firmer hold. During the trial in 1926 of former prison governor, Major Hasting Blake, for breach of the Official Secrets Act, it emerged that all prison governors were forbidden to time executions and, if asked about an execution, were to say that it had been carried out expeditiously and without a hitch.[24] This policy of secrecy enabled the Home Office to keep from the public any embarrassing

---

[22] The drops recommended were intended to produce a blow to the neck of 1260 foot pounds.

[23] On this point they were quickly proved correct. In August 1891 the execution of John Conway at Kirkdale prison resulted in another near decapitation (Potter, op. cit., p. 103).

[24] During the trial there was quoted this extract from a Home Office instruction to prison governors dated January 10, 1925 about executions: 'Any reference to the manner in which an execution has been carried out should be confined to as few words as possible e.g. it was carried out expeditiously and without a hitch. No record should be taken as to the number of seconds and, if pressed for details of this kind, the governor should say he cannot give them as he did not time the proceedings, but 'a very short interval elapsed' or some general expression of opinion to the same effect.' The following year the Home Secretary was asked to publish the memorandum in full. He declined saying 'It would be most undesirable and contrary to established practice to make the terms of such instructions public. The less said at the inquest [on an executed prisoner], either by the governor or anyone else, the better.' (quoted by A Koestler and C H Rolph, *Hanged by the Neck,* Penguin Books, London, 1961, pp 16-17).

details concerning mishaps. In its evidence to the 1948 Royal Commission, the Home Office asserted: 'there is no record during the present century of any failure or mishap in connection with an execution.' The claim was almost certainly false: it is widely believed that something went badly wrong at the executions of Thomas Allaway (1922)[25] and Edith Thompson (1923).[26]

In a memorandum to the Royal Commission, the Home Office described the regime to which condemned prisoners were subject from conviction to execution:

> *Immediately a prisoner sentenced to death returns from court, he is placed in a cell for condemned prisoners and is watched night and day by two warders. Amenities such as cards, chess, dominoes etc are provided in the cell and the officers are encouraged to – and invariably do - join the prisoner in these games. Newspapers and books are also provided. Food is supplied from the main prison kitchen, the prisoner being placed on a hospital diet with such additions as the medical officer considers advisable. A pint of beer or stout is supplied daily on request and ten cigarettes or half an ounce of pipe tobacco are allowed unless there are medical reasons to the contrary. The prisoner may smoke in his cell as well as at exercise.*
>
> *It is the practice for the Governor, medical officer and chief officer to visit a prisoner under sentence of death twice daily, and the chaplain or minister of any other denomination has free access to him. He may be visited*

---

[25] According to W Lloyd Woodland, *Assize Pageant* (Harrap & Co. London, 1952), p 66 Allaway died by strangulation due to a fault in the way the noose had been rigged. He adds that the prison doctor, when asked at the inquest if death had been instantaneous, after a slight hesitation replied, 'Yes, practically.'

[26] See Rene J A Weis, *Criminal Justice* (Hamish Hamilton, London 1988), p 304: '...within hours of Edith Thompson's death rumours about the manner of it are spreading. By the evening of 9 January one rumour in particular is circulating, namely that 'her insides fell out.' As it happens, she had put on over a stone in the period from 11 December 1922 to 9 January, in conditions of extreme mental stress and sparse eating – lending disturbing support to the hypothesis that she may have been pregnant' and pp. 306-07. For another example of a botched twentieth-century hanging see the account of the execution of Goldthorpe at Norwich in 1950, given by assistant executioner Syd Dernley in his book *The Hangman's Tale* (Pan Books, London, 1989), p 139: 'Goldthorpe plummeted down that long 7' 8" drop, there was the boom of the great doors and the man was stopped with a great jerk. I was half turning to walk to the small trapdoor in the corner when I heard the most spine chilling sound I ever heard in an execution chamber. From the pit came a snort, then another snort ... and another and another. The rope was still, the head seemed to be over ... but there were noises coming from under the hood ...The governor had a look of utter horror on his face and the little under sheriff had gone from ruddy red to green.... [when the body was taken down it was found that the white hood] had got caught in the eye of the noose.'

*by such of his relations, friends and legal advisers as he desires to see and as are authorised to visit him by the Visiting Committee and the commissioners, and he is given special facilities to write and receive letters.*

*The executioner and his assistant arrive at the prison by 4 pm on the day preceding the execution and are not permitted to leave the prison until after the execution has been carried out. They see the prisoner at exercise and test the execution apparatus with a bag of sand approximately of his weight. The bag is left hanging overnight to stretch the rope.*

*On the morning of the execution it is usual for the chaplain to spend the last hour with the prisoner and remain with him until the execution is over. Some twenty minutes before the time fixed for the execution the High Sheriff – or more usually the Under Sheriff – arrives at the prison. and a few minutes before it is due, proceeds with the Governor and medical officer to the place of execution. The executioner and his assistant wait outside the condemned cell with the chief officer and the officer detailed to conduct the prisoner to the execution chamber. On a signal given by the Sheriff they enter the cell and the executioner pinions the prisoner's arms behind his back. He is escorted to the drop with one officer on either side. The Sheriff, the Governor and the medical officer enter the execution chamber directly by another door. The prisoner is placed on the drop on a marked spot so that his feet are directly across the division of the trap doors. The executioner places the white cap over the prisoner's head and places the noose around his neck, while the assistant pinions his legs. When the executioner sees that all is ready he pulls the lever.*

*The medical officer at once proceeds to the pit and examines the prisoner to see that life is extinct. The shed is then locked and the body hangs for one hour. The inquest is held the same morning. Burial of the body takes place in the prison graveyard during the dinner hour; the chaplain reads the burial service.*

It was one which had changed little since 1868.

## West Riding Executions

Armley prison, built in 1847, had started life as the Leeds borough prison but, when Leeds was made an Assize town, it became the hanging prison for the West Riding. In the nineteenth century it was a mixed gaol (in 1862 a quarter of its inmates were female). Only one woman was ever hanged there, Emily Swann in 1903.[27]

[27] Emily Swan came from Wombwell. She was 42 years old and the mother of eleven children. In October 1903 she and her lover John Gallagher were convicted of the murdering her husband and sentenced to death. They were hanged at Armley on December 29, 1903. When Emily entered the execution shed Gallagher was already standing hooded on the trap. 'Good morning, John,' she called as she took her place beside him. He did not know that they were to be executed together but, although

The first private execution at Armley was that of the Sheffield murderer William, Smedley in 1875. It took place on a portable gallows erected in a corner of the prison yard near the hospital. To reach it, the condemned man had a walk of about 60 yards and then had to climb up the scaffold steps. By the time Hobson was executed in 1887 for the Montague Street murder arrangements had changed. First, the practice of admitting reporters had been discontinued.[28] Second, the treadmill shed in the prisoner yard had been converted into a permanent execution shed, a deep hole having been excavated in the floor to create a drop.[29] The condemned man still had a long walk to the gallows but now it was, at least, largely under cover.[30] After execution, the body was now removed to another shed where it remained until the jury had viewed it and the inquest was complete.[31] It would then be buried in a corner of the prison yard.

---

completely taken aback, managed to get out the words 'Good morning, love.' Her last words, spoken to him as the noose was being placed around her neck, were 'Good-bye. God, bless you!'

[28] Laycock's execution in August 1884 appears to have been the first at Armley to which the press were denied admission. The *Sheffield Telegraph* suggested that the reason why reporters were kept out was that the authorities feared the hanging might be botched. The hangman Billington was inexperienced and the prison was one at which executions had been bungled in the past.

[29] By the last decade of the nineteenth century execution sheds similar to that employed at Armley were in use at several prisons including Newgate. Cf Oscar Wilde's observation in a letter written to Robert Ross from Reading gaol 'the shed in which people are hanged is a little shed with a glass roof like a photographer's studio on the sands at Margate.'

[30] A further advantage of the new arrangement was that it prevented the proceedings being overlooked from outside the prison. After the first private execution there the authorities at Armley had been discomforted to learn that the upper portion of the gallows could be seen from a vantage point in a neighbouring field. They had also had trouble with spectators climbing telegraph poles in order to look in. The problem was by no means one confined to Armley. In 1878 on the occasion of the execution of Eugene Chantrelle, in order to prevent the proceedings being seen from nearby Calton Hill, the scaffold was erected in a storeroom (*The Times,* June 1, 1868) and, before the execution of Edith Thompson at Holloway, 'a wooden screen [was erected] to prevent [her] last journey being overlooked by the curious from nearby houses.' (Weis, op. cit., p 289}.

[31] At Armley, in the 1920s, coroner's juries conducting inquests upon the bodies of executed prisoners were on occasions allowed to view the condemned cell and the scaffold.

In 1906, Wakefield, which had never previously been used for executions, was pressed into use and from then until 1915 it shared the task with Armley. This appears to have been the result of a Home Office policy of dividing the West Riding into two areas for execution purposes and, while it remained in force, Leeds and Bradford prisoners continued to be hanged at Armley with Wakefield used for the execution of those from other parts of the riding.[32] The first man to die on the Wakefield gallows was Harry Walters, sentenced to death in 1905 for the so-called Sheffield Christmas murder. Those reporting on the execution informed their readers that:

> *The trying walk across the prison yard, which has to be made at most prisons, is obviated at Wakefield where the condemned cell opens directly onto the shed in which the scaffold is placed.*

In 1916 the use of Wakefield discontinued, Armley once again becoming the sole West Riding execution prison. The old treadmill shed was still in use. Eventually, however, the prison got a purpose-built execution block. This was constructed in 1950 and, while it was being built, Strangeways was used for Yorkshire executions.[33] Upon these new gallows Sheffielder, William Smedley, was put to death in 1947. He was the fourteenth Sheffield prisoner and the second of that name to be privately executed at Armley. He was also the last Sheffield man to hang.

---

[32] Amongst the prisoners executed at Wakefield were three from Middlesbrough and one from Pocklington.

[33] See the Report of the Commissioners of Prisons for the year 1951 (Cmnd 8692), Chapter 8, para 13: 'At Leeds a new execution block has been completed.' While the work was being carried out two Yorkshire murderers, Crosby and Inglis (hanged respectively in December 1950 and May 1951) were transferred across to Strangeways for execution (see Dernley, op. cit., pp. 143 and 170).

***Unknown Victorian police officer and charge c. 1860***
*(photo courtesy of South Yorkshire Police).*

*The Sheffield Central Police Office, Castle Green, erected 1864.*

*London Road, Sheffield today. The white painted building was formerly Highfields police station.*

***The Old Town Hall in Castle Street, erected in 1807.***

*Between 1865 and 1965 it housed the town's magistrates' courts. It was also the court house for the town's Quarter Sessions (granted 1884) and after 1955 for the Sheffield Assizes.*

***The Nursery Street Coroner's Court.***

*Until the late nineteenth century inquests were commonly held in public houses. In 1884, however, a public mortuary and coroner's court was built in Plum Lane. This was replaced in 1914 by the Nursery Street building. Since 1977 inquests have been held at the Medico-Legal Centre in Watery Street.*

***Dossey Wightman*** *(1836-1920); solicitor and partner in Wightman and Parker of Change Alley;* ***coroner 1873-1911.***

***Edward M E Welby*** *(1836-1926);*
***Sheffield stipendiary Magistrate***
*1874-1914*

***J Kenyon Parker*** *(1867-1942);*
*solicitor and partner of*
*Dossey Wightman*
***coroner*** *1911-1942*

***Lord Chief Justice Goddard opening the first Sheffield Assize, June 23, 1955.***

***Leeds Town Hall where the Leeds Assizes were held***

**_Armley Prison_**

***A nineteenth-century drawing***

***The gatehouse today***

*A nineteenth-century execution shed. The* ***treadmill shed*** *at* ***Armley*** *was probably little different*

***William Marwood (responsible for the introduction of the 'long drop')***

***Henry Pierrepoint*** *(left) making his way to Swansea gaol for an execution accompanied by his assistant,* ***John Ellis****, whom he loathed.*

*The posting of **notice of execution** outside the prison Gates (1949).*

*Two notices were required to be posted: a **certificate from the prison surgeon** certifying death and a **declaration by the sheriff** that judgment of death had been executed.*

***Twentieth-century hangmen***

***Albert Pierrepoint***

***Steve Wade***

# 2

# The Sheffield Murders 1865 to 1899

| Name | Age and occupation | Date and place of murder | Victim | Date of Trial Judge | Date and place of execution |
|---|---|---|---|---|---|
| 1. William Smedley | 54, table knife hafter | August 28, 1875 Apple Street | Elizabeth Firth | December 2, 1875 Lindley J | December 21, 1875 Armley Prison |
| 2. Charlie Peace | 47, burglar | November 29, 1876 Banner Cross | Arthur Dyson | February 4, 1879 Lopes J | February 25, 1879, Armley Prison |
| 3. James Hall | 55, cutler | March 26, 1881 149, Shelf Street | Mary Ann Hall | May 6, 1881 Kay J. | May 23, 1881 Armley Prison |
| 4. Joseph Laycock | 38, hawker | July 10/11, 1884 No 2 court, White Croft | Maria Laycock and her four children | August 6, 1884 Matthew J | August 26, 1884 Armley Prison |
| 5. Harry Hobson | 53, unemployed | July 23, 1887 99, Montague Street | Ada Stothard | August 5, 1887 Matthew J | August 22, 1887 Armley Prison |
| 6. Robert West | 44, travelling showman | August 17, 1889 caravan at Handsworth Woodhouse | Emma West | December 14, 1889 Manisty J | December 31, 1889 Armley Prison |
| 7. Edward Hemmings | 26, miner | February 16, 1893 Furnace Lane, Woodhouse | Annie Hemmings | March 15, 1893 Bruce J | April 4, 1893 Armley Prison |

## The door key and the polony - William Smedley, 1875 [34]

In 1874 William Smedley[35] suffered two crushing blows. First, his wife died then his eyesight began to fail. After his wife's death, rather than move in with any of his four children[36] he stayed on at the house which he rented in Apple Street, Harvest Lane, employing a local woman to clean for him. She was Elizabeth Firth. Recently widowed, with three children under 12, she needed any work she could get and, as well as charring, she did cleaning at the local baths. But although she was, as neighbours acknowledged, 'an industrious enough little body,' her family was less than respectable.[37] Her dead husband had served a prison term for felony, her eldest daughter was a prostitute and there was also a son who was known to the police.

Soon after starting 'to do' for Smedley, Elizabeth was sleeping with him. Most evenings she would go round to his house at about 11 pm, stay the night and leave at 7 the next morning. He would also call at her home to take her out. Clearly smitten, he asked her to marry him but her children proved a sticking point. He wanted her to leave them and come and live with him; the eldest at 19 was, he argued, more than capable of looking after the four younger ones. But she would not. Smedley's sons, who had taken a dislike to his new mistress, tried to persuade him to give her up but this he stubbornly

[34] See *Sheffield Independent*, Aug. 30, Sept 1, 4, Dec. 3, 22, 1875; *Sheffield Telegraph*, Aug. 28 30, Sept. 1, Dec 3, 22 1875; the *Star*, Aug 28 and Dec 2, 1875; *The Times*, Dec. 3, 1875.

[35] Press reports describe him as 5'6" tall, thick-set and with a florid complexion. He was aged 54 at the date of execution.

[36] Two daughters and two sons.

[37] She would later be described in the *Sheffield Telegraph* as 'addicted to all the vices which fallen womanhood could indulge in.' It was also claimed that on her last visit to Apple Street she had been hooted by all the neighbours.

refused to do. Generally, the couple got on well enough but there were occasional fallings out and twice these ended in blows.

During 1875, Smedley's eyesight got steadily worse until finally he became totally blind. After a three month course of treatment at the Eye Hospital he recovered some vision. A table-knife hafter by trade, he was now quite unable to work and had to get by on the 3/6d a week which the parish authorities allowed him and such help as his children gave. Not surprisingly he became depressed. In August he and Elizabeth quarrelled and she stopped coming up to his house at nights.[38] On Thursday, August 26, he moved in with his married daughter, Mrs Sedgewick, and later that day a broker's man was seen at the house in Apple Street removing his furniture. That evening he went out and did not return until late. His daughter suspected he had been with Elizabeth Firth. Most of Friday, the 27th he spent indoors playing with one of his grandchildren but, at around 6.30 pm, he went out. Shortly afterwards he was seen walking across the Corporation bridge[39] on his way to see Elizabeth. On arriving at her house in Bailey Fields[40] he was invited in. Elizabeth put on her bonnet and jacket, told her eldest son that she was going out for about half to three quarters of an hour, and set off down the street with Smedley. Both were sober and they seemed on good terms.

At around 8 pm they called at the *Bay Horse Inn* in Pea Croft.[41] It was not one of their regular haunts; indeed, the landlady could only remember having seen Smedley once before. To her he did not

---

[38] Her son John told the inquest that she had stopped sleeping over at Smedley's house some three weeks before her death (*Sheffield Telegraph*, Sept. 1, 1875).

[39] The bridge, erected in the 1850s, which carries Corporation Street over the Don.

[40] An area lying between Broad Lane and what is now Trippet Lane and bisected by Bailey Street. Elizabeth Firth's house was in Bailey Street.

[41] West Bar Green.

appear dejected and he was certainly not drinking heavily. In the two hours the couple were there they sat in the tap room, talking quietly, and had just two pints of beer each.

Shortly after 10 they moved on to the *Harrow Inn* in Harvest Lane. At one time they had been regulars there but not during the last six weeks. They went into the tap room where Smedley ordered a whisky and a gin and then took their drinks over to a table where they sat talking. Both appeared sober and there was no hint of quarrelling, although the housekeeper Eliza Gelder did notice that Smedley's eyes were bad. At 11 pm they left, still apparently on good terms, and began to walk slowly up Apple Street.

Shortly after this, Sarah Ann Nutton, looking out of her window at no. 54, saw them standing under a street lamp. She heard Smedley say something and Elizabeth reply 'No.' She then heard the words 'No, Never!' from Elizabeth, followed by a noise which sounded like something striking a door or shutter; 'a great knock' was how she would later describe it. She went to her door and looked out and saw Smedley running off and Elizabeth in the act of falling flat on her face. Noticing blood on the pavement she shouted to a youth across the road to go for help. Neighbours, thinking that Elizabeth was still alive, carried her to the nearby *Greaves Hotel* but when they got her into the light they saw that she was dead. There was a great gash to her throat and a door key in her hand.

Two men set off at once for the Central Police Station. On hearing their story Sub-Inspector Lawton despatched constables Mastin and Broadhead to investigate. When the officers got to Apple

Street they found shocked residents standing around in silent groups. Violence and wife-beating the district was used to but not murder.[42]

Smedley, after fleeing the scene, called in at a shop and bought a small loaf and a polony, which he placed in his hat. He then set off for the Central Police Station. On arrival there he said he wanted to give himself up. The officers noticed that he had a piece of half eaten bread in his hand and that his right hand and right sleeve were bloody. Told he was under arrest, he immediately made a statement under caution admitting the killing.[43]

On Saturday morning he was taken before the borough magistrates. Sub-Inspector Laughton, after explaining the circumstances of the arrest, applied for a remand in custody. 'Have you anything to say why you should not be remanded?' Smedley was asked. 'No sir,' he replied.

In the afternoon, the coroner Dossey Wightman opened the inquest upon the dead woman at the Central Police Office. After the jury had viewed the body at the *Greaves Hotel*, formal evidence of identification was taken and the hearing then adjourned until the following Tuesday.

On Saturday evening, Smedley received a visit from his daughters. In tears they asked 'What made you do it father?' 'I don't

---

[42] Cf *Sheffield Telegraph*, August 28, 1875 'although wife-beatings are frequent in Harvest Lane and assaults of various degrees of brutality are so common as to excite comparatively little notice, it had up to last night been able to claim freedom from the taint of murder.'

[43] The statement was in these terms: 'My name is William Smedley and I live at Orchard St, Harvest Lane. I am 54 years of age and am a table-blade hafter by trade. I have come to give myself up for murdering Elizabeth Firth, a woman I have been cohabiting with.I have cut her throat with a razor in Orchard Street, Harvest Lane. I have thrown the razor away on the slates near the iron bridge.' The iron bridge referred to lies immediately to the south east of the Corporation Street bridge.

know.' 'Was it jealousy?' 'Yes, I found something out and I loved her so much I did it. She was a good woman and I'm sorry I did it.'

Sunday proved a most trying day for the landlord of the *Greaves Hotel.* During the morning a crowd gathered outside the stable of the public house, clamouring to see the body which lay within. At first he refused them admittance but then relented. But this was not enough for some of them who, being unwilling to wait their turn,

> *'battered in the window, forced away the brickwork and generally succeeded in raising what in a very few moments would have assumed the proportions of a riot.'*

It must have been a great relief to him when, on Monday morning, the body was removed to the dead woman's home in Bailey Street.

On the Monday, police officers, searching for the murder weapon, found the haft of a razor and three broken pieces of blade on the roof of the entrance to a converting furnace at Hollins' works in Bridge Street. It had blood and a few hairs on it. They also discovered that the key the dead woman had been holding fitted the door lock of Smedley's house in Apple Street.

On the Tuesday, Elizabeth Firth was buried. At 2 pm a hearse and two cabs for mourners pulled up in Bailey Street and a large crowd watched as the coffin was carried out. As one bystander put it: 'There was a street-full.' As the cortege set off for the General Cemetery the crowd dispersed, only a few of the spectators choosing to make the journey to the burial ground. The funeral service was conducted by the Revd. J. Fisher and the body buried in the unconsecrated part of the cemetery set aside for dissenters.

Some three hours later in the Grand Jury room at the Town Hall, the adjourned inquest got under way. Evidence was taken from Elizabeth's son John, the bar staff at the *Bay Horse* and *Harrow* inns, Sarah Nutton and the arresting officers. Arthur Hallam, the police surgeon who had carried out the post-mortem, said that the deceased had a wound which ran from the left ear to the back of the neck and for some distance to the front of the throat. The trachea, the carotid artery and the jugular vein had all been severed. The cause of death was loss of blood and death must have occurred within two minutes of the throat being cut. Smedley, on the advice of his solicitor, Mr W E Clegg,[44] declined to make a statement. Mr Clegg invited the coroner to direct the jury that they might return a verdict of manslaughter but the latter replied that the case was one of murder or nothing. The jury having returned the inevitable verdict of murder, Smedley, who had shown a great interest in the proceedings but seemed unsurprised by the verdict, was committed in custody for trial.

On the Friday, September 2, there was a committal hearing before Mr Welby,[45] the stipendiary magistrate. Mr Fairburn prosecuted, Mr Clegg appeared for Smedley. Smedley, again on advice, declined to make a statement and, after the depositions had been signed, was committed for trial.

---

[44] **Clegg**, Sir William Edwin (1852-1932); solicitor; Mayor of Sheffield, 1887-89; knighted 1906; CBE 1918.

[45] **Welby**, Edward Montague Earl (1828-1926); 5th son of a Lincolnshire baronet; educ. Eton and Corpus Christi Coll., Oxford; called to the bar in 1863, he practised from London Chambers and then from 42, Bank Street, Sheffield; stipendiary magistrate for Sheffield 1874-1916.

He took his trial at Leeds on December 2, 1875, before Mr Justice Lindley.[46] Messrs. Barker and Heaton Cadman, both of whom had strong Sheffield connections, appeared for the prosecution[47]. When arraigned Smedley answered 'Guilty, but I did not know what I was doing.' The judge recommended him to withdraw his plea and to plead not guilty and requested Mr. Stephen Gatty,[48] one of the barristers in court, to undertake his defence.

Prosecution witnesses cross-examined by Mr Gatty agreed that during the twelve months before the killing, the accused had been in dire straits and had had difficulties with his eye sight. In his closing speech, Mr Gatty contended that every circumstance connected with the case, the prisoner's fondness for the deceased, his lack of motive to kill her, the open manner in which he cut her throat, his immediate confession and the lack of any attempt by him to conceal what he had done, all suggested that he had killed whilst labouring under a fit of temporary homicidal mania and invited them to bring in a verdict of guilty but insane.

Mr Justice Lindley, in his summing up, told the jury that the only possible defence was insanity but there was a legal presumption of

---

[46] **Lindley**, Nathanial Baron (1828-1921); educated University College school; called to the bar in 1850; the author of the leading textbook on the *Law of Partnership*; he was appointed QC in 1872, a High Court judge in 1875, a Lord Justice of Appeal in 1881, Master of the Rolls in 1897 and a Law Lord in 1900. he is described by his biographers as remarkable for his versatility and impartiality.

[47] **John Edward Barker** practised from chambers at 42, Bank Street, Sheffield between 1866 and 1896; the town's best known and most successful barrister, he was appointed Recorder of Leeds in 1880 and QC in 1891.**Heaton Cadman**, born 1839, was the son of Edwin Cadman of Westbourne House, Sheffield; educated at the Sheffield Collegiate School and Worcester College Oxford, he was called to the bar in 1864; he practised from chambers in East Parade, Leeds and in 1877 was appointed Recorder of Pontefract.

[48] **Stephen Gatty** was the son of the Rev'd Dr Gatty, the vicar of Ecclesfield; called to the bar in 1875 he joined chambers at 9, Bank Street, Sheffield; meeting with little success he moved to chambers in London and then in 1883 joined the colonial legal service. In 1895 he was appointed Chief Justice of Gibraltar. In 1904 he was made a QC and knighted.

sanity and it was dangerous to infer insanity merely from the act of killing. The prisoner had gone to the Town Hall eating some bread. Was that a sign of insanity? For himself, he saw nothing in it. A jury ought not to find a man insane without some evidence and to acquit the accused they must be satisfied by evidence - not by guess, by feeling - that he was insane. The jury immediately brought in a verdict of guilty without leaving the jury box. Asked if he had anything to say why sentence of death should not be passed upon him, Smedley replied 'I can't say anything more than what I have said.' Donning the black cap the judge turned to address him:

> *William Smedley, you have been convicted by the jury for the wilful murder of Elizabeth Firth, and I for one am bound to say that I think no twelve reasonable men could come to any other conclusion than they did....there really is no evidence at all upon which any reasonable man could believe you were or are insane. Under these circumstances it is my painful duty to pass sentence upon you.*

Sentence of death having been pronounced, Smedley was removed from the dock and taken by cab to Armley gaol.

His conduct while awaiting execution was exemplary. He made no attempt to deny his guilt and paid the closest attention to the ministrations of the Revd Cookson, the prison chaplain, appearing fully resigned to his fate. On his last Friday, he received a visit from his daughter and brother. Most of the evening before his execution he spent reading scripture and praying. He retired to bed at 11 pm and then slept fitfully until shortly before 6 am when he rose and dressed. At 7 o'clock he took communion after which he declared that he was ready to meet his maker. At 8 he had breakfast but ate little and the warders noticed that he 'was in a state of nervous excitement amounting almost to mania.' At 9 am Askern, the old York hangman, entered his cell and pinioned him. As he did so the prison bell was already tolling. A procession was then formed with the governor and under-sheriff at its head, followed by Askern and then Smedley, with a warder on each side, and began to make its way across the prison yard to the scaffold which had been erected in an alcove by the prison hospital. Warders lined the route. As he crossed the yard Smedley passed the open grave where, in little over an hour's time, he would be buried. Directly he saw the gallows he seemed stricken with partial paralysis and had to be half supported and half dragged to the steps of the scaffold. He was placed on the drop, his ankles were tied and his face hooded. As the noose was being adjusted he was heard to say 'Lord Jesus, receive my soul.' The lever was then pulled and he dropped through the trap. At the same time a black flag was hoisted on the prison's central tower. Outside the gates some 20 to 30 people had gathered and there were a further dozen in Armley road. At 9 15 the bell ceased tolling and three quarters of an hour later Smedley's body was taken down and, after an inquest inside the prison, buried in the yard.

Smedley's was the first hanging to have taken place at Armley since the coming into force of the 1868 Act requiring executions to be carried out inside prison walls. The reporter of the *Sheffield Telegraph* was struck by the drabness of the proceedings:

> *All the excitement of the olden days, when people sat up all night and stationed themselves, provisioned for 24 hours in front of the prison walls has disappeared. ... All is dead and*

*dull and cheerless ... Half a dozen shivering reporters, an equal number of benumbed warders, the gallows which four days has been a building; the chaplain the officials and the culprit.*[49]

Press reports of the execution gave jealousy as the motive for the killing. Perhaps they were right. The fact that Smedley had taken a razor with him that night suggests that he had made up his mind to have a showdown about something. But what are we to make of the fact that the dead woman was found with his door key in her hand? Was she in the act of returning it when he cut her throat or had he pressed it on her in an attempt to persuade her to go inside and have intercourse with him or, as one newspaper suggested, so that he could murder her there? It is impossible to know.

### The Banner Cross Murder - Charlie Peace, 1876 [50]

John Peace and his wife met and married in Rotherham. It was an unlikely match, he a one legged lion tamer working in a travelling show, she the daughter of a naval surgeon. After the wedding the couple moved to Sheffield where John opened a shoemaking business. But it did not pay and he soon gave it up and, after a spell working as a coal dealer and carter, he became the licensee of a beer-

[49] Cf The *Sheffield Independent*, Dec 22, 1875 'Everything had a terribly business-like aspect...Instead of four score thousand people all with their ribaldry and excitement, the spectators other than the officials, did not number a dozen.'

[50] See *The Trials of Charles Edward Peace* (ed by W T Shore), Wm Hodge, London, 1926 (Notable British Trials series); D Ward, *The King of the Lags*, Souvenir Press Ltd, London, 1989, *Sheffield Independent*, Nov 30, Dec 1, 2 and 4, 1876.

house at 2, Love Lane.[51] The couple had four children, the youngest of whom was Charles Edward (Charlie) born on May 14, 1832.

Charlie attended Pitsmoor School and then Hebblethwaite's in Paradise Square. He did not shine at either establishment. By the age of twelve he had left school and was working in Mellard's rolling mill at Millsands. His employment there proved short-lived: on the morning of his thirteenth birthday he was badly injured when a red hot bar pierced his left thigh as it emerged from between two rollers. He was taken to the Royal Infirmary from which, after eighteen months' treatment as an in-patient, he was discharged on crutches classified as 'incurable.' By determination, however, he gradually came to terms with and largely overcame his disability. He got employment at a steel yard in the Wicker but he gave it up when he found he could make more money playing the violin (a newly acquired skill) in public houses and picking pockets.[52] In 1851, caught house-breaking with a 27-year-old, named Campbell, he was sentenced to a month's imprisonment in the Wakefield House of Correction.

Upon his release he supported himself by working from time to time in local rolling mills, playing the violin in public houses and by house burglary. In 1854 he made the mistake of sending his 18-year-old mistress, Emma James to pawn a pair of boots he had stolen in a burglary at the house of Henry Hoole of Crookesmoor.[53] She was detained and the police called. Peace, who was waiting outside, went in and explained that the boots were his and that he had sent the girl

[51] *White's Directory* for 1841 contains the entry: John Peace, shoemaker and beer-house, 2, Love Lane.

[52] 'I was a thief from the age of 14,' he claimed in later life.

[53] Crookesmoor House, Crookesmoor (*Post Office Directory*, 1854).

to pawn them. Any hope he had of bluffing his way out of matters evaporated when the police examined his footwear: he was wearing boots stolen in the Hoole burglary. A police search of his mother's house yielded a large quantity of stolen goods, the proceeds of four recent house-burglaries. For these offences the magistrates at the West Riding Quarter Sessions sentenced him to four years' penal servitude. He served this sentence also in the Wakefield House of Correction. During his time there be made a daring, although unsuccessful, attempt to escape. Put in solitary confinement as a punishment, he tried to kill himself by gashing his throat with a nail. He was clearly a most difficult prisoner more fitted, in the view of some staff, to an asylum than a prison.

On coming out of prison in 1858 he supported himself by playing his fiddle and by crime, and for a time lived at Ripon Street in Bradford. In late 1858 or early 1859, he married Hannah Ward, a widow, whom he met at the Sheffield Feast (according to another story he found her destitute at the roadside and took pity on her). In June 1859, he and a criminal named Newton broke into a house in Rushholme, Manchester. They hid the property stolen inside a drain in a nearby field. When they returned for it, the police were waiting, and, after a fierce struggle in which an officer was badly injured, both were taken. Convicted at Manchester Assizes, following a trial in which his mother testified that he had been home with her in Sheffield every evening during the week of the burglary, Peace was sentenced to six years' penal servitude. He served the initial part of the sentence in Millbank and was then transferred to Portland and Chatham convict prisons. At Chatham he took part in a mutiny which earned him a flogging and transfer to the convict settlement at Gibraltar.

During his incarceration, Hannah, who shortly after his capture had given birth to a child, opened a small shop in Kenyon Alley, Sheffield. When he was released in 1864 on a ticket-of-leave it was to that address he returned[54]. At first, it seemed he had decided to turn over a new leaf. He started a small picture framing business to which he applied himself with great energy. Soon he had two men working for him and took larger shop premises in West Street. This proved to be a mistake and the business was soon in trouble. He now moved to Manchester where Hannah opened a small shop in Long Millgate. While she worked in her shop by day Peace was out at night breaking into houses. In 1866 he was convicted of a burglary in Victoria Park, Manchester. The sentence this time was seven years' penal servitude. Following his trial, Hannah returned to Sheffield and when he came out of prison in 1872 he joined her. Between 1872 and 1875 he lived at addresses in Orchard Street and the Brocco, working as a picture framer and joiner by day. By night he was a highly successful burglar preying on houses all over the north of England. To reduce the risk of being caught, he planned his crimes carefully and made it his policy always to work alone. A master of disguise who 'could transform his facial appearance in an instant,'[55] he would to go about during daylight hours spying out likely premises passing himself off as a

---

[54] Ticket of leave: a 'licence to be at large' granted to a convict towards the end of a sentence of penal servitude as a reward for good and industrious behaviour.

[55] Because he had lost a lot of teeth in prison he was able to push out his lower jaw to 'an amazing extent' whilst contracting the upper part of his face. He once performed this party trick in front of his solicitor, Sir W E Clegg, who observed afterwards: 'He could transform his features and make them utterly unrecognisable [and] could do this instantaneously.' Peace had also inherited his father's way with animals and rarely had difficulty quieting guard dogs.

hawker or itinerant clock repairer. Determined never to serve another prison sentence, he now always carried a firearm when he went out burgling.

In 1875 he and his family moved to 40, Victoria Place, Britannia Road, Darnall. Life at his new address continued much as before, during the day he worked as a picture framer at night he was abroad thieving. He had an unpleasant shock, however, when he discovered that Revd. Littlewood, who had been chaplain at the Wakefield House of Correction when he had been imprisoned there, was the local vicar. Assuring Littlewood that he had put crime behind him, he threw himself on his mercy. The vicar promised that he would keep what he knew to himself provided that Peace showed himself to be a reformed character and a regular church attender.

Living next door to the Peace family, at 36, Victoria Place, were Mr and Mrs Arthur Dyson and their five-year-old son, recently arrived from America. Catherine Dyson, a fine looking woman of 25, had been born in Ireland but had emigrated to Ohio at the age of 15. It was there that she met her husband, a railway engineer born in Sheffield.[56] Smitten with his new neighbour, Peace went out of his way to make friends with the Dysons. According to him, soon after he met her she became his mistress. This she always indignantly denied but there is no doubt that he paid court to her, offering to give her a sealskin jacket and promising to set her up in a shop in Manchester if she would run away with him. Even if she was not

[56] Dyson had returned to England because of health problems. He obtained employment with the North Eastern Railway but was later dismissed for failing to appear at the station to which he had been sent. His relations with Catherine were not untroubled. On one occasion the police were called to an incident in which she had hit him over the head with a hammer and he had hit her back.

willing to sleep with him, she was certainly prepared to let him take her out to public houses and entertainments such as the music hall.[57] Eventually, however, there was a falling out. Arthur Dyson, who was already becoming tired of Peace's constant visits to his home, was appalled when the latter showed him some obscene prints and offered to take him to a brothel. Determined to have nothing more to do with the man, he threw a visiting card over the garden wall on which he had written 'Charles Peace is requested not to interfere with my family.' Peace's response was to try and persuade Catherine to run away with him. When she would not, he began a campaign of persecution against her husband, following him in the street and shouting oaths and abuse. At about 9 or 10 pm on a July evening, Catherine was chatting to neighbours in the street when Peace approached. 'Why do you annoy my husband in the way you do?' she asked. Peace immediately whipped a pistol out of his pocket and held it against her head saying 'I will blow your bloody brains out, and your bloody husband's too.'

This time he had gone too far and the next morning the Dysons took out a summons against him. When he failed to appear in answer to the summons a warrant was issued for his arrest. Shortly after this he decamped with his family to Hull and there opened an eating house.

In the weeks which followed, Catherine received three letters from him, all post-marked Hamburg, pleading with her not to hate him, telling her he loved her and threatening all manner of retaliation if the summons against him was not withdrawn.

---

[57] He also gave her a ring and the two of them were photographed together at the Sheffield Fair.

From Hull he moved to Manchester where he took lodgings. On the night of the 1st to 2nd August, constables Beanland and Cock were on foot patrol in the Whalley Range. Just after midnight they stopped near to the junction of Upper Chorlton Road and Seymour Drive and were talking to a young student, named Simpson, when Beanland saw a man walk quickly into Seymour Drive and disappear down the driveway of a detached house. Although the man was respectably dressed, the officer did not like the look of him and suspected he was up to no good. He told Cock what he had seen and the two of them walked down the drive. Beanland shone his torch but seeing nothing began to turn away. As he did so there were two flashes and the sound of pistol shots and Cock fell down at his side mortally wounded. The man who had fired the fatal shots was Peace, disturbed as he was about to break into the house. Having discharged his gun he made his escape by walking along a railway line in the direction of Manchester.

Before the night was out the police had arrested, on suspicion of being involved in the murder, three brothers called Habron. The trio had been seen in Upper Chorlton Road shortly before the killing and there was bad blood between them and PC Cock, who had taken out summonses against them for being drunk and disorderly. On the morning of July 27, William had appeared in court in answer to the summons and been fined 5s. As he left court, he had been heard to say that he would do for Cock while John had threatened to 'do for the little body.'[58] Against the third brother the police had no

[58] John was fined half a sovereign on the morning of July 31.

evidence, but William and John were committed to Manchester Assizes on a charge of murdering the dead officer.

Back in Sheffield, the Dysons were becoming increasingly troubled by reports of an old woman who had been seen watching their house. Fearing no doubt that the woman was either Peace in disguise or someone in his pay, they decided to get away from Darnall and, on October 25, a furniture van removed them to Banner Cross Terrace on the south western outskirts of the town. Shortly after its arrival Peace, who had followed it from Darnall, visited a grocer's shop in the Terrace kept by a couple, named Gregory,[59] and let rip a diatribe of abuse against their neighbours-to-be. As he was leaving the shop, he came face to face with the Dysons. 'You see, I'm here to annoy you, wherever you go,' he told them. They pushed past him. 'There is a warrant out for you,' said Catherine. 'I care nought for the warrant, nor for the bobbies' Peace told her. The next time they would see him, he told them, there would be murder done.

He was in Manchester for the trial of the Habrons on November 27. The principal planks of the Crown's case were the threats which the brothers had made on the morning of July 1 and the fact that they had been seen in Upper Chorlton Road shortly before the murder. But against William there was other evidence. An ironmonger's assistant gave evidence that, on either July 31 or August 1, William had called at the shop where he worked and asked to be shown cartridges (another shop employee remembered the transaction but was not sure that the customer was in fact Habron). Two percussion caps had been found by the police in the pocket of a waistcoat which William had

[59] The Gregorys' and the Dysons' houses were the last two houses at the north end of the terrace (the end nearer to Sheffield).

been given by his employer. The employer swore that they were not his. Constable Beanland claimed that the man he had seen disappear down the drive appeared to be of the same age, height and complexion as William. Also, it was said that the pattern of the sole of boots taken from William corresponded in certain respect to footprints left at the scene by the murderer. The trial judge, Mr Justice Lindley, was clearly not impressed by the evidence against William and against John there was even less. In his summing up he told the jury that neither the footprint evidence nor Beanland's 'identification' took the matter very far and laid stress upon the fact that William was of good character and that no firearm had been traced to him. On the second day of the trial, after a retirement of two and a quarter hours, the jury returned with verdicts. John was acquitted, William found guilty but with a recommendation to mercy on account of his youth.

On returning to his lodgings after the verdict, Peace told his landlady that the police had sworn Habron's life away. 'He is no more guilty than you are.' He was not alone in this view, for although the *Manchester Guardian* expressed approbation of the verdicts, the city was anything but satisfied that justice had been done. The correspondence columns of the local newspapers were flooded with letters protesting at the verdict and, on December 4, at a meeting, attended by forty prominent Mancunians, the decision was taken to petition the Home Secretary for a reprieve. Two days before Habron was due to hang, he was informed that his sentence had been commuted to penal servitude for life.

On the 28$^{th}$, shortly after hearing the Habron verdict, Peace travelled back to Sheffield. That evening Mrs Dyson was in the *Stag* public house at Sharrow Head. Peace would later claim that she was there with him, a point on which she would prove highly evasive when questioned.

On October 29, he visited his mother, telling her he had come to Sheffield for the fair. In the afternoon he repaired to the *Prince of Wales* at Ecclesall, where he spent several hours playing tunes on a crude fiddle, which he had fashioned out of a poker and a length of string, and being plied with drink by an appreciative audience. At 6 o'clock the Vicar of Ecclesall, the Revd Newman, was sitting down to his tea when his maid informed him that there was a strange man wanting to see him. 'Show him in,' he told her. His visitor was Peace, who had no sooner got through the door than he launched into a tirade against the Dysons. The vicar should be on his guard against them. He, Peace, had been carrying on an affair with Mrs Dyson and proffered letters in proof. The cause of her infidelity was Dyson's jealousy, which had led her to give her husband something to think about. Dyson had taken out proceedings against him and he had become a fugitive, but he would follow them wherever they went. At twenty minutes to seven he was ushered out of the vicarage, having promised the vicar that he would not go near the couple that night.

It was a promise he had no intention of keeping. He at once made his way to the Gregorys' shop. 'My husband's out,' Mrs Gregory told him.

He now settled down to keep watch on the Dysons' house. As he waited Sarah Colgreaves,[60] who lived in nearby Dobbin Hill and had some purchases to make at Gregorys' shop, approached. She noticed

---

[60] The wife of a table-blade maker.

Peace walking to and fro outside the Dysons' house. 'Do you know who lives there?' he asked.

'No. I think they are strangers.'

'That woman is my bloody whore.'

'You ought to mind what you say.'

'Would you mind going to the door and saying that an elderly gentleman wishes to speak to her?'

'I would mind very much,' Mrs Colgreaves told him and with that walked into the shop. Having made her purchases and advised Mrs. Gregory to lock her door, she left the shop. As she did so, she saw Peace emerging from the passage leading to the back yards of the houses in the terrace.

Shortly after 8 o'clock labourer, Charles Brassington, was passing the *Banner Cross Hotel* when he noticed Peace walking up and down in front of it in an agitated fashion.

'Do you know of any strangers living hereabouts?

'No,' he replied.

Peace then showed him a photograph of a man and a woman and handed him some letters to read. 'I can't read,' said Brassington.

'I'll make it warm for them before morning. I'll shoot 'em both,' said Peace, walking off.

Minutes later he was back in the passageway leading to the back of the houses. As he watched he saw Catherine Dyson come out of the back door of her house carrying a lantern and go into a privy. When she came out, Peace was waiting, revolver in hand. 'Speak and I'll fire,' he told her. She screamed and ducked back into the closet. Her cry brought Arthur Dyson out of the house in his carpet slippers. Peace made for the passageway with Dyson in pursuit. Peace fired, his shot striking the stone lintel above the passageway entrance. Still Dyson came on. Peace fired again and this time the bullet found its target and Dyson fell to the ground shot through the temple. Catherine rushed to his side. 'Murder,' she screamed. 'You villain, you have shot my husband.' With the help of neighbours she got the injured man into the house where he was placed in a chair. Dr Harrison, of Cemetery Road, was sent for but Arthur Dyson was beyond help and two and a half hours later he died.

After firing the second shot, Peace hurried across the road, climbed over a wall into a garden and then headed towards Greystones. In doing so, he dropped the bundle of letters which he offered to show Brassington. The first police officer on the scene was PC Sylvester. Having been told what had happened, he made no attempt to follow Peace but, instead, made his way to Highfields Police Station. For this he was roundly criticised by the *Sheffield Independent.* 'It is really astonishing,' it declared, 'that an officer should take refuge behind so much red-tapeism *(sic)*.'

With no officers in pursuit, Peace walked back to Sheffield where he called on his mother and brother and told them he had shot Dyson. He then made his way to Attercliffe railway station and caught a train to Beverley. He got out at Normanton and then travelled on to York. After spending the night on York station, next morning he caught a train to Hull, where he called in at the eating house which his wife ran and asked for food. He had just started his meal when the police turned up. He managed to get away but it was a close run thing and he took immediate steps to alter his appearance. He stayed in Hull for a further three weeks. By now, wanted posters had been issued:

*Charles Peace wanted for murder on the night of the 29th instant. He is thin and slightly built, from 55 to 60 yrs of age. Five feet four inches or five feet high; grey nearly white hair, beard and whiskers. He lacks use of three fingers of the left hand,[61] walks with his legs rather wide apart, speaks somewhat peculiarly as though his tongue were too large for his mouth and is a great boaster. He occasionally cleans and repairs clocks and watches and sometimes deals in oleographs, engravings and pictures. He has been in penal servitude for burglary in Manchester. He has lived in Manchester, Salford, Liverpool and Hull.*

On the Thursday following the murder, large numbers of people visited the murder scene pausing to examine the heavy blood-staining on ground and the chip in the lintel caused by the bullet.

On December 1, Dr Harrison and Mr Benson carried out a post-mortem. They found a hole in the skull near the left temple and, lodged inside the brain, a bullet which had been completely flattened. Later in the day, the coroner, Dossey Wightman, opened the inquest at the *Banner Cross Hotel.* After the jury had visited the Dysons' home to view the body, evidence of identification was taken, a burial certificate issued and the proceedings adjourned for seven days.

While the inquest was getting under way, over in Endcliffe Park the police were draining the dams, there being a theory abroad that following the murder Peace had committed suicide.

At 3 pm on the Saturday, the funeral cortege set out from Banner Cross Terrace for Ecclesall Church. It consisted of a hearse and a single cab. The funeral was conducted by the vicar. The dead man was buried in a grave lying midway between the church and the road

---

[61] He had lost a finger of his left hand (possibly as a result of a firearms accident). To conceal this disability on occasions he wore a false arm, made of *gutta percha*, with an iron hook at the end.

leading to the vicarage. The weather was bad and only a hundred or so persons gathered to watch the proceedings. The following day, however, sightseers were out in force.

On Friday, December 8, the adjourned inquest resumed at the *Stag Inn*, Sharrow Head. The principal witness was Catherine Dyson who described the shooting and also explained to the court the history of her dealings with Peace. Asked by the coroner whether she and her husband had quarrelled over her familiarity with Peace, she replied 'No,' an answer from which she would never thereafter depart. Was she able to help about the bundle of letters, which the police had found in the field opposite her house and which looked like correspondence between her and Peace? No, she was not. She had never written to Peace nor he to her. None of the letters found was in her hand.[62] She was followed into the witness box by Mrs Colgreaves, Charles Brassington, Mrs Gregory and PC Ward who had found the letters. After a brief summing up by the coroner, the jury were soon back with a verdict of wilful murder against Charles Peace.

He next day the *Sheffield Independent* observed that the letters which Catherine Dyson had disowned were 'such as would probably be written by a woman carrying on an intrigue.'[63]

On the day of the inquest Peace was still in Hull but things were getting too hot for him there and, at the end of December, he travelled to Doncaster and later to Nottingham, where he took up with a woman named Susan Gray and resumed his profession as a house

[62] The correspondence is printed in full in Shore, op. cit., Appendix A.

[63] One of the letters contained the sentence: 'Don't know when he will go out again but will sure tell you.' As Shore observes at p 175 'The Americanism was one scarcely likely to be used by Peace.'

burglar. In 1877 he returned to Hull with his new mistress, and took rooms in the house of a police sergeant. After a short and successful burglary campaign he returned to Nottingham.

His next port of call was London. There he took a shop in Lambeth where by day he dealt in musical instruments and by night he was out breaking into houses. Soon afterwards he moved to Greenwich where he took a lease of two adjoining houses; he lived with Susan Gray in one and in the other he installed his wife, whom he had persuaded to move down from Hull, and his son Willie. In May 1877, he took a lease of a house in Peckham.[64] Calling himself Thompson, he claimed to be of independent means. The lavish furnishings of the house seemed to confirm that he was a man of some wealth and his regular attendance at Sunday service his respectability. In reality, he was living with his wife and mistress under one roof and was supporting himself by crime.

At about 2 am on the morning of October 18, 1878, PC Robinson, on patrol in Blackheath, noticed a light suddenly appear at the rear of a large house in St John's Park. Suspecting that there was a burglar at work, he quickly summoned two colleagues. Having instructed one of them to ring the front door bell, Robinson took up position at the back of the house. As soon as the bell sounded, a man climbed out of the dining room window and rushed down the path. Robinson gave chase. 'Keep back!' shouted the intruder 'or by God I'll shoot you.' Robinson ignored the threat whereupon the burglar discharged three shots at him. All missed. Robinson now rushed the

---

[64] While living there Peace devoted some of his time to inventing and he and Henry Brion actually patented an invention for raising sunken ships. Other inventions on which he was working at the time of his arrest included a smoke helmet for firemen, an improved brush for washing railway carriages and a form of hydraulic tank.

man and, despite being shot in the arm, was able to grab and hold on to him. Although he did not know it, had had captured Charlie Peace.

Taken before the magistrates at Greenwich, the burglar refused to give his name but, due to the treachery of Susan Gray,[65] the police quickly learned his true identity.

On November 19, 1878, charged in the name of John Ward alias Charles Peace, Peace stood trial at the Old Bailey for burglary and attempted murder. He was sentenced by Mr Justice Hawkins to penal servitude for life.

As soon as the trial was over, steps were put in hand to indict him for the Banner Cross murder. On January 17, 1879, he was taken from Pentonville Prison to Sheffield for a committal hearing. Catherine Dyson, who had travelled back from the United States to give evidence, was the first witness. On the following day, as the train bringing him from London was passing through Kiveton Park, Peace threw himself out of a carriage window. He was found lying unconscious alongside the track bleeding from a head wound and was taken to the Central Police Office. He later claimed that he had been trying to kill himself.

By January 30, he was sufficiently recovered from his injuries for the committal hearing to resume. It was held in the corridor outside his cell in the Town Hall. Catherine Dyson, who still had to be cross-examined by Peace's solicitor, W E Clegg, was recalled. It was put to her that she had been in the habit of going alone to the accused's house, had been alone with him in public houses and places of entertainment and, indeed, had been photographed with him at the

[65] She later applied for and was paid the reward of £100 offered by the authorities to any person who supplied information leading to Peace's conviction.

Sheffield fair. 'Not to my recollection,' was her reply. Had she not told the licensee of a public house to charge her drinks to Peace? She did not recall that either. As for the letters produced at the inquest they were nothing to do with her. The evidence of the remaining witnesses was taken very shortly. Peace was duly committed for trial and taken to Wakefield gaol whence he was transferred to Armley on the eve of his trial.

The trial took place at Leeds Assizes on February 4, 1879, before Mr Justice Lopes.[66] Mr Campbell Foster QC with Mr Hugh Shield appeared for the Crown.[67] Peace was defended by Mr Frank Lockwood and Mr Stuart-Wortley.[68]

In his cross-examination of Catherine Dyson, Lockwood suggested to her that her husband, before he was shot, had taken hold of Peace. Had she not told the committing magistrate 'I can't say that my husband did not get hold of the prisoner'? 'Put in the little word 'try'' was the tart retort: her husband may have attempted to get hold of Peace but he never succeeded in doing so. Lockwood turned next to the matter of her dealings with Peace and the more she was asked the more evasive Catherine Dyson became. She could not say, one way or the other, whether she had charged to Peace's account drinks she had consumed at the *Half Way* public house at Darnall. She had

---

[66] **Lopes**, Henry Charles, lst Baron Ludlow (1828-1899); educ. Winchester and Balliol; barrister 1852; QC 1869, conserv MP Launceston 1868-74 and Frome 1874; High Court judge 1876, Lord Justice of Appeal 1883; peer 1897.

[67] **Campbell Foster**, Thomas (1813-82); QC 1875. **Shield**, Hugh (1831-1903); educ Bishopwearmouth school, Birmingham GS and Jesus College, Cambridge (Fellow); barrister 1860; QC 1881; MP for Camnbridge 1880-85.

[68] **Lockwood**, Sir Frank; b. Doncaster 1846; educ Manchester GS and Caius Coll, Cambridge; barrister 1872; QC; Recorder of Sheffield 1884-1894; Solicitor-General 1894-95; **Stuart-Wortley**, Charles Beilby; educ Rugby and Balliol; barrister 1876; practised on NE Circuit 1876-85, QC 1892; MP Sheffield 1880-85 and Hallam 1885 and 1916; under-secy of State, Home Office 1885 and 1886-92; 1916 lst baron Stuart of Wortley.

perhaps been with him twice to the *Marquis of Waterford* public house and once to the *Star* Music Hall. Confronted with a girl and a man whom it was suggested she had employed to carry notes to Peace, she claimed that the documents in question were merely receipts for pictures. Yes, on the night before the murder, she had been in the *Stag Inn* and a man had sat with her and left when she did. She could almost swear that man was not Peace. Her prevarications were described by *The Times* as feeble and clearly convinced nobody. She was followed into the witness box by other witnesses who testified to having seen Peace near the Dysons' home on the night of the murder and of hearing a scream and shots. Mrs Gregory said she had heard Mrs Dyson scream and then shots. Brassington described his encounter with Peace and the threat he made to shoot the Dysons. Other witnesses spoke of threats which Peace had uttered against the Dysons in 1875 and 1876. There was also evidence that the rifling on the bullet extracted from Dyson's brain matched the rifling of the revolver taken from Peace on his arrest in October, 1878.

In his closing speech, Lockwood suggested that Dyson may well have been shot accidentally as he struggled with Peace for the gun. He complained of hostile press publicity and ended with an observation (which sounds curious to modern ears) that Peace was in such a state of wickedness as to be unprepared for death and that the jury should therefore be tender with him.

The judge, in his summing, up observed that the theory that the gun had been accidentally discharged was pure surmise. He suggested to the jury that they pick up the gun and judge for themselves whether it was the kind of weapon which was likely to go off accidentally. Mrs Dyson's evidence was corroborated by that of other witnesses and, if the jury found that there was no foundation for the defence put forward, they must do their duty.

The jury retired at 7.15 pm and were back just ten minutes later with a verdict of guilty.

Asked whether he had anything to say why sentence of death should not be passed, Peace replied 'It's no use my saying anything.'

Donning the black cap, Mr Justice Lopes proceeded to pass sentence:

> *Charles Peace, after a most patient trial and after every argument has been urged by your learned counsel which ingenuity could suggest, you have been found guilty of the murder of Arthur Dyson by a jury of your country. It is not my duty, still less my desire, to aggravate your feelings at this moment by a recapitulation of any portion of the details of what, I fear, I can only call your criminal career. I implore you during the short time that may remain to you to live to prepare for eternity. I pass upon you the only sentence which the law permits in a case of this kind. That sentence is that you be taken from this place to the place whence you came and thence to a place of execution and that you be there hanged by the neck until you are dead....'*

After his conviction, Peace spent his time praying and writing letters to and receiving visits from friends and family.[69] To all who would listen he expressed contrition for his misdeeds and his letters to his family were full of exhortations to lead a godly life. On the Wednesday before his execution, he received a visit from the Revd Littlewood, the vicar of Darnall. To the astonished clergyman he confessed that it was he, Peace, who had killed PC Cock at Whalley

[69] The prison authorities fearing that his family would bring him poison with which to kill himself insisted that that visitors have no physical contact with him.

Range and proceeded to give a detailed account of the circumstances. His confession was reduced to writing and handed, along with a plan, to the prison governor for transmission to the Home Office. When it was scrutinised not only did his account fit the known facts but, when the matter was looked into, it was discovered that the bullet which had killed Cock had been fired from a gun of the type which Peace had in his possession when arrested at Blackheath.[70] In the course of his interview with Mr Littlewood, Peace also gave his version of the events leading up to the Banner Cross shooting:

> *I came to Sheffield the night after the [Habron] trial and went to Banner Cross in the evening. I wanted to see Mrs Dyson. I stood on the low wall at the back of the house. I knew the house very well, both back and front, and I knew the bedroom was at the back. While I was standing I noticed a light in the bedroom. The blind was up and I could plainly see Mrs Dyson carrying a candle and moving about the room.*
>
> *I watched her for some time and I then saw that she was putting her boy to bed. I then 'flipped my fingers' and gave a sort of subdued whistle to attract the attention of Mrs Dyson as I had often doe at other places. I had not long to wait Mrs Dyson came downstairs.- she had evidently heard the signal and knew I was there – and in response to my call she came out and passed out to the closet. I then got down off the wall and went towards the closet. I was with her for some time. You may ask what I wanted to do with her. Well I did not do what people think, I went simply for the purpose of begging her to induce her husband to withdraw the warrant which had been issued against me. I was tired of being hunted about, not being able to come and go as I liked. I only wanted the warrant withdrawn. That was my only object and if I had got that done I should have gone away again.*
>
> *Mrs Dyson became very noisy and defiant, used fearful language and threats against me and I got angry. Taking my revolver out of my pocket. I held it up to her face and said 'Now*

[70] After a Home Office investigation, William Habron was granted a free pardon and £800 compensation.

*be careful what you are saying to me. You know me of old and know what I can do. You know I am not a man to be talked to in that way. If there is one man, who will not be trifled with by you, or anybody else, it is Charles Peace.'*

*She did not take warning but continued to use threats against me and angered me. I tried to keep as cool as I could. While these angry words were going on Mr Dyson hastily made his appearance. As soon as I saw Mr Dyson I immediately started to go down the passage which leads to the main road. I was not sharp enough Mr Dyson seized me before I could get past him. I told him to stand back and let me go, but he did not and then I fired one barrel of my revolver wide at him to frighten him, expecting that he would then loose me and then I should get off. He got hold of the arm to which I had strapped my revolver, which I always did, and then I knew I had not a moment to spare. I made a desperate effort, wrenched the arm from him and fired.*

*It was a life or death struggle but even then I did not intend to shoot Mr Dyson...I saw Dyson fall.*

*I did not know where he was hit, nor had any idea that it was such a wound as would prove fatal. All that was in my head at the time was to get away and if he had not so obstinately prevented me I should have got away.*

On Monday, February 24, Peace received a final visit from his wife, stepson and daughter. He produced a will which he had made leaving his estate to the two children in equal shares. 'I have furniture and shares in the London Tramway Company worth about £550 altogether,' he told them. As he took his leave of his wife he handed her a funeral card and a design for a gravestone.[71] During the course

[71] It read

In Memory of Charles Peace
who was executed in Armley Prison
Tuesday, February 25th, 1879, Aged 47
For that I don but never
Intended

He also asked that flowers be placed on a certain grave in a Sheffield cemetery on the day of his execution.

of the day he was disturbed by the sound of hammering. 'That's a noise that would make some men fall to the floor. They are working at my scaffold.,' he exclaimed. Told he was mistaken, he replied 'I am not mistaken. I have not worked so long with wood without knowing the sound of deals; and they don't have deals inside a prison for anything else than scaffolds.'

Tuesday, February 25, 1879, the day fixed for his hanging, dawned icy and bitterly cold. Peace rose at 6 am, spent some time writing letters, made a hearty breakfast but found time to criticise the fare. 'Bloody poor bacon, this,' he complained. He showed no sign of fear. 'I wonder if Marwood [the hangman) can cure this throat of mine,' he joked and when a warder, concerned at the time he was spending on the lavatory, banged on the door, he shouted back: 'You are in a hell of a hurry. Are you going to be hanged or am I?' 'I hope you will not punish me, I hope you will do your work quickly,' he said to Marwood, as the latter entered the cell to pinion him. 'You shall not suffer at my hands,' the hangman assured him. 'I hope to meet you all in heaven. I am thankful to say all my sins are forgiven.'

On the walk from the cell to the scaffold, which had been erected in a corner of the prison yard, he twice almost slipped on the icy path. As the rope was being adjusted he asked to be allowed to hear the prayer the chaplain was reciting. Having done so he asked, and was allowed, to address the reporters present:

> *'Gentlemen, you reporters, I wish to give you notice the few words I am going to say. You know that my life has been base and bad. I wish to tell the world what my death is. I ask – what man could die as I die if he did not die in the fear of the Lord? Gentlemen, tell all my friends that I feel assured that my sins are forgiven me, and that I am going to the Kingdom*

*of Heaven, or else to that place where people rest till the great judgment day. I have no enemies that I feel anything against on earth. I wish that all my enemies would do so to me. I wish them well; I wish them to come to the Kingdom of Heaven, to die as I die. To one and all I say good-bye and Heaven bless you, and may you come to the Kingdom of Heaven at the last. Say my last wishes and my last respects are to my dear children and their dear mother. I hope that no person will disgrace himself by taunting them or jeering them on my account, but will have mercy upon them. God bless you, my dear children; good-be and Heaven bless you. Amen. Oh, my Lord God have mercy upon me!'*

Marwood, who had been waiting patiently for Peace to finish, now began to adjust the noose and place the cap over his head. 'I could do with a drink of water,' said Peace. His request was ignored, 'The rope is very tight,' he complained. 'Never mind, its all for the best,' Marwood told him. 'Hold up your chin I won't hurt you.' 'Good bye and God bless you all:' said Peace and, as he was attempting to repeat these words, the bolts were drawn.[72]

Outside a crowd of about a thousand had gathered to see the hoisting of the black flag.

[72] Marwood said afterwards '...he passed away like a summer's eve.' (B. Bailey, *Hangmen of England*, p 82).

## The Shelf Street axe murder - James Hall, 1881[73]

Living at 149, Shelf Street in the Spring of 1881 were James Hall, his wife Mary Ann and their youngest daughter Selina. The house which stood at the corner of Shelf Street and Leadmill Road was small and cramped. On the ground floor there was a living room and a small kitchen, with a yard at the rear; on the first floor a single bedroom; the only entrance was in Shelf Street. It was poor accommodation but all the family could afford. Fifty-three-year old Hall was a cutler by trade who had in the past worked at Thomas Turner & Company's Suffolk Works. But work was something for which he had little liking. According to neighbours his chief occupation had, for some time, consisted of begging for pence in the street and playing dominoes in public houses. In the words of a local reporter he belonged to:

> *'the fraternity who found it congenial... to stand at street corners and piteously ask people to put a halfpence to another half pence in their hand that they (the beggar) might get bread and, being usually successful in their appeals they soon find themselves with the price of a pint.'* [74]

A heavy drinker, who was not above raising his fist to his wife when in liquor, he had of late started threatening to murder her and their daughter.

If neighbours had little good to say about her husband, not so in the case of Mary Ann.[75] Respectable and hard working she was

[73] See *Sheffield Telegraph*, March 28, 30 and May 7, 1881; *Sheffield Independent*, March 28, 29, 30, 31, Apr 1, May 7 and 24, 1881.
[74] *Sheffield Telegraph,* March 28, 1881.
[75] She was 48 years old at the date of her death.

considered much put upon. For some years she had kept the family afloat financially by taking in washing and going out charring. Selina, who worked at Ibbotsons' edge tool factory, was equally well thought of. She was courting Richard Duckenfield, a young scissor grinder who lived in New George Street.

Saturday, March 26 was much like any other working day in the Hall household. At 8.40 am Selina left to go to work. Next to leave was Mary Ann who had a regular job on Saturdays cleaning for Mrs Sewell at Broomhill. Last out was James Hall heading for the pub.

When Selina returned from work at 2.30 there was no-one in. She had a machine top to polish and was soon busy at work. She was still hard at it when her father came in at around 5.30 smelling of beer.

'What time will your mother be in?' he asked.

'I don't know.'

'What time will tea be ready?'

'Not till I've finished polishing this top.'

'What are we going to have to eat?'

'Dry bread. What there is in the house.'

'Don't say so, let it be some sausage, some steak or something.'

'Oh, you bad un,' exclaimed Selina 'Where do you think my mother is going to get it from? You've done no work and brought no money home for a fortnight. How can you expect anything to eat? You'll not have a home to come to very soon.'

At this Hall walked out. Soon after Mary Ann came in and she and Selina had their tea.

At 8.30 Mary Ann was in a shop across the road buying some frilling for a dress when Hall returned. 'Where's your mother? Has she been in?' he asked. 'You know she has.' Selina told him. Shortly after this Mary Ann came in with some coal for the fire. 'Let us live comfortable together,' she said to Hall. She then asked for his money only to be told he had none. As she went up stairs he shouted after her 'Polly, I'm not going out to night so it's no use thee getting ready.' She ignored him and, after putting the coal on the grate, wrapped herself in her shawl, took the door key and set off for her mother's at Duke Street.

At 9 o'clock, Selina went out to meet her young man in town leaving Hall in the house by himself. Richard Duckenfield took her to the *White Hart* in Waingate where they spent a pleasant evening, he playing billiards and she in another room chatting to the wives of two other men. They left at around 11 pm.

At about this time a neighbour, named Betts, saw Mary Ann standing near the door of no 149. 'Is that Mrs Hall?' he asked. 'Yes, my husband has struck me.' 'Oh nonsense,' he told her. 'Go in and agree.' He was the last person to see her alive. She could only have arrived home a matter of minutes before this exchange for, according to her cousin Mary Ann Staley, she had left her house at 191, Pond Street just before 11 pm.

After leaving the *White Hart* Richard Duckenfield walked Selina home. On arriving at the house she found the door locked and went to the kitchen window where the key was usually kept. As she looked in through the window she saw her father walking towards the door. 'What are you up to now with the door fastened?' she shouted. Hall immediately opened the door and, after looking up and down the street, shouted 'I'll show thee what I'm doing' and aimed a blow at her with a hatchet, catching her on the chin. She fled screaming

'Murder!' Hall chased after her and managed to hit her again but was then grabbed and thrown to the ground by Duckenfield who, having seen what was afoot, had rushed to Selina's aid. He was then held face down on the pavement by Duckenfield and three other bystanders until the police arrived. They were not long in coming. PC Crowe, who had been in St Mary's Road when he heard Selina's cry, was the first officer on the scene. On passing through the kitchen he found Mary Ann lying on her back in the right hand corner of the living room. The whole of the left side of her face had been smashed in and her brains were protruding. Blood and brains were splattered on the walls to a height of between five and six feet. Dr James, a police surgeon living in London Road, was sent for. On examining the body he found that there were seven severe wounds to the head.

Hall in the meanwhile was taken under arrest to Highfields Police Station. He was clearly the worse for drink and unconcerned at what he had done. 'Yes, I did it and I meant to do it. I hope I have done the _______,' he said. When searched he was found to have a purse (later identified as his wife's) which contained 10s. 10 ½d.

On Monday morning, he made a brief appearance before the town's magistrates. 'A post mortem will be required,' the Chief Constable told the bench. He would call one witness and then ask for a remand. The witness was Duckenfield who described the attack in the street. Asked if he had any questions for him Hall said in a clear firm voice 'I mean to say that it is false, sir.' That night Alderman Clegg addressed a temperance meeting in the town. The Leadmill Road murder was he told them the second murder from drink committed in Sheffield in the last three months. His speech was fully reported by the local press.

At 9 am on the Tuesday morning the coroner opened the inquest. It was held at the *Royal Standard* in St Mary's Road. Hall was brought by cab and, as he went in, he was hooted and jeered by the large crowd which had gathered outside. The principal witness called was Selina who, after relating the events of the Saturday night, described what living with her father had been like. He had, she said, threatened to murder her mother many times, a thousand times. He had always said that if he did murder her, he should do all who came near; he should never be hung for he should 'do' himself then. Her mother had said many a time if I ever found her dead I would know who'd done it. She had gone to work for him when she could hardly walk. She had heard him say to her 'Polly is the hatchet in the cupboard?' and when she answered 'Yes,' say 'Then thee be aware.' The hatchet had recently been ground; she (Selina) had snipped it when chipping away ice and her father had told her to get it ground, after which he had it sharpened. He told her mother that it was for her and five weeks since he had it under the sofa. Whilst her deposition was being read over Hall listened attentively with a smile on his face. Asked if he had any questions for her he said 'No. I only wish to say she's a liar: her name is Howson.' 'I am his daughter although my name is Howson,' retorted Selina.[76] 'A man who will call his daughter a liar before company like this is not worth much,' observed the coroner. 'Quite right, sir,' observed one of the jury. The court then heard from Duckenfield, Betts and PC Crowe. The last witness called was William Dale, the police surgeon who had conducted the post-mortem. He had found six wounds to the head and one to the

[76] If Selina had been born before her parents married and her mother's maiden name had been Howson that would have been her surname at birth. Query whether this is the explanation of this rather puzzling exchange.

throat; one of the head wounds had chipped the skull, and two others had fractured the skull exposing the brain; nearly the whole of the left side of the face had been destroyed; the dead woman had been struck many blows with a sharp instrument. He thought she might have been able to walk outside after one of the blows but not after all of them. Invited to put questions to the doctor, Hall said 'Someone else has done all this.' 'That is your look out,' retorted the coroner 'If you can prove that, you will be a very lucky man but it will rest with you to prove it.'

At the conclusion of the evidence the coroner asked Hall if he wished to say anything, stressing that he was not obliged to do so. 'Then I've nothing to say,' he replied. 'I'll save it for another day.' After a short summing up and a ten minute retirement the jury were back with a verdict of wilful murder against Hall. The coroner made out a warrant committing him for trial and he was taken to Wakefield Gaol.

On March 30, he was back in Sheffield before Mr Edward Welby, the stipendiary magistrate, for committal proceedings. Mr Knowles Binns appeared for the prosecution. Again the principal witness was Selina. At the conclusion of her evidence Hall said: 'The reason that caused me to threaten her so often is a circumstance about three years ago.' The stipendiary told him he would have an opportunity to give his version in due course. At the end of the prosecution case Hall was formally charged with murder, cautioned and asked if he had anything to say. 'It will not take me many minutes to say what I have to say.' he replied.

*It is stated by one of the witnesses that I have threatened my wife many a time in my life. That is true.*

The stipendiary: *Do you wish this writing down?*

*Yes, it's true, I say. The reason was this. Three year sin' I lived on Paternoster Row. It war a double house, front door and back kitchen door. There wur a yard behind and a passage coming into the street the back way to make an entrance there. I went home one night. There wur no one in the house and the middle kitchen door wur closed. Well, I thewt where wur my wife. I tried to open t' door an' I couldn't exactly get it open, as there were summat behind. I pushed hard and as I got in't back kitchen door opened. My wife thrust me back into t' house through t'middle door. I thowt there were summat wrong so I went forard to t' back kitchen window and I see a man going down t'passage on his tip toes. Thinks I 'That's William Lowe,' and I runs to t' bottom of t'passage and saw it wur him getting over t'wall into t' front street. So I goes back and says 'Who wur yon man in t'house wi' thee?' She says 'What man?' I says 'The man that's just gone out of t' kitchen door when I came in.' She said 'There was no man with me.' I says 'I see him going down the passage and leap over t'wall out of t'way.' She says 'Who wur it?' I says I know t'man. I says I know his first name, but not his second exactly. She says 'Its queer you should know his first name and not his second.' I says 'Why, because there's two half brothers, both by one mother, but two fathers an' I says I don't know which name it is, whether its Lowe or Booth.' 'Well,' she says 'there's been no one wi' me.' I says 'If I ever catch thee at owt of sort I'll have thee life.' [At this point a woman in the body of the court shouted 'You bad wretch' but was immediately silenced.]. That's all about that. I've seen bits of things many a time after. I says 'Don't let me catch thee else I shall do as I said.' Well , I went home last Saturday night. Well, I saw her about a quarter past eleven and goes through t' kitchen into t' house. There wur a man and her on t' sofa. I says 'What sort of game's this Poll?' I asked flying towards t' man to get hold of him. He kicks t' round table against me and flies out of t' door. I picks t'table up, runs to t' door but he was gone. I comes back and I says 'Now what dost think about thyself?' She says 'Now thou hast done as thou like, I shall do as I like.' I said 'Wilt thou?' 'Ay lad,' she says. So wi me having a drop of beer I goes unto t'cupboard and gets t'hatchet and I says 'I'll do as I like.' Then I struck her. She fell on t' ground. I struck her again and again. Thinks I 'Well she's dead.' Then my daughter came. The door was not locked. It sticks at time. I told her it was not locked. She called me a liar. I was agitated and I struck her.*

His statement having been read over to him he signed it with a cross.

The stipendiary then had Selina recalled. She confirmed that the family had at one time lived in Paternoster Row and that she knew William Lowe. 'He lives in Charles Street, five minutes walk away,' she said. 'I have never heard his name mentioned or any disagreement over him.'

Lowe was then sent for. After a short delay he arrived and was asked to go straight into the witness box. 'I am the man referred to,' he confirmed 'but I have never been in Hall's house in Paternoster Row.' To the reporters in court he appeared to be far more troubled by the loss of half a day's work than by the accusation against him.

Hall conceded that he had never accused Lowe to his face and declined to name any person who could corroborate his allegation of infidelity. The magistrate without hesitation then committed him for trial.

The following day Mary Ann was buried at Heeley. A crowd of around 3,000 gathered in Leadmill Road to watch the cortege set off. It proceeded along Edmund Road, Shoreham Street, Queen's Road, under the railway bridge at Heeley, reaching the church yard by one of the steep streets just beyond it. There an even larger crowd awaited. There was a good deal of feeling against Hall among the crowd, one woman saying he deserved to be flogged and roasted.

Hall took his trial at Leeds on May 6, 1881 before Mr Justice Kay.[77] C B Stuart-Wortley MP and Charles Ellis appeared for the prosecution, J W Vernon Blackburn and Richard Harper for the accused.[78]

At 10 o'clock Hall was put in the dock. He looked unconcerned. The witnesses called at the committal hearing repeated what they had said there and the defendant's statement was read out. From Selina the defence extracted the concession that Hall had been in the habit of questioning her mother minutely on her return home as to where she had been. However, she would not have it that it was jealousy which had provoked the arguments between her parents. The quarrelling she said was because he would not work and she had to keep the home together. Another prosecution witness confirmed that Hall's father had done away with himself.

In his closing speech, Vernon Blackburn, having referred to there being a hereditary taint in the family, suggested that at the time of the killing Hall was in a frenzied state of jealousy and that either jealousy or drink had produced a state of mind where he did not know what he was doing, or that it was wrong, and that he was in that state of mind

---

[77] **Kay**, Sir Edward Ebenezer (1822-97); educ. Trinity Coll, Cambridge; barrister 1847; QC 1866;appointed High Court judge, Chancery Division 1881; Lord Justice of Appeal 1890.

[78] **Stuart-Wortley**, Charles Beilby (see chap 3, n 18); **Ellis**, Charles Edward; barrister, 1878; practised on NE Circuit from chambers in Elm Court, Temple; **Blackburn**, John W Vernon, b 1831, son of Leeds solicitor; educ. Leeds GS and King's College, London; barrister 1837; practised on NE Circuit principally in Leeds but also in 1868-70 from chambers in Sheffield; a great favourite of Sheffield solicitors; **Harper**, Richard Williamson, b 1856 son of George Harper of Lockwood near Huddersfield; barrister 1871; practised on NE Circuit from chambers at 3, Hare Court, Temple.

when he spoke to the police. He invited them to acquit on that ground. In his summing up Mr Justice Kay advised the jury to consider the accused's statement with care. They had to decide if there was any foundation for his claim that he had found the deceased with a man in the house. Lowe denied he was ever in the prisoner's house and the prisoner's statement that the table was kicked over was contradicted by the fact that the table was found standing on its feet. Jealousy was no excuse for such a crime.

After a retirement of just 40 minutes the jury were back in court with a verdict of guilty. It can have come as no surprise to anyone. It was clear from Hall's replies to the police and from the statement which he made at the committal hearing that, when he attacked his wife, he knew what he was doing and knew it was wrong. His claim that he had found her with another man, if true, might have afforded some sort of foundation for a defence of provocation but it was obviously false.

When called upon to say why sentence of death should not be passed, Hall replied 'There has been some false witnesses that is all. If I had been allowed to speak I could have contradicted them.'[79]

In passing sentence of death, Mr Justice Kay warned him not to expect mercy.[80] With that Hall was removed from the dock as apparently unconcerned as he had been at the start of the trial.

While awaiting execution he lost his air of indifference and, under the ministrations of the chaplain, began to express remorse for

[79] The law at this time did not permit an accused person to give evidence in his own defence and it was to this that he was referring when he complained of not being allowed to speak.

[80] I can give you no hope of mercy in this world. I implore you to use the time left to you, which is short, in trying to make your peace with God. There is mercy there for you and for the vilest amongst us. I can but tell you that that is now that is left for you in this world.

what he had done. During a visit from his nephews he admitted that the incident had arisen out of a quarrel at the supper table. He was in a temper and in liquor; his wife complained of his bringing in no wage and of spending all the money he had on drink and threw a table fork at him; at this he went to the cupboard and got out the hatchet. After killing her he decided to throw himself into the Leadmill dyke. He had taken his wife's purse in order to buy a pint of brandy. When he struck at Selina he was not trying to kill her, simply to get away. He told his nephews to ask Selina to forgive him. She sent a message back that she could only do so if he withdrew the aspersions he had cast at her mother. On the Wednesday before execution his sisters visited him. 'I killed her,' he told them 'maddened by drink not because she was faithless. God bless my wife,' he added. 'I hope her soul is in heaven and I shall soon be there with her. I hope you will all pray for me on Monday morning.'

On the evening before his execution he wrote to his sister Sarah Staley:

*Dear Sister,*

*I was glad to receive your letter and to hear that my children had reached home safely and that a lady had been so kind as to ask them to have tea. I hope you will all be able to meet before 8 o'clock tomorrow morning to pray for me the last time on earth. I wish to withdraw my words against my wife. I loved her dearly when I was sober and the sad reason it happened was drunken passion. I hope the Lord Jesus will forgive me for this and all my sins and that you will do the same. Please give my love to Mr and Mrs Allcock; good-bye to sisters, nephews and nieces, to Selina, Abraham and Martha and my last farewell to you all,*

*from your affectionate brother*

*JAMES HALL*

*Abraham, be steady, be steady*

With the letter he enclosed some lines which he asked should be printed as his funeral card:

*In Affectionate Remembrance of*
*JAMES HALL*
*who departed this life May 23rd 1881*
*Aged 53 years*

*Farewell, my friends and children dear,*
*You little thought my time so near,*
*Grieve not for me, grief is all in vain*
*Hope in Heaven to meet you all again*
*JAMES HALL*

The verse which was the same as had appeared on his wife's funeral card had been taken to him by his son Abraham while he was in Wakefield prison awaiting trial.

Soon after writing the letter, he retired to bed. He slept well and, on being roused, ate a hearty breakfast and then spent what time remained praying. When Marwood entered his cell accompanied by two burly warders, he became very agitated crying out 'Oh my God, have mercy upon me.' He then became calm and allowed himself to be pinioned. He was taken out of his cell and escorted across the prison yard to the scaffold. When he saw the gallows he gave a violent start but soon regained his composure and walked with firm unfaltering step to the scaffold. At a signal from Marwood he mounted the steps and placed himself above the drop. As Marwood placed the strap around his legs and the chaplain intoned the words of the burial service, Hall gazed anxiously at the knot of reporters and warders in front of him. His face was ashen. Seconds later the hood was placed over his head and the rope adjusted and then the drop fell. Death according to the medical officer was instantaneous.

Outside the gaol a crowd of about 300 had assembled, some of the more venturesome climbing telegraph poles in the hope of seeing something of the proceedings within. Once the black flag had been hauled up the mast above the gateway the spectators quickly dispersed. After Hall's body had been hanging for the customary hour, it was cut down. Once the inquest had been held and a verdict of death by judicial hanging returned, it was buried within the prison walls.

## Slaughter in White Croft - Joseph Laycock, 1884 [81]

Joseph Laycock was brought up, if not born, in the Harvest Lane area of Sheffield. By age 11 he was working as an errand boy. That was not to his liking and, after trying his hand at pot moulding, he got work at Kelham Island rolling mills where he continued to work off and on for the rest of his life. Never keen on hard work he soon turned his hand to petty crime. First before the courts in 1871, by 1884 he had amassed a total of 13 convictions, mainly for drunkenness and petty theft.[82] He had also a local reputation as a prize fighter - based on an incident in which he fought and beat a man from Leicester who had been offering a sovereign to anyone who could go twenty minutes with him.

In 1875 he had married Maria Green.[83] By the summer of 1884 she had borne him four children and there was a fifth on the way.

---

[81] See *Sheffield Independent*, July 12,14,15,26, 29; Aug 9, 27, 1884; *Sheffield Telegraph*, July 11,12, Aug. 6, 1884; *The Times*, Aug 6, 1884.

[82] He had also been arrested in 1879 on suspicion of stabbing a man.

[83] They were married on May 16, 1875 at St Phillip's Church. She was 16 and a Catholic, he 24 and a Protestant.

Shortly before he married he had joined the militia and Maria soon realised that she could not depend on him to support her and her growing family: if he wasn't in prison or away with the militia he was out of work. After their marriage they lived at a variety of addresses[84] before eventually moving to a three-room house in No 2 court, White Croft near West Bar.

> *'A more squalid poverty stricken abode [could not] be imagined. Situated at the right hand corner at the entrance to the croft [the house had] ... one [room] on the ground floor and two upstairs. ... [had] scarcely a stick of furniture in [it] and [conveyed] the impression of having existed innumerable years in perfect innocence of soap and water.'*

To bring in some money Maria went out with her mother collecting bottles which she would then wash and sell. But though she was more hard working than her husband, she was an indifferent mother. Over-fond of drink she frequently left them on their own, unfed, while she went boozing.

As well as being an idler and a drunk, Joseph Laycock was also a bully. The residents of White Croft had witnessed his violence towards Maria. Twice he had tried to kill her, once by strangling and once by garrotting. On one occasion she had climbed out of a window to escape. Neighbours had remonstrated with him about his treatment

---

[84] According to Maria's mother, Ada Green, the marriage was unhappy from the beginning: 'He ill-used her on the third day after the marriage. He then kicked her. She had him at the Town Hall but it were all of no use. I put them in a furnished house when they were married but they only stopped in it about a fortnight. It was the house we had lived in for 14 years, No 2 court, Queen's Row. He broke everything in the house and nearly killed her. He was had up and got 14 or 21 days. They shifted in the last six months to four or five places.'

of Maria but he claimed that he did it to break her of her drink habit and, certainly, there were those who could testify that, although quiet as a mouse when sober, Maria was a beggar to fight with when drunk. But whatever her faults they did not begin to justify the kind of beatings he handed out.

In late June 1884, he was sent to prison for 21 days for assaulting her. He was released on a Saturday. Within hours of his arriving home there was a dreadful row between them during which he threatened to 'do for her.' The next day he went to a neighbour, Mrs Green, and asked for the loan of a razor. Knowing that he had made two previous attempts on Maria's life, and being in no doubt what he wanted the razor for, she turned him down flat. Over the next few days things appear to have settled down between them but on Thursday there was another flare up of trouble. The morning started well enough with Maria out collecting medicine bottles. Soon after midday she started drinking. In the late afternoon she went into the *Warm Hearthstone Inn* in Townhead Street and called for a glass of beer, but before she could be served her mother came up to her and accused her of spending money which she should be using to buy food for her kids; hearing this the landlord turned her away, telling her to take her money home and spend it on bread for the children.

Shortly after this she was seen in Hawley Croft. She was obviously the worse for drink and had been fighting with another woman. At 6 o'clock a man, named Dixon, saw Laycock fetch her out of an alehouse; he wanted her to come home but she would not; the next minute they were fighting, wrestling on the ground. As they scrapped a policeman walked by. Laycock shouted to him 'She's been drinking with another man. Take her in and me an' all' 'Take yourself off home,' was the officer's reply. At this Laycock got up from the pavement and walked off, saying he was going to give the children something to eat. Maria headed for her mother's house and, soon afterwards, she and her brother Christopher set off for Glossop Road with a sack of medicine bottles, which she hoped to sell. By the time they returned it was raining heavily and they stopped off at *Bearders* in Pea Croft for a pint of beer. Upon leaving the public house Maria bumped into Laycock who was waiting for her outside her mother's.[85] They at once began to quarrel. 'You look well, here, don't you,' he sneered 'the mother of four children.' 'Yes, and you look better,' she replied. Her mother shouted to her 'Don't go home to him or else he'll clout you,' at which she ran off into Pea Croft.

By 10 pm, however, the pair had apparently patched up their differences, for they were seen sitting together drinking in the *Rawson's Arms* in Tenter Street. They appeared on good terms. They put away two or three pints of beer each and listened attentively while one of the customers, James Garratty, read them a report in *The Star* about the storm that day. This led Laycock to comment that he had been at Banner Cross and that the lightning had been so bad that he thought that it would open the ground and swallow him up. Shortly before 11, after consuming a penny cake and a polony which Maria had fetched from a nearby shop, they left and headed home. This was, however, merely the quiet before the storm. Soon after they got indoors they were quarrelling again. The neighbours, to whom such rows were a daily occurrence, took no notice.

---

[85] At No 4 Court, White Croft.

Around midnight a little girl who was crossing the court heard Maria give a loud scream which was followed by the sound of breaking glass. After this all was quiet.

Shortly before 1 am Joseph and Charles Wright, who had just finished their shift at Firth & Co, saw Laycock as they made their way to their home in White Croft. He was walking up and down the street and twice made as if to approach them, only to turn away at the last minute.

The next morning the Laycocks' house was silent and shuttered. Neighbours noticed that the key was in the front door and there was talk of the family having flitted. By 10 o'clock, with still no sound of anyone stirring, curiosity got the better of them and three of them, Mrs Kidnew,[86] Mrs Carr and Mrs Blinn, lifted the latch and went in. The sight which greeted them was not one for those with weak stomachs. Lying against the fireplace of the downstairs room, with her head nearly severed from her body, was Maria Laycock. Mrs Kidnew, braver than her two companions, ventured upstairs. As she pushed the bedroom door ajar she saw a man's feet. The feet moved sending her rushing downstairs in panic. The question on all their minds was where were the children? Fearing the worst but hoping for the best, they hurried round to Maria's mother, Mrs Green. Were the children with her? No. Then the only conclusion to be drawn was that Laycock had murdered them as well. Running as fast as they could they set off to get help. In Tenter Street they came upon Sergeant Hornsey and PC Kimberley. 'Laycock's murdered his wife and children,' they shouted. The officers were soon at the house.

[86] One of men charged with the Princess Street murder in 1925 was named Kidnew. It may be that this is simply a coincidence but then again perhaps not. It is not a common name.

Kimberly went immediately upstairs. In the bedroom he found Laycock lying on a mattress with a fearful gash to his throat. 'Let me die. Don't move me,' he implored. On the floor next to him was a bread knife and, on a second mattress, lay his four children. Their throats had been cut and their bodies were cold. They had clearly been dead for some hours. So savage had been the cut to the throat of the youngest that her head had almost been severed from her body. Returning downstairs Kimberley arranged for a cab to take Laycock to the Public Hospital and Dispensary[87] in West Street for treatment to his wound. The officers then turned their attention to the downstairs room. It was at once clear to them that the mother, Maria, who was dressed in the same clothes she had been wearing at the public house, had not been to bed. On the table lay a plate of bread, cut as though for supper but uneaten, and by the fireplace were the children's shoes.

After the Chief Constable had attended it was arranged for the bodies to be removed to the public mortuary on a corporation dray. There they were laid out and examined. As well as the terrible wound to the neck, Maria had bruising and cuts to her face and her wrists bore marks suggesting that they had been grasped hard; the youngest child, who like Maria had a gaping wound to the throat, also had two cuts to the shoulder, and it was noted that the thumb of one of the other children had been almost severed (doubtless as it put up its hand to try and protect itself). The doctor who conducted the post-mortem examinations was in no doubt that in the case of each of the

[87] Opened in 1832 (in Tudor Place) it would later become the Royal Hospital.

deceased the cause of death was the wound to the throat and that the knife found beside Laycock would have been capable of causing it.

At the Public Dispensary Laycock's wounds were stitched and he was detained for treatment. According to the press he was stricken with remorse for what he had done but blamed what had happened on his wife's drinking. He told a clergyman, who visited him, that when he and Maria had got home on the Thursday night she said that she wished she was dead, to which he had replied that it was better they were both dead than that they should live as they had been. He was then, he claimed, overcome by a fit of madness. He said that he killed the youngest girl last and that she had begged for her life saying 'O Dada, don't do it to me'.

On the Friday the City Coroner, Dossey Wightman, opened the inquest. Before the jury went to the mortuary to view the bodies he warned: 'It is the most awful sight I have seen since I have [been coroner].' Evidence of identification was given by Mrs Green. She said that her daughter was 25 years of age; the children were Sarah, aged eight, Francis, who was six, Mary who was almost four and Joseph who would have been two in October. Having inquired of the police as to how long it would be before Laycock was fit to attend, the coroner issued burial certificates and then adjourned the hearing until August 1.[88]

On Monday July 14, the five victims were buried in a single grave in the pauper section of Intake cemetery.[89] The coffins were

---

[88] Over the weekend White Croft was crowded with sightseers. On the Sunday a local clergyman adverted in his sermon to the murder which he claimed showed the ruin which people brought upon themselves and their offspring by early marriage.

[89] The service was conducted by the Rev AJR Shaw, the chaplain to the workhouse.

carried in a mourning coach, the cost of which had been met by public subscription. Thousands lined the streets as it made its way along Millsands, Blonk Street, Furnival Road, Broad Street and then Duke Street. At the cemetery the crowd was enormous (one reporter's estimate was 25,000). People had begun to gather as early as 7 am and many had brought baskets of provisions with them. Half a dozen young girls, all friends of the dead children, carried their coffins to the grave-side. Each wore a white scarf looped with black and carried a wreath or bouquet of simple flowers. It was only with the greatest difficulty that the police were able to keep the huge crowds back and after the interment 'there was the same unruly scampering to see the mourners as there had been previous to it.' As the *Sheffield Independent* put 'there was some helter-skelter work in the cemetery.'

By July 25, Laycock was sufficiently recovered for the inquest to be resumed. The first witness to be called was Mrs Green who confirmed the truth of her deposition. Asked if he had questions, Laycock said 'Mrs Green, hast tha' owt to say to me at all?' and, when she did not answer, he groaned. Despite initially giving the impression of being too overcome with grief to put questions to witnesses, he was soon to be heard challenging and taking issue with evidence given against him. When Ada Shaw, the 13-year-old daughter of the landlord of the *Rawson's Arms*, told the jury that Maria, on entering the public house, had been told by her husband 'You might as well get drunk tonight while you have the chance...It might be the last time you get any,' he interrupted. 'The girl knows nothing about it. She was only there a few minutes.' A witness, named Wright, said that he had heard a man walking up and down the entry to the court at about twenty to quarter to one, and could tell that it was Laycock because one of his shoes had a loose plate and made a distinctive sound. Laycock told him he was a liar. Mrs Kidnew, who had described seeing three of the children sitting on the doorstep at 9 pm and hearing a pane of glass break soon after he and Maria returned home at 5 past 11, was asked if his wife had had any other men in the house whilst he was in prison. His temper could not have been improved when several of the witnesses called attempted to play down the deceased's drinking habits. After the police and medical evidence had been given, he was asked if he wished to give evidence himself. Heeding the coroner's caution, he declined saying he would reserve his defence. The coroner summed up briefly and the jury immediately returned verdicts of wilful murder.

Four days later he was brought before the stipendiary magistrate. His throat was still bandaged and he appeared weak. Mr Fairburn for the police stated that the previous Friday the prisoner had been committed for trial on a coroner's warrant and, in view of that, he did not propose to offer any evidence but asked that the prisoner be allowed to stand committed on the coroner's inquisition to the Leeds Assizes starting the next day. The stipendiary approved this course, observing that he did not see any use in having two preliminary inquiries.

Laycock stood trial on August 5, 1884, before Mr Justice Mathews,[90] upon the charge of murdering the eldest child, Sarah

[90] **Matthew**, Sir James Charles (1830-1908); barrister 1851; High Court judge 1881; Lord Justice of Appeal, 1901; 'a ready, facile and humorous speaker, an ardent radical and a devout Roman Catholic.'

Ann.[91] Messrs Fenwick and Atkinson appeared for the Crown and, at the judge's request, Meysey Thompson undertook the defence of Laycock, who had no counsel.[92] Brought up into the dock with his throat still bandaged, he 'appeared to feel his position very acutely and trembled violently.' When called on to plead he replied in faltering terms 'I don't know, sir.' During prosecuting counsel's opening he held a handkerchief to his eyes and sobbed bitterly calling out 'Lord, have mercy on me. Oh my child! Lord forgive me.' The evidence for the Crown was that called before the coroner, consisting of testimony from family and neighbours, from the police and the doctor who examined the bodies.

Several witnesses were called for the defence in an attempt to prove that the accused was insane at the time of the killing. His sister, Elizabeth Platts, told how on the Monday before the he had visited her home and behaved so oddly that she thought him deranged, and two other witnesses spoke of the accused talking and behaving oddly in the days before the murder. A doctor testified that an injury to the head which Laycock had suffered when younger would make him more prone to suffer from delusions than ordinary men. The jury were also told that his father and two of his uncles had committed

---

[91] The law prohibited more than one murder being charged in the same indictment and so the prosecution had to decide which of the murders they would proceed try first. The guilty verdict made it unnecessary to proceed with the other charges. The trial lasted some four hours. It excited little interest among the Leeds public. 'There was no crushing to get into the court nor any crowding inside.'

[92] **Fenwick**, Edward Nicholas; barrister 1873; practised on NE Circuit from chambers at 4, Paper Buildings, Temple; **Meysey-Thompson**, Albert Childer; born 1848; 3rd son of Sir Harry Meysey-Thompson late of Kirby Hall, Yorks; educ; Trinity Coll, Cambridge; barrister 1872; practised on NE Circuit from chambers at 1, King's Bench Walk, Temple.

suicide.[93] Finally, his mother was called to say that as a child he had been treated by a Dr Mainwaring for an affliction of the head.[94]

In his closing speech, Mr Thompson submitted that the evidence called demonstrated that at the time the prisoner committed the crime he was not responsible for his actions.

The judge's summing up was more favourable to Laycock than might have been expected. The very atrocity of the crime, he told the jury, rather suggested that it was not the act of a sane man and it was clear that there was insanity in the prisoner's family. The jury were not persuaded and, after fifteen minutes, were back with a verdict of guilty.

Asked why sentence of death should not be passed upon him, Laycock made no reply.

Donning the black cap, the judge proceeded immediately to pass sentence of death. As Laycock listened to the sentence his whole frame shook and he gazed at Mr Justice Mathew in a stupefied fashion. He then muttered 'Thank you, your worship. Thank you.' As he was about to step out of the dock he remarked 'I got my doom. It's all I craved till judgment day.' He was then hurried out of sight.

Following his conviction arrangements for the execution were immediately put in hand. At an early stage the High Sheriff decided that the press would not be admitted and applications from London and provincial papers to attend were all denied. No reasons for the

---

[93] His father had drowned himself, one uncle had been found in bed with his throat cut another had lain on the railway track at Wardsend and been cut to pieces by a train.

[94] When interviewed by a reporter from the *Sheffield Independent* soon after the murder Laycock's mother rejected the notion of insanity out of hand 'He has never shown any sign of insanity in his life.' 'Drink and jealousy that's what's done it' she added.

refusal were given but this did not prevent the press speculating. 'It may be mentioned,' observed the *Sheffield Telegraph*:

> *that Armley is one of those prisons where executions have been bungled and that the hangsman engaged to despatch Laycock [will be performing] his dreadful function for the first time.*[95]

While awaiting execution, Laycock dictated and signed a confession in which he blamed his mother-in-law for the tragedy. She had, he claimed, regularly taken the deceased out drinking and his wife would often return home unfit to look after either him or the children. On the Thursday night, having resolved to kill himself, he went upstairs to kiss the children for the last time. When he came back downstairs his wife attacked and goaded him into a frenzy by her taunts, and he had murdered her and the children one by one. He was seen by Dr Garner, medical inspector of prisons, and Dr Orange, medical superintendent of Criminal Lunatic Asylums. Both concluded that there were no grounds for the plea of hereditary insanity which had been set up at his trial. On the Saturday before his execution he received visits from his mother and his sister and her husband. He had wanted to see his mother-in-law and was disappointed that she refused to visit him. On the Sunday he declared that he wished to die but not by hanging. He was executed at 8 am on

---

[95] *Sheffield Telegraph*, August 27, 1884. The hangman was James Billington, a 37-year-old hairdresser from Farnsworth near Bolton. Some weeks before he had been due to execute Catherine Dooley at Tullamore but she had been reprieved.

Monday on a scaffold erected in the prison yard.[96] As the Sheffield press stressed in their reports, it was the one on which Peace had been hanged. As the hour of execution drew near, Laycock's courage deserted him. He was crying when Billington entered the condemned cell and asked in a piteous tone 'You'll not hurt me?' 'No,' said the hangman 'theaull be eawt of existence in two minutes.' The reassurance was evidently not enough for, immediately on leaving the cell, he fainted and had to be helped to the scaffold. His last words as the rope was being adjusted were 'Oh my children, my children. Lord have mercy on my children.'

## The vengeful engine-tenter - Harry Hobson, 1885[97]

Harry Hobson, although born in Huddersfield, grew up in Button Lane, Sheffield where his father kept a tobacconist's shop. When he was old enough to earn his own living he got a job as a grinder but he disliked the work and decided, instead, to join the Army. After serving for four years with the 1st battalion of the 22nd regiment, he re-enlisted with the 90th regiment for a further ten years. Discharged in February 1868 with a good military character, in 1871 he married Margaret Wright at the Register office at Newport, Isle of Wight. She was the widow of a soldier and had a well-paid job as cook at one of

[96] The *Sheffield Independent*, August 27, 1884, still apparently smarting from the under-sheriff's refusal to admit reporters commented 'It is probable that no execution has ever been conducted as quickly or with as little ceremony as that of yesterday. The only hint outside the gaol that anything unusual was passing was the gathering here and there on the highway side at the bottom of the hill on which the prison stands of small groups of workmen resident in the vicinity who tarried on their way to work for half an hour to see all that could be seen – the hoisting of the black flag on the central tower of the main block of the prison.'

[97] See *Sheffield Independent*, July 25, 26, 27, 29, 30, Aug 6, 23, 1887; *Sheffield Telegraph*, July 26, 27, 30, Aug 6, 1887; *The Times*, Aug 23, 1887.

the principal hotels in the town. After the wedding the couple moved up to Sheffield where Hobson fell on his feet, obtaining well paid work as an engine tenter[98] at Mr Robert Thompson's Horn works in Cambridge Street. This really was quite a cushy billet, not only was the money good but there was free accommodation and fuel thrown in. But soon storm clouds began to gather. Hobson had been a hard drinker throughout his army service and remained so after his return to civvy street. He was kept on when Thompson sold the horn business to his partner John George Stothard but this was more than he deserved, for he was by now regularly drinking to excess and, when in drink, he was frequently insubordinate and quarrelsome. By September 1886, Stothard had had enough and dismissed him. Hobson seems to have blamed his sacking on the latter's son John Henry. 'You will have to suffer for this my lad,' he told him.

For the Hobsons his dismissal was little short of a disaster for, try as he might, he could not get regular work. In the ten months following his sacking he worked for just one month. Living in a small rented dwelling, at 3, Sand's Paviours, the couple were finding it increasingly hard to make ends meet. Margaret managed to get some work office cleaning but it did not bring in enough to pay their bills and, as time went by, she was forced to sell furniture to raise money. As their troubles mounted Hobson became increasingly morose and ill tempered. Neighbours and animals kept well out of his way. By now Margaret was the only friend he had; she must have been bitterly repenting giving up her position in Newport, but she was as

[98] OED: tenter: one who minds or has charge of anything requiring attention as a machine, a flock, etc.

industrious as ever and neighbours noticed that she still kept their small house spotlessly clean.

The Stothards' family home was on the southern edge of the town at 99, Montague Street close by the General Cemetery. In 1887 four generations lived there: John George Stothard, the proprietor of the Horn works, his wife, his mother, his son John Henry, John's 22-year-old wife, Ada, and their six-month-old baby. Ada Stothard had at one time worked as a domestic servant for John's parents but, since the marriage, her place had been taken by a willing young lass named Florence Mosley. She was the daughter of an edge tool grinder and lived in nearby Parliament Street.[99]

On Saturday July 23, 1887, John Stothard and his father set off for the horn works at 9.10am. When they left, Ada and Florence, the young servant, were busy working in the kitchen.[100] Mrs Stothard senior was in bed upstairs reading the newspaper. At 10.30 there was a knock at the door. Ada went to answer it carrying her baby in her arms. It was a man. 'If you please, is Mrs Stothard in?' 'Yes,' answered Ada. 'Will you tell the missus I've opened a shop for rag and bones?' 'Yes I will,' said Ada. After complimenting her on her child the visitor asked if he might have a glass of water. Ada gave him one saying she was sorry she hadn't anything else. 'It'll do nicely,' said the man and, after drinking the water, he left 'That was Hobson,' Ada told Florence 'He used to be the engine-tenter and caretaker at the works.'

---

[99] Parliament Street lay between and roughly parallel to Ecclesall Road and Cemetery Road.
[100] The kitchen door opened onto 'a little asphalt yard reached from street by low dark passage running along the side of house' (*Sheffield Independent,* July 25, 1887).

Quarter of an hour later, as Florence was black-leading the stove, the visitor returned asking for 'a bit of cord.' Ada, anxious to oblige, went down to the cellar to look for some. As soon as she had left the kitchen the man grabbed hold of Florence's head and aimed several blows at her throat with a knife, cutting her on the neck and shoulder and on the hand. She screamed in terror. Her cries brought Ada up from the cellar. As soon as she appeared the man turned on her. Florence now ran out into the back yard and along the passage which led to the street shouting: 'Pray come. A man is in the house and is murdering the missus and everyone.' In Montague Street at the time was greengrocer John Hardy with his dray and, in nearby Cemetery Road, was a stationary coach. On hearing the girl's shouts, Hardy ran to the house closely followed by the coach driver, John Adams. As they made their way along the passage, they met a man running from the direction of the house. 'What a mess that man's done in the house. He's gone upstairs. I'm going for the doctor,' he shouted. With that he ran out into the street and seconds later was seen by two boys running off down Cemetery Road towards town.

In the kitchen the two men found Ada Stothard still on her feet, but almost immediately she collapsed to the floor with blood spurting from a wound in her throat. They bound her throat to staunch the flow of blood, but her jugular vein was severed and within minutes she had bled to death. The only person upstairs in the house was Mrs Stothard senior, who was still in bed, unaware of the tragedy which had been unfolding below. Realising now that the man who had passed them was almost certainly the killer, Adams set off in his coach for Highfields police station. There he reported what he had seen and PC Harris was immediately despatched to the house. By the time he arrived other officers were already at the scene including Womack, a detective officer.

By now Florence was also back. After escaping from the kitchen she had fled to her home in Parliament Street and there insisted that her mother return with her to Montague Street. She was able to give the officers the name of the wanted man. He was the Stothards' former engine-tenter Harry Hobson. Florence, having supplied this important piece of information, was sent off to the hospital in West Street. She had lost a lot of blood but, happily, her injuries were less serious than had been feared and, after her wounds had been stitched, she was taken home and put to bed.

While she was being treated, DO Womack was at the Cambridge Street works. After breaking the news of the murder to John Stothard and his father, he despatched men from the works, who knew Hobson by sight, to his home and to both railway stations with instructions to watch for him. Mr Stothard senior was taken to Highfields police station where a full description of Hobson was taken and immediately transmitted by telegraph to the town's other police station

At 11.30 a police officer attended at Hobson's house at Sand's Paviours. 'He has only just gone out,' his wife told him. He had, she explained, got up that morning at 8 o'clock and when she left at 8.45 for her cleaning job he was still in the house blacking his boots; when she returned home at 10.20 he was out. He came in shortly before 11.30; she asked if he had heard of any work; 'There's nowt lass,' he replied and asked for money for 'a bit of bacca.' After trying and failing to borrow a penny from a neighbour, she suggested to him that he take and sell a sack of old glass which she had collected. After changing his coat and hat [101] he left carrying the sack over his shoulder. He took it to the warehouse of Messrs Turner & Co. in Sussex Street, Park, where he sold the glass for a shilling. The warehouseman who dealt with him noticed nothing unusual in his demeanour.

At 1 pm PC Ford was approached in Furnival Road by one of the men Womack had set to watch for Hobson. 'That man,' he said pointing to Hobson 'is wanted for murder' and explained the circumstances. Seizing Hobson by the collar the officer told him 'I want you for murder'

'What me for murder?'

'Yes, what's your name?'

'My name's Harry Hobson'

'What's your trade?'

'Engine-tenter.'

'You're the man.'

Hobson was then taken to the Central Police Station where he was searched. In his pocket was a knife. There was no blood on it but there was blood staining on his clothes. He was charged with the attempted murder of Florence Mosley, the servant girl.

On the Saturday night he was placed on an identity parade and both Hardy and Gregory picked him out as the man they had seen in the passage.

On the Sunday, sightseers attended in Montague Street in large numbers, adding to the family's ordeal. That day Hobson's wife tried to take him some food but she was turned away. The police would

---

[101] When he came in he had been wearing a dark coat, moleskin trousers and a soft hat; he changed into an old coat and a billycock hat.

neither let her see him nor accept the food. When he heard of her visits Hobson asked his jailers to 'tell the lass not to bother.'

On Monday morning, he was taken before the town's stipendiary magistrate, Mr Edward Welby. The police, who were still awaiting instructions from the Director of Public Prosecutions, asked for a remand. Conscious that the Leeds summer Assizes were due to start the following week and anxious to get Hobson committed in time to stand trial at those Assizes, they asked for and got a short remand. 'You are remanded for eight days or sooner,' Hobson was told. Later that morning a post-mortem examination upon the dead woman's body was performed by Dr Dale Jones, the police surgeon. He found that the knife had penetrated the right side of the neck and severed the jugular vein, producing death in a very few minutes. There were also other small wounds. The injuries were such as a long-bladed pocket knife might produce.

In the afternoon, the inquest was opened by coroner, Dossey Wightman. It was held at the *Vine Inn* in Cemetery road, Hobson being taken there by cab. After swearing in a jury the coroner adjourned with them to the Stothards' house to view the body. This done, they returned to the public house where evidence was taken from Dr Dale Jones and John Stothard junior and a burial certificate issued. The proceedings were then adjourned until 5 pm on the following Friday.

The two court hearings gave the local press their first sight of the accused man. 'He is' the *Sheffield Telegraph* told its readers ' a stiff built man with something of the look of the soldier about him; he has a florid complexion, dark hair, a dark moustache and a grey forelock.'

Tuesday was the day of Ada Stothard's funeral and the town came out to watch. By the time the cortege set out from Montague Street at around 1.30pm a crowd of 700 to 800 persons, mainly women, had assembled to watch it leave.

*Order was kept by a number of police constables under Sergeant Swift ... When the coffin was borne out of the house, there was a buzz of excitement the people pressing forward to catch a glimpse of it... The cortege was followed by a crowd of women and exclamations of pity and horror were constantly heard along the route to Burngreave Cemetery where the interment was to take place. At most of the street ends passed groups of people had gathered and the further the cortege went the greater became the number of people following. The mournful procession went along Ecclesall Road and the Moor into Pinstone street. At the corner where Lewis's shop is situate a very considerable number of women were assembled, probably the wives of the workpeople of Messrs Stothards and acquaintances of the accused and his wife whose house is in that neighbourhood. Along the Wicker and the remainder of the route to the cemetery people assembled to watch the procession.*

But the crowds along the route were as nothing compared to those at the cemetery. There people had begun to assemble as early as 11 o'clock.

*The fact that many of them took provisions showed that they were prepared for a long wait. ...[By mid-day] the cemetery had more the appearance of a public park or a huge picnic area than 'God's Acre.' On the seats and near the graves people sat to eat. The bulk of the gathering assembled [however] between 1 and 2 at which hour there were over 5,000 people present. There were also many persons on the surrounding heights and in the approaches to the cemetery. Of the large numbers in and around some were probably there out of sympathy, but others – and they were undoubtedly in the majority – were there to satisfy a morbid curiosity and their behaviour was not good. On the arrival of the coaches and hearse in the cemetery there was great crushing and the [police] had a difficult task in keeping back the crowds; the people pressed close to the carriage doors, their conduct being painful to witness. After the ceremony in the chapel they broke into the procession and the mourners and friends for a time were separated from one another...The cortege arrived at the cemetery as a quarter past two and the funeral rites were completed in half an hour. The Revd. T Wilkins, vicar of S Michael's, Neepsend officiated.... The grave is on the consecrated side and near the top of the central walk. It is a new one and is intended for the family.*[102]

On the Thursday, Mr Clegg, the local solicitor who had been instructed to act as the DPP's agent, applied to Mr Welby for the case to be listed for a committal hearing the following day. After some wrangling as to the time at which the proceedings should start the application was granted. Since the Saturday the police had put in a good deal of work on the case. From Hobson's neighbours they had been able to build up a picture of his movements on the day of the murder. A blacksmith with a workshop at Sand's Paviours[103] had seen him standing in the doorway of his house between 7 and 8 on the Saturday morning. At 10 am he had called on his neighbour Mrs Wilson and asked to speak to her son Walter. After begging a twist of tobacco off the lad, Hobson had invited him to come for a walk with him down the Moor but Walter, who had been busy putting clothes through the mangle for his mother, declined. At 11.30 he was seen leaving Sand's Paviours carrying a sack (this was clearly the sack of glass his wife had spoken of) and from there he had made his way to

[102] *Sheffield Independent*, July 27, 1887.

[103] Sand's Paviours (originally called Sans Paviours) lay off Orchard Lane close to where the Central Schools then stood and the City Hall now stands.

Sussex Street where he sold the glass. The police were also able to prove that he had been uttering threats against John Stothard prior to the murder. Batt, a silversmith, had actual seen him point to his forehead and say to young Stothard 'I have it here for you, Jack my lad.' According to Mrs Wilson he had had continued to utter such threats after his dismissal. Soon after he came to live at Sand's Paviours, she asked him how he had come to lose his job. He told her that he left it through young Marriott, a former partner in the business, and young John and said he would have a reckoning with them. Later he told her that he had been given ten shillings by the bailiffs for telling them where Marriott lived adding 'I've had a reckoning day with one and I'll have one with the other.' On several occasions after that she had heard him threaten a reckoning, the last time being a matter of two weeks before

On the Friday, the committal hearing, scheduled for 12 noon, got under way half an hour late, owing to Mr Clegg being detained at Rotherham. The public gallery was packed and on the bench with Mr Welby were two other magistrates, Mr Tozer and Mr Skelton. Hobson, who had been undefended at the previous hearing, was now represented by Muir Wilson, a local solicitor. After outlining the case Mr Clegg called his evidence. The principal witnesses were John Stothard, Hardy and Gregory. During Gregory's evidence there was a curious exchange between him and Muir Wilson. After insisting that the accused was the man he had seen in the passage he added 'I would like a round with him.'

'You would like to have a round with him?'

'Yes, for five minutes.'

'Then you have some bad feeling against him.'

'Yes.'

'I suppose you would like to fight him.'

'Yes.'

'Then you must have some bad feeling against him.'

'Well, I think anyone would have.'

'Your indignation is so great you would like to thrash him?'

'He would either thrash me or I would thrash him.'

At the close of the prosecution evidence the charge of murder was put to Hobson. 'I am not guilty, your worship,' he announced in a calm voice. Muir Wilson was then on his feet. He did not wish to say anything now. There was, he was bound to admit, a strong *prima facie* case and in the circumstances he did not resist the prisoner being committed for trial. Judging by Muir Wilson's line in cross-examination, it very much looked as though insanity was the defence to be run at trial. Stothard was asked whether Hobson had mentioned to him suffering from a sun stroke while serving as a soldier in Mauritius and two other witnesses if they had heard it said that the accused was not right in the head. 'No,' he was told. The furthest any of them was prepared to go was to say that he was argumentative and wild in drink.

Having committed him for trial on the charge of murder, the magistrates immediately embarked on a committal hearing in respect of the charge of attempted murder of Florence Mosley. After a short hearing, he was committed on this charge also. During the course of medical evidence about her injuries it emerged that a buckle had deflected one of the knife blows away from the carotid artery thus saving her life. As the *Sheffield Telegraph* observed: 'Had [she] fallen victim to his violence it is likely he would have got off scot free for no-one would have thought of connecting him with the crime.'[104]

From the stipendiary's court, Hobson was taken to the watch committee room in the court-house where, half an hour after the conclusion of the committal hearing, the adjourned inquest got under way. The coroner began by informing the jury that, as Hobson already stood committed for trial, he intended to limit the evidence called before them to the minimum necessary to enable them to reach a verdict. After taking evidence from the police surgeon, Florence Mosley, Hardy and the arresting officer, he summed the case up. The jury immediately returned a verdict of wilful murder. The coroner then signed the committal warrant. After the committal hearing Muir Wilson had seen Hobson in the cells. 'I am not the man who committed this terrible crime,' Hobson told him. 'I am as innocent as that cell door.' Stothard, he said, had at one time been in partnership with a man named Marriott but the partnership had been dissolved as a result of a complaint which he, Hobson, had made, and since that time Marriott had been continually on his track. Charlie Peace committed two murders in one day, one at Manchester and the other in Sheffield, and in that case the wrong man was arrested, and he attributed the fact that he had been singled out for this murder as due to ill-feeling between himself, Marriott and young Stothard. 'Where were you on the morning of the murder?' asked the solicitor.

[104] *Sheffield Telegraph*, July 26, 1887.

'I never went out till I went to Messrs Turner and Co with the sack of broken glass.'

'Why were you wearing your working coat when you went there?'

'Who would carry broken glass in a good coat?'

On the following Friday, August 5, 1887, (a mere 14 days after the murder) Hobson took his trial before Mr Justice Mathew[105] at Leeds Town Hall. Mr West and Mr Gerald Hardy appeared for the Crown and Charley Mellor, the son of a High Court judge, for Hobson.[106]

At 10.30 the judge came into court. Hobson was then brought up and immediately 'walked with a brisk step to the front of the dock' exhibiting 'no sign of fear or serious anxiety.' He looked thinner and more drawn than on his last court appearance but there was the same studied coolness in his demeanour and the same fixed and steady gaze that rarely turned aside. When called upon to plead he replied in a firm voice 'Not guilty.'

After the jury had been sworn, Mr West began his opening speech for the prosecution. It was, he contended, difficult to see who could have committed the murder but the prisoner, adding that it was possible that a defence of insanity would be raised. Mellor was immediately on his feet. 'Insanity is not the defence,' he declared. Nor was it. As the evidence unfolded it became clear that the defence

---

[105] See n 90 above.

[106] **West,** Thomas Edward; b 1814 only son of Joseph West of Lascelles Hall, Huddersfield; educ St John's Coll, Oxford; barrister, 1850; practised NE Circuit from chambers in South Parade, Leeds; **Mellor**, Charles, b 1845; educ Trinity Coll. Cambridge; barrister 1871; practised from 5, East Parade, Leeds.

contention was that the murder had been committed by some third party. The architect called to produce a plan of the house confirmed in cross-examination that it would have been possible for the murderer to have escaped from the house by climbing over a five foot high wall at the rear and dropping down into Pembroke Street.[107] Cross-examination of the police surgeon and of the police officer who seized the accused's clothes established that, although the dead woman and the servant had both bled profusely, the only blood stains found on the deceased's clothing were four very small spots to the trousers and a similar number of small spots to his jacket. Wilson, who had seen Hobson at 10 that morning, and John Ward, who had bought the glass from him at noon, both agreed that when they saw him he had appeared calm and unruffled and the arresting officer testified to his professed astonishment at his arrest. Mellor's real difficulty lay with the identifying witnesses. By his cross-examination of Hardy and Gregory, he was able to show that they had had only a fleeting glimpse of the man who passed them in the passage. But with Florence Mosley he hit a brick wall. It soon became clear that her identification of Hobson was not based simply upon her mistress' naming him as the visitor; she had in fact seen him before the day of the murder during visits to the Cambridge Street works and had heard other people there call him Harry. Mellor was driven in the end to suggest that, in asserting that it was Hobson who called the second time, she was making an assumption and that on this occasion she had been too busy with her work to see who was at the door.

[107] Pembroke Street ran parallel to and was the next street below Montague Street.

In his closing speech defence counsel having urged the jury to approach the case dispassionately proceeded to analyse the evidence:

> *He admitted that the prisoner was annoyed at being discharged and did use threats towards young Mr Stothard but that individual thought nothing of them. It was said truth was sometimes stranger than fiction. Certainly the most extravagant novelist would never dream of making as the motive of a murder such as this, the idle threat of a young man eight months ago. He would not deny that the prisoner went to the house that morning. There could be no doubt that he went at half past ten but there was nothing extraordinary in his conduct. He was cool and collected and seemed on very good terms with the deceased. Was it likely that he would have gone and asked young Wilson to take a walk with him if he intended to kill Mrs Stothard? Besides, he could have murdered her when he saw her at half past ten if he desired to wreak his vengeance on her. Counsel for the Crown suggested that this man was so roused up to a frenzy that he vented it upon this unfortunate woman. But if his theory was correct upon whom did his vengeance fall? Why upon the person of the helpless girl against whom no one could suggest that the prisoner could have had the slightest feeling of rage or envy. It was upon this poor girl that some ruffian fell and committed the outrage that was committed. It was true that Florence Mosley said that it was the prisoner and, no doubt, she believed it. It was very easy when a case had been before the magistrates and the tragedy had been much talked about for a girl to become so confirmed in a belief that it was difficult for counsel to shake it. The girl says that it was Hobson who came and did this. But why? It was because Hobson was there at 10.30. It was difficult to understand how she could have seen the door as she was black-leading the fender though no doubt she believed she did, but when the girl was in peril and danger of her life it would not have been wonderful if she had gone into the box and said she could not tell anything at all about it. But for the fact that she saw Hobson at 10.30 that morning what reliance could be placed upon her saying that she saw the deceased and the prisoner on the floor together? If it were the prisoner*

*would they not expect his coat to be deluged in blood.?.He begged the jury to remember also the fact that when the girl met Gregory and Hardy she simply said that there was a man cutting her mistress's throat and did not mention Hobson's name, although it is said she knew it. Further, if the prisoner was then man who went out of the passage and was the murderer, he was following the girl out into the street when she gave the alarm. Was it not much more likely that a murderer would have gone over a wall 4'10" or 5' in height and in a different direction? He was not going to prove an alibi. It was not for him to prove the innocence of the prisoner but it was for the Crown to prove his guilt. What was the conduct of this murderer? He must have quickened his step very much after passing the two witnesses, Hardy and Gregory. What did a murderer generally do after committing a murder of this character? Did he go home and attend to business or abscond, which if the prisoner was not the man, the real murderer did by going over the wall. The prisoner went home and then visited a place of business in Sussex Street. With reference to the marks of blood on the prisoner's clothes he did not think that the jury on such evidence would convict the prisoner of murder. He laid stress upon the fact that the prisoner gave his right name when arrested and concluded his address with a strong appeal to the jury to give the prisoner the benefit of any doubt which they might feel in their minds.*

It was a powerful speech and in his summing up the judge acknowledged as much, complimenting a very able defence which had not omitted a single point which could be urged in favour of the prisoner. Good though it was, it was not enough. Having retired to consider their verdict at 2.35 the jury were back in court twelve minutes later with a verdict of guilty. The reporters observed that Hobson did not flinch when the verdict was announced. Asked if he had anything to say why sentence of death should not be passed he replied 'No.' The judge then proceeded to pass sentence, adding the warning that he could expect no mercy in this world.

The next day the *Sheffield Independent* remarked upon how quickly conviction had followed crime:

> *Justice has in this case been remarkably fleet of foot. Rarely, if ever has condemnation so closely followed a great crime. Fourteen days ago the family circle in Montague Street was unbroken and the hand of the homicide was still unstained with blood; now the wretched criminal is an inmate of the condemned convict's cell at Armley and little more than a fortnight will elapse before he pays the highest penalty that human tribunals can award to guilt'*

Following his conviction Hobson remained calm and apparently unconcerned. He was, he insisted, innocent of the crime.

He was executed at Armley Gaol at 8 am on Monday August 22, 1887.[108] Roused from his bed at just after 6 am he was served a breakfast of two fried eggs, which he ate heartily. He was then visited by the prison chaplain. To the latter's ministrations he was stolidly indifferent and when reminded of the near approach of death he replied 'The sooner it comes the longer will be the rest.' The execution took place in the treadmill shed, with warders lining the route from condemned cell to scaffold. No reporters were present and such details as the press were able to report were gleaned from prison staff and from the inquest. Outside the prison people stood in small groups watching for the raising of the black flag. An hour after the execution, the body was cut down and removed to a shed where it was viewed by the inquest jury which after a short hearing, in which

---

[108] Billington was the hangman.

evidence was given by the under-sheriff and the prison medical officer, returned the usual verdict. The body was then buried in an unmarked grave in the prison yard.[109]

## Murder at the Handsworth Feast - Robert West, 1889 [110]

Born in Oxford, Robert West had been a travelling showman all his working life and, in the 1880s, his Aunt Sally stall, shooting gallery and swing boats were a familiar sight at Midlands' fairs and feasts. At one time he had lived with a woman, named Houlden, who had borne him three children; after her death he began to court Emma Sketchley a cheerful, good-hearted lass, 14 years his junior, whom he had met at Derby. Her mother, who also kept a shooting gallery and was rumoured to be well off, seems to have taken a dislike to West from the start. But Emma was determined to have him and in 1877 they married, she electing to go on the road with him. It was a somewhat rough and ready life. When they were travelling their home was a two-compartment caravan, the far end of which was fitted out with bunks 'similar to those one would find in a steamer.'[111] Usually they travelled with two other showmen, Charles

[109] Hobson found an apologist in the September, 1887 issue of the anarchist journal, *Freedom*, which described him as 'a man who had laboured during all the best years of his life [and] found himself, as his strength declined, forced to set out on that dreary, sickening, hopeless wandering in search of a job, which English workers know so well. What wonder that after many months his cruel position took fatal hold of his mind, and that finally, in a morbid fit of despairing revenge, he killed the wife of the man who was the immediate cause of his suffering.'

[110] See *Sheffield Independent*, Aug. 19,20,22,23,24 and Dec 14, 1889, Jan 1, 1890; *Sheffield Telegraph*, Aug. 19,20, Dec 14, 1889, Jan 1, 1890; *The Times*, Dec 14, 1889 and Jan 1, 1890.

[111] *Sheffield Telegraph*, Aug. 19, 1889.

Warwick, who had a photographic van and was married to Emma's sister, and Thomas Wigden, who was one of West's oldest friends.

At first they were happy enough, a child was born to them in 1883 and over the next five years two more followed. But in late 1888 the marriage hit trouble. At the Handsworth Feast West was told that Emma had been deceiving him with a showman, named John Baines, known amongst the travelling fraternity as Leicester Jack.[112] He tackled her about what he had heard but she said it was all false. He was not convinced and from then on relations between them soured. Whenever he was drunk he would bring up the subject, she would deny the accusation and he would hit her. On several occasions he talked of killing her.

In summer 1889 things came to a head. At midnight on June 6, PC Hambly was patrolling in the vicinity of East Street, Derby where West's caravan was pitched, when he heard a woman screaming. He rushed to investigate and found Emma standing outside the van, wearing only her chemise, and West at the van door shouting obscenities at her. 'He's accusing me of being intimate with another man,' she told the officer 'and he's thrown me out of the van and

---

[112] The *Sheffield Independent* in its edition for August 24 offered this intelligence concerning Baines: 'Leicester Jack is a very well known man in Sheffield His real name is John Baines and he, like the prisoner, is in the coconut line, besides which he has some swings Although he is a native of Leicester and describes himself on his van as Leicester Jack, he spends a good deal of time in Sheffield He has his own particular corner at the Sheffield fairs which he has occupied for many years and, when not attending fairs and feasts in different parts of the country, he often pitches his caravans on a piece of waste land at Attercliffe. He was formerly connected with the prisoner in his business. He is about 30 years of age and a married man. During the last small pox epidemic in Sheffield, about a year and a half ago, he and wife both fell victim to the small pock, the man being badly scarred by the disease. When he heard of the murder [Baines] put himself into communication with the police He denies that there is any foundation for the jealousy of him entertained by the prisoner.'

won't let me back in.' At this West attacked her. He was immediately arrested and the following morning appeared before the town's magistrates, charged with assault and using obscene language. At the hearing his wife did her best to get the charges dropped but he was convicted and fined 30 shillings, with six weeks' imprisonment in default. To save him having to go to prison, she paid the fine and the two of them then returned to their caravan. Soon afterwards, however, her family persuaded her to leave him and she went back to her mother's. A few weeks later, she went out on the road again with her brother-in-law, Warwick. It was inevitable that sooner or later she would bump into her husband and she did, in early August, at a fair at Riddings[113] in Derbyshire. The two of them talked and agreed to be reconciled, West promising to behave better towards her in future. But within weeks his jealousy returned and they were quarrelling.

In mid August they were at Clay Cross. There they had yet another row during which West threatened to kill her. 'It's only the drink,' Emma told their friends. 'I think the world of him and he would never hurt me.'

On Friday, August 16 they set out from Clay Cross for Handsworth Woodhouse. West had had stalls at the Woodhouse Feast for years, pitching his caravan in a field adjoining the *Royal Hotel* and this year was to be no different. He, his wife and their eldest child set off by road in their van, with a second van containing his side-show equipment following. When the first van reached Dronfield, West got out saying that he was going to catch the train to Sheffield to buy some items he needed for his stall, and told Emma to

[113] A small village approximately one mile from Butterley.

carry on to Woodhouse and to put the van in Hawkesworth's field. This she did.

West's principal purchase in Sheffield appears to have been beer, for when he arrived at Woodhouse by cab at 9.30 pm he was very much the worse for drink. After checking that his caravan was in the field, he repaired first to the *Royal Hotel* and then moved on to the *Cross Daggers* where he stayed until closing time. In the *Cross Daggers,* a showman, named Law, saw him, head slumped on the table. 'What's the matter?' he asked. 'Oh Benny you don't know,' West replied and then added 'Benny I shall do the b____ tonight if they start of me.'

Following her arrival in the village, Emma had been busy tending her sister, Mrs Warwick, who was ill but, by closing time, the invalid was sufficiently improved to be left, and Emma walked across to meet her husband and the two of them then walked back to the caravan. West went straight into his van but Emma remained outside chatting to Twigden who was pitched nearby. Two minutes West came out and called 'Emma are you coming to bed?' 'Yes, I'll be there in a minute,' she replied. 'Well goodnight to you both,' called West going back inside. Emma followed shortly after and then all was quiet.

At 5.30 am there was a knock at the door of Twigden's caravan. It was West. 'Will you get up?' he asked.

'It's too early.'

'Oh, but do get up I have something particular to tell you.'

'What's up?'

'Tom, I've killed my wife.'

'Get away with you,' said the other.

'I've killed her. Come and look she's dead in the waggon. She's in the waggon. Go and have a look.'

Twigden declined to look but asked 'How have you done it?'

'Cut her throat'

'What time did it happen?'

'Soon after we got into the waggon last night.'

West seemed so much in earnest that Twigden decided to go and fetch Warwick. He was equally unwilling to turn out but, on being told what West was saying, agreed to do so. The three of them then set off towards the caravan but when they reached the door West, after repeating that he had killed Emma, said 'I want both of you to go with me to the police station first and I'll give myself up.' They all walked to the police office only to find that the officers were out on their beats. 'Lets go back to the van and see if Emma really is dead,' Warwick suggested. So back they trooped. When they reached the caravan West opened the door and pointed inside. 'There you are,' he said. 'Look at the blood on the bed' and when they looked in they saw Emma West lying on the bed, dressed in her night clothes with her throat cut. She was obviously dead and the floor was covered in blood; sleeping next to her, quite unaware of what had taken place was her young child, its night-clothes sprinkled in blood. Warwick picked the infant up and took it to his own van. As he did so, he noticed that the cut to the dead woman's throat was about five inches long and that there were no signs of a struggle. 'Why did you do it?' he asked. 'We had a row and she said one word when I jumped out of bed and cut her throat. I then left the van.' Soon after this Sergeant Ford came up. Upon seeing him, West got down from a wall he was sitting on and said 'I have done it. You can take me and lock me up or do what you like with me.'

'What have you done?'

'Murdered my wife.'

'Go home,' said the officer 'You're not sober.'

'Sober or not, I have killed her.'

At this point Twigden and Warwick came up and confirmed that West was indeed speaking the truth. Having looked in the van, the sergeant immediately sent to the station for assistance and requested the attendance of Dr Pillow.

When the doctor arrived he at once certified life extinct. His opinion was that death had occurred some two or three hours before. He noticed that the gash to the throat was deepest to the left of the windpipe, which suggested that the weapon which caused it had been introduced at that point and dragged across the throat. The wound, which could possibly have been self inflicted, had severed both the jugular vein and the carotid artery and the deceased would have bled to death within minutes of her throat being cut. Sergeant Ford showed the doctor a knife with a blade with a pointed end which he had found on the floor beneath the bed. The latter confirmed that it could well be the murder weapon.

Soon after this West was removed to the police station.[114] On his way there he said:

> *'This thing has been brewing twelve months. It will be next Sunday twelve months when we were here for the Feast last year when I began to find out her tricks. There's another I*

[114] Before going with Sergeant Ford West kissed his wife on the cheek.

*intended to do first. That Leicester Jack and then her but the b____ kept out of my way. I should have put his light out first.'*

At the police station he was charged with murder. 'Yes, it cannot be helped,' he replied. 'It's better if I make a clean breast of it.' He then admitted that he had killed his wife but said that she had been faithless to him. He should not have killed her but she had said one thing to him which enraged him so that he picked up the knife and cut her throat.

When Superintendent Midgeley of the West Riding police arrived at the station he took immediate steps to have the van removed to the yard of the *George Inn* and the body to the public house. The publican had suggested that it should be placed in an outhouse but he had been forced to yield on the point.

At 8 am, Sergeant Ford took West by train to Sheffield. From Sheffield station they walked on foot to the Central West Riding police office in Burngreave Road. As they walked West said 'I do not wish to live any longer and wish I could be finished off today.' At Burngreave Road his clothes were examined and it was noted that the front of his shirt was covered in blood, with the right sleeve more bloody than the left, and that there was slight blood-staining on the inside of the trousers.

At 2.45 pm, on the Monday, West Riding coroner, Dossey Wightman, opened the inquest at the *George*. The prisoner, who had been brought there by cab, was seated in a corner of the room, well away from the windows and the eyes of the large crowd which had gathered in the street outside. The proceedings lasted a little under two hours, the coroner declaring that it was the simplest case of murder he had had to deal with during his long coronership. The highlight, so far as the press were concerned, was a clash between West and his mother-in-law. As she was about to sign her deposition, Mrs Sketchley turned to him and said 'You are a bad man and the murderer of my daughter.' 'You are ten times worse,' replied West 'for it is you who are the cause of it all. I am glad it is done and over. The only thing I am sorry about is that I didn't do t'other at the same time. I should have done 'em both. She knowed all about it.' It all made marvellous copy for the newspapers but it was not the wisest thing for a man charged with murder to say. After taking evidence from Twigden, Dr Pillow, and Sergeant Ford, the coroner asked the accused if he wished to give evidence He replied that he did not. The coroner then summed up. 'Would evidence of provocation affect our verdict?' the jury foreman asked. 'No,' replied the coroner 'that it is a matter for another court.' This said, the jury immediately returned a verdict of wilful murder by West and the coroner signed the committal warrant, As the accused man was hustled to the waiting police van he called to his friends 'You can see me tomorrow at the police court.'[115] The press reports of the inquest had little good to say of him. 'He appears,' said the *Sheffield Independent:*

> *'... a very determined fellow, a rough looking man with firmly set face that wore an expression of fierceness Attired in long*

[115] During the inquest the body was taken to the railway station and put on a train to Derby. On Wednesday August 21, the dead woman was buried in the Nottingham Road cemetery, Derby. 'The funeral procession started from the *White Horse Inn*, Morledge (of which her brother was the licensee). It consisted of a hearse with glass sides and eight mourning coaches, each drawn by a pair of splendid black horses. The service was conducted by the Revd Marwood, a Primitive Methodist minister. The deceased's youngest child stood at the grave side and dropped a few flowers on to the coffin. Although there was a heavy downpour of rain during the funeral thousands of people assembled in the streets and at the grave side.'

*tweed overcoat reaching almost to his feet and a pair of corduroy trousers [he looked] half gipsy, half horse dealer.'*

The next day there was a committal hearing before two West Riding magistrates, Sir Henry Watson and Mr T W Cadman. Mr Robert Fairhurst, instructed by the DPP, conducted the prosecution, the prisoner being unrepresented. During the hearing West sat with his arm resting on the brass rail at the front of the dock and his head in his hand. The overwhelming impression he conveyed to onlookers was one of disinterest.

> *He frequently looked round the court and once or twice moved in recognition of old friends. Generally, he appeared wholly unconcerned and though listening to the evidence, his interest was not very keen.*

As at the inquest, there was a clash with his mother-in-law. When she told the court that he and Emma had never lived happily, he immediately disputed this saying that they had never had a mis-word until twelve months before.

'But you had,' she insisted 'You bad man, you murderer, you villain. You ought to have your neck stretched.'

'You caused three parts of it yourself. You have no occasion to blame me. Blame yourself. I have done it and I am very glad of it. I want to die, that is what I want. I am glad I have done it. I told you a long while ago I should do it and I have meant to do it.'

'Villain.'

'Blame yourself not me. And Leicester Jack. You and him that is the two.'

The bench, who had had enough, ordered Mrs Sketchley to leave the witness box but she was still not finished. As she passed the dock she turned to the prisoner again and shouted at him:

'You are a villain. I have filled your belly and clothed your back. You owe me £18 10s now.'

'And you owe me £600,' retorted West.

At this she was led out, still shouting 'Villain.'

'You can talk you are as bad as any of them.' West told her. 'I am very glad I did it and only sorry I didn't do both of them. All I want is to die now and the sooner the better.'

As he was being taken from the dock, having been committed for trial, he called to his friends 'Goodbye all of you.' Twigden and several others waved him farewell.

He was tried on December 14, 1889, at the Leeds Winter Gaol Delivery before Mr Justice Manisty.[116] Two Leeds barristers, Mr G Banks and Mr W W Thompson, appeared for the prosecution while two more, Mr Kershaw and Mr Palmer, appeared for West.[117] There being not the slightest doubt that it was the prisoner who had killed Emma predictably the defence run in front of the jury was that of insanity. Twigden, when cross-examined, agreed that the prisoner had suffered a bad attack of brain fever some seven to eight years before

---

[116] **Manisty**, Sir Henry (1808-90) solicitor 1830; barrister 1845; QC 1857; High Court judge 1876.

[117] **Banks**, George James; b 1851, son of Yorkshire clergyman; educ. Trinity Coll, Cambridge; barrister 1876, practised from chambers at 5, East Parade, Leeds; **Kershaw,** Louis Addin; b. 1843; barrister 1872; practised from 39, Park Square, Leeds.

and had been told he should never drink; he and his wife had lived happily down to 1888 but after he had discovered about Leicester Jack he had begun to brood. Dr Pillow confirmed that a predisposition of insanity could be transmitted from parent to child through many generations and that it might skip a generation. He also agreed that brooding over wrongs, real or imaginary, could be a symptom of the approach of a fit of homicidal mania. The defence called just one witness, Fanny Cooper, the prisoner's sister. She told the court that the family came originally from Oxford and that many of its members had suffered from insanity. The prisoner's grandfather had been insane and had had to be confined in an asylum at Abingdon where he died; his great uncle had had to be strapped down in his bed because of insanity and a cousin of the prisoner had been confined to an asylum for 18 years and had recently died there; a son born to the prisoner's mother by a second husband had to be watched day and night because of periodic fits of insanity and had twice tried to take his own life. When cross-examined she agreed that she had not seen the prisoner for 20 years but insisted that when she had known him he had displayed the same restless irritability as others in the family who had become insane.

Kershaw then rose to address the jury:

> *There was not the slightest doubt that the prisoner murdered his wife but he would ask them to say that it was done in a moment of insanity, his blood having being raised to a pitch of excitement by long brooding over the ills which had been wrought to his domestic peace by Leicester Jack. It was at Handsworth where his peace of mind was first destroyed and on returning to the place after an absence of 12 months, it was not difficult to understand that the germ of insanity within him was roused by the terrible thought of the wrong that had been done to him and*

*sprang into full being in one bound. Reason for the time being was thrown from her seat and the prisoner for the time being was in the grasp of an insane impulse – an impulse which he followed blindly to whatever end it might tend. In the present case the man's hand turned against the one whom he loved best in the world and he (counsel) would remind them that prior to the time when he began to doubt the fidelity of his wife he loved her as they were told by Twigden more than life. It was not until Baines came on the scene that the affectionate relations between husband and wife were disturbed and driven to despair by the awful thought of his wife's unfaithfulness, the prisoner grew moody, brooded over the terrible thought, took to drinking and finally, acting on the homicidal impulse within him, committed the deed which had brought him to a position of the most awful peril The learned counsel alluded at some length to the evidence of Mrs Cooper as showing the strong taint of insanity within the family and referring to the evidence of Twigden said the prisoner was obviously under the delusion that his wife was to be found with Leicester Jack and that the two were plotting together against him, although as they knew Leicester Jack had not been seen for a year. He urged upon the jury that the methods pursued by the prisoner were those characteristic of an insane person and, in conclusion, said to them that if they came to the conclusion that the prisoner was not out of his mind it was open to them to return a verdict of guilty of manslaughter.*

Banks, replying for the Crown, submitted that the evidence called by the defence did not begin to prove that the prisoner was insane at the time of the killing. Supposing that every word Mrs Cooper had spoken was true, there was no evidence to show that for the last 20 years the prisoner was otherwise than a perfectly sane man

Mr Justice Manisty in summing up, having directed the jury that drunkenness was no excuse for a crime, said that there was no direct evidence of any apparent insanity in the prisoner though no doubt there had been insanity in the family A very sad tale was told by the prisoner's sister with regard to other members of the family who had been insane but, so far as he could see, there was nothing which could lead the jury to the conclusion that the accused himself had been a victim of the malady.

After a short retirement the jury was back with a verdict of guilty but with a strong recommendation to mercy on account of the great provocation he had received.

Donning the black cap, the judge proceeded to pass sentence:

> *Robert West, you have been found guilty of the murder of your wife. It is not for me to make any observations on the heinousness of that crime. The law imposes on me one duty and one only and that is to pass sentence of death.*

Whilst awaiting execution, West entertained no hope of a reprieve and, when informed, on his last Sunday, that the authorities had decided that the death penalty must be exacted, he expressed no surprise. Under the ministrations of Revd Dr Bowlan, the chaplain of Armley prison, he had become resigned; he showed no open sign of repentance although on one occasion he informed the chaplain that 'if the murder had not been done it never would be done.' In his last week he received a visit from his son who had come to make arrangements for disposal of his effects. Neither showed any emotion and they parted without shedding a tear, West telling the lad that he need not come to see him again

He was hanged on December 31, 1889, together with Frederick Brett, a 39-year-old Halifax murderer.[118] On the morning of the execution both men were astir early. From six o'clock until a few minutes before eight Brett, who was a Roman Catholic, was engaged

[118] The hangman was Billington.

in devotional exercises, three priests being present to give him the last rites. He ate no breakfast and went to his death fasting, West, on the other hand, ate heartily. Only a few minutes elapsed between the pinioning and the fall of the drop and both men walked along the path leading to the execution shed with a firm demeanour. Just before the trap fell, West looked towards his companion and smiled.

The public showed little interest in the event and only a handful of people assembled near the prison for the purpose of morbidly watching the black flag being raised. Once it had been hoisted they quickly dispersed.

At 10 o'clock an inquest was held within the prison. The prison surgeon certified in both cases that the cause of death was strangulation by hanging; death almost instantaneous.

## Talking with Lodgers - Edward Hemmings, 1893 [119]

Annie Haigh was a good looking, high spirited young woman fond of clothes and regarded in her native village of Normanton near Wakefield as a bit of a flirt. Her first job after leaving school was that of general servant at the *Huntsman* public house. There she quickly earned a reputation for honesty and hard work. According to her eldest sister she was a go-getter, anxious to get on in the world and to secure a comfortable home.

At Whitsuntide 1892, aged just 20, she married Edward Hemmings, five years her senior. Why is hard to understand for the pair were as alike as chalk and cheese. A gloomy morose individual,

[119] See *Sheffield Independent*, Feb 17, 18, 20, 21, 23, 25, Mar 16, Apl 1, 4, and 7, 1893; *Sheffield Telegraph*, Feb 17, 18, 20, 21, 23, 25, Mar 16, 1893; *The Times*, Mar 16, 1893.

who had had a strict religious upbringing, Hemmings did not, if what her family were later to say was true, even have the merit of being a hard worker.[120] Soon after the wedding Annie found out, to her distress, that he was up to his eyes in debt.

In August 1892, presumably with a view to escaping his creditors,[121] the couple moved to Woodhouse where, for the first few weeks, they lived with Annie's sister, Annice Jones, at Canary Island. However, as soon as Hemmings had found work (he got a job at Beighton pit) they took lodgings at Robins Lane, furnishing their new home with items bought on hire purchase from the J H Banner Clothing Store in Attercliffe. After only a couple of weeks in their new home they quarrelled and he walked out. One might have expected Annie to return to her sister's but it was Hemmings who did, Annie staying on at the Robins Lane lodgings. To support herself she was reduced to doing washing for neighbours and, being unable to keep up the instalment payments, had to send the new furniture back. All she was able to salvage from the wreck of her home was a walnut chiffonier.

While the couple were separated, Hemmings told Annie Jones that he worshipped the ground his wife walked on, but could not bear to see her talk to anyone else and would sooner kill her than she should do so. 'I should think nothing of it,' he added. Desperate to get her back he besieged her with letters begging for a reconciliation and eventually she yielded and took him back. By February, 1893, they were living in a rented room in the house of Charles

[120] At the date of the marriage he was working as a miner at Pope & Pearson's Altofts colliery.

[121] When they left they were receiving regular visits from bailiffs.

Kennington, a shunter at Beighton railway station. Although they were back together they were still not getting on. Hemmings disliked Annie's habit of spending time of an evening in the communal kitchen, chatting with her landlady and her young male lodgers. She should be spending her time with him in their room not with them he complained. As for Annie, she was fed up with his moodiness and with being constantly in debt. She was anxious to set up a home but Hemmings would seize on the flimsiest excuses for remaining off work: on returning from the pit one morning, he told his landlady that he would not be able to work the next day because his clogs were split. 'I am tired of life,' he said 'and I do not care how soon it is ended.'

February 17, 1889, was Annie's birthday. On the evening of the 15th she and Hemmings stayed in their room. They seemed cheerful and were heard laughing together. When the landlady looked in Hemmings, who seemed to be in a good mood, bantered her. The couple retired to bed at their usual hour and nothing more was heard from them until around 3 am when George Bradshaw, another lodger, heard a moaning sound coming from their room. 'What's wrong Ted?' he called out. 'Nowt. Nowt,' replied Hemmings. Everything then went quiet. At 4 am Bradshaw heard someone leaving the house. Knowing that Hemmings usually left at this time for his work at the pit, he thought nothing of it. At 6 am Bradshaw got up for work himself (he was employed on the construction of a railway line near Chesterfield). As he went past the Hemmings' room, he knocked on the door and asked if everything was alright. Receiving no answer, he looked in. A horrific sight met his eyes: Annie was lying on the floor, her head resting on her left arm; there was a huge wound to her forehead, a great gash to her throat and blood splattered over the walls. He immediately rushed from the room and roused the rest of the house. PC Cole, who lived nearby, was informed and he summoned other officers. Dr Scott of Woodhouse was also fetched; after examining the dead woman's injuries he confirmed what the officers already knew that the injuries were not self-inflicted.

At 9 am, police superintendent Bailby arrived and made a careful examination of the body and of the room where it lay. From the fireplace were recovered the blade and burnt heft of a razor and the burnt remnants of a pair of clogs, all of which bore unmistakeable evidence of blood-staining. He also learned that an axe, last seen on the previous evening, was missing from the house. The nature of Annie's injuries and the distribution of the blood-staining suggested that, as she slept, she had been dealt a terrible blow to the forehead with the missing axe; this may have dazed her but did not kill her; as she tried to rise from the bed she was then attacked with a razor and a struggle followed in which her throat and cheek were cut and the fingers almost severed from her hand.

There was also abundant evidence of the couple's straitened financial circumstances: documents recovered included a number of pawn tickets, an arrears notice from the Prudential Assurance Company relating to a joint lives policy taken out by Hemmings in June of the previous year and letters which showed that the couple were in arrears with payments for a sewing machine.

The question was where was Hemmings? At 4 am he had been seen coming out of his lodgings by a man, named Hill who was on his way to work. Hill followed him as far as Woodhouse Junction railway station then lost sight of him. Later that day the police recovered an axe from a sump near the railway bridge. It was identified by Mrs Kennington as the one missing from her house. The bottle in which Hemmings took cold tea to work was also found in a field, but of the man himself there was no sign.

There was press speculation that he may well have committed suicide. In fact, the truth was more prosaic. On quitting Woodhouse, he had headed for Doncaster where he arrived after dark. Presenting himself as a vagrant to the police at the Guildhall, he was given a ticket which got him a bed in the workhouse. The next morning he set out on foot for Featherstone. There he called at the home of a collier named Fox. The door was answered by Fox's wife Charlotte. 'I never expected to see you alive again,' she told him 'I thought you would drown yourself.' 'I think too much about myself to do that,' he replied. He then told her how he had walked from Doncaster and had had nothing to eat all day but a turnip. She made him some tea. Had he done the murder, she asked. 'Yes,' he told her. He had used a razor. She said that she had read in a newspaper that his wife had been found lying on the bed. No, he said, she was lying on the floor covered by some clothes. Had the lodger anything to do with it? He did not answer and then, showing her a cap belonging to his wife, said he loved the very ground she walked on. After having a wash, he left saying he was going to give himself up. As night fell he headed for Normanton, intending to call on his parents but, when he got to within a mile of their house, realising that a visit would only cause his mother even greater grief, he turned away and made for the police station.

His knock on the station door was answered by the wife of Inspector Turton. He asked to speak to the inspector but was told there were no officers on the premises. 'Can you not do anything?' he asked. 'I have done summat you may be sure but I wanted a policeman.' Knowing that officers were looking for a man called Hemmings, she asked her visitor his name. 'Hemmings,' he told her. With that she invited him into her kitchen and sent her eldest son to fetch Sergeant Ford. Ford arrived within minutes, closely followed by the inspector. 'Hello, Ted,' said Turton 'are you here?' 'Yes I've given myself up to your wife.' He was taken into the office and his wet clothes taken from him. 'Does t'owd hangman get your clothes?' he asked as he took off his stockings. Getting no answer, he started to talk about the murder. He had a very bad temper at times. He had killed his wife but didn't regret the deed in the least. After he killed her a great weight had been lifted from his mind, a sensation resembling that which a man experiences when he undergoes a conversion and receives Christ. If any man did love woman, he loved his wife but he could not bear to see her more fond of other men than her husband and, as his love was not reciprocated, he thought it better that both should be dead. He intended to make a full breast of the affair and go to the gallows like a man. When he was searched he was found to be penniless, his only possession a miners' union card.

At just after 3 am he was taken from Normanton to Sheffield by train. The train got in at 4 and, being unable to get a cab at that hour, the police escort had no option but to march him through the streets from the station to the West Riding police office in Burngreave Road. There he was given breakfast. On his journey to Sheffield, Hemmings had continued to talk about what he had done. He had got a little the worse for drink on the previous Friday night. It was the first time his wife had seen him in that condition and she nagged at him to such an extent that he smacked her face and left the house. The incident had so upset him that he had not the heart to go to work the next morning which led to his losing his job. As he was being taken through the Sheffield streets, he made this chilling admission: 'I struck her, but I didn't think of killing her. Then I thought I should get five years so I thought I would finish her off.'

On the Friday afternoon, while Hemmings was tramping around the West Riding, back at the *Junction Hotel*, Woodhouse, the coroner, Dossey Wightman, opened the inquest into Annie's death. After taking evidence of identification, he issued a burial certificate and then adjourned the proceedings to the following Wednesday.

On the Sunday:

> *[the] villages of Woodhouse and Woodhouse Mill generally so quiet and peaceful on Sundays were thronged with sightseers The trains running from Sheffield took crowds into the villages and vehicles from the surrounding district carried their full quota of people. The chief centre of attraction was the house where the crime was committed and it was found necessary to detail a strong police force to keep intruders out of house Countless applications [were made] to view the interior ... but were in all cases refused. Large numbers ... visited in the hope of seeing the funeral of the murdered woman but to their disappointment the interment takes place today.*[122]

On the Monday the crowds were back for the funeral:

> *Sheffield contributed its quota and Darnall, [Woodhouse's] nearest neighbour seemed to have turned out a large percentage of its female population. Crowds blocked the road leading to the house where the body lay. A subscription had been raised which enabled the coffin to be of a more ornate description than would have been the case if matter had been*

[122] *Sheffield Independent*, February 20, 1893.

*left entirely to the parish. At the church only a small party of mourners was permitted to enter the gates. At the cemetery there was no such restriction .... Just inside the gates people massed six deep [the] crowd spread[ing] over the graves and walks in vicinity of the newly dug grave. The Vicar officiated and the hymn There is a fountain filled with blood was sung by mourners with much earnestness.*[123]

Since the discovery of the murder, reporters had been scouring the area for information about Hemmings and, in its edition of February 17, the *Sheffield Telegraph* related what had been discovered:

*The library of the murderer consists almost entirely of Sunday school prizes received in the years 1874,1875,1879, 1881 and 1882, the last one being a personal gift from his teacher James Harper at the Darleston Wesleyan Sunday School, Staffordshire. They are merely for punctual attendance. There is also a Church of England service and a set of Wesley's hymns. The only work of a fictional kind is The Children of the Abbey. So hard up had [Hemmings] been that he got into arrears with his Union before leaving Normanton and had to leave the colliery in consequence. He had, however, gone back under the name of William Haigh, taking his wife's name.*

On Wednesday, February 22, the inquest was resumed. Arthur Haigh, the dead woman's brother, had new and damning evidence to offer: 'While my sister was at Woodhouse she had to be accompanied by another woman for fear of Hemmings. I have just left a young woman that he paid his addresses to. She belongs to the [Salvation] Army; he threatened to murder her and she had to go from the meetings guarded by two soldiers.' After a brief summing up the jury, in short order, returned a verdict of murder.

---

[123] *Sheffield Independent*, February 21, 1893.

Two days later, Hemmings was at Sheffield Town Hall before the Sheffield West Riding magistrates for preliminary examination.[124] On the bench were Alderman Hunter and Mr T W Cadman. As the case was being opened to the magistrates, Hemmings was observed chatting with the police officers and smiling from time to time. When the court rose for lunch Annie's sister, Annice Jones, went up to him, weeping bitterly. 'I am sorry it has come to this,' she said. 'If you had taken my advice it would not have happened. Speak the truth, Ted.' At this he too began to weep and, before the guarding police officers could intervene, held out his hand to her and said 'Well, I confess I have done it.' The principal witnesses after lunch were Arthur Haigh and Annice's husband, William Jones, both of whom gave highly damaging evidence of past threats.[125] The outcome of the proceedings was never in doubt and at the conclusion of the evidence the accused was committed for trial.

He took his trial on March 15 1893, at Leeds Assizes before Mr Justice Bruce.[126] Cyril Dodd QC and Arthur Bairstow appeared for the prosecution, Walter Beverley for the accused.[127] During the trial,

[124] '[Of] middle height, dark complexion [and] hard features' was the reporters' description of him.

[125] Haigh related how within weeks of the marriage, Hemmings called at his house, produced a razor and said 'She has not returned home and I have bought a razor. Some body will have a taste of this before long.' Jones said that whilst living at his house, Hemmings had produced a razor and talked of finishing his wife and making a job of her. He then added 'I can go and take her life and think I have done nothing wrong.'

[126] **Bruce**, Sir Gainsford, (1834 -1912); educ. Glasgow university; barrister, 1859; Recorder of Bradford, 1877; QC 1883; MP Finsbury, 1888-92; appointed High Court judge, 1892; his appointment attracted considerable criticism (eg (1892) 93 *Law Times*, p 267 'We believe it possible that Mr Gainsford Bruce may make a respectable, if not a good, judge, although we cannot but rebuke those who declared that looking for Mr Bruce's name in the pages of the Law Reports is like looking for a needle in a bundle of hay.' RFV Heuston, *Lives of the Lord Chancellors*, Oxford, 1964, p 65 describes him as being 'as undistinguished on the bench as he had been at the bar.'

[127] **Dodd**, Cyril QC, barrister 1869; QC 1890.; **Bairstow**, Arthur William, educ Cambridge and London universities; barrister, 1878; practised from Calverley St., Leeds; **Beverley**,

which lasted from 10.30 until 6 pm, the public gallery was packed. Amongst the spectators were miners and others from Normanton who knew the prisoner and his wife. It had originally been Hemmings' intention to defend himself but his friends raised money to pay for a defence. The watching reporters noted that he walked into the dock with a firm, almost defiant, step. His face was a little thinner than when last he had appeared in court and, during his three weeks' detention at Wakefield, he had grown a reddish beard. As prosecution counsel was opening the case to the jury, he looked around the court as if searching for the faces of friends and relatives.

In cross-examination Beverley was able to establish that Annie had, on the night before the murder, as on many evenings previously, been in the kitchen joking with the lodgers for at least half an hour and, when Jemima Wilkinson stepped into the witness box to give evidence for the defence, it quickly became clear that the faults in the marriage were not all on Hemmings' side and that he had cause to be jealous. She told the jury that the prisoner and the deceased had lodged with her immediately after their marriage. During the two months they were with her the prisoner was a good husband and was steady and industrious. He used to hand over his wages to his wife for her to spend as she liked. She used to buy him nothing but a little sugar, bread, butter and tea although his wages were 7/6 a day. When they had been married for just three weeks, the deceased asked her to pledge the prisoner's Sunday clothes. One week the deceased went into Rotherham and, when she returned, she said she had been going

---

Walter, son of Wakefield brewer; a one time Leeds solicitor, he was called the bar in 1888 and practised from Chambers at 16, Piccadilly, Bradford.

for walks with her cousins and friends, and had taken off her wedding ring so as to pass for a single woman.

In his closing address Beverley told the jury:

> *Killing was one thing murder was another [The question was did the prisoner] kill with malice aforethought Did he premeditate the act? He invited the jury to bring in a verdict of manslaughter an offence varying greatly in degree and one for which it was competent for his lordship to commit to penal servitude for life. The prisoner was of irreproachable character; he had been well known in Normanton for some years and all his acquaintances gave him a good name. He had got married and the marriage had almost proved to be his death warrant. A more ill assorted union could not have been entered into. He was of a jealous kind who loved his wife dearly and would often coax her when she was in a temper. The wife was often quick tempered, defying the husband and telling him she would do what she liked and take her own course. When the husband complained to Kelly, of his conduct and that of the deceased the latter never resented it but told her husband served him right. She had frequently said she did not care for him. Many circumstances had been mentioned to show that the prisoner was very fond of his wife. Any threats uttered by him were not seriously meant. The night before she was joking with lodgers while prisoner was probably brooding over the old sore. He asked the jury to try and put themselves in the place of this man and they would then perhaps be able to appreciate the amount of provocation the man felt.*

The judge at this point intervened. No words, however opprobrious, could be considered in law provocation sufficient to reduce homicide to manslaughter, if the killing was effected by a deadly weapon.

Beverley suggested it might be so in exceptional circumstances, citing in support a passage in Archbold's *Criminal Pleading and Practice.*[128] 'No,' said the judge.

Beverly tried another tack. It might well be that the prisoner had received greater provocation still. Weapons might have been used by the deceased. There was no evidence to the contrary and there was no knowing what took place in the bedroom on that fatal morning.

This provoked a further interruption from the bench. 'Every homicide was deemed to be murder,' observed his lordship 'unless evidence was given to show it was otherwise.'

Nor, urged counsel, had malice aforethought been proved. There might have been a serious quarrel in the bedroom and, in the heat of the moment, the prisoner might have snatched up the weapon that was nearest to hand and struck his wife. Once again the judge weighed in. 'When a man strikes his wife on the head with a deadly weapon, malice is implied from the act itself. [If you shoot] at a man with a pistol or stab him with a knife the very act is considered malice.'

Beverley now addressed his final words to the jury. All afternoon he had been endeavouring to save a drowning man and he asked them to assist him and to supply any deficiency of which he

[128] The passage was in these terms 'And under special circumstances there may be such provocation by words which will reduce what would otherwise by murder to manslaughter. For instance, if a husband suddenly hearing from his wife that she had committed adultery and having no idea of such a thing before were thereupon to kill his wife it might be manslaughter.' Its citation provoked the judge to observe that there was no case where it had ever been so held and to point out that the authors had used the words 'might be.'

might have been guilty in conducting the case on behalf of the prisoner.

There was considerable applause from the public gallery as he resumed his seat.

Mr Justice Bruce now proceeded to sum up.

The jury must discharge the duty cast upon them, however painful. Counsel for the defence had referred to the absence of express malice but in law every man had to take the consequences of his own acts. When a man struck another on the head with a deadly weapon from the very act there was, in the eye of the law, malice. They had to consider whether what was done was done under such circumstances of provocation as would justify the act If a man killed another in self-defence that was no crime; if done under great provocation the act was not justifiable but the crime might be reduced to the minor one of manslaughter. It was highly improbable that this woman's death was caused by a person in a momentary fit of passion caused by provocation. Even if there was provocation by words, and that was not proved, mere words of reproach were not sufficient to reduce homicide to manslaughter, if effected by deadly weapons. In the present case there was not merely the blow to the head but the terrible gash to the throat. He did not think all this could have been done in a moment of passion produced by provocation by words. The prisoner never, in his numerous conversations, suggested that his wife made an attack on him. The jury could have no doubt how the deceased woman came by her death and who killed her and there was no evidence of sufficient provocation to reduce the crime to manslaughter. It was his duty to tell them that the words the deceased was said to have used were not sufficient for that purpose.

Having been told, in effect, that the accused had no defence, it is surprising that the jury troubled to retire at all. But they did and were out for half an hour before returning with a verdict of guilty of murder, coupled with a strong recommendation to mercy. It was obvious that the judge did not agree with their recommendation.

Hemmings, having been asked if there was any reason why sentence of death should not be passed, immediately launched upon a long rambling statement in which he spoke of his dispute with Kelly[129] and denied that he had ever stopped away from work. Every halfpcnny he earned he tipped up to his wife and if she chose to give him a shilling or sixpence out of it she did so. He would like to be faced with any man who said he was idle and did not work. As to the witnesses Thompson and Hill, he never saw either of them on the morning of the murder. He then began to weep and the judge, believing that he had finished, began to pass sentence. Hemmings at once asked to be allowed to speak further but was told he might not. 'You have.' the judge told him:

> *'been found guilty of a heartless and brutal murder; You have with heartless violence taken the life of a woman whom you were bound by every obligation to succour and protect You sent her without warning to eternity. You will have an opportunity of preparation which you denied her. Let me implore you eagerly to embrace the opportunities of spiritual consolation which will be afforded to you in prison. '*

This said, he proceeded to pass sentence of death.

---

[129] See n 10 above.

After the verdict Hemmings shook hands with Beverley and Lodge[130] saying 'You have done your best for me. Thank you very much and I hope the Lord will reward you.'

In the days which followed, a petition for Hemmings' reprieve was got up which attracted signatures from 6,000 people in various parts of the country but it was not enough to save him. The news was conveyed to him on Friday, March 3. The following day he had a last meeting with his elderly parents and his brother-in-law, John Barber. During the twenty minutes he was allowed with them, he made no reference to the murder but told them he was prepared to die and asked them to meet him in heaven. He urged them to attend chapel and to try and profit by the teaching given. He was hanged at Armley on Tuesday, April 6, 1893.[131] On the night before his execution his sleep was troubled and he was up early. However, he ate a substantial breakfast and was enjoying a pipe of tobacco when the hangman entered his cell. He walked to the scaffold with a firm step with the prison bell tolling. Before his death he handed to the prison authorities a written confession of guilt and the chaplain was convinced that he died penitent.

---

[130] A Wakefield solicitor who had appeared for Hemmings at the committal hearing and had retained Beverley at trial.

[131] Billington was the hangman and the execution took place in the permanent shed adjoining the cook-house. 'It being holiday time the great industrial works in the neighbourhood were all closed, and there was consequently not the usual crowd of workmen out for the breakfast half hour to watch the hoisting of the black flag. But on Gaol Lone, the road leading up to the prison from Armley Road, the crowd was so dense that policemen were necessary to contain them' (*Sheffield Independent*, April 7, 1893).

*Harvest Lane*

*Another view of Harvest Lane*

*The Old Harrow where Smedley and Elizabeth Firth had been drinking just before the murder*

***Apple Street where the murder took place***

***Bailey Street (today).*** *This was where Elizabeth Firth lived.*

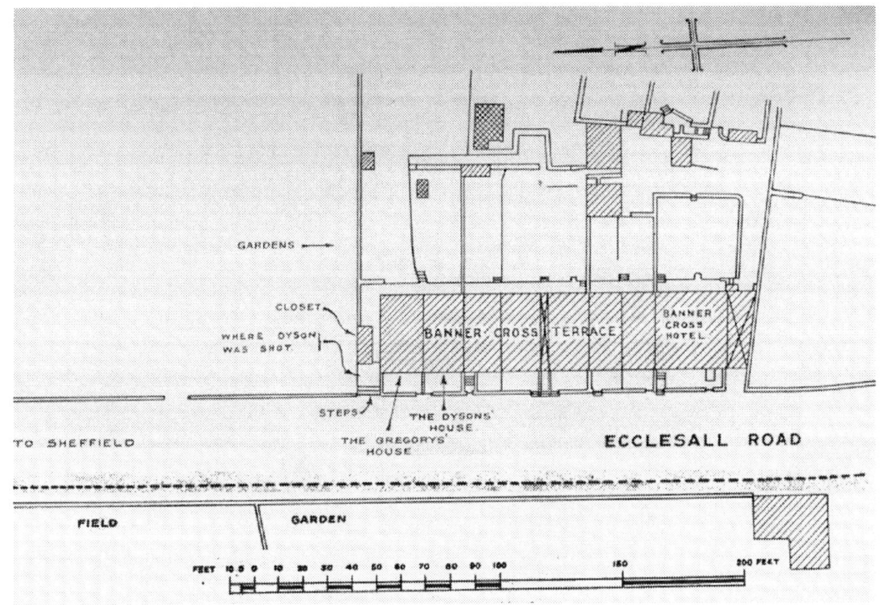


***Map illustrating the Banner Cross murder***

***Banner Cross Terrace today (Banner Cross Hotel top right)***

***Scene of the murder***

POLICE NOTICE

# MURDER

## £100 REWARD.

WHEREAS on the 29th of November. 1876. Mr. Albert Dyson was murdered at Banner Cross, Sheffield, having been shot in the head in the presence of his wife by Charles Peace, who escaped in the darkness of the night, and is still at large

He is a picture framer by trade, occasionally cleans and repairs clocks and watches; sometimes deals in oleographs, engravings and pictures.

*The reward notice*

*The Stag Inn, Sharrowhead were the adjourned inquest into the death of Arthur Dyson was held*

*Sir William E Clegg*
*1852-1932; Peace's solicitor*

*Peace on trial*

*Peace's execution in the prison yard at Armley*
*(Marwood, the hangman, is inset top left)*

***Montague Street** today; the wall of the General Cemetery can be seen on the left; the houses have long since been demolished*

***Sand's Paviours** where Hobson lived*

***The Vine Inn**, Cemetery Road*
*where the inquest into Ada Stothard's death was opened*

*Hobson, the murderer*

*Ada Stothard's grave in Burngreave Cemetery*

*The inscription*

*The Royal Hotel and the Old Cross Daggers where* ***Robert West*** *had been drinking before he murdered his wife Emma (1889)*

*Furnace Lane, Woodhouse, the scene of the* ***Hemmings*** *murder (1893)*

# 3

## The Sheffield Murders 1900 to 1965

| | | | | | |
|---|---|---|---|---|---|
| 8. Harry Walters | 38, miner | December 23, 1905, 7 house, 12 Court, Upper Allen Street | Sarah Ann McConnell (otherwise Jackson) | March 23, 1906 Walton J | April 10, 1906 Wakefield Prison |
| 9. George Edward Law | 34, forgeman | October 21, 1913 17, Bamforth Street | Annie Cotterill | December 2, 1913 Darling J | December 31, 1913 Wakefield Prison |
| 10. Lee Doon (Leong Lun) | 27, laundry worker | September 9, 1922, 231, Crookes | Sing Lee | December 2, 1922 Greer J | January 5, 1923 Armley Prison |
| 11. John William Eastwood | 39, chimney sweep | September 29, 1923 Lister Road | John Joseph Clark (died September 30) | December 8, 1923 Talbot J | December 28, 1923 Armley Prison |
| 12. Wilfred Fowler<br>13. Lawrence Fowler | 23, bricklayer<br>25, bookmaker's clerk | April 25, 1925 Princess Street | William Plommer | July 28-31, 1925 Finlay J | September 3, 1925<br>September 4, 1925<br>Armley Prison |
| 14. Lorraine Lax | 28, miner | August 31, 1925 51, Ripon Street | Elizabeth Lax | December 1, 1925 Fraser J | January 7, 1926 Armley Prison |
| 15. Samuel Case | 24, miner | October 27, 1927 28, Ravencarr Road | Mary Alice Mottram | November 29, 1927, Roche J | January 7, 1928 Armley Prison |
| 16. Armin Kuehne<br>17. Emil Schmittendorf | 21, POW<br>31, POW | March 24, 1945 Redmires POW Camp | Gerhardt Rettig | August 7-13, 1945, Military Tribunal, Kensington | November 16, 1945 Pentonville Prison |
| 18. William Smedley | 38, miner | March 7, 1947 Bridge Street | Edith Simmonite | July 21-22, 1947 Pritchard J | August 14, 1947 Armley Prison |

## The Christmas murder - Harry Walters, 1905 [132]

Until October 1905 Sarah McConnell had been living at Sutton-in-Ashfield with her husband of three and a quarter years. One Sunday after dinner, while he lay snoring on the sofa, she upped and left. He never saw her alive again. Where she went next is unknown but a few weeks later she turned up in Wakefield. There, in a public house, she met Harry Walters and soon they were living together. They made an ill assorted couple, she emaciated and 43, he five years her junior; but they had one thing in common: both were alcoholics. From Wakefield they moved to Barnsley and finally to Sheffield where Walters got work at Orgreave colliery. At first they lived at Darnall but then took furnished rooms in New Street 'a squalid little thoroughfare running off Bank Street.' Shortly after this they were transferred by the landlord's agent to another slum property, no. 7 house, Court 12, Upper Allen Street.[133]

---

[132] See *Sheffield Independent*, Dec 26, 27, 29, 1905; Jan 5, Mar 24, Apl 11, 1906; *Sheffield Telegraph*, Dec 26, 29, 1905; Jan 5, Mar 24, Apl 11, 1906; *Star*, Dec 26, 1905, Jan 4, Mar 24, 27, Apl 10, 1906;The Times, Mar 28, Apl 11, 1906.

[133] One of the many streets of mean unlovely homes which intersect the habited area, bounded on one side by St Phillips Road and on the other by Shalesmoor and West Bar Green. It is but five minutes walk from one of the main arteries from the city to Hillsborough. Allen Street is, on the whole, one of the broadest best paved and most presentable of the uninviting thoroughfares in this district. It stretches from Shalesmoor across Meadow Street and on up the slope to St George's Church. But the dwellers in the houses abutting on the highways in this congested neighbourhood form merely a portion of the population. At the rear are courtyards with human dwellings grouped around them. The scene of the tragedy, no 12 court, is some distance up Allen Street between Well Meadow Street and Jericho St. In relation to some of the courts in the city No 12 is by no means the worst. Reached by a slippery descending passage the court is perhaps 20 or 30 yards long and half that distance across. On either side of the slope are ten or a dozen little houses with a living room on the ground floor and sleeping accommodation upstairs and no 7 house is one of the row facing the entrance passage (*Sheffield Telegraph*, December 28, 1905).

From the day they moved into the house the couple were regularly to be seen returning there drunk and as regularly to be heard rowing. On December 22, the Friday before Christmas, Walters turned Sarah out of the house. At midnight he relented and let her back in, but within minutes they were quarrelling again and continued doing so into the early hours.

At 5.45 pm on Saturday 23rd PC Winfield, on duty in West Bar Green, was approached by a man obviously the worse for drink. It was Walters.

'I want you to come with me,' he told the officer.

'What's the matter?'

'I have been out drinking and came home and found my wife laid on her back with no clothes on and blood coming from her. I don't know how it happened and I thought it my place to come and report the matter to you.'

The officer followed him to Court 12. On entering Walters' house he immediately saw a woman lying on the floor; she had a garment on her upper body but, apart from shoes and stockings, was otherwise naked; lying near the body were a flat iron, a ginger beer bottle and a bloodied broom handle.

A police surgeon was sent for. In the meanwhile the room was examined. Various items of female clothing, some of them bloodstained, were on the sofa and a chair. In the fireplace was a bloodied piece of paper and there was blood on the wall, the fender and the first stair. Part of the floor had been washed in an attempt to remove blood-staining. As the police looked around, Walters stood drinking from a quart bottle of beer. 'My poor Sal Willey,' he exclaimed. 'If she's dead, I'll be dead. I gave her a sovereign this afternoon and we have been drinking I can't do anything with her when she's been drinking. We have had a bit of a quarrel but that's nothing. I fetched you like a man'

When Dr Godfrey, the police surgeon, arrived he made a brief examination of the body. Death, he concluded, had taken place only recently for the body was still warm. The fire brigade ambulance was then sent for to take the body to the mortuary. By this time other officers, including the Deputy Chief Constable, had arrived at the house. Walters was told he was under arrest for murder and taken to the Central Police Office. 'I am not guilty,' he replied.

At the police station he was searched. He had half a crown, a shilling and two half pennies on him. There was blood on his clothing and on his boots which had been washed.

As the investigation got under way, the police did not lack for witnesses. Although no-one in the court had heard any sounds of quarrelling or fighting coming from no 7 house on the Saturday afternoon, the couple had had visitors.

At 5 pm Mrs Bradshaw, who assisted Mrs Drakard in collecting rents, called and asked for 'the missus.' 'She's not in,' Walters told her. The next caller, at just after 5 pm, Margaret Revill, came for 6½d owed for fish. Hearing her knock, Walters shouted 'Come in, if you're a woman.' 'I'm the fish woman,' she explained. 'She's upstairs,' said Walters. 'Call her down.' She did and Sarah then appeared, her hair down and her clothes in disarray She looked as if she had been fighting. 'Pay her,' she said to Walters who was lying on the sofa. He put his hand in his pocked, pulled out 5 ½d and said 'That's all I've got'. He then claimed there was 3s 6d missing from one of his pockets and four shillings and a five shilling piece missing from the other, which he accused Sarah of taking. She ignored him and turning to Revill said 'Never mind lass, come in the morning. It's Good Sunday. I'll pay thee then.' She was obviously the worse for drink and had to use the table to support herself. Walters, who was even more drunk, said to Revill 'As soon as you've gone, I'll kill her stone dead if she does not find me the money.' Realising that she was not going to be paid, the fish wife left.

At 5.30 pm, or thereabouts, Mrs Bradshaw's superior, Annie Drakard, made another attempt to collect the rent. Having knocked and got no reply, she pushed open the door. Lying dead on the hearthrug, with no dress on, was the deceased. She fetched Emily Bradshaw and, having inspected the body, the two women threw a skirt over it for decency's sake.

At around 5.35 pm, twelve-year-old Margaret Osbourne, who lived in the same court, was sent to no 7 to collect three half pence which her mother was owed. Finding the door slightly ajar, she walked in saying as she did so: 'If you please, missus, will you send mamma that three halfpence?' She then saw the deceased lying on her back, with her knees drawn up, and a pool of blood nearby. She had no clothes on, only a skirt thrown over her knees. A man was bending over her and looking at her. Frightened, she ran and told her father what she had seen. 'Don't come here with any of your romancing tales,' he said.

Shortly after 5.30 Walters knocked on the door of his neighbour, Ann Austwick. He was in his shirtsleeves. 'Will you come to my wife?' he asked. 'I believe she is dead.'

A post-mortem examination revealed that the dead woman had bruising to her spine and knees, a large bruise on her right arm, bruising to the right hip, scratches to the face and upper lip and severe internal injuries which had been caused by an implement (in all probability the broom handle) being rammed up her private parts. The cause of death was shock and haemorrhage.

The nature of the dead woman's injuries led the local press to describe the case as Sheffield's ripper murder. 'The Jack the Ripper crimes were horrible enough,' declared the *Sheffield Telegraph* '[but] for downright savagery they were surpassed by the brutality in doing [this] wretched woman to death.'[134]

On December 27, Walters was brought before Sheffield stipendiary magistrate, Mr E M Welby. 'As he stood in the dock he looked,' wrote the reporter of the *Sheffield Independent*:

> *'a picture of misery. A man of medium height carrying some 40 years of rough and ready life, be betrayed signs of feeling his position very keenly. First, he cast his quick restless eyes to a distant corner of the roomy court; then he turned his pale haggard face to the Stipendiary Magistrate and it was a ready reply he gave to a question as to whether he had anything to say 'I am not guilty that is all I have to say.'*

Superintendent Moody told the stipendiary that all the facts of the matter had not yet been put together and the papers were to be sent to the Director of Public Prosecutions that day. He asked for and was granted a seven day remand.

On December 28, the inquest was opened by the coroner, Dossey Wightman. At the Public Mortuary in Plum Lane,

---

[134] Cf The *Sheffield Independent,* Dec 26, 1905: 'Jack the Ripper was never responsible for anything more saddening. Whitechapel in its darkest hours never produced anything so lamentable.' This was nonsense. The Upper Allen Street killing pales into insignificance alongside the last of the Whitechapel murders, that of Mary Kelly in November, 1888.

Corporation Street. Walters was present, having been brought there from the Central Police Station in charge of three officers. Evidence was taken from the deceased's brother, Arthur Wiley, from Margaret Revill, Elizabeth Drakard, Ann Austwick, PC Winfield and Dr Carter. Asked if he wished to give evidence, Walters replied 'I'll reserve it while the court.' After a short summing up, the jury were back within minutes with a verdict of wilful murder. 'There could be no other view to take of the matter,' observed the coroner signing the committal warrant. The prisoner was then hurried out to a waiting cab which took him back to the Central Police Station.

On January 4, 1906 he was back in court – this time in the magistrates' court before the Sheffield stipendiary, Mr Edward Welby.[135] The prosecution were represented by Mr Wing from the DPP's office while local solicitor, Arthur Neal, appeared for the prisoner.[136] The witnesses who had appeared at the coroner's court again gave evidence. At the conclusion of their evidence, Mr Neal rose to address the bench:

> *No doubt an atrocious murder had been committed and the question was whether the prisoner was the person who committed it. The evidence must excite suspicion. But his going to the next door neighbour and asking her to come, his fetching a policeman, the open door and a number of other matters which I need not detail are quite inconsistent with this man being guilty of this crime. It was one of those cases in which the Prisoners' Evidence Act would be of supreme*

---

[135] 'It is an interesting fact that the stipendiary [Mr E M Welby] and the coroner [Mr D Wightman], who [in 1875] both committed for trial [the murderer] William Smedley are holding the same positions today and were responsible for the committal of Walters to the Assizes (*The Star*, April 10, 1906).

[136] **Neal**, Arthur (1862-1933); educ Wesley College; admitted solicitor 1883; senior partner Arthur Neal & Co,, Sheffield; MP (conservative) Hillsborough, 1918-22.

*importance and he had thought it right to advise the prisoner that now was the proper time to give evidence.*

He then called Walters into the witness box. Having explained that he came from Featherstone and that his only criminal convictions were for drunkenness, he related how he had met the deceased in a destitute condition in a public house in Wakefield and they had lived together at Barnsley and Darnall, he getting work at Orgreave Colliery. The deceased, who was known as Mrs Jackson, was a very drunken woman and he never quarrelled with her except on account of her drunkenness. On December, 22 he gave her twenty-four shillings and she was very drunk and noisy all night. When he got up at eight o'clock the next morning, she had gone out and she came in drunk at about 10 o'clock. Afterwards she went out and had more drink. In the afternoon, he went to a certain public house to stop her getting any more drink. He had drunk very little himself up to then: all day he had about five or six pints. He did not threaten the deceased when Mrs Revill was in the house; in fact, he had never threatened her in his life. After Mrs Revill had gone he went out. Up to then he had committed no violence upon the deceased. He went to three public houses, the *Black Man* in Scotland Street, the *Lincoln Castle* in Edward Street and the *Brocco Hotel,* at each of which he had a drink but did not meet anyone he knew. He then described how he found the deceased when he got home. There was a skirt thrown over her. He put his arm under her head and tried to lift her up and called her by her name but got no answer. He went to the neighbour's house and then for the police. He also gave an explanation for the blood on his clothing. The suggestion that money had been taken out of his pocket was untrue. So far as he knew nothing had been taken.

This testimony notwithstanding, he was committed for trial at the Assizes.

His trial took place on March 23 before Mr Justice Walton.[137] J Strachan QC and Mr C L Lowenthal appeared for the Crown. Walters was represented by H T Waddy and VM Coutts Trotter.[138] It quickly became clear that Walters' case was that someone else had done the murder. The most damaging witness called by the crown was the doctor. He told the court that the deceased's injuries suggested to him that she had been assaulted first and then, when trying to escape, knocked down by the broom which had then been used with enormous force to injure her internally. He then went on to deal with the blood on the accused's clothing. His trouser knees were bloody, there was blood on one of his linings and there were also wipe marks. The blood on the clothing was, in his view, in keeping with the character of the crime and could not possibly have been caused merely by the prisoner lifting the dead woman's head, as he had stated he had done in his evidence at the magistrates' court. His boots were literally welting in blood and, although they had been washed, there was still blood all over them. Underneath, it had even extended to the point where the heel joined the uppers. To a suggestion from

---

[137] **Walton**, Sir Joseph (1845-1910); educ Stoneyhurst and London University; barrister 1868; practised from chambers in Liverpool, specialising in shipping and commercial cases; QC 1892; recorder of Wigan, 1893-1901; High Court judge 1901.

[138] **Strachan**, John (1838-1918), son of South Shields JP; barrister 1876; practised from 32, Grainger Street West, Newcastle; QC 1896; playwright; **Lowenthal**, Charles Frederick; barrister 1888; practised on NE circuit; QC 1926; **Waddy**, Harry; son of Samuel Danks Waddy, county court judge for and recorder of Sheffield 1896-1902; **Coutts-Trotter**, Victor Murray; barrister 1901; practised on NE circuit from chambers at 11, King's Bench Walk, Temple.

Waddy that accused might have stepped in blood he replied 'That would not cause it. The boots were covered in blood. There was too much blood on the uppers for that.' Another damaging snippet emerged during PC Winfield's evidence. Having described how the accused, when searched, had half a crown, a shilling and two half pennies on him, the officer added that while in custody Walters remarked 'We have had a bit of a quarrel but that's nothing. I fetched you like a man.' In cross-examination, Waddy got the officer to admit that this was evidence which he had not given at the magistrates' court. Emboldened by the concession, he went further and accused the constable of inventing the reply, only to receive what is known amongst lawyers as 'a nose-ender.' 'It's not invented,' replied the officer angrily. 'I wrote it down in my pocket book at the time.' At this, the judge asked to see the notebook and, after inspecting it, announced that the disputed reply was indeed recorded. The only progress Waddy made was with Revill, who agreed that threats such as she had heard Walters utter were often used by working people.

The prosecution case having closed, Walters was called to give evidence. As he stepped into the witness box, you could have heard a pin drop. Giving evidence in a matter of fact tone and with no trace of nervousness, he said that Mrs Bradshaw had called for the rent just before Mrs Revill. He told her that the missus was out. In fact she was in bed. He denied making any threats against the deceased in front of Mrs Revill, adding that, as soon as she had gone, he went out, going first to the *Black Man*, then to the *Lincoln Castle* and finally to the *Brocco Hotel*. He returned home at half past five and found the deceased lying naked. Saying 'Sarah.' he placed his arm near her head and lifted it up. He did not kneel down nor did he wash anything. He at once asked a neighbour to come and then put his coat on and went for the police.

Prosecuting counsel rose to cross-examine. After getting Walters to repeat his lame explanation for the blood-staining, he turned to the question of money.

'[She had taken 3s 6d from you and] you insisted on getting your 3s 6d back, you searched her and, as you removed the articles of her clothing one after another ,you placed them on the chair and on the sofa while you searched for the money?'

'No.'

'Didn't you say to Mrs Revill that the deceased had taken 3s 6d out of your pocket?'

'No.'

'You had 3s 6d when searched [by the police]?'

'Yes.'

'[But you] told Revill that you only had 5 ½d.'

'Yes, that was all I had in copper.'

'Actually, you had 3s 11½d in your pocket when Revill was at the house?'

'Yes.'

'You spent 6d in the public houses you visited?'

'Yes.'

'How then did you come to have 3s 7d when the police searched you?'

'I felt in my pocket and found another 6d.'

At this answer, which drew a laugh from the public gallery, counsel sat down. The prosecution then called in rebuttal the licensees of the three public houses which Walters claimed he had visited on the fatal afternoon. First, was Robert O' Neill landlord of the *Black Man.* 'As far as I am aware, I have never seen the prisoner in my house,' he said. Jane Hyde of the *Lincoln Castle* told the jury that she had actually seen Walters being taken to the police station by detectives on the 23rd but did not recognise him as anyone who had been to her house that afternoon. David Holmes of the *Brocco Hotel* said his daughter, who was working behind the bar on the afternoon in question, had served the prisoner at about 5.30 pm.

In his closing speech to the jury, Strachan for the Crown laid stress on the amount of blood on the boots and on the fact that someone had attempted to wash the blood up from the floor. It was, he said, inconceivable that a stranger, having killed the deceased, would have stayed to try and wash away the blood. By doing so he would simply be increasing the risk of being caught.

Waddy, in reply, submitted that the Crown case depended entirely upon circumstantial evidence and warned the jury against condemning a man upon such evidence.

The Crown had without doubt presented a powerful case but one person who was left unconvinced was Mr Justice Talbot, who proceeded to sum up strongly for an acquittal. There was no doubt he told the jury that between 5 and 5.45 on day in question a terrible murder was committed. But it was important to make sure that the wrong man was not punished for it. It was true that the prisoner had made a threat against the deceased that day but Mrs Revill, who heard, it attached no importance to it; in that walk of life such expressions were often used and were not to be taken literally. The prisoner's story was that he was out from 5 to 5.35 pm and he thought that the evidence proved he really was out. Mrs Drakard and

Mrs Bradshaw called after the woman had been murdered. A very material question was whether they called before or after the little girl's visit at 5.35, for at that time the prisoner was in. He thought that they called before the girl because they found the body naked and threw over it a black skirt. The skirt was on the woman when the little girl called. Therefore they had it pretty clearly established that between 5.30 and 5.35 the prisoner was out of the house. Perhaps he was not out for long. He might merely to have gone to the *Brocco* which was close and, as the murder did not take long, this did not exclude the possibility of his having committed it. What other evidence was there? The murder was committed by a man in a frenzy, and the murderer could not have committed it without getting a great deal of blood on him; the amount of blood on the prisoner's clothing was not considerable. There was a lot of blood on his boots but the jury should be careful; this was a matter which might give rise to strong suspicion but he questioned whether it was enough to prove the case beyond reasonable doubt.

The jury were out just 35 minutes. Clearly they found the evidence less troubling than did the judge. Surprisingly they attached to their verdict a recommendation to mercy on the ground of the prisoner's drunken and incapable condition at the time.[139]

Asked why sentence of death should not be passed, Walters merely replied: 'I am not guilty. That's all.'

Arthur Neal immediately set about organising a petition for reprieve. He told the press that the grounds of the petition would be

[139] The trial lasted 8 ½ hours.

that the judge in his summing up seemed to take a line favourable to the prisoner and the jury's recommendation to mercy.

The petition proved unavailing. Walters was hanged on April 10, 1906 at Wakefield prison,[140] the first prisoner to be executed there. Since 1864 West Riding murderers had, without exception, been hanged at Armley. The press speculated that the Home Office had decided to divide the riding into two parts for execution purposes, but no official explanation was offered. During his last days Walters had been visited by his mother and other relatives and by the Bishop of Wakefield. According to the *Star,* he maintained a cool and seemingly indifferent demeanour to the last, eating heartily, sleeping soundly and enjoying his tobacco 'apparently quite undisturbed by the fate awaiting him or the atrocity of his crime.' He walked to the gallows as firmly as possible and submitted to the pinioning without a tremor. The *Star* also commended the execution arrangements:

> *The trying walk across the prison yard, which has to be made at most prisons, is obviated at Wakefield where the condemned cell opens directly onto the shed in which the scaffold is placed.*

## The ungrateful lodger – George Edward Law, 1913 [141]

When George Law went downstairs to get his breakfast on the morning of Monday, October 20, 1913, he found waiting for him on

---

[140] Henry Pierrepoint was the hangman. He was assisted by his brother Thomas.

[141] See *Sheffield Independent*, Oct. 22, 23, Dec 2, 1913, Jan 1, 1914; *Sheffield Telegraph*, Oct 22, 29, Dec 2, 15, 1913; *Star*, Oct 20, 22, 23, 28, Dec 1, 1913; *The Times*, Dec 2, 16, 1913.

the kitchen table a letter, giving him notice to quit the room which he rented at 17, Bamforth Street. His landlord George Cotterill had already left for work, but Law wasted no time making known his displeasure.

'He's given me notice,' he shouted up the stairs.

'Well, I can't help it,' Mrs Cotterill called back.

'I shan't go. You'll have to carry me out.'

Shortly after this, the Cotterills' daughter Edith came downstairs and, surprised to find the lodger still there, asked 'Are you going to work?

'No I'm not.'

She saw the notice to quit lying on the table.

Despite his extravagant reaction, Law really had nothing to complain about. Two and a half years before the Cotterills had taken him in when he was homeless and starving. Since then he had got work as a forgeman at The Weir Tilt and Forge in Warren Street, Attercliffe Road and was now earning quite sufficient money to find accommodation of his own. What is more the family needed his room. George Cotterill wanted a normal married life not to have to share a bedroom with Law, which was what he had been doing since Law moved in. Nor was that all. Law's behaviour, which had been always been a little strange, had of late become rather worrying. He had taken badly the news that Edith had become engaged and had started to utter threats. To neighbours he had talked of 'doing two' and leaving only himself and Edith in the house. On the Sunday evening he had bumped into her fiancé, Sydney Peace, at the top of Bamforth Street and had spoken of 'not using a razor or a revolver but something else' adding, pointing at No 17, 'That's the house. Look out, you will see a cross there some morning.'

During the rest of that Monday he stayed in doors. When George Cotterill got home from work he wasted no time tackling him about the notice to quit. Cotterill would not be budged. Law would have to leave. 'It's only right,' he told him 'that I, the father, should have my own place. We have no accommodation for you.' 'You'll have to carry me out,' replied Law 'and 'don't bother hiding the razors. I have something better and sharper.' He then went out, returning later the worse for drink, still uttering threats. By now Cotterill's wife and daughter were so alarmed that they implored him to collect up all the razors in the house. To mollify them he did as they asked, hiding the blades in the cellar head. His wife then reminded him that there was a razor in the bedroom which he and Law shared. 'Go and get it,' she begged. He went up to the room but the razor was not in its usual place. Law, who was in bed, asked what he was looking for. He explained at which Law fetched it out from under the bed and handed it to him. 'Where have you put the razors?' he asked. 'They are downstairs and will be alright till morning,' he was told. 'You don't need to hide my razors, I have something here that is sharper than a razor,' he shouted. Soon after this Cotterill retired to bed himself, but he could not get off to sleep because Law kept talking about razors and spiritualists and would not be quiet. After keeping everyone in the house awake with his ramblings, he eventually fell silent. Around 3 am he started again. 'My life is nothing,' he declared 'there are two more I shall do and leave thee by thisen.'

At 5.30 Cotterill and Law both got up and went downstairs to get ready for work. Law left at 6 am in his working clothes, carrying his packing up and wearing a scarf belonging to Edith. As he departed he said 'Good morning,' as he always did. George Cotterill left minutes later.[142] Edith was the next up. At 7.30 she took her mother's breakfast upstairs, locked the back door, put the key through the back window on a corner of the sink and set off for work.[143] This left Annie Cotterill in the house by herself.

Shortly after Edith's departure, Nellie Smith, who lived at No. 19, noticed Law, standing by the back window of no. 17 talking to Annie, who was in her nightdress. She heard Annie ask if he had his key and him reply 'No.' He was in his working clothes. The episode struck her as rather strange but she dismissed it from her mind.

At around 8 o'clock Mrs Nellie Hollis, at no 21, was lying in bed when she heard moans and cries of 'Oh!' coming from the other side of the party wall, but knowing that Annie was prone to coughing bouts she thought nothing of it.

At 8.30 Law, by now dressed in his best clothes, called in at the *Royal Exchange* public house in Langsett Road and asked for and was given a brandy[144] and soda. 'Is there anything wrong?' asked the landlord, knowing that brandy was not his usual tipple. 'I am feeling faint,' Law told him.

At 10 am, Mrs Armitage called at no. 17 to collect some washing, but the door was locked and she could get no answer. She returned at 2 pm but there was no-one in.

---

[142] He worked as a steel yard labourer for John Wood & Son, steel manufacturers of Wisewood.

[143] She was employed by Messrs Rosefield & Co, tailors' trimming merchants, at their premises in Watson's Walk in the town centre.

[144] Another newspaper report suggests whisky.

When George Cotterill returned home from work at a little before 7 pm he found the house in darkness and the back door locked. He gained entry by climbing through the window of the back room and, once inside, lit the gas fire. On the table was a half eaten morsel of food. He recognised it as part of Law's packing up. But what was it doing there? With a mounting sense of apprehension he went upstairs. In the front bedroom on a bloodstained bed lay his wife. She was dead. A black scarf was tied tightly round her neck, and she had severe head injuries and cuts to her hand. The police were called and, after the police surgeon had certified life extinct, the body was removed to the public mortuary at Plum Lane. In the back bedroom where Law slept were his working clothes, heavily bloodstained (his trousers, waistcoat, shirt and singlet on the bed and his muffler on a chair). In one of the pockets was a note:

> *'Please Mr J R Cotterill withdraw this notice or it will be the worse for you. From G F Law, the end of this.'*

A description of Law was immediately circulated by the police and neighbouring forces asked to keep a look out for him.

Later that day a post-mortem examination was carried out by Dr Payne, the police surgeon. He found that the dead woman had numerous gashes to her head and several small cuts (presumably defence wounds) to her hands. His opinion was that she had died from strangulation and loss of blood and that the head injuries had been caused by a blunt instrument such as a file or a heavy butcher's knife.

At 3 pm on the afternoon of the murder, Law's sister Polly, who had not seen him for two years, was out with her husband in Mansfield where they both lived when they saw him wandering about as if lost. As he would later tell them he was looking for their house. 'Are you George Law?' the husband asked. 'Never, but that is my sister, Polly,' replied Law throwing his arms round her neck and kissing her. 'Now I have finished my dream,' he declared 'I always wanted to see you before I died.'

Later that day, he telephoned the Sheffield police to tell them where he was and, soon after this, was detained by Mansfield officers to await an escort from Sheffield. He appeared in a dazed condition when arrested. He was handed over to Sheffield officers a little after midnight. 'What I have done to Annie. I did in a temper,' he told them. 'Is she dead? I have been expecting you?' On the way back to the city he said that the Mansfield police had been ten minutes later coming for him than he expected. 'I could have got away or done away with myself. I had plenty of time.'

That same morning he was brought before the Sheffield magistrates.[145] After taking evidence from a number of witnesses, including the Cotterills, the magistrates adjourned the hearing until the following Tuesday. One of the most significant questions put was asked by the prisoner himself. 'Was the carving knife in the room? he enquired of the police surgeon. 'We did not find it,' was the reply. As

[145] 'He is,' the *Sheffield Independent* told its readers '34, thin build, 5'6"to 5'7" tall, pale complexion, light brown hair and moustache, high forehead and slightly bowed legs.' According to the *Star* he was born in Bamforth Street, and his parents had died there, which may go some way to explaining why he was apparently so attached to his lodgings with the Cotterills.

he left the dock, he fumbled with his cap and then, looking towards Edith, mumbled something which sounded like 'Cheer up.'

Later that day, the coroner, Mr J Kenyon Parker, opened the inquest. Evidence was taken from the family and the police and, in short order, the jury brought back a verdict of wilful murder against Law. The coroner immediately signed a warrant committing him for trial at the Assizes.

On the 28th he was back in Sheffield before the city's stipendiary magistrate, Mr Edward Welby. Not represented, he was seen to tremble as he stepped into dock. Badly affected by having to give evidence for what was the third time in a week was George Cotterill: as he gave his account he became more and more distressed and, when asked to describe what he found when he went up to his wife's room, he slumped in the chair moaning 'Oh, my head'. The evidence of the Cotterills, father and daughter, was followed by that of the neighbours, police officers and the police surgeon. With the intention of countering any suggestion which might thereafter be made that Law was insane at the time of the killing, the Crown called Professor Dean from the University. The accused was, he told the court, quite a normal person. A number of witnesses, who had known Law since his school days, were then called to say that they had never known him to behave in a strange or unusual manner. At the conclusion of the prosecution case, he made no answer to the charge and was immediately committed for trial.

While on remand at Wakefield Gaol, he wrote a letter to the Cotterills:

*Dear sir,*

*I write a line to you Hoping that you are well, both you and Edith and Sidney. And would like to know how you are Getting on; they tell me you are flitting, so I thought I would write to the Mill so you Would get this.*

*Please write Back and Let me know how you are getting on, for I think hours of you Both and I ham Sory that this has happened. I keep trying to think of who as done it, but I cannot, and what they have done it with, But my mind won't Let me.*

*I must have been out of my mind when this happened. When I got in that morning I hear some one in up the stears, and trying to think who it was but carnt. Please don't make me an enimy of yours. Because you know if I had got my Notic to Leave I shud go, but Little did I think it would be at this place; never been here befour and never had my name in a Poleman Book, but they have got me for the death of Miss Cotterill.*

*But I don't think it is me, for it takes me all my time to kill a foul ore a Blackclock that Edith well knows. But it seems to me that it is me with being at Mansfield but I don't know how I got there. I found little Charley running down the street. So Please write Back and Let me know if you have her anything of Who has Done it.*

[Following was a list of things he wanted sending to his brothers]

*I will close with The best of love to you all, and Forgive me. O plese don't say I threatened Miss Cotterill of her life, becose it is not the true, that you know Well.*

Law took his trial on December 1, 1913 at Leeds Winter Gaol Delivery before Mr Justice Darling.[146] Messrs Coutts Trotter and

[146] **Darling**, Charles John, lst Baron Darling; barrister 1874; QC 1885; appointed High Court judge 1897; his appointment met with unanimous and sweeping condemnation throughout the legal profession; and he won few admirers while on the bench not least because of his levity. Heuston, op. cit., p 55 says of him 'he was quite unable to conduct himself or the proceedings in his court with the requisite degree of dignified detachment' In 1900 his conduct at the Birmingham assizes provoked the editor of the *Birmingham Daily Argus* to write 'There is not a journalist in Birmingham who has anything to learn from the impudent little man in horse-hair, a microcosm of conceit and empty-headedness. [One of

Marsden appeared for the Crown.[147] Law was represented by Lewis Hoare.[148] Reporters noted that he looked considerably more haggard than on his last court appearance. The prosecution evidence followed the same course as in the lower courts but with the defence seeking to extract, where they could, concessions that Law had been considered strange and had been behaving oddly before the murder. To secure a verdict of guilty but insane they required all the help they could get, and some was forthcoming from the Cotterills who agreed that Law had been behaving strangely on the night before the murder.[149] Then it was the turn of the defence. The letter written by Law from Wakefield was put in. His brother, Arthur Law, said that their brother Albert, who was now 24, was in Wadsley Asylum and had been since he was 13 years old; their brother Ainsworth had been in an asylum for about 2 ½ years; and their sister Emily had died of insanity following child-birth. Five years ago his mother died of apoplexy. Her death had upset the accused's mental balance at the time and he had to be in the charge of a brother-in-law as they feared he might commit suicide. Stirling, the brother-in law, said all the family were a bit potty and he had got one of them; on three or four occasions in the past he had had to intervene to prevent the accused drowning himself in a river. His sister Polly described her strange encounter with him in Mansfield on the day of the murder. There was also evidence from schoolmates and acquaintances that the accused had always been

---

his biographer's] states that an eccentric relative left him much money. This misguided testator spoiled a successful bus conductor.'

[147] **Coutts Trotter**, see Walters n.7; **Marsden**, George, barrister 1910; practised on NE Circuit from chambers at 2, Garden Court, Temple.

[148] **Hoare,** Louis Gurney, barrister 1905; practised on NE Circuit from chambers at 2, Harcourt Buildings, Temple.

[149] At the inquest Mr Cotterill said that the family had considered him 'a bit rum but we took it to be his 'soft.'

'odd.' James Hawley, a publican of Harvest Lane, said that if the accused had a pint of beer he lost himself and was not conscious of his surroundings. Workmate, Thomas O'Mear, said that Law was sometimes not right in the head and, on one occasion, had attacked a foreman at work without provocation. In rebuttal, the Crown called Dr Benson Cook, the medical officer of the gaol. He had observed the prisoner every day since his arrival at the prison and, on some days, had seen him two or three times. He had seen nothing to suggest that he suffered from epilepsy or any form of mania. In his view, his mental condition was normal.

In a highly emotional closing speech defence counsel asked the jury whether it was conceivable that a sane man would commit a horrible and gruesome murder on a woman who had been a good friend to him.

> *What sane man would have slashed her all over, a wild continuous slashing, none of which wounds in themselves attacked a vital part? It is the act of a maniac and now he is here silently appealing to you to give him back his life. It would have been better if he had been let go and sleep where his mother is or that he be locked up in a lunatic asylum than that this should happen.*

As counsel was speaking, Law wept bitterly and at one point had to be supported by warders in his chair

In the judge's summing up the defence arguments received exceedingly short shrift. 'Insanity in law,' said Mr Justice Darling 'did not mean a man not being able to control himself. Nor did it mean having a brother or sister in an asylum or having been there himself. To reap the benefit of the special plea it must be shown that a prisoner was suffering from a mania or incapable of distinguishing between right and wrong.' He especially directed the jury's attention to the motive behind the crime as shown by the threats made. The prisoner simply said 'I got into a temper and killed someone'. If that were to be allowed [as a defence] no-one would be safe. [The jury should also ask themselves] whether the prisoner's actions after crime, his changing clothes and removing from himself all traces of the murder, were not actions of a sane man. Even the defence, he reminded them, had not contended that prisoner was insane five minutes after crime was committed or subsequently, but only when the murder was done. He made no reference to the letter which Law had written from prison and pooh-poohed the evidence of Stirling.

After half an hour's retirement the jury were back in court with a verdict of guilty

As sentence of death was passed Law was seen visibly to stagger. Seemingly dazed and half supported by the warders he was hurried below.

Notice of appeal was immediately lodged on his behalf. His appeal came on for hearing on in the Court of Criminal Appeal on December 15, 1913 before Lord Chief Justice Reading, Mr Justice Bray and Mr Justice Lush. Hoare, addressing the court on his behalf, said that the prisoner desired to appeal on the ground that, though he was guilty of the act charged, he was insane at the time and the defence of insanity was insufficiently left to the jury. 'Are you complaining of the summing up of the judge?' asked the Lord Chief Justice.

*I am. The summing up was objectionable on two grounds: the first was that it was extremely insufficient, that it dealt hardly at all and in a way calculated to brush it aside with the general case for insanity, and it dealt with Stirling's evidence as though it were the only serious evidence called for the prisoner and because Stirling had said the whole family were dotty therefore other witnesses were not to be believed.*

*It threw the evidence of the defence into altogether false perspective because it looked as if the evidence of insanity was based entirely on the evidence of Stirling, and that the evidence of Stirling was not to be believed, or so open to comment as to be worthless.*

*The judge had rather airily dismissed the general body of evidence called by the defence which ought to have been led with great care before the jury.*

Without calling upon the Crown, the Lord Chief Justice gave judgment dismissing the appeal.

*The court was asked to say that the summing up was unsatisfactory and that the conviction ought to be quashed because the learned judge did not point out in more detail the whole of the evidence called on behalf of the defence, and rested his comment upon the criticism of one witness whose statement was too general.*

*There was a good deal of force in the observations made by Mr Hoare with regard to that evidence, and no doubt he urged it upon the jury, but it must be borne in mind that the case was tried in one day and that all the witnesses and all the evidence were before the jury on that day.*

*They knew exactly what point they had to consider, and they had the witnesses in front of them.*

*The Court must take the summing up as a whole, and it could not be said to have been unfavourable to the prisoner. There were passages in the earlier part of the summing up which were distinctly favourable to the prisoner and were as fairly put as would be possible. The Court could not say that any fault could properly be found in the summing up.*

*Attention had been directed by Mr Hoare to the evidence called on behalf of the prisoner to establish insanity at the time of committing the action. There was a considerable amount of evidence of what one might call a bad family history in this respect, and some very cogent evidence was called on this point.*

*A body of evidence was also called to show that the prisoner at the time was moody and depressed and that, after his mother died which was some five or six years before this act was committed, he had not looked the same. He had been to use the expressions of witnesses, 'dotty,' 'barmy,' depressed and melancholy. Evidence was given that within 12 months before he committed the act a door fell on him, which in some way injured him and affected his head.*

*It was right to say that there was a considerable body of evidence of that character upon which the jury could have acted if they had accepted it in its entirety, rejecting a considerable body of evidence called for the Crown and they could have found that he was insane at the time he committed the act. But it was not possible for their Lordships, sitting in the Court of Criminal Appeal, not having had the opportunity of hearing and observing the witnesses to interfere with the verdict which there was ample evidence to support and which was given upon a right direction.*

*In these matters, The Home Secretary had opportunities, which their Lordships had not, to seek and get reliable advice; all the Court could say was that they could not interfere with the verdict appealed against, and they must leave it to such inquiry as the Home Secretary might think to make and to act upon in any way he might think proper.*

Following the dismissal of the appeal, a medical commission was sent to the prison to examine Law. Having considered its report, the Home Secretary announced that there would be no reprieve.

On the last day of 1913 Law was executed at Wakefield prison.[150] 'He walked unflinchingly to his fate' the *Sheffield*

[150] Thomas Pierrepoint was the hangman.

*Independent* told its readers. During his final days he had received no visit from any of his family or friends.

### The Chinese laundry murder - Lee Doon, 1922 [151]

When Sing Lee arrived in England he was just 25 years of age. His aim was to better himself and by hard work he did just that. In 1919, already the owner of a successful Chinese laundry in Liverpool, he opened a second at 231, Crookes Road, Sheffield, a seven room house, the ground floor of which had been converted into shop premises. The new business thrived and was soon taking up most of his time. By summer 1922, working there in addition to Sing Lee were Lee Doon, who lived in,[152] and shop manager Lily Siddall,[153] who had been there since February. By now Sing Lee was a familiar figure in the neighbourhood. He lunched most days at Wilkinson's' refreshment shop and was an occasional patron of a local hotel and a local wine and spirits shop, from which he would purchase stout, whisky and wine. He was extremely well thought of. Customers were impressed by the cleanliness of his shop, his pleasant manner and his scrupulous honesty and his fellow countrymen knew they could turn to him for help and sound advice.

So far as the laundry staff were concerned, Saturday, September 9, was a day like any other. The shop was busy and everyone was glad when closing time arrived. As Miss Siddall was leaving at 8.30

---

151 See *Sheffield Independent*, Sept 18, 22, Dec 2, 21, 1922; *Sheffield Telegraph*, Sept 23, Dec 2 1922; Jan. 5, 6, 1923; *Star*, Sept 16, 18,19, 21, 22, 1922; *The Times*, Dec 21, 1923.

152 Aged 27 and also known as Leong Lun.

153 Aged 23 and living with her parents at 154, Forncett Street, Sheffield.

pm, Sing Lee asked if she would call in on Sunday as usual and open the shop up for a couple of hours. She readily agreed and bade him good night, leaving him on the premises with Lee Doon.

When she arrived at 11.30 am on the Sunday she was surprised to find Lee Doon up and about. Usually he and Sing Lee slept late on a Sunday. 'Where is the boss?' she asked.

'Gone away.'

'Where has he gone?'

'I not know, I think he go back to China. This business belong to me now.'

It all struck Lily Siddall as very strange.

When she turned up on Monday another surprise awaited her; from the cellar there were sounds of digging. She asked what it meant. 'Not your business Lee Doon,' told her.

'Has the landlord sent the men?'

'Not your business.'

Determined to get to the bottom of the matter she went down to the cellar. There she found two men[154] hard at work with pick and shovel. 'What are you doing?' she asked. They told her that Lee Doon had approached them on the Sunday and said that he wanted a hole digging in the cellar. When they went into the cellar they saw that somebody had been digging near to the front wall. Fearful that the pavement would come in, they had bricked it up and begun the present hole well away from the wall.

---

[154] They were Walter Thornhill of 44, Toyne Street and a friend of his, named Crookes. Doon told them that the hole was to hold a water tub, a supply of water being needed in the cellar to keep down coke dust.

A little time after this Lee Doon went out. While he was gone Miss Siddall went into Sing Lee's bedroom. In it were his hat, attache case and other belongings which he always took with him when he went away on business. Later in the day a van from Proctors' store delivered two parcels which Lee Doon opened. One contained a quilt, the other two sheets and a pillow. 'Do you like them?' he asked.

When she arrived at the laundry on Tuesday, Lee Doon told her that someone had fetched the boss's trunk and taken it away in a taxi, but he did not know where. He was wearing a pair of Sing Lee's trousers. 'Why have you got those on?' she asked. 'Mine are dirty I am washing them,' he told her. She also asked him why the boss's bedding was being washed and why there was blood on one of the windows. 'Bedding dirty. Blood from chicken.'

In the afternoon two more parcels addressed to Lee Doon arrived; one contained a new hat, the other a pair of shoes. At tea time Lee, after making an indecent suggestion to Lily, offered her 30 shillings to look after the shop for the rest of the week. She angrily pushed him away and made for the door. 'Who'll look after the shop?' he called after her. 'Look after it yourself,' she replied. On the Wednesday morning, after inquiring whether there had been any letters from Sing Lee, and being told 'No,' she announced that she did not intend coming back to work until Sing Lee returned.

Somebody else who was by now asking about Sing Lee was his friend, Thomas Marshall, who lived at 7, Toftwood Road, Crookes. On the previous Friday he had suggested to him that the two of them go to the *Hippodrome* on Monday, first house. 'I'll think about it,' said Sing Lee. On Monday, he called in the shop to find out whether he was going or not. There he found Lee Doon, on his own, singing from a Chinese song book. 'Where's Sing Lee?' he enquired. 'Had telegram. Gone to London, Took £100 with him,' Lee Doon told his astonished enquirer. On the Monday night, Marshall called again. The shop door being locked, he looked through the window and saw Lee Doon struggling with a trunk. He called again on the Wednesday asking if there was any news of Sing Lee. There was not.

On the Wednesday, Miss Siddall, who was extremely troubled by the turn events had taken, decided to make some inquiries of her own. She called first on Sing Sai, a friend of her boss who lived in Barnsley Road. 'Had he heard or seen anything of Sing Lee?' 'Nothing at all,' he told her. She then sent off a telegram to the shop in Prescott Road, Liverpool asking if Sing Lee was there. 'Not here,' came back the reply. On Thursday she called in again at the shop at Crookes. 'Has there been any letter from Sing Lee?' she asked. 'No,' said Lee Doon. 'Don't think boss come back any more. Perhaps go to China.[155] Perhaps go to Liverpool.' After consulting further with Sing Sai she set out for Liverpool. There she spoke to Sing Lee's cousin, Sun Kwong Lee. After listening to her story, he agreed immediately to come back with her to Sheffield.

Having arrived in the city in the early hours of Saturday morning, they went immediately to the police and, within a short time, police officers were hammering on the door of the laundry. The door was eventually opened by Lee Doon. 'Where is Sing Lee?' they

---

[155] According to Miss Siddall, Sing Lee had a wife , a child and an adopted child in China and had been intending to take a six-month holiday with them the following year. 'He must have saved a good deal of money. Although he said he should sell the Liverpool shop, he intended to keep the shop at Crookes. He liked England too well to go back to China to live and said there was not enough money to be made there.' (*Sheffield Independent*, Sept 18, 1922).

asked. 'Gone away,' he told them. They asked to look at the cellar. It was well stocked with coal and coke with nothing seemingly out of order. However, when the coke was removed, it immediately became apparent that the clay floor had recently been disturbed. As dawn began to break, the officers started to dig. Lee Doon looked on, affecting disinterest. Soon one of the shovels struck something hard. It quickly became clear that what it had hit was a metal trunk. The trunk was dug out, carried upstairs and opened. Inside was a man's body. Doon was immediately told he was under arrest. 'I no understand,' he replied and, with that, he was taken off to police headquarters. When searched he was found to have on him £30 in cash, including two five pound notes, and to be wearing a sovereign ring. The ring was later identified as Sing Lee's and it was also established that Sing Lee had had two five pound notes paid over to him in the week before he disappeared

Soon after Lee Doon had been taken off, Dr Carter, the police surgeon and university lecturer in forensic medicine, arrived at the premises. At just before 7.30 am be began his examination of the trunk and contents. The trunk when measured was 29½ inches long, 18 inches wide and 22 inches high at the top of the domed lid. The body inside was lying on its back and trussed up with rope, with its knees flexed and a running noose round the neck; it was dressed in singlet and drawers. There were gaping wounds to the head, including a deep wound which extended from the lower end of the ear to beneath the jaw; also in the trunk were a pillow and pillow case much stained with blood. On later post-mortem examination the doctor found extensive fractures of the skull, including severe fractures at the base of the skull on the left side. Death had taken place seven to eight days previously and had occurred about one and a half hours after the deceased had taken a meal of rice and lentils. The injuries had been caused by a blunt instrument and could not have been self inflicted. The cause of death was head injury and haemorrhage. The amount of blood on the bedding suggested that the deceased had been killed in bed.

At 10.30 that morning, Lee Doon appeared before the city magistrates. Smartly dressed and turned out, when asked if he understood English, he shook his head. After hearing evidence from police officers as to the finding of the trunk, the magistrates remanded him in custody until the following Friday. [156]

On Monday, September 18, the coroner, Mr Kenyon Parker, opened the inquest upon Sing Lee. There were at once language difficulties, with a brother of the deceased, called to identify the body, struggling to understand the questions asked of him. However, enough evidence having been given to establish identity the coroner issued a burial certificate and, observing that an interpreter would be needed next time, adjourned the hearing until 2.30 pm on the Friday.

On Thursday the 20th the dead man was buried in the section of Anfield cemetery reserved for Chinese burials. The funeral had been scheduled for 1 pm but, owing to the hearse breaking down en route from Sheffield, it got under way two hours late. A vast concourse of people had assembled in the Chinese quarter to greet its arrival, and from many business premises the Chinese republican flag was being flown draped in black. The coffin was transferred to a horse-drawn

[156] During the morning large inquisitive crowds gathered outside the laundry. Even the *Star* was caught up in the excitement. 'Fiction has not produced a more thrilling and dramatic sequel to a mysterious disappearance,' it declared (September 16, 1922).

hearse, which then set off for the cemetery, followed by three carriages and seven taxis carrying friends and family of the deceased. The burial was carried out in accordance with the rites of the Church of England, with the Revd Hutchinson, the vicar of St Bartholomew's, Liverpool, officiating.

On Friday afternoon, the inquest was resumed. After an interpreter had been sworn, the coroner addressed the jury briefly. Lee Doon was then brought in, handcuffed to a policeman. The reporters noted that he was shaking a little. After evidence had been taken from Miss Siddall, the police surgeon and the officers who found the trunk, Lee Doon was asked if he wished to give evidence. To everyone's surprise he indicated that he did.

> *Sing Lee wrote to me in Manchester and asked me to come to Sheffield I saw him taking morphia and I told him not to do it and he started fighting with me. We had a fight and I struck him. I found I had killed him. At the time I did not know the consequence. I was afraid and put him in the box. Then I took the box down to the cellar. I then engaged two men to dig a hole so that I could hide it and no one would be any the wiser. I covered the hole up. The deceased is one of my relatives and I leave it to the bench.*

Following a brief summing up, the jury instantly returned a verdict of murder Saturday saw the prisoner back before the city magistrates. The case had attracted enormous interest and, at 10.30 am, there was a huge crowd outside the court-house. Just before 11, they were let in, with spectators, for the first time in years, being admitted to the upper galleries. The magistrates were Sydney

Robinson and J W Flint, Mr Wing appeared for the DPP and local solicitor, Keeble Hawson, for the accused.

In opening the case, Mr Flint commended Miss Siddall for her detective work. He also referred to the claim which the accused had made at the inquest that the dead man was a morphia user. As at the inquest Miss Siddall was the principal witness. Mr Marshall, who had been hoping to visit the *Hippodrome* with the deceased, told of seeing the prisoner trying to drag a trunk upstairs. He had, he said, never heard of the deceased using morphine and police officers testified that a search of the laundry premises, carried out since the inquest, had failed to unearth any evidence of the drug. This time, when charged and asked if he wished to make any statement, Lee Doon reserved his defence. He was committed for trial.

That trial took place at Leeds Winter Gaol Delivery on December l, 1922, before Mr Justice Greer.[157] Mr W J Waugh KC, with Mr H V Rabaghati, appeared for the prosecution, Mr W P Donald for the accused.[158] Opening the case Mr Waugh referred to the explanation proffered by the accused at the inquest. Even if the two men had quarrelled, he argued, the amount of force used to inflict the injuries went far beyond anything necessary for the accused's own defence, but the doctor's evidence that the dead man had been killed in his bed negatived the suggestion that there had been a

[157] **Greer**, Frederick Arthur, baron Fairfield (1863-1945); educ Aberdeen GS and university; barrister 1886; practised in Liverpool and London; KC 1910; High Court judge 1919; Lord Justice of Appeal, 1927; baron 1939.

[158] **Waugh**, William James, (1856-1931); barrister 1880; practised on NE Circuit from chambers in Bradford; KC 1906; Recorder of Middlesborough 1910; Recorder of Sheffield 1915; retired from bar 1927; **Rabagliatti,** Herman Victor, barrister 1908; practised on NE Circuit; QC 1937; **Donald,** William Pennington, barrister 1904, practised on NE Circuit from 42, Bank Street, Sheffield.

quarrel. The same witnesses having given evidence as in the lower court, the Crown closed its case. The only new fact to emerge had been evidence from the police surgeon to the effect that he had found no trace of opium or morphia in the dead man's body on post-mortem examination, which he would have expected to find if the dead man had been addicted to these drugs.

Lee Doon now went into the witness box:

> *On the Saturday after closing the shop at 9 pm I went into the drying room at the back of the house and lay on a sofa there. Sing Lee, after removing the silver from the till upstairs, came into the drying room and stood in front of the stove. He said 'I wish I had an opium pipe so that I could have a smoke. It would be worth 3s to have a smoke.' I asked him what he wanted to smoke opium for. I said 'You have only £300 or £400 saved up and, if they get to know, you will be arrested.' Lee replied his smoking had nothing to do with him. He got vexed and made use of abusive language. I retorted by calling him a few names. He rolled up his sleeves and said he wanted to fight. He came for me and then there was a fight and in the fight we fell to the ground, Lee striking his head on the stove. A flat iron fell from the stove and hit Lee on the head. Lee had said I was illegitimate and had no ancestors and that made me very angry. When I saw Lee was bleeding I wrapped his head up in two towels and took him back upstairs and put him on the bed. I put two pillows under him to raise him up, took his shirt and trousers off and covered him up with a blanket. I went for a drink for him and on my return I found him dead. I got frightened, saw the trunk and put him in it He was too long for the trunk so I put one rope round his neck and the other round his feet to pull him together so that he would fit into the box He had then been dead an hour. I got frightened. I knew I should be held responsible for his death so I thought I would bury him. I washed up the blood.*

In cross-examination, he said that he had battered the dead man's head against the flat iron five or six times. 'I took him by the armpits to get him upstairs. At that stage he had the use of his legs.'

In the light of this claim, Dr Carter was recalled. He said that he did not believe that Sing Lee would have been conscious after being struck with the iron or could have taken any part in going upstairs.

In his closing speech, Mr Donald argued that the blows the accused struck were in self defence and that, in any event, it was not proved that when he struck them he intended either to kill or to cause grievous bodily harm to the Sing Lee.

In his summing up the judge drew the jury's attention to a contradiction in the prisoner's evidence; he had said that the iron had fallen on the left side of Sing Lee's face and, also, that during the struggle Sing Lee was lying on his left side.

The jury returned with a verdict of guilty just before eight o'clock. As sentence of death was passed the Town Hall clock was just striking the hour. The prisoner's face was expressionless as he was sentenced, but he appeared dazed as he was taken below.

Notice of appeal against conviction was duly lodged on his behalf, alleging that the judge had misdirected the jury and urging the court to substitute a conviction for manslaughter. The appeal came on for hearing in the Court of Criminal Appeal on December 20, 1922. It was dismissed in short order without the Crown being called upon. Delivering the judgement of the court, Lord Chief Justice Hewart said that there was no doubt who committed the murder because many of Sing Lee's goods, including his wallet with money in it, had found on the prisoner.

A petition to the Home Secretary for a reprieve proved equally unavailing.

During the time he was awaiting execution, Lee Doon was visited by a Chinaman living in Leeds. He interpreted the condemned man's requests to the prison governor and, by this means, was been able to secure a change of diet for him (he preferred vegetables to potatoes and also wanted bacon for breakfast) and books to read. To his visitor Lee Doon made no confession but insisted that he never intended to kill Sing Lee. He repeatedly expressed his dismay at the fact he was to be hanged, saying he would prefer to be beheaded. Described by the *Sheffield Telegraph*[159] as the loneliest man in England, he was hanged at Armley prison on January 5, 1923.[160]

The jurymen attending the prison inquest were shown his cell. The floor was strewn with cigarette ends and there was a beer bottle top on the floor. They were told that Lee Doon had had a very good night before his execution. He had risen in good time the next morning, eaten a hearty breakfast and then smoked several cigarettes. He had walked to the scaffold, gazing calmly at those present, and on the drop had arranged his feet very carefully and precisely next to the chalk marks.

The morning was dismal and cold with drizzling rain. Shortly before 9 am there was only a small knot of people assembled outside the main gates but, as the hour of execution approached, the crowd swelled. A few moments after 9 am the prison bell began to toll, signifying that the execution was in progress. When the statutory notices were posted at the gates spectators rushed forward to read

[159] December 28, 1922.
[160] The hangman was Thomas Pierrepoint.

them. They included a man 'with two small girls both of whom evinced a morbid interest in [perusing them].'

Before Lee Doon only two Chinamen had hanged in England: Pong Lun and Sem Lee both executed at Walton Gaol on May 31 1904 and March 30, 1909 respectively.[161]

## A disastrous elopement - John William Eastwood, 1923 [162]

On June 30, 1923, 39-year-old John William Eastwood, the licensee of the *Bay Horse* in Daniel Hill Street, Walkley[163] ran away to Liverpool with Mildred Parramore, one of his customers. The romance quickly soured and by July 12 both were back in Sheffield. Mildred's husband took her back. Ethel Eastwood, however, proved less forgiving and, when her errant husband turned up on the doorstep of the public house, she refused to let him in. In his absence she had, or so it was suspected, struck up a relationship with her barman, John Clark, a 48-year old steel works stamper, who had helped out behind the bar for some years. Eastwood, desperate to get his wife to change her mind, asked Clark to plead his cause with her. When this produced no result he took to calling in at the public house of an evening for a drink, but Ethel simply ignored him. Sometimes at the

---

[161] 'Come on, Ping Pong,' was the insulting remark which the unfeeling Billington addressed to Pong Lun when he entered the condemned cell to pinion him. At least Lee Doon was spared that kind of boorishness.

[162] See *Sheffield Independent*, Jly 30, 31, Aug 4, Dec 8, 28, 1923; *Sheffield Telegraph*, Aug 1, 6, 11, Dec 28, 29, 1923; *Star*, Jly 31, Aug 6, 11, 22, 27, Dec 7, 8, 28, 29, 1923; *The Times*, Dec 29, 1923.

[163] According to the *Sheffield Independent*, the couple had taken the public house some 18 months before. Prior to that he had worked as a chimney sweep and his wife had a buffing shop which she managed very successfully. It stood at the corner of Daniel Hill Street and Harworth Street.

end of the night he tried to force the issue by refusing to leave and the police had to be called. His hopes for a reconciliation took a severe knock when on July 26, at the transfer sessions, the beer-house licence was transferred into Ethel's name. It was just over a fortnight since his return from Liverpool and his situation was desperate. He was sleeping where he could: either at the home of Arthur Hilton and his wife in Conduit Street; or at no. 1, court 8, Greaves Street; or on the settee at Clark's home at 41, Ripon Street. He was eking out a living as a chimney sweep..

On morning of Saturday, July 28, he bumped into Mildred in Wallace Road. 'If my wife won't have me back, I'll do him,' he confided but didn't explain who it was he was talking about. At lunchtime he was in the *Bay Horse* where he spent some time chatting, apparently amicably, to Clark. He was back at the bar in the evening drinking steadily. His wife would later, irrelevantly, recall that one of his drinks was a lemon dash. He asked her to let him stay but was turned down. At closing time he time he showed a marked reluctance to leave but eventually did so after some 'peaceful persuasion.' Just after midnight, using his latch key, he let himself into his lodgings in Conduit Street. Arthur Hilton and his wife were asleep when he walked into their bedroom. 'I'm going to knock him up,' he announced. He then threw his latch key on the table saying 'I shan't want that any more.' Hilton, who could see an axe sticking out of his trouser pocket, shouted 'Don't be a fool,' but Eastwood took no notice and they heard him descend the stairs and let himself out.

At about 1.30 am Clark and his wife were in bed when Mrs Clark was awoken by the sound of someone throwing pebbles at the window. She looked out and saw it was Eastwood. She roused her husband and sent him downstairs to see what he wanted, surmising that he probably had nowhere to sleep. Minutes later she heard the door bang and the sound of a scuffle. She hurried down and found her husband rolling on the kitchen floor next to the wringer, bleeding from his head, and Eastwood standing over him with a hatchet in his hand. Eastwood then turned heel and made his way to the police station at Burgoyne Road where he spoke to Hughes, the duty inspector. 'I want you to go to 20, Lister Road,' he said. 'I believe I have done John Clark in with a hatchet, which I have thrown away probably in the chapel yard in Walkley Road.' The inspector ordered him detained. To PC Peach, the officer who placed him in the cells, Eastwood volunteered further detail:

> *He let me in the back door. As he was locking the door, I hit him on the head with the hatchet. He fell on the floor and then I hit him twice more.*

The Inspector had, by now, set out for Lister Road. On arriving at no. 20 he saw that all the lights were on. The back door was closed but it opened a little when he pushed it. Looking in, he could see a man's foot. Pushing the door further ajar, he stepped inside and saw, lying on the floor, a man, dressed in shirt and trousers; he was unconscious and there were two wounds to the back of his head, one very deep. Mrs Clark, who was on the stairs, told him 'Jack Eastwood has done this. I don't know what he has done it for.' An ambulance was sent for and Clark taken to the Royal Infirmary. There he was found to have three wounds and a severe fracture to the skull. He underwent an emergency operation but to no avail: at 8.48 am he died.

At 10.05 Eastwood was charged with murder. ‘Yes sir,’ he replied.

In the meanwhile a hatchet, on the back of which was a large quantity of fresh blood, was recovered by the police from the chapel yard at the junction of Walkley Bank and Walkley Road. It was later identified as having come from the *Bay Horse* where it was kept in the back yard.

Local reporters were soon on the scene. One of their ports of call, in their search for copy, was the public house and there they found Eastwood’s wife more than willing to talk. The dead man had, she said, repeatedly tried to effect a reconciliation between her husband and herself. When her husband returned to Sheffield from Liverpool, the deceased was the first person he had gone to see. Since then he had allowed Eastwood to stay at his house on several occasions. She intended to visit Mrs Clark. ‘I am thinking of [her] and his children,’ she said, bursting into tears ’their breadwinner is gone.’[164]

On July 29, Eastwood was brought before the city magistrates. A heavily built man, with stern, bronzed features, wearing a blue suit but no collar or tie, he appeared both cool and collected. Evidence was given by Inspector Hughes of the events of the Sunday morning. A request that the hearing be adjourned until Saturday was granted, with the accused remanded in custody.

---

[164] Clark had two sons Jack, aged 18 and Henry, aged 10. Also, living at no. 20 was Clark’s 74 year-old- father.

The following day an inquest into Clark's death was held by the coroner, J Kenyon Parker, Evidence was taken from the dead man's widow, Arthur Hilton, Mildred Parramore, Inspector Hughes and PC Peach. Dr Clarke from the Infirmary testified that a skull fracture was the cause of death. After a brief summing up, the jury returned a verdict of wilful murder. Eastwood received the verdict with his head bowed and, when the coroner announced that he was committed to Leeds Assizes for trial, his whole body trembled and his hands twitched feverishly.

On the Friday, August 3, large crowds assembled outside the dead man's house and at Walkley cemetery to watch the funeral cortege and the burial. Among the mourners, noted the *Sheffield Independent,* was Ethel Eastwood.

The magistrates' committal hearing was finally resumed (after several adjournments) on August 21. Mr J E Wing appeared to prosecute. Eastwood was represented by local solicitor Charles Nixon.[165] It quickly became clear that the defence strategy was to try and lay the ground for a defence of insanity. The dead man's widow was cross-examined about the terms the two men had been on before the killing. 'Relations between them were good,' she replied. 'I know of no reason why he should want to hurt my husband.' Inspector Hughes was asked about the prisoner's medical and family background. 'My inquiries show that he was admitted to the Ecclesall institution in February 1915 suffering from syphilis. His father and uncle both died in Wadsley asylum, the former from paralysis, the latter from melancholia following war service.' Dr Brockam, from

---

[165] Charles Wyril Nixon, Queen Street Chambers, Queen Street, Sheffield.

the Royal Infirmary, called to give evidence about the deceased's injuries, found himself being asked about the link between syphilis and insanity. 'Many people,' he said 'with a history, such as Eastwood had, were mentally normal. Syphilis would not predispose a sufferer to suicide until he was quite off his head and if a man so suffering did go insane he did not recover.' The prosecution, even at this stage, were ready with witnesses in rebuttal. Particularly damaging evidence was given by William Weeks, a young man who was keeping company with the Eastwoods' 20-year-old daughter Ethel.[166] He claimed that on July 15 (less than a week after his return from Liverpool) the prisoner had produced a razor and said 'This is for Jack Clark. He has told me to find somewhere else to sleep today. His wife objects to me sleeping on their couch and it means I shall be homeless. That's after promising to find me shelter.' Later that day he had again taken out the razor saying 'I'm going to finish the job.' Weeks immediately took it off him. In cross-examination, he agreed that Eastwood's conduct had always been queer in the 14 months he had known him. He had several times heard him threaten his wife and he was always talking about doing the whole lot of them in, himself too. Indeed, Mrs Eastwood had become so fearful that he would do some harm to someone in the house that she had asked him, Weeks, to sleep there to protect them. Mildred Parramore, who had the embarrassing experience of having to admit her infidelity in public, said, in the course of her evidence, that while they were in Liverpool Eastwood had talked of killing himself. At the conclusion of the prosecution case, which had broadly followed the lines of the inquest

---

[166] As well as Ethel, there was a younger child, 14-year-old John William.

evidence, the accused announced that he had nothing to say and intended to reserve his defence. The magistrates thereupon committed him for trial. His solicitor asked the court to grant a defence certificate: Eastwood was entirely without means; his wife allowed him nothing and he did not think that, in any event, she had the funds to pay for his defence. The application was granted.

Eastwood took his trial on December 7, 1923, at the Leeds Winter Gaol Delivery before Mr Justice Talbot.[167] W J Waugh QC and T Hedley appeared for the Crown, FJO Coddington for the prisoner.[168] Opening the case for the prosecution, Mr Waugh told the jury that the motive for the killing was jealousy. From the evidence to be given and from statements made by the prisoner himself they would be left in no doubt that the deceased and the prisoner's wife were on intimate terms. As he was addressing them one of the jurors collapsed. After a brief adjournment a replacement juror was sworn and the trial resumed. This was but the first of several untoward incidents which would occur during the trial. When the name of Dr Clayton, one of the Crown's medical witnesses was called, there was no answer. Counsel, with some embarrassment, rose to explain that since the police court hearing Dr Clayton had sailed for China. The judge, less than impressed, ordered that he forfeit the sum of £50. During the trial, while the other medical evidence was being gone, through Eastwood became extremely agitated and began to clutch at

[167] **Talbot**, Sir George John (1861-1938); educ Winchester and Christ Church, Oxford; Fellow of All Souls 1886; barrister 1887; KC 1906; High Court judge 1923; Heuston, op cit, p 436 describes him as 'deeply respected by the bar.'

[168] **Waugh**, see above; **Hedley**, Walter, barrister 1904; practised on NE Circuit; Recorder of Richmond; **Coddington,** Fitzherebert John Osborne, barrister 1912, practised on NE Circuit from chambers At 42, Bank Street, Sheffield.

his throat. 'The accused is feeling ill,' Coddington explained and the proceedings were halted until he recovered. The concentration of the jury was also disturbed from time to time by noise from the street. Outside the Town Hall several thousand people were waiting to learn the results of the city's contests in the General Election and, as each result was given, there was loud cheering.

The evidence took predictable form, the witnesses called being those who had testified at the inquest and committal hearing. To deal with any suggestion that the prisoner was insane the Crown called Dr R D Worsley, the medical officer at Armley. He said there was nothing to suggest that the prisoner's mind was unhinged at the time of the killing. With this, his assistant, Dr Hoyland Smith disagreed. In his view, at the time of the killing, Eastwood had not known the quality of the act he was committing although he knew an hour afterwards what he had done. The defence by their cross-examination of Crown witnesses were able to get in evidence the accused's medical history (as well as having suffered from syphilis in the past he had also been rejected for army service because of neurasthenia), the history of insanity in his family and a good deal of more general evidence to the effect that he was generally considered queer.

In his closing speech, Coddington invited the jury to return a verdict of guilty but insane. He must have known, as he spoke, that the most he could hope for was a sympathy verdict. Within half an hour of the killing Eastwood had presented himself at a police station and given a clear and accurate account of what he had done and how he had disposed of the murder weapon. In the light of that how could it realistically be argued that, at the time of the killing, he did not know what he was doing or, alternatively, that he did not know that it was against the law, which is what the defence had to prove if he was to escape the death sentence? The jury were back in half an hour with a guilty verdict coupled with a recommendation to mercy. Mr Justice Talbot, whose first murder trial this was, told Eastwood that he had been convicted on evidence which left the jury no alternative but to bring in a verdict of guilty and, donning the black cap, he proceeded to pass sentence of death. He warned Eastwood that he must not count on the sentence not being executed, and beseeched him to use the short time he had 'to seek mercy where only it can be found.' Eastwood immediately collapsed and had to be carried from the dock.

His lawyers did not seek to appeal his conviction but a petition was got up for his reprieve. The petition, bearing several thousands of signatures including those of a number of professional men, placed heavy reliance upon the evidence given by Dr Hoyland Smith at trial. It was presented at the Home Office by the Sheffield Hillsborough MP, M A W Alexander. The outcome was announced in a telegram sent by the MP to the *Sheffield Telegraph* on December 27:

> *H Secretary unable to grant reprieve Eastwood. ALEXANDER*

The condemned man was executed at Armley Gaol at 9 am the next day.[169] The Leeds public showed little interest in the event. There was no crowd outside the prison and the posting of the notice of execution attracted no more than passing interest. Reporters were told by the prison staff that Eastwood passed a fair night before his execution but had to be assisted to the scaffold.

---

[169] John Ellis was the hangman.

## The Princess Street gang murder
## Wilfred and Lawrence Fowler, 1925 [170]

In the early 1920s organised pitch and toss betting in Sheffield was controlled by the infamous Mooney Gang based in West Bar. The best known tossing ring was that at Skye Edge, an area of high ground above the Park which still offers panoramic views of the city. At such meets the gang would post look-outs to watch for the police and provide a 'tosser' to toss the coins. Their profit came from the toll which they levied on bets placed and was considerable. In his running of the ring Mooney was assisted by a Park villain, named Sam Garvin, and a number of other Park criminals. By 1923, owing to the economic slump, profits from the Sky-Edge ring had dropped so much that Mooney decided to dispense with Garvin and his henchman. The latter's response was to form his own gang, known as the Park Brigade, which quickly seized control of the ring. Over the next eight months Mooney was twice attacked in his home after which he left the city for a time. His departure did not, however, mark the end of gang violence. In December 1924, the Park Brigade smashed up the home of his associate Tommy Rippon. Five months later one of the Park gang was attacked with an iron bar outside Edmund Road drill hall. Nor did the big gangs lack imitators: in the East end there were, by 1925, several gangs operating protection rackets enforced by ready resort to the razor. In April 1925, gang

[170] See J.P. Bean, *The Sheffield Gang Wars*, D & D Publications, Sheffield, 1981; J. Morton, *Gangland, Vol. 2*, Little Brown & Co, London 1994, pp. 185-95; *Sheffield Independent*, Apl 28, 29; May 19, 20, 21, 22, 26, 27, 28, 29, 30; Jne 17, 18, 20: Jly 29, 30, 31; Aug 1, 17, 19, 1925; *Sheffield Telegraph*, May 19, 26, 27, 29; Jly 29, 30, 31; Aug 17, 1925; *The Star*, Apl 28, 30; May 2, 6, 20, 21, 25, 27; Jly 28, 29, 30, 31; Aug 1, 18, 20; Sept 3, 4, 1925; *The Times*, Aug 1, 19, 1925.

violence took its most serious turn yet when a man was stabbed to death yards from his home in Princess Street, Attercliffe.

Today Princess Street is home to a number of small firms and businesses. In 1925 it consisted of dismal back-to-backs and courts. One of the places where its inhabitants did their drinking was a beer-house in nearby Windsor Street, known to locals as the *Windsor Hotel* or more simply the *Windsor*. Near there on the evening of Sunday April 26 occurred an incident which the next night would lead to a fatal street attack. In the *Windsor* that Sunday were Garvin, gang member William Fowler, with two of his associates, and Harold Liversidge, a stranger to the district. At around 10 pm, Liversidge went outside and stood across the road with his back to the wall and his hands in his pockets. Shortly afterwards Fowler came out, went straight up to him and struck him in the face. According to the landlady, Mrs Addis, when he struck the blow Fowler said 'There's a gang here.' Other witnesses claimed that they heard him say 'You will remember me. I am Spinks Fowler.' A remark made to or about some women had apparently triggered the attack.

Liversidge, with his nose bleeding heavily, beat a hasty retreat and made his way to the home of William Francis ('Jock') Plommer at 42, Princess St. Thirty-three-year-old Plommer was a labourer at Bessemer & Co. Strong and well built, he had served in the army through the Great War, emerging with the rank of sergeant and also had boxing experience. Having explained to Plommer how he had been attacked, Liversidge asked for his help, and shortly afterwards the pair of them set off for the *Windsor* accompanied by Albert Cooper, who had been at No 42 when he called. Following behind were Mrs Plommer, Mrs Cooper and the Plommers' eleven-year-old son. Liversidge would later claim that his object in returning was to fight Fowler man to man, and that he had asked Plommer and Cooper to accompany him to keep Fowler's companions off and ensure a fair fight. "I said to Fowler,' he told an inquest jury 'You have struck me in face for nothing. I want to have a fair fight with you.' Then each of us took his coat off and we started fighting.[171] Plommer did not take part he just said 'This has to be a fair fight.' By the time it was over, Fowler had a cut to the back of his head which needed stitches. How he got it would be the subject of much dispute. He always insisted that when he started to get on top, he was struck on the head with a poker and that the man who hit him was Plommer. 'Nonsense,'claimed Liversidge 'the fight was between me and Fowler. Plommer took no part in it and certainly had no weapon.' This much is clear, however: Fowler's parting words, after Plommer, had helped him to his feet were 'Jock, you are in for a tanning for this.' Why he should have made Plommer the target for his anger, if all he had done was merely to hold the ring, has never been explained. Did Plommer, in fact hit him, or was Fowler's grievance that he had made him fight man to man?

That Fowler had been worsted in the fight outside the *Windsor* was soon common knowledge in the East End, and Sam Garvin, if his actions on the following evening are anything to go by, seems to have regarded it as an opportunity for his gang to make their presence felt. Not only would Plommer be made to pay but so too would his pals, particularly any who had played a part in Sunday night's events.

---

[171] The fight drew a number of spectators including James 'Spud' Murphy.

The first sign of trouble on the Monday evening came when gang members turned up in public houses in the vicinity of Princess Street and the Wicker, asking for the addresses of Plommer, Cooper and Liversidge. As 8 pm approached, there were at least ten gang members in the area including Wilfred Fowler, his elder brother Lawrence and gang leader Sam Garvin. Both the Fowlers were easy to pick out in the crowd: Wilfred had a bandaged head and Lawrence was wearing a light coloured coat and a bowler hat. At around 8 pm, Sam Garvin and two of his henchman suddenly left and caught a tram to the Wicker. They were after Harry Rippon, who had a singing engagement that night in the *Bull and Mouth*. They caught up with him outside the public house and slashed his face with razors.

Meanwhile, in Princess Street tension was growing. By about 8 15 there were at least six gang members parading up and down, watched by an apprehensive and growing crowd. Plommer, realising why they were there, bravely if somewhat foolishly, went out and offered to fight them one by one. He was quickly knocked to the ground and attacked. Eventually he managed to break free and, bleeding heavily from head wounds and from gashes to his stomach, managed to get back to his doorway where he was struck by a child's scooter. He was helped inside and placed in a chair. He asked his young son to get him a drink of water but when it was brought he could not drink. His sister-in-law placed her arms round his neck in an attempt to comfort him; when she got up her clothes were covered in blood. It was obvious he was dying.

By now PC Hogan was on the scene. While on patrol in Attercliffe Road, he had noticed fighting in Princess Street and had gone across. On seeing him, those fighting ran off and by the time he got into the street only the Fowlers and a man named Wills remained. Wilfred Fowler was sitting on the step of a fish and chip shop and the other two were standing next to him. The officer noticed that Lawrence Fowler was holding a razor in one hand and a poker in the other, both of which had traces of fresh blood on them and that Wilfred had a cut to his thumb and a head injury. He went across and relieved Lawrence of his weapons. 'Look what they've done to Wilfred,' complained Lawrence 'they've nearly took his finger off.'

'Who has?'

'Jock.'

'Who's Jock?'

'The steward of the club.' [172]

The officer, having telephoned for an ambulance from the fire-box at the top of the street, took the Fowlers into the nearby *Rawson's Arms.* At this point a woman came in and told him he was wanted up the street. Having instructed the bar staff to detain the Fowlers, he went along to no. 42 where he found Plommer lying unconscious in a chair, bleeding from a head wound. He helped to get him on to a couch and then hurried back to the *Rawson's Arms,* where he had asked the ambulance to call, and told the Fowlers that they and Plommer were going to the Royal Infirmary. 'I hit him with a poker,' said Lawrence. The officer warned him that it looked like being a serious affair. 'Oh well, I didn't hit him then,' said Lawrence. Shortly after this the ambulance arrived and the trio were taken to the Infirmary with the constable in attendance.

---

[172] Whether this was a job Plommer had in addition to his employment at Bessemers is not clear.

Plommer died within minutes of his arrival at hospital. Wilfred Fowler's injuries were dressed, following which both brothers were handcuffed and told they were under arrest. 'I did it in self defence,' said Lawrence. Wills and a fourth man Goddard were arrested later and the next morning, Frank Kidnew surrendered. That same morning all five were charged with murder. 'I reserve my defence,' declared Lawrence Fowler.

On the late evening of the 28th, Dr James Ewart Schofield, a resident surgical officer at the Infirmary, carried out a post-mortem examination on the dead man at the public mortuary. He noted that the body was well-built and muscular. There were two wounds to the abdomen about five to six inches deep, which had been caused, in his opinion, by a two-edged pointed weapon about an inch wide. A straight blow had caused one of the wounds and a slanting blow the other. One of the blows had severed a large vein. In addition to the abdominal injuries, there were three scalp wounds all about an inch long and clean down to the bone. The cause of death was haemorrhage from the severed vein and shock..

On Tuesday morning, the five men who had been charged were taken before the city magistrates at Castle Street. Detective Inspector Naylor, having called PC Hogan to give evidence of the events leading to their arrest, asked that they be remanded in custody until the following Tuesday, which application was immediately granted. Reporters present in court were struck by the prisoners' seemingly casual attitude to the proceedings. As soon as the five had been taken down, their place was taken in the dock by Sam Garvin, his brother Robert and William Furniss. Charged with wounding Rippon outside the *Bull and Mouth*, they too were remanded in custody for a week.

In asking a remand, Inspector Naylor told the bench that further inquiries needed to be made and that it might be possible 'to connect this affair with something else which happened later in the evening.'

In the afternoon, the city coroner Mr Kenyon Parker, opened the inquest on Plommer at Nursery Street. Having empanelled a jury, he told them that the deceased had died at the Royal Infirmary on Monday night from wounds inflicted shortly before his death near Norfolk Bridge. There were extensive police inquiries still to be made, and today all they would hear would be evidence of identity and part of the medical evidence, after which he would adjourn the hearing until May 18. This said, he launched into a stinging denunciation of gang violence. From the statements taken by the police, he told the jury, the dead man:

> *was without provocation violently assaulted by a gang ...some of [whom] were armed and [he received] such severe and terrible wounds that he died in a very short time... if the evidence in court bore that out, the case was one of a cowardly murder perpetrated in the main streets of Sheffield as early as 8 o'clock in the evening... There ought ...to be ... indignation and anger that such a crime should be possible in such a place as [Sheffield].*
>
> *[The] city is acquiring an unenviable notoriety through crimes of violence committed by gangs of men, and I know that an impression is growing among law-abiding citizens that even the main streets and roads are not safe at night for ordinary people to go about their business... If, as is said in some quarters, the Police Force is too small to carry out its duties adequately, that force must be increased and to my mind the Force should be encouraged and upheld and not discouraged, as I am sometimes told it is, by misplaced leniency by magistrates or by juries at the Assizes.'*

Ellen Akers was then called to give evidence of identity of the body and Dr Schofield to testify as to the injuries and the cause of death. Having issued a burial certificate, the coroner then adjourned the hearing.

His remarks which were fully reported in the newspapers which were qui ck to add their own words of condemnation. 'It is,' observed the *Star*:

> *'little short of a miracle that there have not been deaths before. Good luck rather than good management has prevented them*
>
> *Before the war ... gangs caused trouble in Sheffield but to a very large extent it was mere hooliganism compared with the highly organised gang system of today, which seeks to laugh at the law. The gangs have no compunction about making an attack within the precincts of the police courts while gang cases are on, or of hunting down men who have given evidence or helped the police.*
>
> *Criticisms have been made that magistrates have been far too lenient in dealing with [gang men] when they have been brought before the court, and the Chief Constable has advocated the cat as the only effective cure for the trouble, especially as juvenile gangs such as the Park Junior gang are growing up.'*

These broadsides seem to have had little effect. On both Tuesday and Wednesday nights large crowds gathered in the Princess Street district, with gang members amongst them and only police vigilance prevented trouble breaking out afresh. There were also attempts at intimidation afoot.

On Saturday May 1, Plommer was buried at Burngreave Cemetery. The funeral, which was attended by the Chief Constable and his Deputy, attracted huge crowds. As the cortege, with an escort of ex-servicemen, made its way from Princess Street to the cemetery, a disabled serviceman and a young boy moved amongst the dense crowds which lined the route, soliciting contributions for the support of the dead man's family. When it reached the cemetery there was more than a little disorder. As the coffin was carried into the chapel women gathered outside, loudly demanding admission, and as soon as the funeral service was finished hordes of people rushed across the graves, in an attempt to get as close as they could to the graveside. But such behaviour was the exception. Most of the 8,000 or so crowd present at and outside the cemetery stood in respectful silence. For many one of the lasting images of the day was the dead man's elder son, wearing his father's war medals and fighting to keep back his tears.

The funeral was not, however, the only news item about the murder which the *Star* carried that night. The number of men charged with the murder now stood at nine, it announced. Amos Stewart had recently been picked out on an identification parade as one of those present at the time of the affray and, earlier that day, the police had also charged the Garvins and Furniss with the murder. None of this trio had of course been present in Princess Street at the time of the killing, but the police had statements from a number of witnesses to the effect that on the night in question they had been in the area asking for Plommer's address and saying that they were going to kill him. That, in the view of the police and the prosecuting authorities, was sufficient to justify charging them as accessories before the fact (i.e. as persons who, although not present at the killing, had incited it).

Over the next two weeks the police continued with the work of gathering evidence, applying successfully for further remands of the accused. By the start of the third week, however, they were ready to go to court and on May 18 the twice-adjourned inquest finally got under way. By this date the number of accused had swollen to eleven. Stanley Harker had been charged on May 1, and shortly before the inquest an eleventh man, William Wild, was charged (both were alleged to have been party to the attack on Plommer). The eleven, who had spent the previous night in the Sheffield police cells, were brought to the Nursery Street court in a black maria. Once they had taken their places, the coroner, addressing the jury and the lawyers[173] who had been retained to represent the DPP and the accused, announced that, although statements had been taken from some 62 witnesses, only 45 of them would be called, he having taken the view that the evidence of the other 17, which related principally to the events of the Sunday, was not relevant to the issues they had to decide.

The first witness called was Elizabeth Plommer, the dead man's widow. "I was standing in my doorway,' she told the jury 'when I saw seven or eight men go up to my husband and attack him. One of them with bandages round his head struck him but I couldn't see what with because I was too far away. I started running up the street and, just as I got there, a man in a light tweed overcoat, who I was told afterwards was Lawrence Fowler, hit my husband on the back of the head with a poker. My husband tried to get onto a passing motor

[173] Mr Frederick William Scorah (of Arthur Neal & Co.) of Hoole's Chambers, Bank St. represented Furniss; Mr James William Fenoughty of Compton Chambers, Effingham Street, Rotherham and 7, Bank Street represented the other prisoners.

car but they pulled him off. My husband shouted 'Come one at a time'. I then heard Lawrence Fowler say 'Come on. Let's do him while we have him.' I shouted to my husband 'Run Jock, they won't fight fair.' He ran and the Fowlers chased after him. William Fowler took a scooter off a boy and threw it at my husband." Asked if she could see the Fowlers in court, she pointed to the two brothers in turn. As she looked at Lawrence, she sobbed 'You.' She also picked out Wills and Stewart. 'They were there too,' she said. No, her husband had no weapon on him when he left the house that night.

Next into the witness box was ten-year-old Thomas Plommer. 'I saw them dash at my father,' he said. 'Lawrence Fowler had a poker and Wilfred Fowler a leather truncheon. When my father was down several men kicked him. One of them was Harker. As my father was running away I heard Lawrence shout 'Come on let's do him.'

Things were already looking bad for the Fowlers but they were looking blacker still by the time Mrs Rose Lemm left the witness box. 'Ten men were involved in the attack,' she told the jury (almost certainly an over-estimate) and they were led by Wilfred Fowler, who had something which looked like a poker up his sleeve' and, turning excitedly towards Lawrence Fowler, she exclaimed 'I saw you jab him in the stomach.' At this several of the prisoners laughed. Ignoring them, she continued: 'Plommer was knocked down by the Fowler brothers and, while he was on the ground, Lawrence jabbed him in the stomach till his mouth opened wide.' Afterwards she saw the other Fowler brother, the one with the bandaged head, putting something which looked like a bayonet in a leather case.' Unfortunately for the Fowlers, she was not the witness who spoke of seeing them with a bayonet and case that night. Miriam Lycett said that she saw Lawrence with a black leatherette case about a foot long by two inches wide. Company director, Percy Playfair, who was a passenger in the motor car which Plommer had tried to board, also recalled seeing a bayonet and his impression, he told the jury, was that 'it was being carried by a man with a bandaged head.' John Rigg, the car driver, related how he had braked to avoid running down the men who were fighting. One of them, who was bleeding, put his hand on the car as if he was going to jump on, but then seemed to change his mind. At this point his passenger shouted to him 'Move on. They have knives and bayonets in their hands.'

When Dr Schofield was called he confirmed that the two wounds to Plommer's stomach could have been caused by a bayonet or something similar.

Mrs Plommer's identification of Wills as one of her husband's attackers was amply borne out by the evidence of several other witnesses, not least PC Fort. He had arrived on the scene as the gang were running off. He chased after them and managed to catch and detain Wills whom he promptly handcuffed to some railings. Having relieved Wills of a small iron jemmy, he set off after the others. When he later examined the spot where Wills had been detained he found a razor.

According to labourer, Harry Pollard, Gardner and Harker also took part in the attack. That Harker was at least present was not open to doubt, for he admitted as much to the police on his arrest.

No witness described either Garvin brother as present during the affray but there was an abundance of evidence that they had been in the Princess Street beforehand, uttering threats against Plommer. A little before 8' o clock they had called in at the home of bookmaker,

George Thompson. Thompson claimed that Garvin asked him what he knew about the bother the previous night, adding 'If we see Jock Plommer tonight, he will be for it.' Spinks Fowler had been done last night and those who did him would get done themselves tonight. 'If you were working with a mob like I am and one of them got done, what would you do?' Thompson's account was confirmed by his wife and two other people present in his house at the time. According to Mrs Thompson, before he left Sam Garvin kissed her baby and, as he leaned forward to do so, she could see a razor in his pocket. She also recalled him saying: 'We have been quiet long enough and we are going to be quiet no longer. Someone did Spinker last night and we are going to do him tonight. We will make Princess Street flow with blood.' The Thompsons and their guests were not the only persons who spoke of hearing threats. The witness Pollard said that at about 8 o'clock Sam Garvin had come up to him at Norfolk Bridge and asked 'Where's all these fighting men?' adding 'We will do Plommer in and Whitham, Spud Murphy and Frank Rhodes.' When he said this Bob Garvin, Kidnew and a fourth man were with him.

The inquest evidence was eventually concluded on Tuesday, May 19. During the proceedings neither of the solicitors representing the eleven accused asked a single question. They would make their move at the committal hearing and, for the present, were content simply to note what evidence came out. On Thursday, the coroner summed up the evidence to the jury.

> *'You have not the common difficulty of having to decide between conflicting witnesses. There has been very little conflict... and what there has has been only on matters of detail. Very ample evidence has been put before you of the*

*broad facts of this case: Plommer, an unarmed man standing quietly in a street, was attacked by a number of men armed with various murderous weapons [and received fatal injuries]. In law this amounts to wilful murder on the part of those proved to have taken part in the attack.*[174] *It may be that one is more responsible than another for inflicting the abdominal wounds which actually caused death, but, in law, I have to direct you that the others are equally guilty as aiders and abettors. In your verdict you may wish to distinguish between the man or men who inflicted the abdominal wounds and to say that he or they are guilty of wilful murder and that the others aided and abetted.*

*No question of manslaughter arises in this case and no question of killing in self defence.*

*[In his view] there was no evidence affecting William Furniss and Robert Garvin.*

*There was ample evidence to warrant a verdict of 'Wilful murder' against both Wilfred and Lawrence Fowler; ample evidence to justify them in finding that Stewart, Goddard and Wills aided and abetted.*

*It was for them to decide whether Kidnew and Wild were aiders and abettors and, if they accepted the evidence, Kidnew should be included as an aider and abettor.*

*There was one name left Sam Garvin.*

*There was evidence that he was seen in Princess Street at 6.30, 7 pm and 7.45.*

*A large number of witnesses had stated that they had heard Sam Garvin using threats to kill or 'do in' Jock, They had no evidence that he was in the gang that attacked.*

*But if you accept the evidence about these threats and about his presence in the vicinity at the time of the affair and the evidence that he was in possession of a razor, you have ample evidence to say that this man, Sam Garvin, either conspired with others to murder Plommer or aided and abetted others in this murder.*

Seven minutes after retiring to consider the case, the jury were back with verdicts of wilful murder against the Fowlers and verdicts

[174] Later in his summing up he observed that if the gang had intended just to give Plommer a thrashing they would not have gone about with such murderous weapons.

of aiding and abetting murder against all of the other defendants, save for Bob Garvin and Furniss against whom no verdict was found. The coroner immediately signed a warrant committing the nine against whom verdicts had been returned for trial at Leeds Assizes.

Hard on the heels of the inquest came the committal hearing before the city magistrates. This got under way on Monday, May 25. The whole week had been set aside for it. Mr Wing appeared for the DPP, local solicitor, Mr Fenoughty for the ten accused (following the inquest jury's verdict the prosecution had decided to drop the murder charge against Furniss). In opening the case, Mr Wing told the bench that the fatal blow could have been given by one of six or seven of the men who attacked Plommer, but it was impossible to say who. (This was, in reality, a very pessimistic view to take. The evidence given at the inquest strongly suggested that it was one of the Fowlers who had killed Plommer and, indeed, the inquest jury by its verdict had identified them as the killers). The first witnesses called was again the dead man's widow. When Mr Fenoughty rose to cross-examine her it quickly became clear that the gloves were now off, and that the accused intended to put their version of events to the court. It was suggested to her that her husband had been involved in a gambling ring, and that on the Sunday night he had been fetched out to give Wilfred Fowler a thrashing and had done just that, hitting him with a poker. 'No,' she insisted 'he was just there to see fair play and he did not attack Fowlers at all.' Her version of the events of the Sunday night was corroborated by Liversidge, by Cooper and his wife, and by the licensee of the *Windsor* and her niece. Oddly, Liversidge, who according to the prosecution was the person responsible for the wound to the back of Fowler's head, could offer no explanation as to how it had been caused. 'I couldn't say how he got it,' he declared. After the fight Fowler had told Plommer 'Jock, you have got to have a tanning for this.' Also put in at this point was a written statement which Wilfred Fowler made to the police [apparently on the Sunday]. This read:

> *Jock and Harold [Liversidge] said to me outside the Windsor Hotel: 'We will serve you as we served Butler.' I intend to find out who Jock and Harold are and have a straight set to today. Harold and Jock are part of Spud Murphy's gang.'*

The last witnesses to be called on the Monday were Princess Street residents, Mrs Beaver and William Holden. Mrs Beaver said that after the gang had set about him she had shouted to Plommer, who was bleeding badly, 'I should run, Jock.' 'No,' he replied 'I will fight them single.' It was suggested to her that it had been Plommer who had started the fight by taking a poker from his sleeve and hitting Wilfred Fowler with it. But she would not have it. Holden having described how the gang had all got Plommer on the ground and started batting him about the head, added 'He fought like a lion.'

On the second day of the hearing the prosecution called further evidence as to the events of the Monday. Most of those called, such as young Thomas Plommer and Mrs Rose Lemm, merely repeated the accounts which they had given at the inquest. During his cross-examination of a witness called Hazlewood, Mr Fenoughty, having extracted the concession that a man in a light suit, whom he had seen with a razor in his hand and whom he had heard say 'Look what he has done to my brother,' was wearing a bowler hat, immediately produced such a hat. 'This,' he told the bench 'is Lawrence Fowler's and you can see it bears what is obviously the mark of a poker.'

From Garvin's point of view one of the least helpful of the day's witnesses was Ishmael Pollard, a labourer, of 45, Carlisle Street East. "I was standing at Norfolk Bridge," he told the bench "when Sam Garvin came up with some other men and I heard him say 'We will kill Whitham, Plommer and Murphy.' As he walked away he said 'We have a mob here to do Plommer.' "

When the court sat on the Wednesday, Mr Wing was immediately on his feet asking the bench to take steps to prevent witness intimidation. 'I wish to state,' he said ' that the night before last, as some witnesses were going home after the hearing, certain persons got on a tramcar and intimidated them. I hope the police will assist in putting down this sort of thing.' 'That will be done,' the chairman told him. The rest of the morning was occupied taking further evidence. Ten witnesses were called including the car driver, Rigg, and his passenger, Playfair. As he had done the previous day, Mr Fenoughty suggested to witnesses that Plommer had been armed and that it was he who had started the fight. But he got nowhere.

Thursday saw him get yet another 'nose-ender' in cross-examination. Having obtained confirmation that no bruises to the deceased's body were found on post-mortem examination, he suggested to the two doctors called by the prosecution that this meant that eye-witness evidence that the deceased had been given a kicking whilst on the ground simply could not be true. 'Not so,' he was told 'if a man lost a considerable quantity of blood and died soon afterwards that would make bruising less likely.' 'I recall a case,' said Dr. Carter 'of a man run over by a lorry. His liver was cut in two but there was no external bruising.' Much of the day's hearing was taken up by police evidence and by evidence as to the attack on Rippon in the Wicker (called to corroborate Mrs Thompson's claim that Sam Garvin had a razor on him on the Monday). In the afternoon, 75 witnesses having been called over the four days, Mr Wing announced that he did not propose to call any further evidence. Mr Fenoughty immediately requested that the case be adjourned until the following morning to give him opportunity to consult with his clients and decide what course to take, which application was granted.

On the Friday morning, he rose to address the bench. 'There were,' he submitted 'major contradictions in the evidence. Some witnesses had spoken of there being kicking, another said there had been none. Some witnesses had said that all those involved had weapons. Others had seen no weapons. The picture of one man being set upon by many inevitably produced prejudice and may have led witnesses to exaggerate. The suggestion that there had been a betting gang in Thompson's yard was, on the evidence, not without foundation. A large number of witnesses said that the Garvins, Kidnew and Ward had left the scene before Plommer was attacked. So far as Robert Garvin was concerned, it was not suggested he did anything or took part in anything at all except the affair in the Wicker. As for the suggestion that Garvin had asked for Plommer at Thompson's house, Kidnew who was with Garvin knew full well where Plommer lived and had actually stayed at his house, so what need was there for Garvin to go asking where he lived.? The injuries found on post-mortem examination were not consistent with Plommer having been savagely kicked. More than one witness said that Stewart did nothing and he had gone along voluntarily to the police station to make a statement. It was not sufficient for the prosecution to throw a welter of facts and contradictions at the magistrates and ask them to commit these men for trial. Turning to the position of the Fowlers, Wilfred Fowler was not in a physical condition on the Sunday to make to threats against Plommer; he had been struck and knocked out. He was intending to have a fair fight with Plommer on the Monday and was making arrangements to do so. As for Lawrence Fowler, he knew nothing of the attack on his brother until the Monday. On the question of weapons, he asked if it was likely that Plommer, who had injured Wilfred Fowler the day before, would go out unarmed on the following day. In fact, he had a poker up his sleeve and, when the Fowlers asked him for an explanation of his behaviour on the Sunday, he pulled it out and hit Wilfred on the head with it. It was obvious that Wilfred had been roughly handled in the affray because afterwards he collapsed and, when the officer found Wilfred sitting on a step, what did Lawrence say 'Look what he's done to our kid.' Later on he said 'I did it in self defence.' If he did actually kill Plommer, it was justified if done in self defence. He submitted that there was no evidence against the Garvins and Kidnew and asked them to consider very carefully the evidence of the others. Fenoughty, having intimated that he had a large number of witnesses to call, the magistrates then adjourned the proceedings until after the bank holiday.

When the court re-assembled on Monday, June 16, Mr Fenoughty immediately called Lawrence Fowler to give evidence and, over the next two days, he was followed into the witness box by five more of the accused and two alibi witnesses. Why he decided to take this course is not easy to understand. In order to secure the committal of the prisoners, all the prosecution had to do was to satisfy the magistrates that there was a *prima facie* case against them, a case for them to answer and, given the weight of the prosecution evidence, it was hard to see how they could conclude otherwise, whatever the accused might say. Further, nine of the ten already stood committed for trial on the coroner's inquisition so that, even if the magistrates threw out the case, they could and undoubtedly would be put on trial on that. If the solicitor's object was to secure publicity for himself he certainly succeeded but how his clients' position was improved by disclosing their hand and tying themselves to a version of the facts, well in advance of trial, is hard to see.

Lawrence Fowler claimed in evidence that he was a bookmaker's clerk and had, on the Monday, been working at Uttoxeter racecourse. At around 8.10 on the Monday evening he was with a number of others at the top of Princess Street when his brother Wilfred said 'There's Jock there.' He then noticed Plommer standing at the junction of Princess Street and Sutherland Road and a group of about twenty men standing against a wall. "I went up to Plommer," he explained "and told him 'Our kid is going to have a fair fight tonight and there's going to be no poker. At this Plommer pulled a poker out of his trousers saying 'I will use it on you an all' and hit me twice on the head with it. I went down. Plommer then hit my brother on the side of the head – on his bandages. As soon as he struck my brother I ran and grabbed hold of the poker. I swung him round. He kicked me on the leg and bruised it. It was for these bruises that I was taken to the hospital. He let go of the poker and I went down on my back. When I got up I saw Wilfred struggling with Plommer [who] I saw, had a razor. He swung my brother off and made for me. I hit him on the side of the head. He then went back, slipped on the tram line and went to the floor. A motor car then came by and Plommer made for it and shouted at us 'Come on you ______'. He ran off down Princess Street and I ran after him. I shouted 'Drop that razor' and he dropped it near the chip shop. Wilfred picked it up and gave it to me. I saw Wilfred was going to faint so I sat him down on the chip shop step. There was a crowd about. I held up the poker and the razor and said 'Look what the fighting man has been using.' When a policeman came up and said 'Who's done it?' I said 'Jock, and these are what he has been using.' Asked if any of the other prisoners took part in the scuffle, he replied 'Only my brother.' Cross-examined he said that he had heard that Whitham had offered to lay £20 that Plommer, Cooper, or Liversidge could tan Wilfred. Wilfred was going to ask them to fight fair but he didn't intend that there should be any fight that night. Plommer, he said, associated with gamblers who had been part of the Mooney gang, who since the gang had been knocked out by Garvin, had settled in Princess Street. 'Members of a gang,' he added 'get training in the use of razors for acts of violence.' He was not himself a member of the Garvin gang but had heard that Kidnew and Furniss were. Others had taken part in the fight besides him and his brother but he did not know who they were.

He was followed into the witness box by his brother, Wilfred. He denied belonging to any gang; he was a bricklayer's labourer. He had first met Plommer and his wife at a party a month before the fight and next saw him on Sunday 26th. He had been in the *Windsor Hotel.* When he came out he saw three young women quarrelling. Liversidge, who was there, said to him 'What have you to do with this row? You are one of the Alfred Road gang' and struck at him. He remained outside the hotel and talked to the three women for about half an hour. Liversidge then reappeared with Plommer and two others. Liversidge said 'You have had one go. Let's have another one now.' He replied he would 'have a go one at a time' and he fought with Liversidge. Spud Murphy was one of those present. He had been paying all round the room for beer. Cooper was there and struck at him (Wilfred) and, while he was closed with Cooper, Jock got hold of his throat and said 'We have done Buck. We will do you the same as we have done him.' Plommer then struck him on the head with a poker and felled him. He didn't remember anything more until he found himself in a house where there was a policeman and someone bathing his head. He was taken to the Royal Hospital and four stitches were put into his head. He told the policeman he would not prosecute but would have a fair fight.

His description of the events of the Monday matched that given by his brother and he confirmed that neither Stewart, Wills, Goddard nor Harker had taken part in the affray. He had no connection with the Garvins but had been to the tossing ring in Thompson's yard, where he had seen Harry Pollard, Whitham, Murphy and Ishmael Pollard. In cross-examination, he said he had worked for two hours in the last twelve months and was kept by his brother John. He conceded that he also made money out of the Alfred Road tossing ring, which was attended by thousands of people every week.

Wills was next to testify. The reason why he had had a case opener on him when arrested by PC Fort was that he was on his way to commit a burglary at Staniforth Road stores with Goddard. Goddard, the last witness of the day, confirmed this story and said that the reason he ran away when the police shouted to him was that he had two flash lamps and Wills had a jemmy. In cross-examination, he admitted that he had only worked one week in his life and earned a living carrying parcels (a reply which the other prisoners seemed to find highly amusing).

At the next day's hearing Stewart and Harker gave evidence. Stewart admitted being present during the affray but said that, as soon as he saw there was going to be trouble, he walked to a horse trough 18 to 20 yards away. Plommer was the first to strike a blow, knocking Wilfred Fowler to the ground with a poker. He then struck Lawrence twice to the head. In all about 15 to 20 men seemed to be taking part in the struggle. He could not say who they were or who struck the fatal blow

Harker denied taking any part in the fight. He saw Plommer with a poker and a razor. He saw the Fowlers go up to him and Plommer strike them with a hammer,

Last to testify were Mrs Sarah Jane Cooper and her sixteen-year-old daughter Alice. They claimed that Goddard, who was courting Alice, was at their house in Alfred Road from 7.50 until nearly 9 o'clock on the night of the affray.

Mr Fenoughty then told the court that no further witnesses would be called and that the prisoners Sam and Bob Garvin, Wild and Kidnew reserved their defence.

The Magistrates, after a brief discussion, announced that all ten accused would be committed to the Assizes to stand trial on the charge of murder, and granted a poor prisoners' defence certificate to all except the Garvins and Kidnew on whose behalf no application was made.

The trial took place at Leeds Town Hall before Mr Justice Finlay.[175] It started on July 28 and lasted four days. Because the dock was too small to accommodate all ten accused, four of them, the Garvins, Wild and Kidnew were placed immediately below it flanked by warders. If the dock was full to overflowing, counsel's bench was no less crowded. In all seven counsel had been retained. Mr Mortimer KC, Mr A Morley and Mr L R Lipsett appeared for the Crown.[176] Mr G H B Streatfield represented the Fowlers, Mr J W Jardine appeared for Garvin, Kidnew and Wild, Mr R Burnand for Stewart, Wills and Harker and Dr E C Chappell for Goddard.[177]

There were some fifty witnesses to be called for the prosecution and on the first day of the trial extra coaches were attached to the Leeds train to accommodate them and the various officials connected

---

[175] **Finlay**, William, 2nd Viscount; (1875-1945); educ. Eton, Trinity College, Cambridge; barrister 1901; KC 1914; High Court judge 1924; his appointment caused a storm of criticism (see e.g. (1824) 158 *Law Times*, p 481 'Sir William Finlay must be accounted a singularly fortunate man. Called [to the bar] in 1901, in 1905, being the son of the then Attorney-General, he was appointed counsel to the Inland Revenue, an important an lucrative post previously held by counsel of standing an experience. Now after 23 years at the bar, for no apparent professional reason, he is passed over the heads of those who have undoubted prior claims for consideration and whose appointment would have strengthened the High Court Bench.' In the event he turned out to be a respectable judge' (Heuston, op. cit, p 436) and served on the Nuremburg War Crimes Commission.

[176] **Mortimer**, George Frederick Lloyd (1866-1928); educ Birkenhead sch., Balliol Coll, Oxford; barrister 1891; practised on NE Circuit from Chambers at 4, Harcourt Buildings, Temple; KC 1919; recorder of Rotherham, 1905-28. **Morley**, Arthur M; barrister 1913, practised on NE Circuit from 4, Harcourt Buildings; **Lipsett**, Lewis Richard; Irish KC called to English bar, 1918; practised on NE Circuit from 1, King's Bench Walk, Temple.

[177] **Streatfield,** Geoffrey Hugh Benbow (1897-1979); barrister 1921; practised on NE Circuit from 1, King's Bench Walk, Temple; recorder of Rotherham 1932; Huddersfield 1934; QC 1938; recorder of Hull, 1943; High Court judge, 1947; **Jardine**, James Willoughby (1879-1945); educ Eton, King's College Cambridge; KC 1927; recorder of Halifax 1923-31; Newcastle 1931-32; Leeds 1932-40; county court judge 1940; **Burnand**, Richard Frank (1887-1969); educ Uppingham, Pembroke Coll, Oxford; OBE 1918; barrister 1919; recorder of Richmond 1928-30; senior master Supreme Court and Queen's Remembrancer, 1930-60; CBE 1946; knighted 1960; **Chappell**, Ernest Charles; LL D; barrister 1917; practised on NE Circuit, 1923-63 from Chambers in Sheffield, including 42, Bank Street.

with the case. As the train passed the end of Princess Street, a large crowd waved them good luck.

During the trial security arrangements were strict. The prisoners were brought to court each day in a fleet of taxis accompanied by warders and police outriders, while outside the court room there were officers posted to keep out undesirables.

The prosecution evidence which followed the same lines as at the committal hearing concluded at the end of the second day. The morning of the third day saw the judge direct the jury to acquit Bob Garvin, Wild and Kidnew. None had been present at the time of the affray and they had accordingly been charged as accessories before the fact but, to convict them of being accessories, the jury would have to be satisfied that they had incited the attack on Plommer. There was simply no evidence to show that they had. In the case of Sam Garvin, however, also charged as an accessory, there was evidence to for them to consider: witnesses claimed that before the attack he had said 'We have a mob to do Plommer.'

Garvin, Wild and Kidnew having left court, counsel for the remaining seven accused commenced to call the defence evidence. The six defendants who had given evidence at the committal hearing did so again, as did Goddard's two alibi witnesses. The story which each told was the same as in the lower court. Significantly, none of the accused was able to offer any explanation of how Plommer came by the two wounds to his stomach and Wilfred did his case no good when he smirked at prosecution counsel, drawing the rebuke that the case was no laughing matter.

Sam Garvin's evidence was listened to with particular interest by the Sheffield reporters, for he alone had reserved his defence at the committal hearing. He told the jury that he knew the Fowlers slightly. He had spoken to Lawrence on three or four occasions, the last time being at a race meeting at Gringley-on-the-Hill. Lawrence had never worked for him. As for Wilfred, he had spoken to him twice. The other four prisoners he did not know at all. On the night of the affray he had called to see Thompson who owed him £17, as Kidnew had told him it would only take a few minutes to get there. Thompson asked him if he had heard about the bit of bother on Sunday night. 'It was the Alfred Road lads and one of the Fowlers had got done.' I said 'They look quiet enough. Has Murphy started his messing again? There are four of us and we could beat any four amongst them.' After that he, his brother, Kidnew and Wild went up Princess Street and, as they were getting on a tram, they saw a number of people there and he said to them 'I suppose you had the fighting men here last night. There are four of us. We will fight any four amongst them.' He had never said 'We have a mob down here to do Plommer.' He did not know Plommer.

The final day of the trial was devoted to counsels' closing speeches and the judge's summing up. A point stressed by Mr Mortimer, in his speech and by the judge, in his summing-up. was that not a single independent witness had been called by the defence to support their version of the affray. All the bystanders had been called by the prosecution. The judge's summing up lasted some three and a half hours. He counselled the jury that they must consider the case of each accused separately. He said that, in his view, against Garvin and Goddard there was suspicion only. So far as those alleged to have taken part in the affray were concerned, the questions they had to decide in relation to each were did he take part in the attack on

Plommer and, if so, with what intent. Any of the attackers who shared a common intent either to kill or do grievous bodily harm to Plommer was guilty of murder; if his intent was merely to give Plommer a beating he was guilty of manslaughter only. Armed with his direction the jury retired. It took them the remarkably short time of three quarters of an hour to arrive at verdicts. They acquitted Garvin and Goddard, convicted both the Fowlers of murder and Wills, Stewart and Harker of manslaughter. Asked why sentence of death should not be passed, Wilfred was silent but Lawrence said 'I spoke the truth. I only struck one blow with the poker. I am innocent. If only his wife would speak up. It is an impossible decision.' The judge immediately proceeded to pass sentence of death.

When the Fowlers had been taken down, their place in the dock was taken by Wills, Stewart and Harker. Telling them that it was an extremely serious case of manslaughter which demanded a very serious punishment, the judge sentenced Wills and Stewart to ten years' penal servitude and Harker, who unlike the other two was without previous convictions, to seven years' penal servitude. The next day, Sam and Bob Garvin stood trial before Mr Justice Finlay on the charge of wounding Rippon. Both were convicted and received sentences of 21 and nine months' imprisonment, with hard labour, respectively.

For the Fowlers, their only hope of escaping the noose lay in a successful appeal. Notices of appeal were duly lodged and their appeals came on for hearing on August 18 before Lord Hewart, the Lord Chief Justice, Mr Justice Swift and Mr Justice Talbot. Their counsel, Mr Streatfield, submitted to the court that the trial judge had been guilty of both misdirection and non-direction and that the murder convictions were against the weight of the evidence. The only difference between the case against the Fowlers and that against those whom the jury convicted of manslaughter was that there was a suggestion that one of the Fowlers had a short bayonet. The evidence was so confusing that it was impossible for any jury to make up their minds with reasonable certainty as to which of the Fowlers had it and as to who had struck the fatal blow. The evidence was that all five took an equal part in the attack and, the jury having acquitted the other three of common intent, must have come to the same conclusion with regard to the Fowlers, if they had been properly directed. The court would have none of it. It was tolerably clear that the jury had picked out the two Fowlers as the ringleaders. They had taken a merciful and lenient view in the case of the other three, who might well have been found guilty of murder, and had found them guilty of manslaughter. The simple answer to the appeal was that the jury could very well have believed – indeed they could hardly have resisted it – that the appellants were the ringleaders in the murderous affray and were inspired from first to last with the intent to kill Plommer. The jury might have believed that a blow or wound, administered by one of them, undoubtedly did kill Plommer and that both were equally guilty. No possible complaint could be made about the summing-up which was as favourable as it could be to the defendants. At this point Wilfred Fowler was heard to observe 'But others are guilty as well.' As one of the warders touched him on the shoulder to indicate he should leave the dock, he exclaimed 'But they won't believe it will they? None of them.' Reporting the outcome of the appeal the *Sheffield Independent* carried the headline 'Fowler

Brothers' Last Hope Gone.' It was right. The case was not one in which there was any likelihood of a reprieve.

On September 1, Mr Fenoughty was informed by letter that the Home Secretary had been unable to find any grounds sufficient to advise the granting of a reprieve. But officialdom was not quite finished with the brothers. On September 2, it was announced that Wilfred would be executed the next day along with Dalton murderer, Alfred Bostock, and Lawrence on September 4.[178] On hearing the news, Lawrence pleaded to be allowed to die alongside his brother. His request was refused but the brothers were allowed to share the same cell on the night before Wilfred's execution.

By 9 o'clock on the morning of September 3, a crowd of about 1,000 had gathered outside the prison. Among them were several Sheffield racing men. Unusually (and possibly out of consideration for Lawrence the prison bell was not sounded during the execution). Meanwhile, inside the prison, Wilfred was making a last minute confession. It was he who struck the fatal blow. Lawrence had no part in it. By 9.20 notices announcing his execution were posted at the prison gates. Back in Sheffield, Mr Fenoughty, who had learned of the confession, renewed his appeal for clemency for Lawrence. It fell on deaf ears. 'Jix' (as Home Secretary, Joynson Hicks, was contemptuously known) was not a man noted for his humanity. During the day Lawrence received a final visit from his mother. Before they parted he gave her a lock of his hair as a keepsake. The crowd which assembled outside the gaol for his execution was smaller than on the previous day but there were more Sheffielders

[178] The last double hanging at Armley was that of John Henry Roberts and Thomas Riley on April 18, 1952.

present. Inside the prison Lawrence, who had been in a state of collapse since Wilfred's execution, had to be helped to the scaffold.[179]

## Workhouse on Monday - Lorraine Lax, 1925 [180]

Badly injured at the battle of Loos in 1915, Lorraine Lax, a Woodhouse lad with a French sounding Christian name, returned from the First World War with his nerves shattered, or so his mother claimed. Like many war veterans he seems to have found it difficult to adjust to civvy street. If his detractors are to be believed, he certainly had no liking for manual toil, regarding drinking and gambling as activities far preferable to work down the pit. In April 1920, he married Elizabeth Bedford, a good looking Darnall lass a year his senior. They started their married life in a rented house at 71, Ripon Street but, after a fortnight, Lax went to the Warwickshire Furnishing Company and told them to take the furniture back and returned to his parents' home at Woodhouse.[181] Elizabeth obtained a maintenance order against him in the magistrates' court but he did not pay regularly.

After fifteen months the couple got back together. For a time they lived with his parents and then moved to a house at 54, Ripon Street. But things were little better between them: there were many

[179] The hangman at both executions was Thomas Pierrepoint.

[180] See *Sheffield Independent*, Sept 1, 3, 8, 9, Dec 2, 22, 25 1925; Jan 1, 1926; *Sheffield Telegraph*, Sept 1, 3, Dec 2, 1925; *Star*, Aug 31, Sept 1, Dec 1, 1925; *The Times*, Dec 22, 1925.

[181] At 16, Birks Avenue, Woodhouse.

angry scenes and on one occasion neighbours saw Elizabeth climb out of a window to escape.

In 1923 there was a further separation and, after living with her parents for a time, Elizabeth, who by now had three dependant children, took a room in the house of the Antcliffe family at 31, Ripon Street. Shortly before Christmas 1924 the couple again became reconciled and Lax moved in with her. The room in which she was living was on the ground floor and had its own access to the street (via the front door of the house),[182] but it had little else to commend it. It was far too small for a couple with three young children, but it was all they could get and they had to make the best of things. At night, two-year-old Frank slept in his parents' bed and the two other children, four-year-old George and Lorraine aged three, slept in a cot.

It was a miserable existence made worse for Elizabeth by lack of money: her mother, who lived in the same street at no. 61, gave what help she could, but she was still forever hard up. If she believed that things could get no worse, she was wrong. By August she was pregnant again and, at the end of that month, Harry Antcliffe, from whom they rented the room, gave them notice to quit for rent arrears. On Sunday, August 30, she called at her parents' home 'I've got no money,' she told them. 'We shall have to go to the workhouse.' On the Sunday evening, the Antcliffes, who appear to have had a soft spot for her, and would later describe her as respectable and hardworking, invited her to join them for a spot of supper and she poured out her woes to them.

[182] The room had two doors, one leading to the street, the other to a passage at the back of the house. The Lax family always used the front door, the other door being kept locked to give the families some privacy. Consequently the two families saw little of each other (*Sheffield Independent*, September 1, 1925).

At about 6.30 the next morning (August 31), the landlord's son, Norman, was upstairs in no. 31 when he heard a strange gurgling sound coming from the Laxs' room. He then heard the children screaming. He shouted 'Stop that, or I'm coming round.' Shortly after this, his father who had gone down to find out what was going on, heard Lax shout 'Lie down you.' Being unable to gain access to the room, he walked round to the front of the house. As he did so, Lax emerged from the front door fully dressed. He had a wound to his throat and was pulling his coat collar up to cover it. 'Take me to the police station,' he said. Asked where Lizzie was, he replied 'I expect she's dead.' Antcliffe immediately called Norman down and told him to take Lax to Attercliffe police station. His daughter, Clara, he sent round to no. 61. 'Tell them to come up and see to Lizzie,' he instructed. She came back with Lizzie's brother-in-law, Harold Gardner. They passed Lax on the way. 'It's no use,' Lax told them 'she is dead. I'm going to give myself up.'

On entering the Laxs' room, Harold found Elizabeth lying on the bed in a crouching position. She was close to the wall and looked as if she was dead. Her body, which was still warm, was partly covered by bedclothes but there were tell tale splashes of blood on the wallpaper and the bedding. Lying at her side was the two-year-old; the other children were in a cot. Harold immediately got all of them out of the house and round to their grandmother's.

Meanwhile Lax and Norman Antcliffe were walking steadily to the police station. Before they set off Lax had tried to cadge a cigarette and, as they walked, he remarked 'I am parched and could drink a pint.' 'Buck up,' Antcliffe told him 'you can have a drink when we get there.' As they neared the station, Lax took three halfpence out of his pocket and handed it to Antcliffe saying 'It's all I have. Give it to the children.' Inside the station he heard Lax say, in an undertone, 'It's murder. Send a cab up at once.' The officers to whom he surrendered immediately took him to the Royal Infirmary, where the wound to his throat was stitched and then to Firvale Hospital where he was admitted as an in-patient.

Back in Ripon street, detective officers were examining the murder scene. After a police surgeon had certified life extinct, the body was taken by the Fire Brigade ambulance to the Public Mortuary in Nursery Street. There police surgeon, Dr Carter, carried out a post-mortem examination. He found that both sides of the throat had been cut, severing the jugular vein and exposing the bones of the spine, embedded in which was a broken piece of razor blade.

On September 2, Colonel Connell, the deputy coroner, opened the inquest into Elizabeth's death. After taking evidence from Harry Antcliffe and Dr Carter, he adjourned the proceedings to await Lax's discharge from hospital. The hearing was resumed on the 8th with Lax present. Harry Antcliffe and the police surgeon again gave evidence, Antcliffe adding some further details. He had, he said, frequently heard Lax and his wife quarrelling over money matters and, on the night of Sunday, August 30, when she was taking some supper with them, Elizabeth had said that she would not live in a house alone with her husband as she would be in fear for the lives of herself and the children. Alice Gardner, the dead woman's sister, said that as she was making her way to no. 31 she passed Lax, who said 'Don't be alarmed. She's dead.' She added that her sister had frequently complained that her husband did not provide her with sufficient money to carry on. He earned enough but preferred to spend it on drink and gambling. At the conclusion of the evidence the jury returned a verdict of wilful murder against Lax who was committed for trial.

The following day, there was a committal hearing in the magistrates' court. Mr G Banwell appeared for the prosecution and local solicitor, Mr L Siddons, for Lax. The same evidence was gone through as at the inquest. At the conclusion of the prosecution evidence, Lax declined to make any statement and reserved his defence. He was at once committed for trial and granted legal aid.

He took his trial at Leeds Winter Gaol Delivery on December 1, 1925, before Mr Justice Fraser.[183] Mr Frank Beverley appeared for the Crown. Lax was represented by Mr W P Donald.[184] At the close of the prosecution case, Lax was called to give evidence in his own defence. Speaking in a voice so low that he could scarcely be heard, he gave his version of the events leading up to the killing:

> *'As I was getting up, I accidentally caught my wife on the shoulder and she said 'You are up to your old games again.' I then crossed the room and when I turned round I saw my wife with a razor in her hand. I went across to take it from her and she struck out at me and wounded me across the right side of my throat. We struggled and I hit her and stumbled. I got hold of the razor and thrust it at her throat. I was not in full control of myself. I was very angry. I had no intention of killing her when I went across to take the razor from her. It was just done on the spur of the moment.'*

[183] **Fraser,** Hugh (1886-1927); educ. Charterhouse and Trinity Hall, Cambridge; appointed High Court judge 1924.

[184] **Beverley**, Frank, barrister 1908; practised on NE Circuit from chambers at 9 Park Square Leeds and Old Post Office Chambers, Bradford; **Donald**, see above p 174n.

In his closing speech Donald submitted to the jury that it was a killing under provocation. Lax had been provoked into losing his self control by his wife's attack and so his crime was not murder but manslaughter.

Mr Justice Fraser, in his summing up, directed the jury on the law of provocation, explaining that great provocation which caused a man to lose his self-control and kill might reduce what would otherwise be murder to manslaughter.

The jury, having retired at 4.42 pm, were back at 6.03 with a request for clarification of the law of provocation. 'Great provocation,' the judge told them 'reduces to manslaughter the act of killing, even though it may be done with some dangerous instrument such as is likely to kill.' At 6.10 they returned to court. 'We find the Defendant guilty,' announced the foreman in answer to the Clerk of Assize's question 'but with a very strong recommendation to mercy.'

According to the reporter of the *Sheffield Independent*, Lax received the verdict 'in the same depressed and disinterested spirit that he had taken the whole of the trial.' Asked why sentence of death should not be passed upon him he replied: 'My sympathies still lie with my wife.'

Within days of the verdict, notice of appeal against conviction was lodged on his behalf alleging that the judge had misdirected the jury on the law of provocation. The appeal came on for hearing in the Court of Criminal Appeal on December 21, 1925 before a court comprising Lord Chief Justice Hewart, Mr Justice Salter and Mr Justice Sankey. Mr Donald, after outlining the facts of the case, submitted that the judge ought to have told the jury fully how provocation affected the verdict which they were to bring in. The vital question was how much provocation was there, and did it produce such passion that the man was prevented from exercising the mental judgment which would have told him the quality and nature of the act he was committing. The judge simply did not deal with the point adequately.

The Court was not impressed and dismissed the appeal without calling on counsel for the Crown.

'There was no doubt' said Mr Justice Sankey, delivering the judgment of the court,

> *'that terrible wounds were inflicted upon the woman and they were committed with great violence. The point now raised was that the judge did not fully state the law about the effect of provocation upon the verdict. The law was that a man could plead provocation with success if he proved that he committed the act immediately he was provoked and not after a lapse of time, during which he could have cooled down. As a matter of fact, the judge put the position to the jury in the clearest and simplest of terms and no fault could be found with the summing up which was admirable and clear.'*

Lax's only hope was now the prerogative of mercy. A petition seeking a reprieve had been lodged. The jury's verdict had been accompanied by a strong recommendation to mercy. Might that not be sufficient to win a reprieve? It was not and at 9 am on Thursday January 7, 1926, he was executed at Armley Gaol.[185] On the morning of the hanging only a handful of spectators gathered outside the prison gates. One of them was a boyhood friend of Lax's from Sheffield who, as the clock struck nine, stood with head bowed tears

---

[185] The hangman was Thomas Pierrepoint

streaming down his face. He had visited Lax on the Monday and found him in good health and awaiting his end calmly. 'I never felt better in my life,' he said. On the Wednesday before the execution he had written to his mother:

> *This is my last letter and keep sake in remembrance. Sister Nellie and Charlie have been to see me today and I am pleased that the kiddies are well again. Well, mother, I can honestly say that I have been well looked after here and, under the circumstances, I am very grateful to the prison officials and officers. I have been confirmed and now I shall go in a good spirit and may my soul see the heavenly land. I also wish to thank George what he did for me re petition.*
>
> *All I now ask is for a prayer.*
> *May God bless you all and my kiddies.*
>
> *Your ever loving son,*
>
> *Lorraine*
>
> *Good bye.*

### The Wages of Sin – Samuel Case, 1927 [186]

George and Alice Mottram were a quiet young couple who kept themselves to themselves. He worked as a miner at Tinsley Park Colliery, she as a buffer girl at the Sheffield Plate and Printing Company works in Priestley Street. They had married on March 13, 1926. They had lived first in rooms on the Manor estate before finally

---

[186] See *Sheffield Independent*, Oct 22, 24, 27, 29, Nov 3, 5, 30, Dec 7, 21, 22, 1927; *Sheffield Telegraph*, Oct 22, Nov 3, 5, Dec 21, 22, 1927; Jan 9, 1928; *Star*, Nov 4, 29, 1927; Jan 7, 1928; *The Times*, Oct 22, Nov 30, 1927.

getting a house of their own on Ravencarr Road in April 1927. According to her mother, Alice was very much a home bird who never went out to dances and much preferred to stay in and read a book. Neighbours at Ravencarr Road hardly ever saw her. The only friends the couple had away from work were Samuel Case and his wife. Mottram had known Case all his life and, when Case got married Mottram was best man and Alice a bridesmaid. After the wedding the two couples had kept in touch, visiting each other's homes and occasionally going out to the cinema as a foursome.

On Thursday October 20, 1927, George, who was working afternoon shift, did not leave the house until about 12.30 pm. By then Alice had already been at work for several hours. When his shift finished at 10 he caught the 10.30 bus from Darnall and by quarter to 11 he was walking up his front path. As he neared the house he was surprised to see that it was in darkness and, when he tried the back door it was unlocked, which was unusual for Alice always kept the door locked when she was alone in the house. On entering the kitchen he found her lying on the floor with her head near the kitchen table and her feet towards the scullery door. Thinking she had fainted he ran for help and seeing a neighbour, Leonard Cutts, walking up the path to his house at 30, Desmond Crescent he shouted across to him 'I think my wife has had a fit.' Cutts ran across and joined him and both entered the house.

On close examination, it was clear that Alice was not ill but dead. Her body was cold and tied tightly around her throat was a towel and, on top of the towel, was a short piece of clothes line also knotted. Her spectacles were hanging from one ear and were broken. The two men set out for the nearby fire station to seek help. There a telephone call was made to a local doctor, Dr Finklestone Saylis. He was at the scene by 11 and, after a brief examination, pronounced life extinct. He noticed that the dead woman's face was swollen, congested and of purplish hue. He thought that she had been dead for some two hours. In the kitchen itself there were no signs of a disturbance. On the table were a partly eaten egg and a half drunk mug of tea, and there was a book propped up against the tea pot. The only thing which appeared to be missing was Alice's purse.

After the doctor and the police had completed their examination of the scene, the Fire Brigade ambulance was sent for and the body removed to the public mortuary.

On the following day the purse was handed in by a member of the public who had found it on waste ground. It was empty.

Police inquiries at Alice's workplace established that she had left work at 5 35 pm with two of her workmates. She had seemed in good spirits and said that she was going straight home. It was estimated that she would have arrived home at around 6.15.

A post-mortem examination revealed that she had been strangled. Death had occurred within half an hour, possibly less, of her consuming food.

This tended to confirm the police theory that she had been sitting down, having a bite to eat and reading her novel, when someone had called at the door, been admitted to the house and then strangled her. But who was the mysterious caller? The police had received reports from several persons living on the road of a woman, who had been going from door to door asking for a young married couple who had lived in the street about five months. The woman described as '45 to 50 years of age, tall, with a longish face, a dark complexion and dark hair turning grey, and dressed in a long brown coat with three buttons down the front and a large black hat with silk trimmings' was never traced.

On the Friday, the coroner opened the inquest. After receiving evidence of identification and issuing a burial order, he adjourned the hearing for two weeks in order to give the police the opportunity to make further inquiries. On the Friday evening, with the police no nearer finding the killer, there was what the local newspapers, without exaggeration, described as 'a sensational development.'

At around 11.25 pm a man walked up to PC Kirbyshaw in Snig Hill and said 'I want to give myself up for murdering a woman at Intake.' It was George Mottram's childhood friend, Case. He was arrested and taken to the police office where he was seen by Inspector Flint, who cautioned him. 'I murdered Mrs Mottram. I want to make a statement,' he told the inspector. He then proceeded to dictate and sign a written confession of guilt. It was in these terms:

> *I left home about 12.30 on the 20th to go to work but I did not go. I had seen Mrs Mottram on the previous day at her house about 6.45 and I then made arrangements to go again to her house on the following day. I went there arriving at 6.30. I saw a light in the house. I could see through a chink in the blind, Mrs Mottram came to the door and asked me in. I sat down but she did not sit down again for her tea but talked to me.*
>
> *The subject of the conversation was that she was in a certain condition and I was responsible for it. She burst out crying. She knew I was responsible. She said how miserable she was and how she felt like doing what another woman did on the estate – drowned herself in a bath. She said she was thinking what would my wife and her husband think. We went on*

*talking about the same thing. I asked her why she didn't finish her tea. She said she did not feel like eating, as all her thoughts were on what my wife and her husband would think. She said that she would rather be dead than her husband know. After she had said that, she bent down to put some coal on the fire. At that time I was standing with my back to the table and it seemed as if I lost control of myself then, for I pulled my scarf off my neck and put it over her head and round her neck She was bent down at the time. Before I realised what I had done she was black in the face. On the handle of the door was a towel or tea cloth. I got hold of this and tied this towel or tea cloth round her throat. Then I saw a piece of rope on the floor and I tied that around her throat.*

*After I had done that, I seemed to realise the seriousness of what I had done and my one thought was to get away. I noticed her purse on the table and it seemed to flash through my mind that, if I took the purse, when she was found robbery would perhaps be thought the motive. Then I switched the light off after I had picked up the purse.*

*I have known Mrs Mottram about five years. Her husband and herself, when my wife and myself got married, she was bridesmaid and her husband was best man. We have always been the best of friends though neither my wife nor her husband knew what was taking place between us.*

On the Saturday morning he was taken before the magistrates' court. Dressed in an old blue suit and without collar and tie he had a dejected air. The hearing lasted less than five minutes. Superintendent Hollis, the chief of the CID, asked for and was granted a seven day remand to enable the police to make further inquiries. The press, by now, had unearthed some detail about the accused's background. He was they told their readers 'a 31-year-old miner, married with a child, a boy of nearly two. He was employed at Orgreave colliery and lived at 74 Woodhouse Road, Intake.' After a further remand on October 29, the case was adjourned until Friday, November, 4, when the police assured the court they would be ready to present their evidence.

On November 2, the coroner further adjourned the inquest until the conclusion of the criminal proceedings. Two days later, Case was brought back to the magistrates' court for the committal hearing. On the bench were Mr. W. Farren and Councillor Nunn. Mr G Banwell of the D P P's office appeared to prosecute and the defendant was represented by local solicitor, Mr F W Scorah.[187]A packed court-room listened intently as Mr Banwell told the justices how Mrs Mottram believed herself to be in a certain condition and that Case, whom she said was responsible, had at her request called at her home on the Tuesday night to discuss the situation and that, while they were talking, he had attacked and strangled her. George Mottram, Dr. Saylis and the police officers to whom Case had made his confession were all called to give evidence, and the statement of Dr Carter who had performed the post-mortem was read. The only one to be cross-examined was Dr Saylis, from whom Mr Scorah extracted the concession that episodes of temporary insanity could be brought on by sudden shock, with the recovery almost as sudden as the onset of the illness. The doctor further agreed that a predisposition to depression made the onset of insanity slightly more likely. Clearly, the defence team were inclining to insanity as a possible line of defence. Case, described by reporters as looking weak and ill, having

[187] Frederick William Scorah of Arthur Neal & Co, solicitors of Hoole's Chambers, Bank Street.

stated that he reserved his defence, was committed for trial in custody.

In its report of the hearing the *Star*, referring to the adulterous affair between Case and the dead woman, said that the case was one of gross intrigue. But were the press assuming too readily that Case's account of events was the truth? No-one had, apparently, ever seen him visiting the house when Mottram was at work. More to the point Alice was not pregnant. It was, of course, possible that her period was late and that this had made her fear that she was pregnant. At Case's trial it was suggested, somewhat faintly by the prosecution, that the explanation for the murder might be that he had a desire for her, with which she would have nothing to do. Against that, however, there was the evidence that her clothing had not been disturbed. Also, she was, according to the post mortem findings, a strongly built woman who, had she been sexually assaulted, would have been able to give a good account of herself.

Case took his trial at Leeds Town Hall on November 29, 1927, before Mr Justice Roche.[188] Mr J. C Paley Scott appeared for the prosecution and Mr John Neal for the defence.[189] The prosecution were in no doubt that insanity was the defence which would be run and, after calling evidence to prove the killing and Case's confession to it, set about ruling it out. Dr Carter, who had performed the post-mortem was asked by Paley Scott whether there was anything in the

---

[188] **Roche**, Sir Alexander Adair (1971-1956); educ Ipswich GS, Wadham Coll, Oxford; barrister 1896, practised on NE Circuit, specialising in maritime cases; KC 1912; High Court judge 1917; Lord Justice of Appeal 1934.

[189] **Scott,** Charles Paley; educ St Peter's school, York, King's College, Cambridge; barrister 1906; practised NE Circuit; Recorder of Doncaster, 1923-33; KC 1933; Recorder of Hull, 1933, Recorder of Leeds, 1943.

history of the case which made him think that the prisoner was not of sound mind at the time of the crime. 'No,' he replied. He was followed into the witness box by Dr Worsley, the medical officer at Armley Prison. The prisoner, he told the court,

> *has been kept under observation day and night and I have seen him twice a day during his time in the prison; I have sat and talked to him, watched him and found that he was perfectly normal in his conduct and showed no sign of insanity.*

In cross-examination, the doctor conceded that some forms of insanity were intermittent. He further agreed that, if it could be proved that the prisoner had, in the past, made two unprovoked sudden attacks on others, this might be some evidence of insanity.

The prosecution having closed its case, Mr Neal called witnesses to put flesh on the allegation of insanity. First, to be called was Case's wife. Looking very pale she told the court that her husband had always been in poor health. Earlier that year he had had all his teeth out because of pyorrhoea. On the Monday and Tuesday before the murder he stayed off work, complaining of pain in his head. On the Wednesday and the Thursday he had left, as if to go to work, and returned late at night. On the Thursday night, the two of them went to bed at midnight and she heard him say he was fed up and wished he was dead. His uncle, Samuel Dunne, was next. He said that the prisoner's mother had always been very highly strung and sensitive; also there was insanity in the family. His own brother, Arthur, had died in the South Yorkshire mental asylum in 1905 and an uncle of his had died in the Doncaster Infirmary, having been mentally deficient from birth. Case's sister told the jury that he had called at her house on the Thursday afternoon; he was very quiet and looked worried and ill; she was struck by how strange he looked; his eyes were heavy and he had a vacant expression. His father confirmed that his son had not been himself for several weeks before the tragedy. He had last seen him on the Sunday when he had called at his house. He looked ill and had lain down on the sofa. Vincent Clarke, a colliery filler, said that he had worked with Case for many years and that he was a man whom it was impossible to offend. One day in August this year he had been working near Case when a boy shouted 'Fetch these tubs up' to which he, Clarke, replied 'Fetch them yourself.' At this Case rushed at him, grabbed him round the throat and threw him to the ground. Another miner, named Percival, described an occasion when Case had rushed at him at the pit bottom and grabbed him by the throat. 'What did you do?' asked counsel 'I clouted him. His eyes seemed to be coming out of his head.' This reply caused some laughter in the public gallery, drawing an immediate rebuke from the judge:

> *I cannot understand people who can laugh in a miserable case like this. They come here as if it is some sort of entertainment.'*

Armed with this material, Neal rose to make his closing speech. As he must have realised, securing an acquittal would be a tall order. Even if the evidence called was enough to persuade the jury that Case was suffering from mental illness (and it was for the defence to prove insanity not for the Crown to disprove it), how could he convince them that that illness was of such a degree that at the time of the killing he either did not know what he was doing or that he did not know it was legally wrong? Had he not, in his written confession, described not only how he had killed his victim and but also how he had stolen the dead woman's purse to put the police on the wrong track? After reminding them of the evidence which pointed to insanity, counsel argued that the killing was motiveless.

Paley Scott for the Crown reminded the jury that there was nothing to confirm the prisoner's account of events; nothing to confirm his claim that he and the deceased had been keeping company.

In his summing up, Mr Justice Roche said that the evidence showed that the prisoner was a man of indifferent health, melancholy temperament and uncontrollable temper. If uncontrollable impulse was the explanation for the killing that was not of itself insanity. It must be proved, for the plea of insanity to succeed, that there was a disease of the mind. Few criminals were normal but abnormality was not insanity.

The jury were out just half an hour before returning with a verdict of guilty. As the judge assumed the black cap, there was a cry from the crowded women's gallery of 'God help him.' After sentence Case was half-helped, half-carried from the dock.

His lawyers immediately lodged notice of appeal. The notice alleged that the trial judge had misdirected the jury on the law as to insanity. However, when the appeal came on for hearing on December 19 before Lord Chief Justice Hewart and Mr Justice Avory, the focus of the defence's attack had changed.

On the eve of the hearing, Case's solicitors had been supplied with a seven page typed copy of a statement made prior to Case's trial by a prisoner in Strangeways confessing to the Mottram murder.

As soon as he got to his feet in the appeal court, Neal drew it to the judges' attention and asked leave to call evidence of the confession. He invited them to say that anybody instructed for the defence in a murder case, which at least presented certain queer features, would have been likely to raise a very different defence to that of insanity, had he known that there had been another confession of equal detail in existence at the time of the trial. The judges were less than impressed. 'If Case did not murder the woman,' asked Mr Justice Avory 'why did he not go into the witness box and say so?'

'The defence then was one of insanity,' Neal replied.

'Is it,' asked the Lord Chief Justice, 'that the existence of the confession tends to support the defence of insanity or, is it that, since there are two confessions, nobody is guilty of this murder?'

'Had I known of its existence at the time of the trial, the defence would have taken a different course,' Neal repeated.

Paley Scott, for the Crown, confirmed that he had been aware of the confession at the time of the trial but said that, after investigating it, he had concluded that it was untrue. The evidence given by Case's wife as to his movements in the days before the murder is inconsistent with it. 'Also,' observed Lord Hewart, 'in the second confession the rope was said to be tied at the back of the woman's neck whereas, in fact, it was tied in front; and the new confession speaks of rushing out into the garden to cut the clothes line whereas the clothes line was across the ceiling of the room.'

'There are,' observed Paley Scott,' small differences which look as if the man's information may have come from the newspapers.' If [the man] was called, he would seek leave to call further evidence in rebuttal.

Hewart thereupon announced that the appeal would be adjourned until the following day and steps would be taken to secure the attendance of the maker of the confession.

Its author was a Liverpool criminal, named William Hartle, then a serving prisoner. At 10.30 on the 21st he stepped into the witness box in the Lord Chief's court. After confirming his name and home address, acknowledging that he was the maker of the confession and was willing to give evidence, he launched into an account of the murder. He began by describing how he and Case had travelled to Sheffield from Liverpool October 18 or 19. At this point, he was asked if he could see Case in court. He looked around and said he could not. 'Look at every part of the court,' Hewart told him. After staring at the dock where Case sat sandwiched between two warders, he said 'I cannot see the man. He is not here.' He then continued with his narrative:

> *In Sheffield, his companion suggested that they should break in somewhere. They went to a Council house in Ravencarr road, opened the front door and went inside. The room which he entered was unoccupied, but then a young woman came in. He hid himself inside a coal hole or cupboard but the air in the cupboard was bad and made him cough. As he coughed, Case came running into the room. The woman said 'What are you doing here? You have no right here. I will call the police.' At this he placed a bath towel, as long as himself, round her face to quieten her. Case told him to be careful and warned him about her condition. By this time the woman was lying on the floor. He thought she had fainted. He ran out into the garden, clutched a piece of clothes line and wrapped it loosely round her throat. She was lying near a corner of the room. She made no movement. Case said 'She is dead.' He picked something to eat up off the table and went. We took the main road out of Sheffield. Case gave him a ten shilling*

*note and he went back to Liverpool. He took a pair of patent shoes which fitted and a ring. He thought Case took a purse because he saw him throw one away.'*

Asked the young woman's name, he declined to say. 'You mentioned a name in the statement,' it was put. 'I think otherwise now,' he replied.

Paley Scott rose to cross-examine. He showed Hartle a photograph of the room where the murder had been committed. 'I do not recognise it,' he replied. Nor did he recognise the tea cloth or the cord which had been found wrapped around Mrs Mottram's neck. Asked to describe the wallpaper in the room he said it had a pattern of red and blue roses on a white background, the woman wore her hair in a bun and the towel he placed round her neck was a big one with a coloured border. The diamond ring he stole had three stones two white and one red. He had pawned it at Liverpool. He had been arrested on October 19 for stealing cheques and had been arrested before for larceny and had been to Borstal

The Lord Chief then asked him about the man Case. 'I've known him about four years and seen him a great many times,' claimed Hartle. 'His hair is sandy and the man sitting in the dock is not anything like him.' He confirmed that the man Case was in the room when he tied the towel round the woman's throat, watching him. He said 'Go easy,' but didn't do anything to stop him. Afterwards, he helped me remove things from the house. He saw me take the ring and shoes. 'And that,' asked the Lord Chief 'is the man you say is innocent?' 'Of course he is innocent, he took no part in the murder.'

By now Hartle, as a witness, was hopelessly discredited, but Paley Scott was still not satisfied.

With the court's leave he called George Mottram and took him one by one through the points on which Hartle's account strayed from the facts: the wall paper in the room where the murder was committed had a reddish brown check design; there was no cupboard in the room; there was no clothes line in the garden; the piece of cord wrapped around his wife's neck had been cut from a line in the kitchen; there was no Turkish towel in the house; the cloth around his wife's neck was a tea towel which had been tied tightly; his wife did not have a bun; no shoes were missed after the murder.

As Neal rose to address the court, the Lord Chief observed that the murder which Hartle had described was clearly not the murder with which the court was concerned:

> *'I submit that there is something in the confession.' said Neal.*
>
> *'What after his evidence in the witness box? Give us credit for having as much intelligence as a jury. How could Hartle mix up his friend Case with the prisoner here?'*
>
> *'Perhaps,' suggested Neal somewhat desperately 'there were two Samuel Cases. It was quite logical that Hartle should think that the man he knew and with whom he committed the murder was the prisoner here. Hartle, after all, made a very careful and detailed statement to the Governor and was not like a lunatic who would confess to a murder [he had not committed]. Had the evidence been before the jury the defence might have been quite a different one.*

*Do you seriously suppose that the testimony of Hartle would have done your client any good? It was obvious if he was speaking of a Samuel Case it was not the Samuel Case we see in this court.*

Neal, recognising, not before time, that he was on a losing wicket, changed tack.

*The defence of insanity was not as hopeless as some we see in the court.'*
*'The jury heard the defence,' retorted Hewart 'and would have none of it.'*

After the briefest of consultations with his brother judges, the Lord Chief Justice gave judgment:

*The defence put forward at the trial was not that the appellant was elsewhere at the time of the murder or that he was not the man whose hand committed the act, but that he was insane and did not know what he was doing. The summing up was not unfavourable to the defence On the contrary, it would not be wrong to say that the appellant had the advantage conferred upon him of a view, or something like a view, as to the onus of proof to which he was not at all entitled. It could not be too clearly and permanently remembered that there was no burden of proof on the Crown to prove that he was sane. The law presumed that every man was sane and responsible for his acts unless and until the contrary was proved. The jury negatived the defence and most properly found that the appellant was guilty of murder. [As to the evidence of Hartle] not one of the members of the court believed a word of his story. Whether the story was concocted for the sake of getting a day out of prison or for some other reason, or whether it had some relation to things that had happened [at some time and somewhere else] the court did not know, but one thing was perfectly obvious; it had no bearing on this case. If Hartle was speaking of a real person whom he had known as Samuel Case, it was quite obvious that the appellant was not that Samuel Case. It would be idle to enumerate the matters upon which [his] testimony ...failed to strengthen the argument on behalf of the appellant. There is nothing in [this appeal and it] is dismissed.*

The Hartle confession having proved to be a cruel attention-seeking hoax, Case's only hope now lay in a reprieve. Even as the appeal hearing was getting under way, a petition was being got ready for dispatch to the Home Secretary. Bearing upwards of 7,000 signatures, it urged the following grounds:

*That the convicted man was young, he being 24 years of age.*

*That he is a married man.*

*That he was a man of previous good character and was held in high esteem by his fellow workmen, as was shown by the evidence given at the trial.*

*That the crime was not premeditated and was apparently motiveless.*

*That the only evidence of the crime was the perfectly truthful confession volunteered by the condemned man.*

*That the condemned man suffered from ill health and melancholy and had twice recently made attacks at the throat of a workman, without any sort of provocation or motive, and, although not insane, he must have been afflicted with mental and emotional instability approaching insanity.*

But no reprieve came and on Saturday, January 7, 1928, Case was hanged at Armley prison.[190] By 9 o'clock, the time of execution, about 50 people were standing outside the gates of the Gaol in the drizzle. As the clock began to strike the hour, the men bared their heads. Several of the women were in tears. Within a few seconds after the clock had ceased to strike, the prison bell began to toll. Ten minutes later the notices of the sheriff and the prison doctor certifying death were posted outside the gate-house.

## POW Camp justice - Armin Kuehne and Emil Schmittendorf, 1945 [191]

Redmires has long had military associations. In the 1880s the Old Militia used to fire their artillery pieces from Stannington at targets in Wyming Brook. During the first World War an army camp was built there and used in the training of the volunteer Sheffield City Battalion.[192] At the end of the war it was decommissioned and in 1926 the huts and other equipment sold off by auction.

---

[190] Thomas Pierrepoint was the executioner.

[191] See *Sheffield Telegraph*, Aug 9, 10 and 14, 1945; *Star*, Aug 9, 1945; *The Times*, Aug 8, 9,10, 14, Oct. 10, 11, 1945.

[192] On August 7, 1914, the day after his appointment as Secretary of State, Lord Kichener, foreseeing that the coming war would be a long one and that the army would need to be expanded considerably, launched an appeal for volunteers to enlist for three years or the duration of the war. Public response was overwhelming. In Sheffield, HAL Fisher, the vice-chancellor of the University, encouraged the formation of a local unit. Following a series of public meetings, enlistment began on September 10 and by the end of the next day 900 men had been accepted. Thus was born the Sheffield City Battalion. Training began in earnest on September 15 at the Bramall Lane football ground. For some months the men lived at home, assembling daily for drill and training. Soon, however, a new hutted camp was under construction at Redmires, on the site of an old racecourse. Local contractors did the bulk of the construction. The accommodation huts housed 34 men apiece and adjacent to them were showers

The 1940s saw the site pressed into service as a Prisoner of War Camp. After D Day, it had more prisoners than the huts could accommodate and tents had to be put up to house fresh arrivals. Standing in bleak moor land, at a height of 1,000 feet above sea level and far from the coast, the camp did not offer obvious escape opportunities and, by 1945, with Germany on its knees, one might have expected that the inmates would have been happy enough to sit out the rest of the war there. Not so, however. The camp had a hard core of Nazis who regarded it as their patriotic duty to escape. On December 20, 1944, seven prisoners broke out[193] and escape attempts continued into 1945.

March was a particularly bad month for escapees. First, on March 14 camp guards shot and fatally wounded a prisoner who tried to escape.[194] Then, on March 24, a tunnel which was nearing completion was discovered. The guards, who knew exactly where to look, had clearly been tipped off and there was not much doubt as to the identity of the informant: earlier that afternoon a prisoner, named Gerhardt Rettig, had been seen passing a note through the wire to the

---

and ablution blocks. Bad weather caused delays in completing the camp and towards the end of November nightly work parties were sent up to Redmires to help finish the camp. The Battalion moved up to the camp in December and remained there until May 12, 1915, when after a warm send off from the Midland station, they went to Cannock Chase to continue their training. The City Battalion officially designated the 12th (Service) Battalion of the York and Lancasters became part of the 94th Brigade, together with the lst and 2nd Barnsley Pals (13th and 14th Battalions, York and Lancasters) and the Accrington Pals (11th Battalion, E Lancs). The battalion was disbanded at the end of the Great War. The building and opening of the camp gave a marvellous, if temporary, boost to the trade of the nearby *Three Merry Lads* and *Sportsman Inn.* (See generally C Binfield (ed) *The History of the City of Sheffield 1843-1993,* Sheffield Academic Press, 1993, Vol 2, p 236 and Paul Gibson and Paul Oldfield, *The Sheffield City Battalion,* Wharncliffe Press Ltd 1988, pp 37-39).

[193] *Star*, December 20, 1944.

[194] *The Times*, March 16, 1945.

guards. When the German camp leader learned of this he arranged for Rettig and a second man to be transferred to another camp for their own safety. 'Pack up your kit immediately,' they were told. As they were doing so, roll call was sounded. Having attended this, Rettig returned to his hut to complete his packing and, this done, he ventured outside. He was immediately spotted and seconds later dashed into the hut pursued by a baying mob of 20 or 30 prisoners. He was given a bad beating and then pushed outside, his face covered in blood and his eyes almost closed. An even larger crowd, variously estimated at 100 and 200-300, now gathered, shouting 'Hang him. Beat him to death.' He fled towards the wash house, where he was cornered and beaten into unconsciousness. Revived by having a bucket of cold water thrown over him, he staggered to his feet and ran off, again with the mob hard on his heels. Then a shout went up 'The Tommies are coming,' at which the crowd of pursuers melted away.

A medical orderly found Rettig lying on a rubbish bin. His head and face were so badly swollen that he was unrecognisable; he had severe wounds to the head, a tear to the upper lip, and was bleeding profusely from the nose and mouth. He was taken to the camp hospital and almost immediately despatched to the Wharncliffe Emergency Hospital. He died at 8.15 pm that night. A post-mortem was carried out and established that he had died from asphyxiation caused by inhalation of blood. This finding came as no surprise. The medical orderly, who had accompanied Rettig in the ambulance, said that there was so much blood pouring from his mouth that it must have been impossible for him to breathe. The source of the bleeding was the severe wounds to the face and head which the doctor, conducting the post-mortem, thought had been caused by a weapon.

Investigation of the incident by the British military authorities resulted in four men being charged with Rettig's murder: Armin Kuehne, Heinz Ditzer, Juergen Kersting and Emil Schmittendorf.

On August 7, 1945, they were put on trial before a military tribunal held at the London District Prisoner of War Cage at Kensington Palace Gardens, presided over by Colonel W.H.E.L. Fox Pitt. The prosecution was conducted by Major R.A.L. Hillard. Lieutenant A.C. Brands represented the accused.

None of the four was under any illusion as to what was at stake. As Kuenhne had written to a fellow prisoner 'Six comrades of mine from Camp 21 [at Perth] have been condemned to death and the same thing is going to happen to us.'

Because of the fear of reprisals against witnesses, press reporters admitted to the hearing were required to give an undertaking not to publish the names of those who gave evidence.

The hearing extended over five days.

During the second day, Lieutenant Brands informed the tribunal that he had been given the name of a witness, who was in hospital in Yorkshire with pleurisy, and had sent off a list of questions which he wanted putting to him. He asked the court to adjourn the hearing to enable these inquiries to be completed which was granted.

When the hearing resumed, several German witnesses pointed the finger at Schmittendorf. One said that Rettig had crumpled up after being struck several blows to the face by Schmittendorf, who had then taken hold of his hair and kicked him in the face twice. Another claimed that Schmittendorf had described the affair as 'very successful.' A third witness said that when he and Schmittendorf had been in a camp at Doncaster, Schmittendorf had pointed him, the witness, out as a scoundrel and a criminal for saying that Germany had lost the war. Against Kuehne and Ditzer, it was said that they punched Rettig on the head. Kuehne was also said to have explained afterwards that Rettig had been attacked because he 'had given away about the escape tunnel.'

All the prisoners gave evidence in their own defence. Lieutenant Brands, opening the case for Schmittendorf and Kuehne, said that their defence was 'a denial that they attacked Rettig. Schmittendorf would say that he was present at the fight inside the hut, during the course of which he had attacked one of the prosecution witnesses. He later saw a large crowd outside, but could not find out what it was doing. Kuehne's defence was that he was in the hut when the fighting outside was taking place.'

Schmittendorf told the tribunal that shortly after the tunnel had been found by a British sergeant who appeared to know where to look for it, he, Schmittendorf, went into one of the huts. He was told who the betrayer was and could see a man being beaten up. He was being knocked from one side to the other and, when he came to my side, I hit his head. The man he hit was not Rettig, who was being beaten up by others in the hut. He did not hit Rettig at all. In cross-examination, he agreed that he had spent many nights working on the tunnel and that all who had worked on it were very angry at the betrayal. They had suspected that there must be a traitor in the camp because, in the past, every time prisoners had tried to break out it had always gone wrong. A number of letters were put to him, in one of which it was stated ‘It is important you saw me in the hut.’ He admitted that he had written it.

Kuehne, described in press reports as ‘a diminutive figure with a large Red Cross armband,’ said that he was in his hut when about twenty men rushed in upsetting the beds. ‘I was carried along with the crowd and then saw two men being beaten up. I straightened up my bed and went to the end of the hut to escape the tumult.’ Asked if he knew that Rettig was anti-Nazi he replied ‘I am not interested in whether a man is a Nazi or anti-Nazi. When one is a soldier one has nothing to do with politics.’ He added that, being in the Red Cross, he had no interest in escape tunnels; in fact, he and several others thought it rather a joke that the escapers had worked on the tunnel to no avail. He too was confronted with a letter which he had written whilst awaiting trial. It was in these terms

> *It is only a matter of two points: during the beating up I was in the hut and, secondly, I fetched the rations. If you can give testimony accordingly, I will be very grateful. Please do anything you can. Things might go wrong. Please destroy contents when read. If you cannot, remain silent.*

Next to be called was Ditzer. He claimed that he took no part in the beating up of Rettig. He admitted that he had helped to dig the escape tunnel, and that two days after the discovery of the tunnel he and Schmittendorf had escaped from the camp. He agreed that he knew, at the time of the escape, that Rettig was dead. He asked permission to make a statement to the court to help Schmittendorf. At this, Lieutenant Brands was given the opportunity to speak to him, but having done so refused his offer of help.

Last to testify was Kersting. He denied taking any part in the killing.

When it sat on August 13 the tribunal announced that Ditzer and Kersting were acquitted. Lieutenant Brands then proceeded to address them on behalf of the remaining two accused. He said that Rettig had been attacked by a yelling milling crowd and it was vital to identify the accused accurately. The only witness who alleged that Schmittendorf kicked Rettig was not sure which he was when asked to identify him in court. Schmittendorf was 31; his wife and children were in Berlin but he knew no more than that. He was a regular soldier, having joined up in 1934, and that would explain the intense feeling he would have towards anyone whom he considered a traitor. To escape is not a dishonourable thing but to prevent your comrades escaping is, in the minds of most of us, a beastly thing to do.

Turning next to the case of Kuehne, the Lieutenant, said that he joined the Hitler Youth movement at the age of nine, left home when he was twelve and had not seen his parents since he was eighteen. By the time he was fifteen he was engaged in the instruction of the National Socialist philosophy, with particular emphasis on the life of the Fuhrer, to young Germans who were being incorporated into the Reich as German conquest spread eastwards and south-eastwards. He had a school at Lodz. instructing these men how to be good Germans. Having spent his formative years in those unnatural surroundings is it strange that Kuehne reacts to treachery to the Fuhrer in the way he was trained to act over the years?

His pleas proved unavailing. Both men were convicted and sentenced to death.

On October 9 the War Office announced that Schmittendorf and Kuehne were to hang.[195] They were executed at Pentonville prison on October 10, 1945.[196] The hangman was Albert Pierrepoint.

## Murder in the Snow - William Smedley, 1947 [197]

In March 1947 Britain was in the grip of the worst winter within living memory. To make matters worse there was a coal shortage.[198]

At around 2.30 on the afternoon of Saturday, March 8, while out scavenging for wood amongst the bomb damaged buildings in the city centre, eleven-year-old Peter Johnson[199] made a grim discovery. In a derelict outbuilding in Spring Street, less than 50 yards from the busy Bridge Street bus station, he came across a woman's body.[200]

> *I looked through the doorway and saw [a] woman lying face downwards at one end of the room. I ran and fetched Ronnie (ten year old Ronald Higgins who was collecting wood with him), who was in Bridge Street, and then we went to tell a bus man.'*

At the bus station, they told their story to the traffic controller who sent for the police and an ambulance. Officers from the Central Police Office were quickly on the scene and it was at once obvious to them that they had a murder on their hands. The dead woman had

---

195 *The Times*, October 10, 1945. Four days before five of the German prisoners of war involved in killing a fellow prisoner at Comrie Camp, Perthshire in December, 1944 (this was the murder referred to by Kuehne in his letter) had been executed at Pentonville (*The Times*, October 5, 1945).

196 *The Times*, October 11, 1945.

197 See *Sheffield Telegraph*, March 10, 12, Jne 11, Jly 22, 1947; *Star*, Mar 10, 13, 24, May 14, 22, 30, Jne 10, Jly 23, Aug 14, 1947.

198 'Paralysing grip of winter continues its stranglehold on transport' (*Star*, March 8, 1947).

199 The lad was the son of the licensee of the *Stag Inn* in Wilson Street, Neepsend.

200 The building was known as 'the cottages.' Outside the snow was 18" deep.

been strangled with her own headscarf and one of the officers recognised her - she was 27-year-old local prostitute, Edith Simmonite. Near to the body were footprints made by a man's Wellington boot. An ambulance waited by the building for two hours while the police surgeon examined the body and police officers searched the interior of the building and took photographs. The corpse was taken to the nearby public mortuary in Nursery Street.[201]

The police started to make door-to-door inquiries, concentrating, in particular, upon public houses, and lodging houses in West Bar, trying to establish where and with whom the dead woman had been in the last 24 hours.

Edith was well known in the area.[202] She had for the last six or seven years lived in a women's hostel at West Bar Green. The landlord of the hostel, Charles Fisher, told the police that during the time she had lived there she had not had regular work, spending most of the day in the hostel but going out to public houses at midday. In the evenings she went to cinemas and then to public houses, returning late at night or in the early hours of the morning. She had gone out on Friday evening and he had not seen her since.

---

201 The inquest took place on March 13 and the funeral on March 17.

202 According to the *Star*, both her parents had died when she was young and she had in consequence spent a good deal of her childhood at various institutions in the city. For the last six or seven years she had lived at the Women's Hostel in West Bar Green. During the war she had served in the ATS; after the war she had worked as a hospital domestic and latterly in the cutlery trade. The matron of a city nursing home told the *Star* 'She was a splendid worker, always bright and cheerful. She was with us for some months and once returned after leaving us. She said 'It's no good matron. I'm too bad to mend.' We knew all about her past and did our best to rescue her.'' Her last job was at A H Risby & Co Ltd of Portobello Place, Sheffield where she worked for a short time as a scratch brusher in the plating shop. A spokesman for the firm said 'she left last November without giving any reason either to the firm, or to her workmates.' She had eight convictions for prostitution, the first in 1941.

One of the places she had visited that night was the *Sun Inn* in West Bar. 'She often came in alone or with different men,' the licensee's daughter told the *Sheffield Telegraph*. 'Usually she was very quiet but some times when she was very merry she would sing.' She had come in with a man on the Thursday and on the Friday. The police made two visits there on the Saturday evening. On each occasion a man left with the officers and accompanied them to the CID headquarters, only to be released after questioning.

A police superintendent told the *Star* that, at around 10.30 pm on the Friday night, Edith had been seen talking to a man wearing a light coloured overcoat and Wellington boots, with the tops turned down, outside the Civic Restaurant in Bridge Street. After that, she had, it was believed, walked through or around the bus station.

An appeal was put out for witnesses. The dead woman was '5'½" tall with a fresh complexion brown hair and medium build. She was wearing a rough brown coat, a coloured scarf, rubber high-heeled overshoes and her legs were bare'. Anyone who had seen her on the Friday evening was asked to contact the police. The police said that they were particularly anxious to speak to anyone who had been queuing at Bridge Street on Friday night between 10.20 and 11 pm for a bus to Parson Cross, Stocksbridge, or High Green.

Two weeks on, despite exhaustive inquiries, the police were no nearer finding the killer. 'Officers had,' *The Star* told its readers 'travelled to Lancashire to interview two men known to have been in Sheffield at the time of the murder, and they were still anxious to trace three men, who had been overheard discussing the murder in a city cafe at least three hours before the body was found. The trio were described as follows: man no 1: aged about 35, well built, well-dressed wearing a blue pin-stripe suit and a dark overcoat; man no 2: aged about 30, 5'7" dirty appearance; man no 3: aged about 40, 5'10" well built, very dirty appearance, wearing a blue Melton overcoat and cap, possibly a coal man.' This unlikely trio were never traced.

One man who had been seen in Edith's company on the night in question was 38-year-old West Bar hostel resident, William Smedley. Taken to the police headquarters for questioning on the Saturday night, he admitted he had been with her on the Friday but insisted that he had left her at 10.15 pm and had not seen her after that. Unable to break his story, the police were obliged to let him go. On March 27 they saw him again, but he stuck to his story and was again released.

On Friday May 9, with the investigation apparently going nowhere fast, the police got a break. Smedley turned up asking to speak to Detective Sergeant Naylor. He had some information for him. After he, Smedley, had left Edith at 10.15 she had headed off towards Bridge Street in the company of a man he knew by sight who was stopping at the same hostel as he was. This man had spoken to him on the Saturday morning. He said he had murdered Edith and was clearing off to Rhyl.[203] He had now received a letter from the man, asking about the progress of police inquiries into the murder and requesting that Smedley meet him outside the Miners' Convalescent Home at Rhyl on the following Monday. He did not explain why he had not mentioned any of this before. The police paid him £3 for the information and told him that he would receive a further £7 if the man kept the appointment.

[203] I...saw the man on the morning of Saturday, March 8, in the reading room [of the hostel]. I was sitting at a table and the man came up to me and said 'I have done her. 'I will let you know when I am going to see you, and will write to you.' I have not seen him since.

Later that Friday, Smedley sent a telegram to his married sister, Doris Butler, in Doncaster: 'Come Saturday morning. Urgent. Brother in terrible trouble.' The next day she and her husband, Jack, met him outside the hostel. He took them to a nearby public house.' 'What have you done?' asked Jack. 'The police are pulling me in for the murder of Edith Simmonite?' At first, the Butlers thought that the he was joking but, when it became clear that he was not, his brother-in-law asked 'Did you do it?' After some prevarication, he admitted that he had. When the time came for the Butlers to set off for home, Smedley turned to his sister: 'I don't care what happens now I have seen you,' he said.

On the Monday, he was taken over to North Wales in a police car but, although he was at the meeting place at the appointed time, his correspondent did not turn up. He and Sergeant Naylor spent the rest of Monday and part of Tuesday in Rhyl, making enquiries trying to trace the man, but to no avail. On the Tuesday afternoon, at Colwyn Bay, the police got the breakthrough they had been seeking. 'I killed her,' Smedley told the Sergeant and went on to dictate and sign a statement under caution:[204]

> *I went out of the Sun Inn with Edith Simmonite on March 7 at 10 o'clock, and I was talking to her at the bottom of the hostel steps. She was nagging at me.*
>
> *I went down Spring Street at about 10.15. I went into an old building in Bridge Street [The statement then described a conversation which he had with her and continued] I then got hold of her scarf and pulled it tight but I didn't mean killing her.*

[204] It was dictated and signed in the police car.

*She had the scarf round her neck and I pulled it tight in a single knot. I took the scarf round the top of her head but I cannot remember whether I tied the ends or not. Suddenly, she dropped back and stopped struggling. I got back to the hostel about 11.20.*

*The reason I did it was she gave me a disease and was always tantalising me. My intention was to frighten her so she would keep away from me. I was getting fed up.*

*I had a letter from an Irishman last Wednesday to go and see him at Rhyl outside the Yorkshire Miners' Convalescent home. This man was at the hostel on March 8, 1947, and I told him I had killed Edith.*

*I also told Matthew Frayne the same day.*

*What I have written is the truth. I am not pleading guilty to murder but I admit that it was me who killed her.*

Back in Sheffield he said to one of the custody officers 'This means the rope. I don't want a reprieve.' At 8.45 pm he was charged with murder. 'Not guilty,' he replied.

The following morning he appeared before the Sheffield magistrates who remanded him in custody for seven days. He appeared in the dock wearing a blue tunic jacket and an open neck shirt. 'I have nothing to say,' he told the bench 'until I have legal aid.' After successive remands, committal proceedings finally got under way on June 10. By this time he was represented by local solicitor Mr B. Beale. Opening the case to the magistrates, Mr J F Claxton, for the DPP, took the magistrates through the signed statements Smedley had made to the police. The accused interrupted him several times and, when the May confession was read out, he shouted 'That is all lies, that paper.' For all his protests, the confession did not lack corroboration. His brother-in-law, Jack Butler, told the bench that Smedley had confessed to him and hostel resident Matthew Frayn confirmed having heard some of what was said.[205] There was also evidence that Smedley had not returned to the hostel on the night of the murder (the next morning the domestics found that his bed had not been slept in). Dr Forster, who had carried out the post-mortem examination, said that death was due to asphyxiation caused by the ligature around the neck and that there was slight evidence that the dead woman was suffering from venereal disease. At the conclusion of the evidence, Smedley reserved his defence. The bench, without hesitation, committed him for trial.

He was tried at Leeds Assizes on August 14, 1947, before Mr Justice Pritchard.[206] Raymond Hinchcliffe KC prosecuted, Alastair Sharp defended.[207]

Called to give evidence in his own defence, Smedley told the jury of nine men and three women that on the night of the murder he was jolly. Towards the end of the evening, Simmonite, with whom he had been intimate before, said 'Are you going with me, Billy?' When he refused she said 'If you don't go, I'll get you chucked out.' He then went with her to the derelict building. After a time she asked if he knew she had given him a disease at which he lost his head and pulled at her scarf. He pulled at it for three or four minutes and then went home. 'I just did it to frighten her. I had no intention of killing her, no intention of hurting her.'

---

[205] Mrs Smedley, however, would not have it that any confession had been made. She claimed his reply was 'No. I was in bed at the time.'

[206] **Pritchard**, Sir Fred Ellis (1899-1982); educ Shrewsbury and Liverpool university; barrister 1923; practised on N Circuit; KC 1937; High Court judge 1947.

[207] **Hinchcliffe**, Sir George Raymond; b Huddersfield, 1900; educ Leys school and Trinity Hall, Cambridge; barrister 1924; Recorder of Berwick on Tweed, 1939-47; QC 1947; Recorder of Middlesborough 1947-50; Leeds 1950-57, High Court judge 1957; **Sharp**, Alastair George, b 1911, educ Aberdeen GS, Fettes school, Clare College, Cambridge; barrister 1935; MBE 1945; ecorder of Rotherham 1960-62; QC 1961; county court judge 1962.

Cross-examined, he insisted that he had not known that he had a disease until Simmonite told him, but was then forced to admit that he had attended a Sheffield clinic for treatment in November, 1946, and had named Edith Simmonite as the person who had given him the disease. Asked to describe the strangulation, he said he was standing up when Simmonite spoke to him. He dropped down astride her and pulled her scarf. She was kicking and when she stopped he had an idea he had killed her. He admitted he had told lies to put the police off the scent.

In his closing speech, Mr Sharp asked the jury to bring back a verdict of manslaughter. It was in doubt whether Smedley intended either to kill or to cause grievous bodily harm and, in any event, he was provoked. 'Were there any circumstances more extreme than for a man to be told he had been given a loathsome disease?' he asked.

The jury were out for just over an hour before returning with a verdict of guilty. Asked if he had anything to say why sentence of death should not be passed upon him, Smedley replied 'Nothing.' But when sentence was passed he buried his face in his hands and collapsed. He had to be carried from the dock.

He was visited after his conviction by Mr Sharp who told him there were no grounds of appeal but he would draft a memorial to the Home Secretary asking for clemency. This came to nothing and on August 14, 1947, Smedley was hanged at Armley prison. The execution attracted no interest, not a single person being present at the prison gates when the statutory notices were posted outside.

Smedley was the last man to be executed for a Sheffield murder and the second Sheffielder of that name to be hanged at the gaol.

*Harry Walters*

*Upper Allen Street*

*Rippon Street (now demolished) in the 1950s*

*George Edward Law*

*The Chinese Laundry murder, 1922*

*A policeman stands guard outside 231, Crookes after the murder*

*Today 231, Crookes is a Barnado's charity shop*

***Sing Lee***

*The trunk in which **Sing Lee's** body was found being carried into the coroner's court*

***The Walkley Murder, 1923***

***No 41, Lister Street,** the scene of the murder (No 41 is the house nearest the camera) and the victim **John Clark***

***Princess Street** today*

***Norfolk Bridge** today (Princess Street is off the picture to the left)*

***The Rawson's Arms where** the Fowlers were taken after their arrest*

*'Jock' Plommer*

*Lawrence Fowler*

*Wilfred Fowler*

*Sam Garvin*

*Robert Henry Garvin*

*Elizabeth and Lorraine Lax*

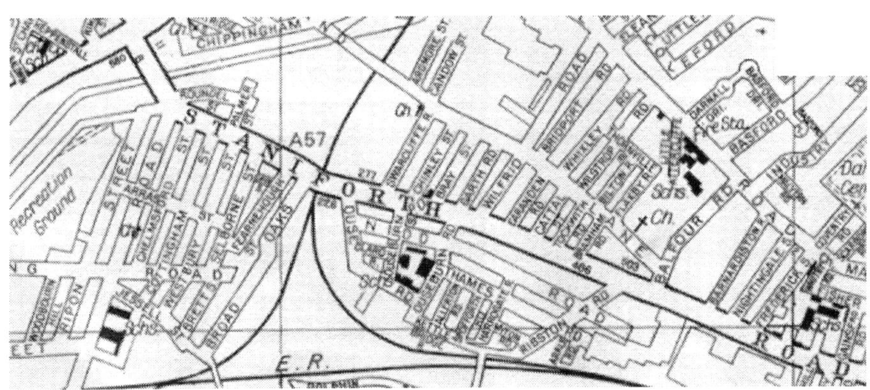


***Ripon Street, a side road running off Staniforth Road, is to be found on the left hand side of the plan.***

*Alice Mottram*

*Samuel Case*

*No. 28, Ravencarr Road*

***Today, the site of the POW camp is covered by a wood but the concrete bases of and entrances to the huts can still be seen among the trees.***

*The Bridge Street murder, 1947*

*The victim,* ***Edith Simmonite***

***Bridge Street bus station in the late 1940s.***
***Edith's body was found in a derelict building, a short distance away.***

***This building was formerly the Sun Inn, West Bar. Edith and Smedley had been drinking there shortly before he strangled her.***

***Thirlwell Road, Heeley today. Kate lived in Thirlwell Terrace a side-street off to the left***

***Glover Road, Lowfields today. Thomas Skinner lived at no 27.***

*Cresswell Street where Phyllis Staton lived*

*Dr John Blakeley's home at 203, School Road, Crookes*

# 4

# After Smedley

## *a. The end of capital punishment*[208]

Capital punishment for murder continued in Britain for eighteen years after the execution of William Smedley. At the date of its abolition in 1965 public opinion was three to one in favour of retention.

The campaign for abolition had been a long one. In 1925 a National Council for the Abolition of the Death Penalty had been established under the energetic leadership of Roy Calvert, but all it had to show for its efforts by 1939 was the raising of the age limit for capital punishment from 16 to 18.

By 1945 the climate had changed. During the committee stage of the 1948 Criminal Justice Bill, the House of Commons passed an amendment that the death penalty be suspended for a trial period of five years. The majority was 114 to 89 and the vote was followed by an announcement by Home Secretary, Chuter Ede, that he intended to advise the King to commute all death sentences to life imprisonment. The House of Lords, however, would have no truck with the amendment which was rejected by 181 votes to 28, Lord Chief Justice Goddard claiming that the announcement by the Home Secretary that he would reprieve all murderers was an alteration of

[208] See J B Christoph, *Capital Punishment and British Politics*, George Allen & Unwin, London, 1962; E.O. Tuttle, *The Crusade against Capital Punishment in Great Britain*, Stevens, London, 1961.

the law through administrative action – an exercise of ‘a dispensing power which has been repudiated by Parliament ever since the days of James II.’ When the Bill came back from the Lords, the Government proposed a compromise clause retaining the death penalty for certain murders but abolishing it for all others. The clause passed in the Commons but was rejected by the Lords and, rather than lose the Bill, the government gave way.

Later in the year the government announced the appointment of a Royal Commission on Capital Punishment charged with considering whether capital punishment should be limited or modified. Its report published in 1953 recommended alteration of the M’Naughten rules, a widening of the definition of provocation, abolition of the felony-murder rule (also known as the doctrine of ‘constructive malice’) and the raising of the age limit for capital punishment from 18 to 21. In the Commons’ debate on the Report an abolitionist amendment was defeated.

By the end of 1955 there was increasing unease about the use of the death penalty. It had always been claimed by those opposed to reform that there was no risk of an innocent man being hanged. During the debate on the 1948 Bill, Sir David Maxwell Fyfe (soon to achieve notoriety as the Home Secretary who refused to reprieve Derek Bentley) had ridiculed claims to the contrary. ‘There is,’ he declared:

> *no practical possibility [of an innocent man being put to death]. Of course, a jury might go wrong, the Court of Criminal Appeal might go wrong as might the House of Lords and the Home Secretary: they might all be stricken mad and go wrong. But that is not a possibility which anyone can*

*consider likely ... it is impossible for anyone who views and examines fairly the facts of any murder case of which he has knowledge to say that such a miscarriage has taken place.'*[209]

However, the conviction of John Halliday Christie for murder in 1953 had given rise to strong suspicions that he had committed the murders for which Timothy Evans had been hanged three years before.[210] The executions of Derek Bentley in January, 1953 and Ruth Ellis in July 1955 had also caused widespread unease.

In 1956 a bill for abolition, introduced by the veteran campaigner, Sidney Silverman, was passed by the Commons only to be rejected by the Lords. In November the Government intervened and introduced its own Homicide Bill. Passed by both Houses it became law in 1957. Under the Act the only categories of murder which would henceforth be capital were: (i) murder in the furtherance of theft; (ii) murder done in the course of resisting or preventing arrest or effecting or assisting in an escape from legal custody; (iii) murder of a police officer in the execution of his duty; (iv) murder of a prison officer by a prisoner; (v) murder by a person previously convicted of murder. It was hardly a well thought out list, omitting as it did child sex murders and murder by poisoning. The Act also introduced a new defence to murder of diminished responsibility and adopted the recommendations of the Royal Commission as to the redefinition of provocation and the abolition of the felony-murder rule.

Following the return of the Labour Government in October, 1964 Sidney Silverman, with government encouragement and support

[209] PD 1947-48, vol,. 449, col. 1077.
[210] As to the Evans case see L Kennedy, *10 Rillington Place*, Grafton, London, 1971.

introduced a bill proposing that the death penalty for murder should be abolished for a period of five years and that, at the end of that period, the abolition should become permanent if both Houses of Parliament passed an affirmative resolution. The Bill passed in both Houses and in December 1969 resolutions were passed making abolition permanent.[211]

The reintroduction of capital punishment was made more difficult by the conversion of condemned cells to other uses and the destruction of execution apparatus at all prisons except Wandsworth. This refurbishment and dismantling was complete by March 1967.

Arson in the royal dockyards ceased to be capitally punishable in 1971;[212] the death penalty for treason and piracy with violence was abolished by s. 36 of the Crime and Disorder Act, 1998.

### *b. Sheffield gets it own Assize*

While the debate as to capital punishment was proceeding on the national stage, in 1955 Sheffield got its own Assize court. Henceforth all South Yorkshire murders would be tried there, although, since the city had no prison, those sentenced to death would still be executed at Armley. In 1930 the City Council had submitted a memorandum to the Royal Commission of the Despatch of Business at Common Law, urging that Sheffield be granted its own Assize. In its Third Report (1936) the Commission urged that the city's claims be given 'the most sympathetic consideration,' and later the same year the Circuit

---

[211] The last persons to be hanged for murder were Peter Allen at Liverpool and Gwynne Evans at Manchester on August 13, 1964 for a murder at Workington.

[212] Criminal Damage Act, 1971, s 11 and sch. Part III.

Towns Committee recommended that Sheffield become an Assize town in August, 1940. The City Council immediately busied itself with plans for a new court-house. Initially, the site of the old *Albert Hall* in Barkers Pool (where Cole Bros now stands) was considered. Eventually, however, a site was chosen in Eyre Street close by the Central Library and a compulsory purchase order obtained and an artist's impression of the new building appeared in the *Sheffield Telegraph.* But then came the Second World War which brought the scheme to a halt.

In 1953, with a new court-house as far away as ever, Lord Chief Justice Goddard visited the Castle Street courts and declared that they would serve as a temporary home for the Assizes. Alterations were put in hand and Whirlow Court, which had been acquired for use as Judges' Lodgings, was refurbished (pre-war the Council had been contemplating acquiring nearby Parkhead House).

In 1955 an Order in Council was made creating Sheffield a new Assize Division, and on June 23 the first Assize was held, opened by the Lord Chief Justice. At this Assize Alec Wilkinson, a 21-year-old from Wombwell, was tried and convicted of the murder of his mother-in-law. He and Rotherham lecturer, Bernard Hugh Walden (tried in 1959), were the only two person convicted at Sheffield to be put to death. In 1962 the Sheffield Assize Division was by Act of Parliament made a separate judicial county (Hallamshire) with its own High Sheriff, provoking this comment in the *Solicitors' Journal*:

> *'the provisions [of the Act] are unique in that they create a shire for the sake of the assizes in reverse of the*

*historical process of instituting assizes for the benefit of shires.'*[213]

Sheffield Assizes, so long in coming, were destined to have but a short life. In 1971, the government adopting the recommendations of a report by Lord Beeching, abolished Assizes and replaced them with the Crown Court. Today Sheffield Crown Court tries all South Yorkshire murders but the city still has no prison of its own in which to house them pending trial.

---

[213] (1962) 106 Sol. Jo. 381-82.

# 5

## Overview

Between 1865 and 1965 18 men were put to death for Sheffield murders. Of their 20 victims 10 were women, 4 were children and just 6 were men. Although, unsurprisingly, half were domestic murders, the list is not without interest including, as it does, a 'ripper murder,' a trunk murder, a gang slaying and a prisoner of war camp execution.

The youngest of those hanged was 21-year-old German prisoner of war, Armin Kuehne. James Hall, at 55, was the oldest. No fewer than five were miners.

Peace, one of the nineteenth century's master criminals, was the most notorious, with the Fowler brothers the next best known. In no fewer than ten of the pre-1930 murders a cut throat razor was used; only one victim was shot: Arthur Dyson at Banner Cross. The decline in the use of the razor as a murder weapon is, almost certainly, linked to the invention of the safety razor[214] and then the electric razor,[215] following which cut throat razors gradually passed out of general use.

The police can rightly claim credit for bringing Smedley to book for the murder of prostitute, Edith Simmonite, in 1947. He was an obvious suspect and, by keeping the pressure on him, they eventually achieved the break through they were seeking. But in none of the other cases was the detection and conviction of the killer due to

---

[214] Gillette and Nickerson patented the first safety razor in 1901.
[215] The electric razor was invented by Joseph Schick in 1928.

skilled or painstaking police work. In a third of the cases, the murderer simply walked into a police station and gave himself up. Had Samuel Case not done so, he would never have been caught and had Hobson killed the Stothards' servant girl, as he had intended, and not merely wounded her, he would undoubtedly have escaped.

It is difficult to contend that any of the 18 was the victim of a miscarriage of justice. Six (having no other arguable defence) took refuge in a plea of insanity but although two, Law and Case, probably were suffering from mental illness, neither was M'Naughten insane: each clearly knew at the time of the killing what he was doing and that it was against the law.

Had Walters been guilty of a less horrific murder, he might well have been reprieved. The trial judge plainly had doubts as to his guilt and the jury recommended him to mercy. But in his case, as in those of West, Lax and Eastwood, the jury's recommendation was ignored. In 1921 a Bill had been introduced into the House of Commons seeking to prohibit the passing of the death sentence upon those whom a jury had recommended to mercy, but it failed to pass.[216]

The geographical spread of the murders (Banner Cross, Redmires, Darnall, the Manor Estate, Handsworth and Woodhouse were all the scene of killings) reflects the expansion of the city during the century in question. The most horrifying were undoubtedly those committed by Laycock and Walters and it is no coincidence that they occurred in slums close by the town centre, where heavy drinking, poverty and desperation were part of the everyday fabric of life.

[216] PD 1921, Vol 130, col. 1255.

# Appendix 1

## Charlie Peace's last letter

*HM Prison, Leeds, 7$^{th}$ February, 1879*

*My dear Son-in-Law, - I hope this letter will find you as well it can do I am still very weak and ill but a little better than I have been. You will know that I have been perged (perjured) by three persons in Darnall whar I wish to say to you is this do not make any attempt to avenge the wrong that was done to me by Jim and his wife and Mrs Padmore, for under my Present feelings I feel no imbetterness against no Person in this world, for if i must be forgiven i mushin t forgive. So my Dear Son. Do you Not Commit yourself in either thought, word or deed against any of these Persons, but in Place of being in their Company do all you Can to avoid them, and this will keep you from doing anything at each other that will be offencive. I do Send you a form of Prayer that I Compiled Myself before I left Pen ton vile Prison.*

*O Lord, turn not Thy face from me, but have mercy. Good Lord have mercy on me. I need not Confess my life to thee, for thou knows what I have been and what I am. So O my blessed Lord and Saviour Jesus Christ have mercy upon me, and wash and cleanse me from all my Sins and Make Me Clean, and save me from the danger of sin and from the Power of Hell. O God do not despise me nor Cast me from thee, but have mercy Good Lord have mercy upon me, and make me what thou would have me be, to enter into the Kingdom of heaven and then receive my Poor Soul at the last for Jesus Christ his Sake. Amen. "The Lord have mercy upon me, Christ have mercy upon me, Amen."*

*My Dear Son,*

*I have sent you this Prayer to Show you all the State of Mind that I do now feel myself to be in.i do not feel no trouble so great as I do my Sinful life agains my God I begin to feel that my God will have mercy on me and forgive me all my Sins and receive my Poor Soul into the Kingdom of heaven i send my best love, thanks and Good Wises to all friends that Came up on my trial to Speak for me I do want to see all my family as often as I can before I die you Can see me any week day but you will have to bring this letter with you and go to the Leeds Town Hall and enquire for Mr John Thornton the magistrates clerk and he will give you every information you require to see me you cannot see me without an order from him So to Save time and trouble go and see him before you Come to the Prison.*

*I send my Dearest love to my Dear, dear Wife and all of you my loving children*

*I am,*

*Your Wretched Husband and Father,*

*CHARLES PEACE*

# Appendix 2

## Kate Dover, The Queen of Heeley[217]

In April 1880, 28-year-old Kate Dover struck up an acquaintanceship with Thomas Skinner, a widower old enough to be her father. His was a well known name in Sheffield. An engraver and amateur painter of considerable merit, he had some years before been presented by his fellow townsfolk with a gold medal in recognition of his achievement in inventing a method of etching pictures on steel. He lived at 27, Glover Road, Lowfields where a Mrs Jones kept house for him. He had, if servants were to be believed, an eye for young women, particularly servant girls. When Kate met him she was running a confectionery shop in London Road. She lived with her mother at 4, Thirlwell Terrace, Thirlwell Road, Heeley. Because of her fondness for smart clothes she was known in the area as the Heeley Queen.

In September 1880, Mrs Jones left Glover Road; she would later claim that this was because Kate had started to interfere in the running of the household and because her husband disapproved of Skinner's taking up with her. In November 1880, Kate became Skinner's day housekeeper. At first they got on well enough but soon there was friction. She complained that he would not pay her a salary and kept her short of money, and certainly she was no longer dressing as smartly as she once had. He, for his part, accused her of pawning

[217] See the *Sheffield Independent*, December 8, 9, 10, 17, 21, 22, 23 and 24, 1881 and February 7, 8, and 9, 1882 and *The Times*, February 7 and 8, 1882.

his property. In June 1881 there was a furious row in which he accused her of pledging his tea service and best suit of clothes. But their life was not all quarrelling. He often took her out of an evening and had talked of altering his will in her favour. Days before his death she had told a young servant that she was going to marry him. 'He's too old for you,' said the girl. 'I would rather be an old man's darling than a young man's slave,' rejoined Kate. On December 5, the day before his death, the two of them were seen together in the *Big Tree* at Woodseats. They were on the most friendly terms and Skinner was heard to offer to buy Kate a pony.

On December 2, Mrs Jones had received a basket of vegetables from the country and had sent a portion of them, including some onions, to Skinner.

At around dinner time on Tuesday, December 5 Kate asked a little girl, named Charlotte Booker, to go to Learoyd's chemist's shop in Lowfield for three pennyworth of laudanum and three pennyworth of chloroform. She came back with the message that the chemist would not supply her unless she brought a note. Kate gave her a note stating that she wanted the items for the tic. The chemist then served her but kept the note.

Later the same day, Kate went round to another chemist's in Lowfield and asked the assistant for two pennyworth or arsenic. 'What do you want if for?' he asked. 'To colour some artificial flowers,' she replied. He told her he could not supply it unless she brought a witness. A few minutes later she returned with a Mr Wood and, having signed the poisons book, was supplied with the arsenic.

The following morning she sent a young servant out to Wood's butchers in Highfields to buy a fowl. In the note to the butcher she asked that the neck and giblets be removed.

When the servant returned she set about cooking the fowl in a pudding tin; in the tin was also some thyme and onion stuffing cooked separate from the fowl.

At midday she and Skinner sat down to dine. After consuming a Yorkshire pudding, they started to eat the fowl. They were soon both taken ill and began to vomit. After remarking 'She's done for us this time,' Kate sent out for an emetic and for a doctor. As chance would have it Dr Harrison of Cemetery Road was nearby and arrived very quickly. On examining Skinner he concluded that he had consumed a metallic irritant, possibly arsenic. Kate looked ill but her symptoms did not appear to be due to poisoning. He administered an emetic. Skinner got steadily worse and at around 8 pm he died. The doctor immediately took possession of the fowl, the stuffing in the fowl, the stuffing in the tin and some vomit which Kate had disgorged. He also sent for the police. While they were in the house Kate was seen to burn in the grate a document which looked like a will and to pass a packet and some small items to her mother. She told the police that the deceased did not keep arsenic on the premises or use it in his work and that she had burnt the will on the his instructions.

A post-mortem examination was carried out on Thursday, December 7, by Dr Harrison and Mr James, a surgeon. The appearance of the internal organs was consistent with arsenical poisoning. The deceased's stomach and contents, and were sent along with other specimens, including the items seized on the Wednesday, to the public analyst.

On the Friday, the inquest was opened at the *Royal Hotel*, Abbeydale Road by the coroner, Dossey Wightman. After taking evidence of identification and issuing a burial certificate, he adjourned the hearing until the following Friday by which time he hoped to be in possession of the analyst's report.

On the Monday the deceased was interred in a vault in Ecclesall church yard in which his wife was buried.[218]

The inquest was resumed on December 16 but not finally concluded until December 22. The borough analyst informed the court that he had found arsenic to be present in the deceased's stomach, stomach contents, liver and intestines, in the chicken and the stuffing taken from the tin but not in the stuffing inside the chicken nor in the specimen of Kate Dover's vomit. Evidence was given by Mrs Jones and by the butcher who sold the chicken that they had consumed respectively, without ill effects, vegetables from the pack sent from the country and the giblets of the fowl. A considerable sensation was caused when it came to light that some love letters between Kate and another man had been found at the house. The coroner refused to allow them in evidence but the local press managed to get hold of copies which they promptly published. In the course of a two and a half hour summing up, the coroner told the jury that there were three possible verdicts open to them: accidental death, if they felt that the arsenic had been administered accidentally, murder if it had been administered with intent to kill, manslaughter if it had been administered deliberately but not with the intent of

---

[218] *Sheffield Independent*, December 17, 1881 'a brick grave erected in the new portion of the graveyard [with] a memorial of considerable artistry erected over it.'

causing serious harm. The jury returned a verdict of murder by Kate Dover who was committed for trial in custody.

On December 24 she appeared before Mr Edward Welby, the town's stipendiary magistrate. Muir Wilson, the solicitor who had represented her at the inquest, suggested that in the light of the verdict a hearing was unnecessary. 'It is impossible to dispense with it,' he was told. Nonetheless, the evidence was taken in short order and the defendant again committed for trial. As she left the crowded court-room, she smiled and bowed to several of her friends.

She took her trial at Leeds Assizes on February 5 and 6, 1882 before Mr Justice Cave. Mr Waddy QC, with Mr Barker and Mr J L Watson appeared for the Crown. The prisoner was defended by Mr Frank Lockwood and Mr. Stuart-Wortley.[219]

Just before the court was due to sit the scene outside the court-room was one bordering on chaos:

'The corridors and the staircase above were,' reported in the *Sheffield Independent*:

> *crowded with women anxious to see Kate Dover Some ... were young and pretty others old and plain, but they nearly all had commodious luncheon baskets How these ladies, some in fashion's dress, some in rags, push their way rudely past the police in their eagerness to witness another woman's misery. ....the fingers of the clock pointed to 5 to 11; there was a great hustling outside the court, then pell mell, like a lot of schoolboys escaping from their lessons,*

[219] **Cave**, Sir Lewis William (1832-97); educ. Rugby and Lincoln Coll, Oxford; barrister, 1859; recorder of Lincoln 1873; QC 1875; High Court judge 1881-97; **Waddy**, Samuel Danks (1850-1902); barrister 1858; QC 1874; recorder of Sheffield, 1894; county court judge for Cheshire and then Sheffield, 1896; **Barker, Lockwood** and **Stuart-Wortley** see biographical details given in main text. The prisoner appeared in the dock heavily veiled. She was kept overnight in the lock up at the Town Hall. On the second day a rumour swept the press benches that she was about to address the jury in her own defence (i e make an unsworn statement).

*the ladies stormed the galleries, one of two of them haggling in loud voices for seats, as if they had descended from the witches of MacBeth.'* [220]

Opening the case, Mr Waddy told the jury that the deceased had died of arsenic poisoning and it was the Crown's submission that the deceased had administered it to him. She had purchased arsenic the day before his death, the giblets of the fowl had been found to be free of arsenic as had other vegetables in the consignment received by Mrs Jones, but the fowl and the stuffing both of which the prisoner had cooked were full of poison. True she had become ill after eating the fowl but not from poison; her vomit, when analysed, had contained no arsenic. The Crown then proceeded to call its evidence.

Mr Lockwood was able to demonstrate that there was mutual affection between the couple and that on the night before his death the deceased had offered to buy her a pony but that was all.

At the conclusion of the evidence he rose to address the jury:

*The prosecution had undertaken to prove the prisoner had committed the most awful crime known to the law and he contended they had not done so. They had failed. He had never heard a case before in which the jury had been asked to disregard utterly all questions of motive. There never was a case in which it was more essential that a motive should be shown, as the prisoner had everything to gain by the prolongation of the life of the deceased and as no living man or woman had seen the act committed. He would be able to show the jury that the prosecution had stated facts that they*

---

[220] Cf also *Sheffield Independent*, February 7, 1882: " 'If we don't get to the front, we shall hear nothing,' said a stout lady with a large hamper ... as she struggled to get into the ladies' gallery;" also February 9, 1882: 'Monday and Tuesday saw the court crowded in every part of the galleries with ladies carrying luncheon boxes and directing opera glasses at the dock, bench, and bar.'

*were not in a position to prove. It was stated that there were many quarrels, yet only two nights before Skinner's death, he was seen sitting in a chair with the prisoner's head on his knee. The very night before his death he was talking about giving the prisoner a pony, and the prisoner had said some time before that the deceased was going to marry her. It was stated that Mrs Jones and her husband were compelled to leave the deceased, owing to the improper conduct of the prisoner with the deceased. This was a base and groundless charge, unsupported by one tittle of evidence. It was stated she had pawned Mr Skinner's property. Why? Because the allowance given her for the support of the household was insufficient. There was everything to show that she loved the deceased and expected he was going to marry her. Why then should she murder him? The prisoner had brought to the house on the very day the alleged crime was committed Emma Bolsover as a servant. This extraordinary conduct surpassed conception if she had at the very time made up her mind to take the life of the deceased. ... As soon as they were taken ill the prisoner sent for some tincture of lobelia. She immediately sent for medical assistance and, not content with that she herself rushed off and brought back a medical man and displayed the greatest anxiety that Mr Skinner should be attended to. From beginning to end her conduct was consistent; she kept nothing back but informed the constables exactly what they had had for dinner and where the things came from. More than that, when asked, she at once said that the dinner was cooked by her, and that, too, without any assistance. The arsenic was purchased by the prisoner in a perfectly straightforward manner and no attempt was made in any way to conceal her name which she gave in full.*

*The jury would no doubt believe that the prisoner was herself suffering from poisoning by arsenic, that her symptoms were the same as those from which the deceased was suffering and her symptoms were not feigned as suggested by the prosecution. He repudiated the suggestion that Mrs Jones had anything to do with the matter. It was possible that the prisoner was jealous of the influence of Mrs Jones over the deceased man, whom the prisoner wished to marry and that a small amount of arsenic may have been scattered by her over the stuffing in order to produce sickness only, and that the expression made use of by the prisoner with regard to Mrs Jones was employed with the purpose of producing in the mind of the deceased the impression that Mrs Jones had done it, since, if the influence of Mrs Jones over the deceased was undermined, the prisoner would have a better chance of marrying him. This view would entirely explain the whole conduct of the prisoner and her intense anxiety when she discovered that the effects produced by the arsenic were so different to what she had intended and expected. If the jury adopted this view the prisoner clearly could not be convicted of murder. In conclusion, he most earnestly implored the jury to give the case the most serious consideration, stressing that if a mistake were once made it could not be remedied.*

The judge then summed up.[221]

After a two hour retirement the jury returned with a verdict of Not Guilty of Murder but Guilty of Manslaughter.

Mr Justice Cave, who was doubtless as astonished by the verdict as everyone else in court and plainly disagreed with it, now proceeded to pass sentence:

*'Felicia Dorothea Kate Dover, the jury have taken a merciful view of the case and adopted the suggestion of the learned counsel who had defended her. Nevertheless, the circumstances of the case were so atrocious that only a fine line divided the case from one of wilful murder. I feel it my duty to pass upon you the heaviest sentence which lies within my power and that sentence is penal servitude for life.'*

Upon hearing her sentence, Kate collapsed in the dock and was carried below apparently insensible. The *Sheffield Independent*

[221] The summing up, like defence counsel's speech lasted 1½ hours.

reported that, after being given restoratives, she was taken back to Armley Gaol to await transfer to one of the convict establishments, probably Pentonville.

# Appendix 3

## Trunk Murders

Lee Doon's was not the first and it was certainly not the last English trunk murder.

In January, 1905, 24-year-old chemist's assistant, Arthur Devereux was in dire financial straits. Seeing no way out, he brought home some chloroform and morphine, which he induced his wife Beatrice to take and to give to their two youngest children with fatal results. He put the three bodies in a trunk, made the lid tight and had it taken to a warehouse at Harrow. He then moved with his other child to a new address. His mother-in-law, disbelieving his explanation of his wife's disappearance, learned by asking round that a Harrow furniture company's van had called at the couple's home shortly before Beatrice disappeared. She then visited the firm's warehouse, found the trunk and had it opened. Devereux was quickly arrested. Tried and convicted of murder at the Old Bailey, he was hanged at Pentonville Prison on August 15, 1905.

In May 1927, staff at the left luggage office at Charing Cross railway station noticed an unpleasant smell. It was found to be coming from a trunk which had been deposited six days before, When the trunk was opened up, it contained the dismembered parts of a woman's body, each wrapped in brown paper and string. Post-mortem examination established that the cause of death was asphyxia. A photograph of the trunk was published in the newspapers and this led to several witnesses coming forward. Soon it was traced to John Robinson. At first he denied any knowledge of it, but then said that a Mrs Bonati had called at his office asking for money. They quarreled, he pushed her away and she fell, hitting her head. Realising she was dead, he panicked cut up the body and hid it in the trunk.

Tried and convicted of murder at the Old Bailey in July, 1927 he was hanged at Pentonville on August 12, 1927.

On June 17, 1933, the body of a woman minus head, legs and arms was found in a trunk at the left luggage office of Brighton railway station. The victim's identity was never discovered. In the course of their inquiries into the crime, the police interviewed 26-year-old waiter, Tony Mancini, whose girl friend, 42-year-old Violet Saunders, had not been seen for over a month. When they called back at his lodgings a few days later, he was not there but in the basement of the building was a trunk. The police opened it. Inside was Violet's decomposing body. Post-mortem examination established that she had a fracture to the left side of the skull, caused in all probability by a blow from a hammer or similar weapon. Arrested on July 17, Mancini said 'Yes, I'm the man but I didn't murder her though.'

At his trial at Lewes Assizes in December 1934, he told the jury that he had found Violet lying dead on the bed and in panic had decided to hide the body. Asked why he did not call the police, he replied 'Where the police are concerned, a man who's got convictions never gets a square deal.' Much to everybody's surprise he was acquitted. No-one was more astonished than Mancini himself. When he saw his counsel in a side room after the verdict, the only words he could get out were 'Not guilty, Mr Birkett? Not Guilty?'

# Appendix 4

## Ruth Ellis – the Sheffield connection

Ruth Ellis was born in Rhyl in 1926 moving to London in 1941. By 1943 she was pregnant by a Canadian serviceman named Clare who, unbeknown to her, was married with three children. Following the birth of the child she supported herself first by photographic modelling and then by working as a nightclub hostess. In 1950 she married recently divorced dentist, George Ellis. The marriage proved a disaster from the start and the following year they separated. By this time she was pregnant again. When the child was born it was given for adoption.

In 1953 she was still working as a hostess and through her work she met David Blakely. In late October, by which time she was managing a night club in Brompton Road, the two became lovers. Blakely who was a motor racing enthusiast was in the process of building his own racing car, a venture which took most of his money and left him constantly hard up. The relationship did not run smoothly. Ruth felt slighted when Blakely refused to introduce her to his mother and there were quarrels over money. In 1954 he drove in the Le Mans 24 Hour Race. He was late returning from France and Ruth decided to pay him back by sleeping with a man named Cussens. Blakely was furious but did not break with her. By October 1954 the club she was running was doing badly and suddenly Ruth found herself without a job or accommodation. Cussens took her in but she continued to see Blakely. In February 1955 they decided to move in together and took a flat at 44, Egerton Gardens. On April 2, Blakely's racing car blew up during a race and he took his anger out on Ruth, punching her in the stomach causing her to lose the child she was carrying. He was by now spending a lot of time with a couple named Findlater, and Ruth suspected, rightly, that he was having an affair with the wife. On April 8 he decided to finish with Ruth but, rather than tell her, he simply failed to keep a date with her and spent the weekend at the Findlaters'. Ruth knew he was there but when she telephoned asking to speak to him, she was told he was not. She spent the Sunday brooding and by the evening had decided to kill Blakely. At 9.30 pm she came upon him as he was leaving the *Magdala Tavern* in South Hill Park. She called his name, pulled a Smith and Wesson revolver out of her handbag and fired six shots. Blakely died almost instantly. Although he denied it, there is little doubt that Cussens had supplied the gun.

Ruth was tried for murder at the Old Bailey on June 20 and 21, 1955. The case against her was overwhelming and she made no effort to help herself. Asked in cross-examination what she intended to do when she fired the gun at Blakely, she replied 'It is obvious when I shot him I intended to kill him.' The jury took just fourteen minutes to convict her. Sentenced to death, she refused to appeal her conviction and was hanged at Holloway on July 13, 1955. Her execution caused a considerable public outcry[222] and was undoubtedly a factor in hastening the end of capital punishment.

[222] When he left Holloway after the execution, Pierrepoint needed protection to get him through a 'storming mob' (A. Pierrpoint, *Executioner: Pierrepoint*, Coronet Books, London 1977, p 205.

The link between Ruth Ellis and Sheffield is that her victim had strong connections with the city. The son of a Sheffield doctor, David Moffatt Drummond Blakely, was born on June 17, 1929 at Oakdale Nursing home, 33 Collegiate Crescent. The youngest of four children, he lived until his parents' divorce in 1940 at 203, School Road, Crookes where his father had his surgery. After the divorce he moved to Buckinghamshire with his mother who had been awarded custody of him. In 1941 she remarried. Her new husband was Humphrey Wyndham Cook, the wealthy son of a wholesale draper who before the war one had been one of England's best known racing drivers. David was sent off to public school (Shrewsbury). On leaving school he was called up for national service and obtained a commission in the Highland Light Infantry. When he came out of the army his stepfather got him a job as a trainee at the *Hyde Park Hotel*, but this was not to his liking and he soon turned his attention to motor racing. He still kept in touch with his father and from time to time would drive up to Sheffield to see him.

That one of Dr John Blakely's children should have ended up being murdered had a certain irony about it, for in 1934 he had himself been charged with murder.[223]

In 1934, the 47-year-old doctor had begun an affair with Phyllis Staton, a 19-year-old unemployed waitress. Clearly infatuated, he saw her almost daily, regularly took her out to dinner and just as regularly had sexual intercourse with her. 'I usually picked her up near her home,' he would later tell the police 'but we stayed together only one night which was at Grantham.' Her father, Harry, a foreman

[223] See *Star*, February 12, 20 and 23, 1934; *Sheffield Telegraph*, February 10, 13, 14, 20 and 22, 1934; *Sheffield Independent*, February 13, 21 and 23, 1934

joiner, knew that she was keeping company with a married man but he did not know who. She merely referred to him in conversation as 'the Doc.' He left her in no doubt that he disapproved of what she was doing.

On January 15, 1934, Phyllis left home, telling her mother that she had got a position and would write. The following Sunday she came back to get some clothes. 'I've been nursing a lady at Bamford,' she told her mother. After two hours she left saying she was going back to Bamford. The next time her family saw her was on Saturday, February 3. Shortly after 6 pm there was a knock at the back door of their home at 91, Cresswell Road, Darnall. When the door was opened it was Phyllis. She immediately collapsed into her sister's arms saying 'Oh mother, I shall die.' Her father ran to the door and was in time to see a car driving off; it was a vehicle which he had seen call for her before. 'Who brought you?' her sister asked. 'The Doc,' she replied. Clearly very ill, she could hardly walk. She was immediately put to bed and Dr Gilmore of 669, Prince of Wales Road sent for. He found her to be acutely ill and feverish. When he called the next day she was no better and he at once arranged for her to be admitted to the City General Hospital.

Dr Clark, the medical superintendent of the hospital, saw her following her admission. She was dangerously ill with septicaemia following a miscarriage. Within hours she was dead. A post-mortem examination revealed no natural cause for the miscarriage but neither was there any evidence of an illegal operation or the use of drugs. Dr Clark thought that she had been pregnant for just over four months and that she had miscarried five to ten days before he saw her.

The coroner was notified of the death and he contacted the police.

At 10.18 on the evening of February 7, Detective Superintendent Bristow, the head of the Sheffield CID, and Chief Inspector Flint, approached Dr Blakely in Tudor Court and told him that they wished to speak to him, either at his home or at the police station, about the death of Phyllis Staton, a woman they believed he knew. 'I will tell you anything you want to know,' he replied. He was taken to the Central Police Office where he made a statement in which he admitted his association with the dead girl, said that he had learned of her condition, had given her a drug and taken her to a house in Sheffield on January 15; on January 30 he was told that she had suffered a miscarriage and on February 3 had driven her to her home and left her in the backyard. He denied 'any criminal responsibility for the girl.'[224]

The next day Phyllis' bedroom was searched. In it the police found a diary, inside which was a note (identified by local chemists as being in Dr Blakely's handwriting) which contained a timetable for inducing labour. From a cupboard they recovered a phial of liquid which, on analysis, was found to be pituitrin.

On February 11 Dr Blakely was arrested on suspicion of murder.[225] On entering the police office he said 'I may be morally

[224] He claimed in his statement that three married men had had intercourse with Phyllis and that she had asked him if something could be done about an abortion, adding 'She probably picked on me because I was fairly well off. I told her I was prepared to take my share if the other men would.' He had made clear to her that he would not under any circumstances treat her as a patient or carry out an abortion.

[225] Where a woman died as a result of an illegal abortion, it was open to a jury to convict the person who performed it if they were satisfied that he, as a reasonable man, must have contemplated death or grievous bodily harm as a likely result – see *R v Lumley* 22 Cox 635.

responsible. I certainly have no criminal responsibility towards her.' When charged he replied 'Not guilty to that.'

The following day he was brought before the city magistrates. Superintendent Bristow, after outlining the facts, asked for an eight day remand in custody to enable the chief constable to communicate with the Director of Public Prosecution's office. The application was granted. Mr Eric Scorah, for the doctor, asked that the prisoner be kept in custody in Sheffield rather than being sent to Leeds Prison as was generally done. The chairman of the bench told him that the place of custody was a matter for the police.

When the doctor next appeared before the magistrates on February 20, Mr Chant of the DPP's office told the bench that the prosecution had decided to prefer additional charge, namely one of supplying pituitrin to the dead girl knowing that it was intended to be used for an unlawful purpose, the date of the alleged supply being November 1.[226]

Mr Chant then began to outline the Crown's case. On January 15 the defendant had taken the dead girl to 279, Holme Lane, a house occupied by Gladys Bailey and her female lodger. Phyllis Staton had shared a bedroom with one of them. In a statement to the police, the defendant had told them that she had asked him to take her to the house. She thought she was going to have a miscarriage and did not want to have it at home. After taking her to the house, the defendant, according to Gladys Bailey, visited three times a day at first, bringing food when he called. On Saturday, January 27, Gladys went out to

[226] Contrary to s.59 of the Offences against the Person Act, 1861 (the section makes it an offence to supply a poison or other noxious thing knowing the same is to be ... employed with intent to procure the miscarriage of any woman).

the pictures with her lodger, leaving Phyllis and the defendant alone in the house. When she got back at 6.45pm the defendant had gone.

Later that evening Phyllis showed her a mark on her arm like a pin prick. The following morning she stayed in bed and did not get up at all during the next week. During this period, the defendant called to see her twice a day, bringing with him an attaché case. On one occasion he left with a parcel although Gladys Bailey had not seen him bring one with him. He suggested that she should call in another doctor. She replied that if the girl was ill she should go home. On Saturday February 3, Phyllis got up and dressed herself; she looked pale but seemed alright and did not complain of anything and the defendant then took her away in his car.

In his statement to the police the defendant had said that he had learned on Tuesday, January 30, that she had had a miscarriage. On Saturday, February 3, he had suggested that it was time for her to go home and offered to take her after he had been to the football match. He left her at the back door. She could walk with a little assistance and he did not consider her condition to be 'sufficiently serious to be drastic.' The girl was to have written to him and he was surprised to learn from the police that she had died the day after he had left her.

The prosecution case was that, while at the house in Holme Lane, the dead girl had suffered a miscarriage which had been procured by an injection of pituitrin which had led to her developing blood poisoning. Pituitrin, the action of which was very rapid, was used to induce labour in maternity cases. 'It is the latest method known to medical science,' Mr Chant explained. Pituitrin is normally given by injection. It can not be detected because everybody had certain quantities of the drug naturally occurring in their bodies. A curious feature of the case was that no trace had been found of the body of the dead child, and yet the dead girl could not have disposed of it and the two women in the house would say that they had not seen it.

M/s Bailey, Drs Gilmore and Clark and Superintendent Bristow were the principal witnesses called. Asked 'Would you give a phial of pituitrin to a pregnant woman?' Dr Clark replied emphatically 'I would not.' Asked if he would give a pregnant woman a copy of the timetable for inducing labour, he gave the same answer.

At the close of the prosecution case, Mr Scorah for Dr Blakely submitted that there was no case to answer. There was not the slightest evidence on which a charge of murder could be brought. There was no evidence that the dead girl's miscarriage was not perfectly natural. The magistrate agreed. The prosecution had failed to prove that the miscarriage was other than natural. There was no evidence of any instrument having been used or drug taken. 'No jury would convict,' he declared, ordering the defendant discharged.

Dr Blakely was, beyond doubt, a very lucky man. On the charge of supplying pituitrin with the intention that it be used for an illegal purpose, the evidence was extremely strong. A phial of pituitrin had been found amongst the dead girl's belongings together with a document detailing the timetable to be followed when it was used to induce labour. The defendant admitted that he had supplied her with the drug and the timetable was in his handwriting. He knew that she was pregnant. For what purpose other than inducing an abortion had these items been supplied? It was a question which called for an answer. There was also compelling circumstantial evidence that the miscarriage had been procured by an injection of pituitrin. After the defendant had left on the Saturday the dead girl had shown Gladys Bailey the mark to her arm. The following morning she did not get up and for the next week she never got out of bed. The defendant had been seen taking a parcel away from the house. On post-mortem examination, no natural reason had been found for the girl to have had a miscarriage and, if pituitrin had been used it would have been undetectable, as the defendant, as a medical man, would have well known. Again there was sufficient against him to call for an answer. A more astute magistrate would have realised this and sent the doctor for trial on both charges.

# Appendix 5

## Capital murder convictions at Sheffield Assizes

Of those convicted of murder at Sheffield Assizes two - Alec Wilkinson and Bernard Hugh Walden - went to the gallows.

### Alec Wilkinson [227]

Alec Wilkinson and Maureen Farrell were married on August 21, 1954 at Wombwell Parish Church. After the wedding they moved in to 21, Bradbury Back Walk, a house two doors away from Maureen's mother, Clara. At first, Mrs Farrell, a former prostitute, was helpful to the young couple but soon relations between her and Alec became increasingly strained. He took offence at the crude sexual remarks which she was for ever making while she, for her part, seems quickly to have come to the conclusion that he was a useless husband who would be better off out of the way. 'It doesn't matter about thee working for Maureen,' she told him during one argument 'she can always go out hawking her duck.' She now began to put pressure on Maureen to leave him and to come and live with her and eventually she did. Alec did everything he could to get her back but to no avail.

On April 30, 1955 he spent the whole day drinking. At closing time he visited a late night café where he decided to make one last attempt to win his wife back. He telephoned for a taxi and, when it

[227] For a full account of the case see J Parris, *Most of My Murders*, Frederick Muller Ltd, London 1960, chapter 10.

arrived, told the driver to take him to Bradbury Back Walk. As it pulled up, he saw Clara Farrell in her front window. He guessed, correctly, that she was waiting up for Maureen. Minutes later Maureen came down the street with two girl friends. After she had entered the house, he went to the door and knocked. Clara answered the door. When she saw who it was she hurled a tirade of abuse at him and tried to push him out. At this he snapped. Having felled her with a punch he got astride her and began to batter her head against the floor, Maureen came to her rescue but was immediately punched and knocked unconscious. Alec now got a knife from the kitchen and stabbed Clara to death. His attack with the knife was particularly savage, one of the woman's breasts was cut off and the knife had also been pushed into her vagina. Once he had finished attacking her, he piled furniture on her body and set it alight.

The noise of the struggle brought neighbours running round and they quickly put out the fire. Alec in the meanwhile had fled out of the back but soon afterwards he gave himself up to the police.

His trial took place at Sheffield between June 20 and 29, 1955 before Lord Chief Justice Goddard. Sir Russell Vick QC and Felix Denny prosecuted, John Parris and Richard Hutchinson defended. The defence case was that this was a killing under provocation. In the witness box, Wilkinson was asked if he was sorry for what he had done. 'No sir, I'm not,' he replied. It was an honest answer but one which did him no favours with the jury, several of whom gasped when he gave it.

After an hour's retirement the jury returned with a verdict of guilty.

The conviction was appealed and 35,000 people signed a petition for reprieve. The appeal was dismissed and the petition ignored and on August 12, 1955 Wilkinson was hanged at Armley Prison.

A few weeks after his execution the House of Commons passed a Bill for the abolition of capital punishment and, although the Bill did not become law, all executions were suspended.

## Bernard Hugh Walden[228]

On April 7, 1959 lectures were in progress at Rotherham Technical College. At around 7.30 pm, Bernard Hugh Walden, a 33-year-old assistant lecturer at the College. left the class he was taking and passed on the way to his locker 21-year-old student Neil Saxton, who was talking to his girl friend, Joyce Moran, through a window. Returning from his locker, where he had a revolver secreted, he shot Saxton through the back and then went into the office and shot Joyce Moran six times in the back. Both died within minutes. He then fled. A week before he had asked Joyce to marry him but she had turned him down.[229]

The following day his car was found abandoned in Leeds and in it were firearms. Other firearms were also found in the bedroom of his home at Spinneyfields, Rotherham. For some weeks he managed

---

[228] See *The Times*, July 1 & 2, 1955, *The Guardian*, July 1 & 2, 1959 and [1959] 43 Crim App Rep 201

[229] Joyce was a secretary at the College. Walden lectured in physics.

to give the police the slip but was finally arrested at Reading on May 1.[230]

He was tried at Sheffield Assizes on June 30, 1959 before Mr Justice Paull. The trial lasted for two days. Mr G S Waller QC[231] and Mr JB Willis appeared for the Crown, Walden was represented by Mr H Scott QC[232] and Mr J F S Cobb.[233]

Opening the case for the defence Mr Scott told the jury that there was no dispute about the facts, the issue was diminished responsibility. Diminished responsibility was a new defence introduced by the Homicide Act, 1957 and available only in murder cases. If made out, and the burden of proving it lay with the defence, it had the effect of reducing what would otherwise have been murder to manslaughter. To establish the defence, the accused had to satisfy the jury that it was more probable than not that, at the time of the killing, he was suffering from a gross abnormality of mind which substantially impaired his mental responsibility for his acts. It had been introduced because insanity was so narrowly defined in law as not to be available as a defence to many of those who suffered from serious mental illness.

Mr Scott explained that, after contracting poliomyelitis while he was at Oxford, Walden had suffered two disasters: he was unable to study at a vital time and finished with a third-class degree, and the disease had withered his leg, a condition of which he was bitterly conscious and rather ashamed.

---

[230] He was found by an officer in a shelter.

[231] Later a High Court Judge and Lord Justice of Appeal.

[232] The son of Paley Scott QC who prosecuted Case. Henry Scott.

[233] Later a QC, and Leader of the North Eastern Circuit. Shortly before his death he was appointed to the High Court bench.

He called for the defence psychiatrist, Dr James Valentine who told the jury that Walden was suffering from chronic paranoiac development and he considered him to be grossly abnormal. The abnormality had reached such a stage that in his view it impaired his responsibility. Walden had told him that he wanted to marry Miss Moran but at the same time he showed no remorse for what he had done to her. He bore Neil no ill will. He shot him not to kill him but to paralyse him from the waist down. At a recent interview he had explained his motive saying 'It was more a question of striking against God and faith than against any particular person. I felt I had to make a stand. I was looking all along the line.' It was an explanation hardly likely to endear him to the jury any more than his assertion that 'since he was a cripple he had the right to carry a gun to put him on equal terms and a right to kill.'

The prosecution called in rebuttal Dr Walker, the senior medical officer at Armley prison, and Dr Fraser, a consultant psychiatrist. Dr Walker, who had had the accused under observation from the time of his arrest until the trial, said that he had been unable to detect any signs of mental disorder or defect and was of the opinion that Walden was not suffering from any abnormality of mind. Dr Fraser agreed: all his reactions were within normal limits.

The prosecution in their closing submissions argued that the case was one of simple jealousy.

Walden was duly convicted and sentenced to death. An appeal against conviction on the grounds of misdirection failed and he was hanged at Leeds on August 14, 1959.

# Appendix 6

## The Hangmen

The hangmen who executed the 18 murderers with whom this book is concerned were Askern, Marwood, Billington, three of the Pierrepoints, Ellis ands Wade.

Thomas Askern from Matlby, was appointed York hangman in 1853. By accepting the position he secured his release from the debtors' side of York Castle gaol. In 1864 he was appointed Leeds hangman. He had little skill: when he attempted to execute a prisoner, named Johnson, at Armley in 1877 the rope broke and this was not the first bungled execution to which he had been party.[234] His other claim to notoriety is that he carried out the last public execution in Scotland, when he hanged 19-year-old Robert Smith outside Dumfries Prison on May 12, 1868. Another of his victims was **William Smedley.**

Marwood who executed **Peace** in 1879 and **Hall** two years later had succeeded Calcraft as Newgate hangman in 1874. He was the first English hangman to employ 'the long drop' and also made improvements to the method of pinioning the arms of the condemned man and securing the noose in place. Of his predecessor Calcraft, he always spoke with contempt. 'He hanged them. I execute them,' he boasted. But despite his pride in his work, hangings at which he

[234] The incident, which was quite horrific, is described in *The Times*, April 4, 1877, p 4c 'As soon as the drop fell, the rope, which was an old one supplied by Askern snapped, throwing the condemned convict to the ground where he lay groaning. After a delay of about ten minutes a newer and thicker rope was procured and fastened to the cross-beam. Johnson was then led from beneath the drop back on to the scaffold and turned off a second time. This time the rope held and after five minutes of convulsive struggling he expired.' Not surprisingly, this execution proved to be Askern's last.

officiated did not always go without a hitch. When he executed Vincent Knowles Walker at York in May 1878, he gave him too short a drop and Walker died very hard. He died in 1883 three months after hanging the Phoenix Park murderers. 'If Pa killed Ma, who would kill Pa?' was a popular riddle in the 1880s. The answer, of course, was Marwood.

Between 1884 and 1965 the country's leading hangmen were either Yorkshiremen or Lancastrians.

James Billington, a hairdresser from Farnworth near Bolton was appointed York hangman in 1884. His first execution was that of **Laycock** at Armley later that year. He also executed **Hobson, West** and **Hemmings**. In 1896 he hanged Trooper Charles Wooldridge at Reading; it was this execution which inspired Oscar Wilde to write *The Ballad of Reading Gaol.* He died in 1901 with a tally of 147 executions to his credit.

The Pierrepoint family 'dominated the English hanging trade from 1900 to 1956.'[235] The first to take up the work was Henry, a former butcher from Huddersfield. He retired in 1916 having carried out 99 executions. Among his victims was **Walters**, the Christmas murderer. Henry was often assisted by his son Tom who, after Ellis's retirement, became principal executioner. With a fondness for sucking sweets during executions, he served as a hangman for 45 years, retiring in 1948. It was he who executed **Law, Lee Doon,** the **Fowlers**, **Lax** and **Case.**

[235] O Cyriac, *The Penguin Encylopaedia of Crime*, Penguin Books, London, 1996, p. 444. Cf also Albert Pierrepoint 'It's in the family really' (cited by B Bailey, *Hangmen*, True Crime, London 1993).

The third member of the Pierrepoint family to take up the work was Albert who began in 1933 by acting as assistant to his uncle Tom and rose, in due course, to become the country's principal and certainly best known executioner. When applying to the Home Office for the post of assistant, he wrote that the job was 'something to take pride in' and referred enthusiastically to the opportunities for travel which it afforded. An extremely fast worker, he was in much demand after the Second World War, dispatching some 200 war criminals. On one occasion he hanged 22 American servicemen at Shepton Mallett Military Prison in one morning. In 1946 took over a pub named *Help the Poor Struggler* at Hollinswood near Manchester. It soon became known locally as Help the Poor Strangler. In 1974, after 30 year career in which he had executed 530 men and 20 women both here and abroad, he wrote 'Capital punishment, in my view, achieves nothing but revenge.' It was he who executed the German prisoners convicted of the **Redmires** camp murder.

John Ellis, a hairdresser from Rochdale, was appointed assistant executioner in 1901 and senior hangman in 1907. In 1923 he executed Edith Thompson; the experience affected him badly. In March 1924 he resigned his post and wrote his reminiscences for Thompson's *Weekly News.* In August of the same year he shot himself in the jaw. He was charged before the Rochdale magistrates with attempted suicide, the proceedings ending with him being bound over for 12 months to keep the peace. In 1927 he played part of the hangman in a play at the *Grand Theatre* Gravesend and after this went on a short lecture tour. In 1932 took his own life with a cut throat razor. One of his last men he hanged was **Eastwood**, the former Walkley publican.

Steve Wade, who hanged **William Smedley** for the Bridge Street murder in 1947 was a Doncaster motor coach dealer. He applied for the post of executioner in 1918 when he was only 21. He was told that he was too young. However, he continued to make applications and during the Second World War was appointed assistant executioner. In 1955 he was made principal hangman but retired the following year due to ill health.

# Index